THE ANCIENT EGYPTIANS

VOLUME ONE

THE ANCIENT EGYPTIANS

THEIR LIFE AND CUSTOMS

VOLUME ONE

J. GARDNER WILKINSON

SENATE

The Ancient Egyptians Volume One

First published by John Murray, London

This edition published in 1994 by Senate, an imprint of
Studio Editions Ltd, Princess House, 50 Eastcastle Street,
London W1N 7AP, England

ISBN 1 85958 052 1
Printed and bound in Guernsey by
The Guernsey Press Co Ltd

PUBLISHER'S NOTE
The Ancient Egyptians – Their Life and Customs was
previously published in one volume. Senate have now
reprinted this work into two companion volumes,
The Ancient Egyptians – Their Life and Customs Vol. One and
The Ancient Egyptians – Their Life and Customs Vol. Two.

PREFACE.

THE present account of the "Ancient Egyptians" is chiefly an abridgment of that written by me in 1836; to which I have added other matter, in consequence of my having re-visited Egypt, and later discoveries having been made, since that time.

I have here and there introduced some remarks relating to the Greeks, thinking that a comparison of the habits and arts of other people, with those of the Egyptians, may be interesting; and the impulse now given to taste in England has induced me to add some observations on decorative art, as well as on colour, form, and proportion, so well understood in ancient times. And as many of the ideas now gaining ground in this country, regarding colour, adaptability of materials, the non-imitation of natural objects for ornamental purposes, and certain rules to be observed in decorative works, have long been advocated by me, and properly belong to the subject of Egypt, I think the opportunity well suited for expressing my opinion upon them; while I rejoice that public attention has been invited to take a proper view of the mode of improving taste.

Attention being now directed towards the question of the precious metals, some observations, on the comparative wealth of ancient and modern times, have also appeared to be not out of place.

Of the Religion and History of Egypt, I have only introduced what is necessary for explaining some points connected with them; being persuaded that a detailed account of those subjects would not be generally attractive, and might be omitted in a work not intended to treat of what is still open to conjecture. For the same reason I have abstained from all doubtful questions respecting the customs of the Egyptians; and have confined myself to as short a notice of them as possible.

References too are mostly omitted, having been given before.

Several new woodcuts have been added, and others have been introduced instead of some of the lithographic plates in the previous work; and as an Index is more useful than a mere list of contents, I have given a very copious one, which will be found to contain all the most important references.

August, 1853.

CONTENTS OF VOL. I.

——◆——

CHAPTER I.

PAGE

Character of the Egyptians — Original populations — Social life — Houses — Villas — Farmyards — Gardens — Vineyards — Winepress — Wines — Beer — Furniture of rooms — Chairs 1

CHAPTER II.

Reception of guests — Music — Various instruments — Sacred music — Dance 73

CHAPTER III.

Amusement of the guests — Vases — Ornaments of the house — Preparation for dinner — The kitchen — Mode of eating — Spoons — Washing before meals — Figure of a dead man brought in — Games within, and out of, doors — Wrestling — Boat-fights — Bull-fights . 141

CHAPTER IV.

The Chase — Wild animals — Dogs — Birds — Fishing — Chase of the hippopotamus — Crocodile — Its eggs — The trochilus — List of the animals of Egypt — Birds — Plants — Emblems — Offerings — Ceremonies 212

CHAPTER V.

Origin of the Egyptians — Population of Egypt and of the world of old — History — The king — Princes — Priests — Their system — Religion — Gods — Triads — Dresses and mode of life of the priests — Soldiers — Arms — Chariots — Ships and navy — enemies of Egypt — Conquests 302

LIST OF WOODCUTS

In Vol. I.

*Those with ** prefixed are new woodcuts; with * new woodcuts copied from lithographs of the previous work.*

** **Frontispiece.**

A complete Egyptian Temple, surrounded by the *Temenos*, or " grove," planted with trees. A procession, with the sacred boat, or ark, advances from the hypæthral building at the extremity of the paved *dromos*.

A wooden model of the *grove* was sometimes carried in these processions, as behind the statue of Khem. It was doubtless similar to the "*grove*" which the Israelites "brought out" and "burnt."—2 Kings, xxiii. 6; Isaiah, xxvii. 9. The real grove is also mentioned, Exod. xxxiv. 13; Judges, vi. 26, &c.

CHAPTER I.

Vignette   Page

A. Part of Cairo, showing the *Mulkufs* on the houses   .   .   1

Woodcut

1. House with a *Mulkuf* 6
2. Over the door, a sentence, "The good house" . . . 7
3. Doorway, with a king's name 7
4.
5. Plans of houses 8
6.
7. Tower of a house 9
8.
9. Porches of private houses 9
10. Entrance to a house 10
11. Plans of houses and a granary 12
12. Model of a house 13
13. Model of a house (showing the court) 14
14. Bronze pins (serving as hinges) 15
15. A folding-door 15
16. Mode of fastening doors 16
17. An iron key 16
18.
19.
20. Painted and sculptured doorways 17
21.

Woodcut   Page

22. Roof representing palm beams 18
23. Position of the rafters in the wall 18
24. Arches, roof, and floor over it 18
25. A painted house 20
26. House with a battled parapet, from the sculptures . . 23
**27. Man in a boat on a lake, drawn by servants, from a tomb at
    Thebes. 25
28. Entrances to large villas 26
29. Ornamental summit of walls 26
30. Villa, with obelisks and towers, like a temple . . . 27
30a Panelled walls of an Egyptian building 29
31. Farm-yard, and plan made from it 30
32. Rooms for housing grain, apparently vaulted . . . 31
33. Granary, showing how the grain was put in . . . 32
34. Steward overlooking the tillage of the lands . . . 32
35. Men watering the ground with pots of water . . . 33
36. Wooden yoke and strap found at Thebes 33
37. Water-buckets carried by a yoke on the shoulders . . 34
38. Shadóof, or pole and bucket, for watering the garden . . 35
39. Water-skins suspended at a tank ; and square beds of a garden 35
40. Tree with earth raised round the roots 36
41. Hieroglyphic signifying " a tree" 36
42. A pomegranate tree 36
43. A large garden, with vineyard and other enclosures, tank and
    house 38
44. Palm-trees on each side of a tank 39
45. The vineyard and orchard contiguous 40
46. Plucking the grapes; vines trained in bowers . . . 41
47. Figurative hieroglyphic signifying "vineyard" . . . 41
48. Vineyard, with a large tank of water 42
49. Frightening away the birds with a sling 43
50. Basket containing grapes 43
51. Monkies assisting in gathering fruit 44
52. Kids allowed to browse on the vines 45
53. A winepress 45
54. Large footpress and asp, the protecting deity of the store-room 46
55. The new wine poured into jars 47
56. Wine-jars with covers 48
57. Vase supported by a stone ring 49
58.
59. } Ladies at a party caricatured by the Egyptians . . . 52
60. Men carried home from a drinking party . . . , 53

Woodcut   Page

61. *Dôm* nut, used for the head of a drill 56
62. Positions of Egyptians when seated on the ground . . 58
63.
64. } Chairs 59
*65.
*65a } Fauteuils painted in the tomb of King Remeses III. . . { 60
61
66. Double and single chairs 62
67. Stools on the principle of our camp-stools 63
68. Seat made of interlaced thongs 64
69. Different forms of chairs 64
70. Other forms; one is a kangaroo chair 65
71. Stools 65
72.
73. } Other stools, one with a leather cushion 66
74. Three-legged stools 66
75. Low stools 67
76. Ottomans from the tombs of Remeses III. . . . 67
77. Carpets or mats 68
78. A couch, head stool, and steps 69
79. Round tables, one supported by a figure 69
80. Wooden table 70
81. Tables from the sculptures 70
82.
83. } Wooden pillows, or head stools 71
84. *Caffass* bedstead, and bier 71
Vignette.
B. The modern *shadóof*, end of Chapter I. 72

CHAPTER II.

Vignette
   C. Pavilion of Remeses III. at Medeenet Haboo, Thebes . . 73
Woodcut
85. An Egyptian gentleman driving in his curricle to a party . 74
**86. A chariot with an umbrella 75
87. Military chief carried in a sort of palanquin. . . . 75
88. Golden ewers and basins in the tomb of Remeses III. . . 77
89. A servant anointing a guest 78
90. Servants bringing necklaces of flowers 78
91. Wooden stand 79
92. A case containing bottles supported on a stand . . . 80

Woodcut   Page

93. Offering wine to a guest 81
94. Harps, pipe, and flute, from a tomb near the Pyramids. . 85
95. The harp and double pipe 86
96. Harp, guitar, and double pipe 87
97. Harp, and a smaller one of four chords 87
98. Harp, guitar, double pipe, lyre, and square tambourine . . 88
99. Men and women singing to the harp, lyre, and double pipe . 89
100. Harp and two guitars 89
101. Two guitars, a harp, and double pipe, and a woman clapping
     her hands 90
102. The flute, two harps, and men singing 91
103. Two harps, and another instrument, probably with a jingling
     sound 92
104. An unusual kind of instrument 93
105. Women beating tambourines and the *darabooka* drum . . 93
106. Egyptian harper and blind choristers 95
107. The *darabooka* drum of modern Egypt 98
108. Cymbals. 99
109. Striking the clappers and dancing 101
**110. Buffoons 102
111. Men dancing in the street to the sound of the drum . . 103
112. A military band 104
113. The trumpet 105
114. The drum 105
115. Mode of slinging the drum 106
116. A drum-stick 107
117. A drum and drum-sticks 107
*118. } Harpers in the tomb of Remeses III., called Bruce's tomb . { 108
*118a}   { 109
119. Head of a harp from Thebes 110
120. Painted harp on a stand, a man clapping his hands, and a player
     on the guitar 110
121. Minstrel standing while playing the harp 112
122. Harp raised on a stand, or support 112
123. Harp of the Paris Collection 114
124. Lyre ornamented with the head of an animal . . . 115
125. Lyres played with and without the *plectrum* . . . 116
126. Lyre in the Berlin Museum 116
127. Lyre of the Leyden Collection 117
128. } Triangular instruments 118
129. }
130. Other instruments 119

Woodcut   Page
131. A standing lyre 120
132. An instrument played as an accompaniment to the lyre . . 120
133. A light instrument borne on the shoulder 121
134. Instrument, differing from the harp, lyre, and guitar . . 121
135.} Another kind of instrument of four strings 122
136.}
137. Female playing the guitar 123
138. Dancing while playing the guitar 124
139. Guitar supported by a strap 124
140. Instrument resembling the guitar 125
141. Flute-player, standing 127
142. Reed pipes found 128
143. A woman dancing while playing the double pipe . . . 128
144. Sacred musicians 130
145. Sistrum 131
146. Sistrum of unusual form 131
147. Sistrum in the British Museum 132
148. Model of a sistrum in the Berlin Museum 132
149.} Sistra in the Berlin Museum 133
150.}
151. Different attitudes in the dance 134
152. The Pirouette and other steps 136
153. Figure dances 137
154. Men dancing alone 139
155. Man dancing a solo to the sound of the hand . . . 139
Vignette
D. The Palace-temple of Remeses II. at Thebes during the inun-
        dation 140

CHAPTER III.
Vignette
E. The two Colossi of Thebes during the inundation . . 141
Woodcut
156.} Parties of guests . . . . {142
157.}   {143
158. A black and white slave waiting upon a lady at a party . 144
159. Ladies talking about their earrings 145
160. Gold vases of the time of Thothmes III. 147
161. Bags, generally containing gold dust, tied up and sealed . 148
162. Vases, with one and two handles 149
163. Ornamented vases 150
164. Richly ornamented vases 151

Woodcut	Page

165. Vases with the head of a bird and of a Typhonian monster . 152
166. Vases, jugs, drinking-cups. 154
167. Various vases, one of cut glass 155
168. Bronze and other vases 156
169. Large bronze vase, like a caldron 156
170. Alabaster and porcelain vase 157
171. Vases of alabaster, porcelain, and glass; some for holding ointment 157
172. Bronze vase, with elastic cover 158
173. A glass bottle 158
174.
175. } Ornamental carved boxes 159
176, 177, 178, 179,
180, 181, 182, 183. } Ornamental wooden boxes . . . . { 160 / 162
184. A box, with lid carved also, belonging to the toilet table . 163
185. Curious substitute for a hinge 164
186. Terra-cotta bottle, held on the thumb 165
187. Butcher cutting up an *Ibex*, another sharpening his knife on a steel 169
188. Peculiar joint of meat 171
*189. A head given to a beggar 171
190. An ox and bird placed entire on the altar 173
191.
191 a } The kitchen 175, 176
192. Cooking geese and various joints. 178
193. Drinking cups, or saucers 180
194. A table brought in with the dishes on it 181
195. A cake of preserved dates 181
196. A dinner party, of very early time 182
197.
198. } Spoons 183, 184
199.
200. Alabaster shell and spoon 184
201. Bronze simpula 184
202. Figure of a mummy, brought to an Egyptian table . . 187
**203. Tumblers 189
204. Feats of agility 189
205. Playing at *mora* 190
206. Games of draughts and *mora* 190
**207. Draughtsmen (*figs. 3, 4, 5, lately found*) . . . 191
208. Game of draughts 192
209. A game like a Greek *kollabismos*, a sort of " forfeits" . . 192

Woodcut   Page
209a. Remeses III. playing at draughts 193
210. A game with a hoop 194
**211. Other games 194
**212. Wooden game boards, of *Dr. Abbott's Collection* . . . 194
213. Dice found in Egypt 195
214. Wooden dolls 196
215. Children's toys 197
216.
217. } Games of ball 198, 199
218.
219. Balls, found 200
220. Men swinging women round by the arms . . . 201
221. Game of men rising from the ground 201
222. Game of throwing knives into a wooden block . . 202
223. Thimble rig 203
224. Dwarfs and deformed persons in the service of grandees . 204
225. Wrestling 205
226. Single stick, or cudgelling 206
227. Feats of raising weights 207
228. Boatmen fighting with the *nebóot*, or long pole . . . 208
229.   (209
230. } Bull fights . . . . {210
231.   (211

CHAPTER IV.

Vignette
F. View of Philæ 212
Woodcut
232. Hyæna caught in a trap 213
233. Mode of carrying young animals 215
234. Gazelles and other animals kept in the preserves . . 216
235. Marking cattle 217
236. Huntsman bringing home game with coupled dogs . . 219
237. Gazelle, porcupines, and hare, caught, and brought home . 219
238. Catching a gazelle with the *lasso* 220
239. Catching a wild ox with the *lasso* 220
240. Hunting with a lion 221
241. Shooting at the wild ox 222
242. Animals from the sculptures 223
243. A chase in the desert 225
244. Monsters, or fabulous animals 226

Woodcut   Page
  245. Various dogs of Egypt   230
  246. } Various birds of Egypt 232, 233
  247.
  248. } A sportsman using the throw-stick   .   .   .   . { 235
  249.   { 236
  250. Fowling and fishing scene 237
  251. A gentleman fishing 238
  252. Attendant carrying a *corbag* whip   240
  253. Spear used in the chase of the hippopotamus   .   .   . 241
  254. A reel held by an attendant   241
  255. The Trochilus 243
  256. } The name of "Egypt" in hieroglyphics   244
  257.
  258. } Emblems   257
  259.
  260. Various flowers from the sculptures   258
  261. Offering ointment   259
  262. Offering a figure of Truth   260
  263. Emblematic offerings   261
  264. Offerings on the altar   262
  265. Stands for bearing offerings   263
  266. Joints placed on the altars, or the tables   .   .   . 264
  267. Offering of incense   265
  268. Offering of incense and libation 265
  269. Wine offered   .   .   .   .
  270. Vases used for libations   .   .   .   .   .   . } 266
  271. Offering of milk   .   .   .   .
**271a Shrine or ark 267
  272. One of the sacred boats or arks 270
  273. Dedication of the *pylon* of a temple   271
  274. Sceptre of a Queen 276
  275. *Tau*, or sign of life 277
  276. "Lord of the assemblies" 280
  277. Bronze figure of Apis   289
  278. Hieroglyphical name of Apis,—*Hapi*. (It is remarkable that
       the Nile, and one of the Genii of Amenti, are also called *Hapi*) 290

CHAPTER V.

Vignette
  G. The Pyramids during the inundation, from near the Fork of
     the Delta   302

Woodcut   Page

279. Princes and children, head-dress of 311
280. People throwing dust on their heads 315
281. King and Queen offering 317
282. Sacred offices held by women 318
283. Priests clad in the leopard skin 320
284. Onions and other vegetables; and figs in a basket, the hieroglyphic of " wife ". 323
285. Mode of tying up onions for some offerings . . . 324
286. Dresses of priests 334
287. Alabaster pillow for the head 335
288. Allies of the Egyptians 338
289. Disciplined troops 339
290. Phalanx of heavy infantry 341
291. Egyptian standards 343
292. Officers of the king's household 344
293. Shields 345
294. Boss of the shield 346
295. Thong inside the shield for slinging it 346
296. Concave form of the shield 347
297. Grasping the spear while supporting the shield . . . 347
298. Handle of the shield 347
299. Bucklers of unusual form 348
300. The large shield 349
301. Bow of the Koofa 349
302. Egyptian bows 350
303. }Mode of stringing the bow 350
304. }
305. A guard worn on the wrist 351
306. Spare arrows carried in the hand 352
307. }Arrows made of reed 352
308. }
309. Metal heads of arrows 353
310. Javelin and spear heads 356
310 a Spear head 356
311. Heads of small javelins 356
312. Slingers 357
313. Daggers in their sheaths 358
314. Stabbing an enemy 359
315. Mode of wearing a dagger 359
316. Dagger with its sheath 360
317. Another dagger 360
318. Axes and hatchets 361

Woodcut   Page
319. Battle axes 362
320. Pole-axe 363
321. Maces 364
322. Curved stick or club 365
323. Helmets or head pieces 366
*324. Corslets, with and without metal plates 367
**324 a Plates of scale armour with name of Sheshonk (Shishak) . 368
?25. Egyptian soldiers of different corps 369
326. The royal princes in their chariots 370
327. The son of King Remeses with his charioteer . . . 371
328. Whips 372
329. Whip suspended from the wrist of the archer . . . 373
330. Making the pole and other parts of a chariot . . . 374
331. A war chariot with bow cases and complete furniture . . 376
332. Chariot of the Rot-ñ-n 376
333. Cutting leather and binding a car 377
334. Bending and preparing the woodwork of a chariot . . 378
335. Chariots in perspective, from a comparison of different sculptures 380
335 a An Egyptian car and horses in perspective . . . 382
**336. A wheel and shafts 383
337. Singular instance of a four-wheel carriage 384
338. An Ethiopian princess travelling in a *plaustrum*, or car drawn
       by oxen 385
339. Car at Florence 385
340. Use of the testudo 388
341. Assault of a fort 389
342. Some of the Asiatic enemies of the Egyptians . . . 391
343. Carts of the Tokkari, at the time of their defeat . . . 392
344. Prisoners of Tirhaka 396
345. Other enemies of the Egyptians 398
346. Phalanx of the Sheta (or Khita) with their fortified town,
       surrounded by ditches, on a river, over which are bridges . 400
347. Other Asiatic and African enemies of the Egyptians . . 402
348. A body of archers drawing their bows 405
349. A guard at the gates of an encampment 407
350. A captive secured by a handcuff 410
351. War galley; the sail pulled up during the action . . . 412
352. Large boat with sail, apparently of the papyrus, a double mast,
       and many oars 414
353. Women of the Rot-ñ-n sent to Egypt 416
354. Black slaves, with their women and children . . . 417
355. Egyptian arms 419

MANNERS AND CUSTOMS

OF

THE ANCIENT EGYPTIANS.

A.   Part of Cairo, showing the *Mulkufs* on the houses of modern Egypt.

CHAPTER I.

CHARACTER OF THE EGYPTIANS — ORIGINAL POPULATIONS — SOCIAL LIFE —
HOUSES — VILLAS — FARMYARDS — GARDENS — VINEYARDS — WINEPRESS
— WINES — BEER — FURNITURE OF ROOMS — CHAIRS.

THE monumental records and various works of art, and, above all,
the writings, of the Greeks and Romans, have made us acquainted
with their customs and their very thoughts; and though the
literature of the Egyptians is unknown, their monuments, especially the paintings in the tombs, have afforded us an insight
into their mode of life scarcely to be obtained from those of any
other people. The influence that Egypt had in early times
on Greece gives to every inquiry respecting it an additional
interest; and the frequent mention of the Egyptians in the Bible

VOL. I.

connects them with the Hebrew records, of which many satis-factory illustrations occur in the sculptures of Pharaonic times. Their great antiquity also enables us to understand the condition of the world long before the era of written history; all existing monuments left by other people are comparatively modern; and the paintings in Egypt are the earliest descriptive illustrations of the manners and customs of any nation.

It is from these that we are enabled to form an opinion of the character of the Egyptians. They have been pronounced a serious, gloomy people, saddened by the habit of abstruse specu-lation; but how far this conclusion agrees with fact will be seen in the sequel. They were, no doubt, less lively than the Greeks; but if a comparatively late writer, Ammianus Marcel-linus, may have remarked a " rather sad " expression, after they had been for ages under successive foreign yokes, this can scarcely be admitted as a testimony of their character in the early times of their prosperity; and though a sadness of expression might be observed in the present oppressed population, they cannot be considered a grave or melancholy people. Much, indeed, may be learnt from the character of the modern Egyptians; and not-withstanding the infusion of foreign blood, particularly of the Arab invaders, every one must perceive the strong resemblance they bear to their ancient predecessors. It is a common error to suppose that the conquest of a country gives an entirely new character to the inhabitants. The immigration of a whole nation taking possession of a thinly-peopled country, will have this effect, when the original inhabitants are nearly all driven out by the new-comers; but immigration has not always, and conquest never has, for its object the destruction or expulsion of the native population; they are found useful to the victors, and as necessary for them as the cattle, or the productions of the soil. Invaders are always numerically inferior to the conquered nation—even to the male population; and, when the women are added to the number, the majority is greatly in favour of the original race, and they must exercise immense influence on the character of the rising generation. The customs, too, of the old inhabitants are very readily adopted by the new-comers, especially when they are found to suit the climate and the peculiarities of the country they have been formed in ; and the habits of a small mass of settlers living in contact with them fade away more and more with each successive generation.   So it has been in Egypt ; and, as usual, the conquered people bear the stamp of the ancient inhabitants rather than that of the Arab conquerors.

Of the various institutions of the ancient Egyptians, none are more interesting than those which relate to their social life ; and when we consider the condition of other countries in the early ages when they flourished, from the 10th to the 20th century before our era, we may look with respect on the advancement they had then made in civilization, and acknowledge the benefits they conferred upon mankind during their career.   For, like other people, they have had their part in the great scheme of the world's development, and their share of usefulness in the destined progress of the human race ; for countries, like individuals, have certain qualities given them, which, differing from those of their predecessors and contemporaries, are intended in due season to perform their requisite duties.   The interest felt in the Egyptians is from their having led the way, or having been the first people we know of who made any great progress, in the arts and manners of civilization ; which, for the period when they lived, was very creditable, and far beyond that of other kingdoms of the world.   Nor can we fail to remark the difference between them and their Asiatic rivals, the Assyrians, who, even at a much later period, had the great defects of Asiatic cruelty—flaying alive, impaling, and torturing their prisoners ; as the Persians, Turks, and other Orientals have done to the present century ; the reproach of which cannot be extended to the ancient Egyptians.   Being the dominant race of that age, they necessarily had an influence on others with whom they came in contact ; and it is by these means that civilization is advanced through its various stages ; each people striving to improve on the lessons derived from a neighbour whose institutions they appreciate, or consider beneficial to themselves.   It was thus that the active

mind of the talented Greeks sought and improved on the lessons
derived from other countries, especially from Egypt; and though
the latter, at the late period of the 7th century B. C., had lost its
greatness and the prestige of superiority among the nations of
the world, it was still the seat of learning and the resort of
studious philosophers; and the abuses consequent on the fall of an
empire had not yet brought about the demoralization of after times.

The early part of Egyptian monumental history is coeval with
the arrivals of Abraham and of Joseph, and the Exodus of the
Israelites; and we know from the Bible what was the state of the
world at that time. But then, and apparently long before, the
habits of social life in Egypt were already what we find them to
have been during the most glorious period of their career; and
as the people had already laid aside their arms, and military men
only carried them when on service, some notion may be had of
the very remote date of Egyptian civilization. In the treatment
of women they seem to have been very far advanced beyond
other wealthy communities of the same era, having usages very
similar to those of modern Europe; and such was the respect
shown to women that precedence was given to them over men,
and the wives and daughters of kings succeeded to the throne
like the male branches of the royal family. Nor was this privilege rescinded, even though it had more than once entailed upon
them the troubles of a contested succession: foreign kings often
having claimed a right to the throne through marriage with an
Egyptian princess. It was not a mere influence that they possessed, which women often acquire in the most arbitrary Eastern
communities; nor a political importance accorded to a particular
individual, like that of the Soltána Valídeh, the Queen Mother,
at Constantinople; it was a right acknowledged by law, both in
private and public life. They knew that unless women were
treated with respect, and made to exercise an influence over
society, the standard of public opinion would soon be lowered,
and the manners and morals of men would suffer; and in acknowledging this, they pointed out to women the very responsible
duties they had to perform to the community.

It has been said that the Egyptian priests were only allowed to have one wife, while the rest of the community had as many as they chose ; but, besides the improbability of such a license, the testimony of the monuments accords with Herodotus in disproving the statement, and each individual is represented in his tomb with a single consort.　Their mutual affection is also indicated by the fond manner in which they are seated together, and by the expressions of endearment they use to each other, as well as to their children.　And if further proof were wanting to show their respect for social ties, we may mention the conduct of Pharaoh, in the case of the supposed sister of Abraham, standing in remarkable contrast to the habits of most princes of those and many subsequent ages.

From their private life great insight is obtained into their character and customs ; and their household arrangements, the style of their dwellings, their amusements, and their occupations, explain their habits ; as their institutions, mode of government, arts, and military knowledge illustrate their history, and their relative position among the nations of antiquity.　In their form and arrangement, the houses were made to suit the climate, modified according to their advancement in civilization ; and we are often enabled to trace in their abodes some of the primitive habits of a people, long after they have been settled in towns, and have adopted the manners of wealthy communities ; as the tent may still be traced in the houses of the Turks, and the small original wooden chamber in the mansions and temples of ancient Greece.

As in all warm climates, the poorer classes of Egyptians lived much in the open air ; and the houses of the rich were constructed to be cool throughout the summer ; currents of refreshing air being made to circulate freely through them by the judicious arrangement of the passages and courts.　Corridors, supported on columns, gave access to the different apartments through a succession of shady avenues and areas, with one side open to the air, as in our cloisters ; and even small detached houses had an open court in the centre, planted as a garden with palms and other trees. *Mulkufs*, or wooden wind-sails, were also fixed over the terraces of the upper story, facing the prevalent and cool N.W. wind, which was conducted down their sloping boards into the interior of the house. They were exactly similar to those in the modern houses of Cairo; and some few were double, facing in opposite directions.

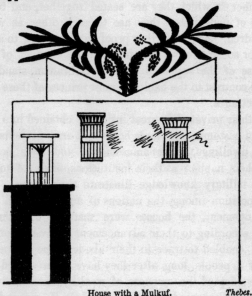

1.   House with a Mulkuf.   *Thebes.*

The houses were built of crude brick, stuccoed and painted with all the combinations of bright colour, in which the Egyptians delighted; and a highly decorated mansion had numerous courts, and architectural details derived from the temples. Over the door was sometimes a sentence, as "the good house;" or the name of a king, under whom the owner probably held some office; many other symbols of good omen were also put up, as at the entrances of modern Egyptian houses; and a visit to some temple gave as good a claim to a record, as the pilgrimage to Mekkeh at the present day. Poor people were satisfied with very simple tenements; their wants being easily supplied, both as to lodging and

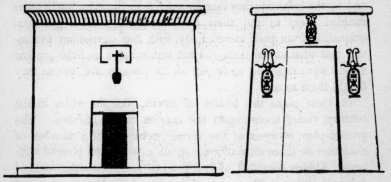

2. Over the door is " The good house." 3. Doorway, with a king's name.

food; and their house consisted of four walls, with a flat roof
of palm-branches laid across a split date-tree as a beam, and
covered with mats plastered over with a thick coating of mud.
It had one door, and a few small windows closed by wooden
shutters. As it scarcely ever rained, the mud roof was not
washed into the sitting room ; and this cottage rather answered
as a shelter from the sun, and as a closet for their goods, than for
the ordinary purpose of a house in other countries. Indeed at
night the owners slept on the roof, during the greater part of the
year; and as most of their work was done out of doors, they
might easily be persuaded that a house was far less necessary for
them than a tomb. To convince the rich of this ultra-philo-
sophical sentiment was not so easy ; at least the practice differed
from the theory ; and though it was promulgated among all
the Egyptians, it did not prevent the priests and other grandees
from living in very luxurious abodes, or enjoying the good
things of this world ; and a display of wealth was found to be
useful in maintaining their power, and in securing the obedience
of a credulous people. The worldly possessions of the priests
were therefore very extensive, and if they imposed on themselves
occasional habits of abstemiousness, avoided certain kinds of
unwholesome food, and performed many mysterious observances,
they were amply repaid by the improvement of their health,

and by the influence they thereby acquired. Superior intelligence enabled them to put their own construction on regulations emanating from their sacred body, with the convenient persuasion that what suited them did not suit others; and the profane vulgar were expected to do, not as the priests did, but as they taught them to do.

In their plans the houses of towns, like the villas in the country, varied according to the caprice of the builders. The ground-plan, in some of the former, consisted of a number of chambers on three sides of a court, which was often planted with trees. Others consisted of two rows of rooms on either side of a long passage, with an entrance-court from the street; and others were laid out in chambers round a central area, similar to

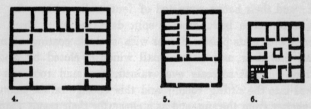

4.   5.   6.

the Roman *Impluvium*, and paved with stone, or containing a few trees, a tank, or a fountain, in its centre. Sometimes, though rarely, a flight of steps led to the front door from the street.

Houses of small size were often connected together, and formed the continuous sides of streets; and a court-yard was common to several dwellings. Others of a humbler kind consisted merely of rooms opening on a narrow passage, or directly on the street. These had only a basement story, or ground-floor; and few houses exceeded two stories above it. They mostly consisted of one upper floor; and though Diodorus speaks of the lofty houses in Thebes four and five stories high, the paintings show that few had three, and the largest seldom four, including as he does the basement-story. Even the greater portion of the house was confined to a first-floor, with an additional story in one part, on which was a terrace covered by an awning, or a light roof supported on columns (as in Woodcut 25). This served for the

ladies of the family to sit at work in during the day, and here
the master of the house often slept at night during the summer,
or took his *siesta* in the afternoon. Some had a tower which rose
even above the terrace.

The first-floor was what the
Italians call the "*piano nobile;*"
the ground rooms being chiefly
used for stores, or as offices, of
which one was set apart for the
porter, and another for visiters
coming on business. Sometimes
besides the parlour were receiving apartments on the base-

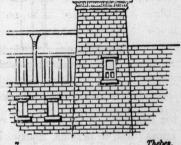

7.   *Thebes.*

ment-story, but guests were generally entertained on the first-
floor; and on this were the sleeping rooms also, except where the
house was of two or three stories. The houses of wealthy citizens
often covered a considerable space, and either stood directly
upon the street, or a short way back, within an open court; and
some large mansions were detached, and had several entrances
on two or three sides. Before the door was a porch supported on
two columns, decked with banners or ribands, and larger porticos
had a double row of columns, with statues between them.

Other mansions had a flight of steps leading to a raised platform, with a doorway between two towers, not unlike those before

8.   Porch. *Tel el Amarna.*   9.   Porch. *Thebes and Tel el Amarna.*

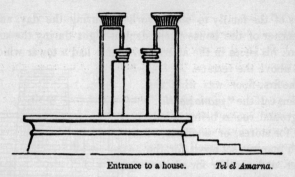

10.   Entrance to a house.   *Tel el Amarna.*

the temples. A line of trees ran parallel to the front of the
house; and to prevent injuries from cattle, or any accident, the
stems were surrounded by a low wall, pierced with square holes
to admit the air.* This custom of planting trees about town
houses was common also at Rome.

The height of the portico was about twelve or fifteen feet,
just exceeding that of the cornice of the door, which was only
raised by its threshold above the level of the ground. On either
side of the main entrance was a smaller door, which stood at an
equal distance between it and the side-wall, and was probably
intended for the servants, or those who came on business. On
entering by the porch you passed into an open court (*aula*, or
hall), containing a *mándara*, or receiving room, for visiters.
This building, supported by columns, decorated with banners,
was closed only at the lower part by inter-columnar panels, over
which a stream of cool air was admitted, and protection from the
rays of the sun was secured by an awning that covered it. On the
opposite side of the court was another door, the approach to the
mándara from the interior; and the master of the house, on the
announcement of a stranger, came in that way to receive him.
Three doors led from this court to another of larger dimensions,
which was ornamented with avenues of trees, and communicated
on the right and left with the interior of the house; and this,
like most of the large courts, had a back entrance through a central

* As in Woodcut 11, *fig.* 2, *c.*

and lateral gateway.   The arrangement of the interior was much
the same on either side of the court : six or more chambers,
whose doors faced those of the opposite set, opening on a corridor
supported by columns on the right and left of an area, which was
shaded by a double row of trees.

At the upper end of one of these areas was a sitting-room,
which faced the door leading to the great court ; and over this
and the other chambers were the apartments of the upper-story.
Here were also two small gateways towards the street.

Another plan consisted of a court, with the usual avenue of
trees, on one side of which were several sets of chambers opening
on corridors or passages, but without any colonnade before the
doors.   The receiving room looked upon the court, and from
it a row of columns led to the private sitting apartment, which
stood isolated in one of the passages, near to a door communicating with the side chambers ; and, in its position, with a corridor
or porch in front, it bears a striking resemblance to the "summer
parlour" of Eglon, king of Moab,* "which he had for himself
alone," and where he received Ehud the Israelite stranger.   And
the flight of Ehud "through the porch," after he had shut and
locked the door of the parlour, shows its situation to have been
very similar to some of these isolated apartments in the houses,
or villas, of the ancient Egyptians.   The side chambers were
frequently arranged on either side of a corridor, others faced
towards the court, and others were only separated from the outer
wall by a long passage.

In the distribution of the apartments numerous and different
modes were adopted, according to circumstances ; in general,
however, the large mansions seem to have consisted of a court
and several corridors, with rooms leading from them, not unlike
many of those now built in Oriental and tropical countries.†
The houses in most of the Egyptian towns are quite destroyed,
leaving few traces of their plans, or even of their sites ; but
sufficient remains of some at Thebes, at Tel el Amarna, and other

---

* Judges, iii. 20.   † Woodcut 11, *fig.* 1.

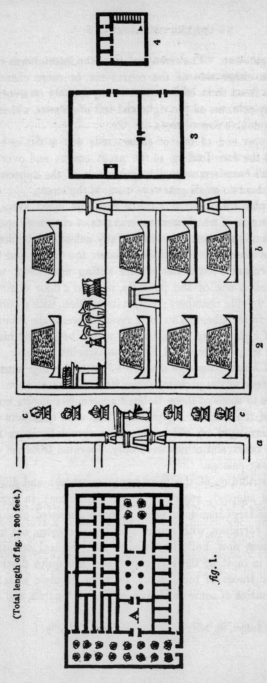

Tel el Amarna

Fig. 2 shows the relative position of the house, *a* ; and the granary, *b*. *cc*, trees surrounded by low walls.

Plans of houses and a granary.

fig. 1.

(Total length of fig. 1, 200 feet.)

11.

places, to enable us, with the help of the sculptures, to ascertain their form and appearance.

Granaries were also laid out in a very regular manner, and varied of course in plan as much as the houses, to which there is reason to believe they were frequently attached, even in the towns; and they were sometimes only separated from the house by an avenue of trees.

Some small houses consisted merely of a court, and three or four store rooms on the ground-floor, with a single chamber above, to which a flight of steps led from the court; but they were probably only met with in the country, and resembled some still found in the *fellah* villages of modern Egypt.* Very similar to these was the model of a house now in the British Museum,† which solely consisted of a court-yard and three small store-rooms

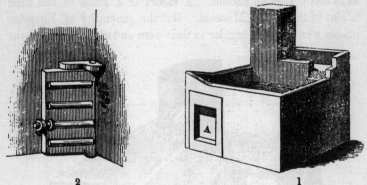

12.
2   1

    Fig. 1. Model of a small house.   *From Thebes.*
    Fig. 2 shows how the door opened and was secured. *British Museum.*

on the ground-floor, with a staircase leading to a room belonging to the storekeeper, which was furnished with a narrow window or aperture opposite the door, rather intended for the purposes of ventilation than to admit the light. In the court a woman was represented making bread, as is sometimes done at the present day in Egypt, in the open air; and the store-rooms were full of grain.

   * Woodcut 11, *fig.* 4.   † Woodcuts 12, 13.

Other small houses in towns consisted of two or three stories above the ground-floor. They had no court, and stood close together, covering a small space, and high in proportion to their base, like many of those at Karnak. The lower part had merely the door of entrance and some store-rooms, over which were a first and second floor, each with three windows on the front and side, and above these an attic without windows, and a stair-case leading to a terrace on the flat roof. The floors were laid on rafters, the end of which projected slightly from the walls like dentils ; and the courses of brick were in waving or concave lines, as in the walls of an enclosure at Dayr el Medeeneh in Thebes. The windows of the first-floor had a sort of mullion dividing them into two lights each, with a transom above ; and the upper windows were filled with trellis-work, or cross bars of wood, as in many Turkish harems. A model of a house of this kind is also in the British Museum. But the generality of Egyptian houses were far less regular in their plan and elevation ; and the

13.   Showing the interior of the court, and upper chamber in the same.

usual disregard for symmetry is generally observable in the houses even of towns.

The doors, both of the entrances and of the inner apartments, were frequently stained to imitate foreign and rare woods. They were either of one or two valves, turning on pins of metal,

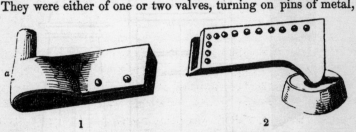

14.

Fig. 1. The upper pin, on which the door turned.
Fig. 2. Lower pin.   *British Museum.*

and were secured within by a bar or bolts. Some of these bronze pins have been discovered in the tombs of Thebes. They were fastened to the wood with nails of the same metal, whose round heads served also as an ornament, and the upper one had a projection at the back, in order to prevent the door striking against the wall. We also find in the stone lintels and floor, behind the thresholds of the tombs and temples, the holes in which they turned, as well as those of the bolts and bars, and the recess for receiving the opened valves. The folding doors had bolts in the centre, sometimes above as well as below : a bar was placed across from one wall to the other ; and in many instances wooden locks secured them by passing over the centre, at the junction of the two folds. For greater security they were occasionally sealed with a mass of clay, as is proved by some tombs found closed at Thebes, by the sculptures, and in the account given by Herodotus of Rhampsinitus's treasury.

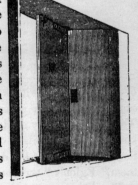

15.   A folding-door.

Keys were made of bronze or iron, and consisted of a long

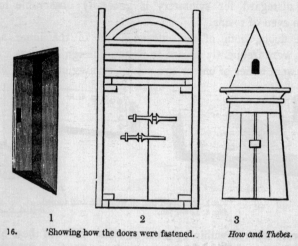

1   2   3

16.   'Showing how the doors were fastened.   *How and Thebes.*

straight shank, about five inches in length, with three or more
projecting teeth; others had a nearer resemblance to the wards

17.   Iron key.   *From Thebes.*

of modern keys, with a short shank about an inch long; and
some resembled a common ring with the wards at its back.
These are probably of Roman date. The earliest mention of a
key is in Judges (iii. 23-25), when Ehud having gone "through
the porch, and shut the doors of the parlour upon him and locked
them," Eglon's " servants took a key and opened them."

The doorways, like those in the temples, were often surmounted
by the Egyptian cornice; others were variously decorated, and
some, represented in the tombs, were surrounded with a variety
of ornaments, as usual richly painted. These last, though sometimes found at Thebes, were more general about Memphis and
the Delta; and two good instances of them are preserved at the
British Museum, brought from a tomb near the Pyramids.

18.   Painted on a coffin at *Thebes*.   19.   *Thebes.*

Even at the early period when the Pyramids were built, the doors
were of one or two valves ; and both those of the rooms and the
entrance doors opened inwards, contrary to the custom of the
Greeks, who were consequently obliged to strike on the inside

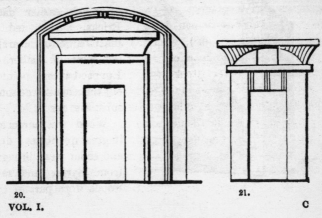

of the street-door before they opened it, in order to warn persons passing by; and the Romans were forbidden to make it open outward without a special permission.   The floors were of stone, or a composition made of lime or other materials; but in humbler abodes they were formed of split date-tree beams, arranged close together or at intervals, with planks or transverse layers of

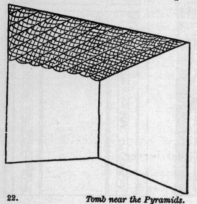

22.   *Tomb near the Pyramids.*   23.   *Thebes.*

palm branches over them, covered with mats and a coating of mud. Many roofs were vaulted, and built like the rest of the house of crude brick; and not only have arches been found of that material dating in the 16th century before our era, but vaulted granaries

appear to be represented of much earlier date. Bricks, indeed, led to the invention of the arch; the want of timber in Egypt having pointed out the necessity of some substitute for it.

Wood was imported in great quantities; deal and cedar were brought from Syria; and rare woods were part of the

24.   *Thebes.*

tribute imposed on foreign nations conquered by the Pharaohs. And so highly were these appreciated for ornamental purposes, that painted imitations were made for poorer persons who could not afford them ; and the panels, windows, doors, boxes, and various kinds of woodwork, were frequently of cheap deal or sycamore, stained to resemble the rarest foreign woods. And the remnants of them found at Thebes show that these imitations were clever substitutes for the reality. Even coffins were sometimes made of foreign wood ; and many are found of cedar of Lebanon. The value of foreign woods also suggested to the Egyptians the process of veneering ; and this was one of the arts of their skilful cabinet-makers.

The ceilings were of stucco, richly painted with various devices, tasteful both in their form and the arrangement of the colours ; among the oldest of which is the Guilloche, often mis-called the Tuscan or Greek border.

Both in the interior and exterior of their houses the walls were sometimes portioned out into large panels of one uniform colour, flush with the surface, or recessed, (as in Woodcuts 25 and 30,) not very unlike those at Pompeii ; and they were red, yellow, or stained to resemble stone or wood. It seems to have been the introduction of this mode of ornament into Roman houses that excited the indignation of Vitruvius ; who says that in old times they used red paint sparingly, like physic, though now whole walls are covered over with it.

Figures were also introduced on the blank walls in the sitting-rooms, or scenes from domestic life, surrounded by ornamental borders, and surmounted by deep cornices of flowers and various devices richly painted ; and no people appear to have been more fond of using flowers on every occasion. In their domestic architecture they formed the chief ornament of the mouldings ; and every visiter received a bouquet of real flowers, as a token of welcome on entering a house. It was the pipe and coffee of the modern Egyptians ; and a guest at a party was not only presented with a lotus, or some other flower, but had a chaplet placed round his head, and another round his neck ; which led the

Roman poet to remark the "many chaplets on the foreheads" of
the Egyptians at their banquets.   Everywhere flowers abounded;
they were formed into wreaths and festoons, they decked the
stands that supported the vases in the convivial chamber, and
crowned the wine-bowl as well as the servants who bore the
cup from it to the assembled guests.

Besides the painted panels there were other points of resemblance to Pompeian taste in the Egyptian houses; particularly the
elongated columns sometimes attached to the building, sometimes
painted on the walls, which were derived by the Greeks either
from Egypt or from Asia.   Their long slender shafts were made
to reach the whole way from the ground to the very roof of

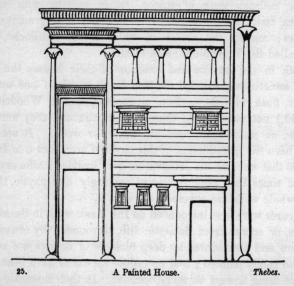

25.   A Painted House.   *Thebes.*

the house, in utter defiance of proportion or the semblance of
utility; performing no more office than many of the pillars and
half columns which, having nothing to support, may be said to
hang up against the fronts of our modern houses, with two tiers
of windows, like pictures, in the vacant space between them.

And though in their temples the horizontal line predominated, as in Greece, the Egyptians were not averse to the contrast of the vertical with it, which they managed by means of the long line of their lofty pyramidal towers, and of their obelisks; and indeed in the lengthy columns that extended up the whole front of their houses they may claim the first introduction of the vertical principle. This was afterwards adopted by the Romans also; and is very obvious in their arches of triumph, where the column, rising from the ground on a pedestal, extends the whole way up the front, forces the entablature to advance, and break its uniform straight course in order to accord with the capital, and is surmounted by a statue or a projecting attic, extending to the summit of the edifice.

The same slender columns, or " reeds for columns," considered so inconsistent by Vitruvius, found their way into the houses of Rome; and we see them painted in those of Pompeii, as well as the " buildings standing on candelabra," he equally condemns. Incongruous they certainly were, having been merely called in from another and proper office, in order to assist in developing a new element of architecture; which long afterwards introduced numerous vertical lines, in the form of towers, minarets, and other lofty edifices, that now rise above our roofs, and give so much variety to the external aspect of modern European and Saracenic towns. This contrast was wanting in the low and very uniform outline of Greek buildings, scarcely relieved by the triangular pediment of a temple; for, however beautiful each monument itself, a Greek city was singularly deficient in the combination of the vertical with the horizontal line. But the endeavour to obtain this effect at Rome, by isolated columns bearing a statue, which towered above the roofs, was not such as taste could justify; for we may well condemn the inappropriateness of extracting from a temple one of its legitimate members, and of magnifying it to an extravagant height; and the same Roman poverty of invention, and inapplicableness, were shown in this as in the maimed " truncated column," called upon to support a bust in lieu of its own head. Nor can any justification be found for the erection of monstrous colossi, such as Egypt, Greece, and Rome produced; and we are now happily freed from the dilemma, of exaggerating what ought to be limited to its proper dimensions, by the resources of modern architecture, whenever we seek the harmonious contrast of vertical and horizontal lines.

The windows of Egyptian dwellings had merely wooden shutters of one or two valves, turning on pins; and these, like the whole building, were painted. The openings were small, because where little light is admitted little heat penetrates; coolness was the great requisite, and in the cloudless sky of Egypt there was no want of light. And though, as in most of our modern houses, the windows were little more than square holes, unrelieved by ornamental mouldings, the Egyptians did not spoil the external appearance of the house by making them of unreasonable size, in order to admit the light, and then inconsistently do all they possibly could to exclude it by numerous dust-catching hangings, such as are inflicted on innocent Englishmen by tasteless and interested upholsterers.

The palace of a king was generally of more durable materials than a private house, and, like the temple to which it was often attached, was of stone, as at Medeenet Haboo in Thebes. It was then placed at the outer end of the avenue that led to the sacred building; and the principal apartments stood, in two stories, immediately over the gateway, through which all the grand processions passed towards the temple. The rest of the building extended a considerable distance on the right and left before this gateway, forming an outer approach from two lodges at the very entrance, occupied by the guards and porters. Some of the chambers looked down upon this passage; others faced in opposite directions; and the whole building was crowned with battlements, like the walls of fortified towns. The apartments were not large, being only 14 feet long by 12 feet 8 inches in breadth, and 13 feet 6 inches in height; the walls being 5 to 6 feet thick were a protection against the heat, and currents of air circulated freely through them from opposite windows. The walls were ornamented with subjects in low relief, or in intaglio, representing the king and his household, with various ornamental devices, particularly the lotus and other flowers.

Pavilions were also built in a similar style, though on a smaller

scale, in various parts of the country, and in the foreign districts
through which the Egyptian armies passed, for the use of the
King; and some private houses occasionally imitated these small
castles, by substituting for the usual parapet wall and cornice
the battlements that crowned them, and which were intended
to represent Egyptian shields. The roofs of all their houses,

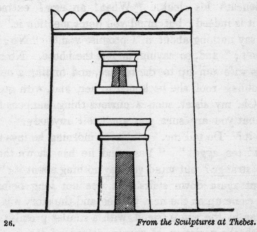

26.   *From the Sculptures at Thebes.*

whether in the town or country, were flat, like those of the
modern houses of Cairo, and there (as at the present day) the
women often held long conversations with their neighbours on
the scandal and gossip of the day. Many a curious subject was
doubtless discussed at these animated meetings, and report affirms
that some modern Cairene stories have been founded on those
recorded of Pharaonic times, one of which is thus related.

A man, digging in his vineyard, having found a jar full of
gold, ran home with joy to announce his good fortune to his
wife; but as he reflected on the way, that women could not
always be trusted with secrets, and that he might lose a treasure
which, of right, belonged to the King, he thought it better
first to test her discretion. As soon therefore as he had entered
the house he called her to him, and, saying he had something of
great importance to tell her, asked if she was sure she could

keep a secret. "Oh, yes," was the ready answer; "when did you ever know me betray one? What is it?" "Well, then,—but you are sure you won't mention it?" "Have I not told you so? why be so tiresome? what is it?" "Now, as you promise me, I will tell you. A most singular thing happens to me; every morning I lay an egg!" at the same time producing one from beneath his cloak. "What! an egg! extraordinary!" "Yes, it is indeed: but mind you don't mention it." "Oh, no, I shall say nothing about it, I promise you." "No; I feel sure you won't;" and, so saying, he left the house. No sooner gone than his wife ran up to the terrace, and finding a neighbour on the adjoining roof, she beckoned to her, and, with great caution, said, "Oh, my sister, such a curious thing happens to my husband; but you are sure you won't tell anybody?" "No, no; what is it? Do tell me." "Every morning he lays ten eggs!" "What! ten eggs!" "Yes; and he has shown them to me; is it not strange? but mind you say nothing about it:" and away she went again down stairs. It was not long before another woman came up on the next terrace, and the story was told in the same way by the wife's friend, with a similar promise of secrecy, only with the variation of twenty instead of ten eggs; till one neighbour after another, to whom the secret was intrusted, had increased them to a hundred. It was not long before the husband heard it also, and the supposed egg-layer, learning how his story had spread, was persuaded not to risk his treasure by trusting his wife with the real secret.

The villas of the Egyptians were of great extent, and contained spacious gardens, watered by canals communicating with the Nile. They had large tanks of water in different parts of the garden, which served for ornament, as well as for irrigation when the Nile was low; and on these the master of the house occasionally amused himself and his friends by an excursion in a pleasure-boat towed by his servants. They also enjoyed the diversion of angling and spearing fish in the ponds within their grounds, and on these occasions they were generally accompanied by a friend, or one or more members of their family. Particular

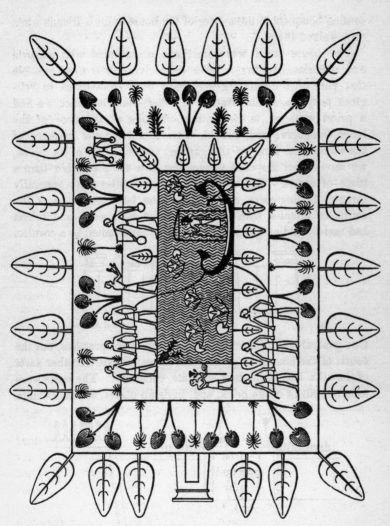

27.　　　Painting in a Tomb at Thebes.

care was always bestowed upon the garden, and their great fondness for flowers is shown by the number they always cultivated,
as well as by the women of the family or the attendants pre-

senting bouquets to the master of the house and his friends when they walked there.

The house itself was sometimes ornamented with propyla and obelisks, like the temples themselves; it is even possible that part of the building may have been consecrated to religious purposes, as the chapels of other countries, since we find a priest engaged in presenting offerings at the door of the inner chambers; and, indeed, were it not for the presence of the women, the form of the garden, and the style of the porch, we should feel disposed to consider it a temple rather than a place of abode.   The entrances of large villas were generally through folding-gates, standing between lofty towers, as at the courts of temples, with a small door at each side; and others had merely folding-gates, with the jambs surmounted by a cornice.

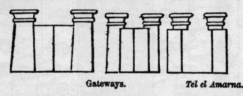

28.   Gateways.   Tel el Amarna.

One general wall of circuit extended round the premises, but the courts of the house, the garden, the offices, and all the other parts of the villa had each their separate enclosure.   The walls were usually built of crude brick, and, in damp places, or when within

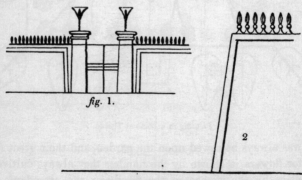

fig. 1.

2

29.   Tel el Amarna and Thebes.

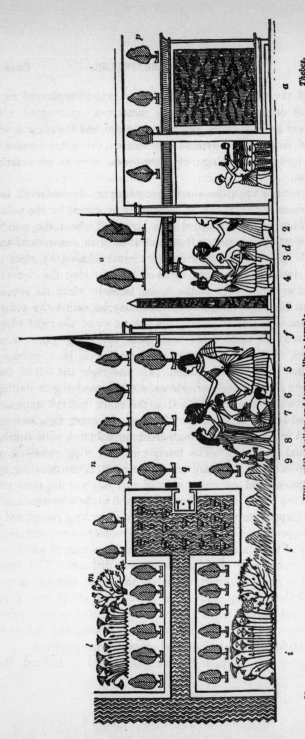

Villa, with obelisks and towers, like a temple.

Thebes.

30.

reach of the inundation, the lower part was strengthened by a basement of stone. They were sometimes ornamented with panels and grooved lines, generally stuccoed, and the summit was crowned either with Egyptian battlements, the usual cornice, a row of spikes in imitation of spear-heads, or with some fancy ornament.

The plans of the villas varied according to circumstances, but their general arrangement is sufficiently explained by the paintings. They were surrounded by a high wall, about the middle of which was the main or front entrance, with one central and two side gates, leading to an open walk shaded by rows of trees. Here were spacious tanks of water, facing the doors of the right and left wings of the house, between which an avenue led from the main entrance to what may be called the centre of the mansion. After passing the outer door of the right wing, you entered an open court with trees, extending quite round a nucleus of inner apartments, and having a back entrance communicating with the garden. On the right and left of this court were six or more store-rooms, a small receiving or waiting room at two of the corners, and at the other end the staircases which led to the upper story. Both of the inner façades were furnished with a corridor, supported on columns, with similar towers and gateways. The interior of this wing consisted of twelve rooms, two outer and one centre court, communicating by folding gates; and on either side of this last was the main entrance to the rooms on the ground-floor, and to the staircases leading to the upper story. At the back were three long rooms, and a gateway opening on the garden, which, besides flowers, contained a variety of trees, a summer-house, and a large tank of water.

The arrangement of the left wing was different. The front gate led to an open court, extending the whole breadth of the façade of the building, and backed by the wall of the inner part. Central and lateral doors thence communicated with another court, surrounded on three sides by a set of rooms, and behind it was a corridor, upon which several other chambers opened.

This wing had no back entrance, and, standing isolated, the

Panelled walls of an Egyptian building.

Thebes.

30 a.

outer court extended entirely round it ; and a succession of doorways communicated from the court with different sections of the
centre of the house, where the rooms, disposed like those already
described, around passages and corridors, served partly as sitting
apartments, and partly as storerooms.

The stables for the horses, and the coach-houses for the travelling chariots and carts, were in the centre, or inner part of the

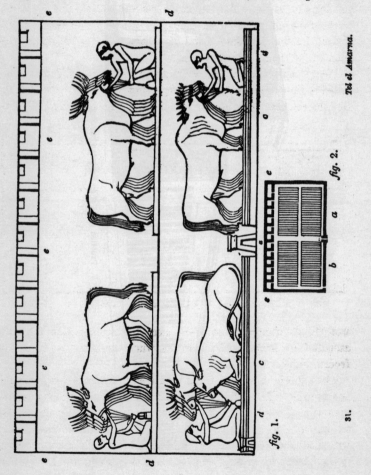

building; but the farm-yard where the cattle were kept stood at some distance from the house, and corresponded to the department known by the Romans under the name of *rustica*. Though enclosed separately, it was within the general wall of circuit, which surrounded the land attached to the villa; and a canal, bringing water from the river, skirted it, and extended along the back of the grounds. It consisted of two parts: the sheds for housing the cattle, which stood at the upper end, and the yard, where rows of rings were fixed, in order to tie them while feeding in the day-time; and men always attended, and frequently fed them with the hand.

The granaries were also apart from the house, and were enclosed within a separate wall; and some of the rooms in which they housed the grain appear to have had vaulted roofs. These

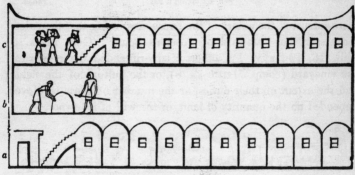

32.   Rooms for housing the grain, apparently vaulted.   *Beni Hassan.*

were filled through an aperture near the top, to which the men ascended by steps, and the grain when wanted was taken out from a door at the base.

The superintendence of the house and grounds was intrusted to stewards, who regulated the tillage of the land, received whatever was derived from the sale of the produce, overlooked the returns of the quantity of cattle or stock upon the estate, settled all the accounts, and condemned the delinquent peasants to the bastinado, or any punishment they might deserve. To one

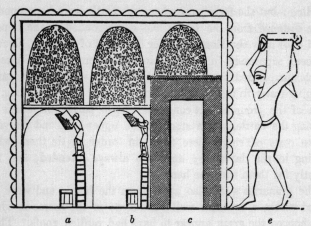

a   b   c   e

33.—Granary, showing how the grain was put in, and that the doors *a b* were intended
for taking it out.   *Thebes.*

were intrusted the affairs of the house, answering to " the ruler,"
" overseer," or " steward of Joseph's house " (Gen. xxxix. 5 ;
xliii. 16, 19 ; xliv. 1) ; others " superintended the granaries,"
the vineyard (comp. Matth. xx. 8), or the culture of the fields ;
and the extent of their duties, or the number of those employed,
depended on the quantity of land, or the will of its owner.

2   3   4   *fig.* 1   5   6

34.   Steward (fig. 1) overlooking the tillage of the lands.   *Thebes.*

The mode of laying out their gardens was as varied as that of
the houses ; but in all cases they appear to have taken particular
care to command a plentiful supply of water, by means of reservoirs and canals. Indeed, in no country is artificial irrigation
more required than in the valley of the Nile ; and, from the cir-
cumstance of the water of the inundation not being admitted into
the gardens, they depend throughout the year on the supply
obtained from wells and tanks, or a neighbouring canal.

The mode of irrigation adopted by the ancient Egyptians was exceedingly simple, being merely the *shadóof*, or pole and bucket of the present day ; and, in many instances, men were employed to carry the water in pails, suspended by a wooden yoke they bore upon their shoulders. The same yoke was employed for

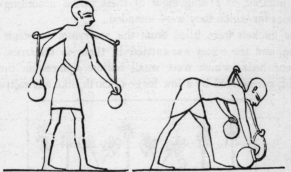

35.   Men watering the ground with pots of water.   *Beni Hassan.*

carrying other things, as boxes, baskets containing game and poultry, or whatever was taken to market ; and every trade seems to have used it for this purpose, from the potter and the brick-maker, to the carpenter and the shipwright.

The wooden bar or yoke was about three feet seven inches in length ; and the straps, which were double, and fastened together

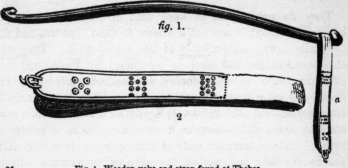

fig. 1.

2

a

36.   Fig. 1. Wooden yoke and strap found at Thebes.
                 Fig. 2 is the strap *a*, on a larger scale.

at the lower as well as at the upper extremity, were of leather,

VOL. I.

and between fifteen and sixteen inches long. The small thong at the bottom not only served to connect the ends, but was probably intended to fasten a hook, or an additional strap, if required, to attach the burden : and though most of these yokes had two, some were furnished with four or eight straps ; and the form, number, or arrangement of them varied according to the purposes for which they were intended.

The buckets were filled from the reservoirs or ponds in the garden, and the water was carried in them to the trees, or the different beds, which were small hollow squares on the level ground, surrounded by a low ledge of earth, like our saltpans.

37.   Water-buckets carried by a yoke on the shoulders.   *Thebes.*

They do not appear to have used the water - wheel very generally ; though it was not unknown to them ; but this and the hydraulic screw were probably of late introduction. They may also have had the foot-machine mentioned by Philo ; and it is either to this, or to their stopping the small channels which conducted the water from one bed to another, that the sentence in Deuteronomy (xi. 40) refers—" Egypt . . . . where thou sowedst thy seed, and wateredst it with thy *foot* as a garden of herbs ;" but the common mode of raising water from the Nile was by the pole and bucket, the *shadóof,* so common still in Egypt.

Skins were much used by the Egyptians for carrying water, as

38.   Shadóof, or pole and bucket, for watering the garden.   *Thebes.*

well as for sprinkling the ground before the rooms or seats of
the grandees, and they were frequently kept ready filled at
the tank for that purpose.

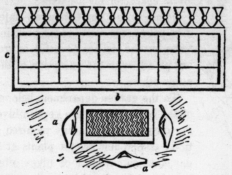

a a a Water-skins suspended close to the tank *b.*
c Beds of a garden, laid out as at the present day in Egypt, very like our saltpans.
39.   *Thebes.*

Part of the garden was laid out in walks shaded with trees,
usually planted in rows, and surrounded, at the base of the stem,
with a circular ridge of earth, which, being lower at the centre
than at the circumference, retained the water, and directed it

more immediately towards the roots. It is difficult to say if trees were trimmed into any particular shape, or if their formal

40.   1. Tree with earth raised round the roots.
             2. The same according to our mode of representing it.

appearance in the sculpture is merely owing to a conventional mode of representing them; but, since the pomegranate, and some other fruit trees, are drawn with spreading and irregular branches, it is possible that sycamores, and others, which presented large masses of foliage, were really trained in that formal manner, though, from the hieroglyphic signifying "*tree*" having the same shape, we may conclude it 41. was only a general character for all trees.

Some, as the pomegranates, date-trees, and *dôm*-palms, are easily recognised in the sculptures, but the rest are doubtful, as are the flowering plants, with the exception of the lotus and a few others.

To the garden department belonged the care of the bees, which were kept in hives very like our own. In Egypt they required great attention; and so few are its plants at the present day, that the owners of hives often take the bees in boats to various spots upon the Nile, in 42.   quest of flowers. They are a smaller kind than our own; and though found wild in the country, they are far less numerous than wasps, hornets, and ichneumons. The wild bees live mostly under stones, or in clefts of the rock, as in many other countries; and the expression of Moses, as of the Psalmist,

" honey out of the rock," shows that in Palestine their habits were the same. Honey was thought of great importance in Egypt, both for household purposes, and for an offering to the gods; that of Benha (thence surnamed *El assal*), or Athribis, in the Delta, retained its reputation to a late time; and a jar of honey from that place was one of the four presents sent by John Mekaukes, the governor of Egypt, to Mohammed.

Large gardens were usually divided into different parts; the principal sections being appropriated to the date and sycamore trees, and to the vineyard. The former may be called the orchard. The flower and kitchen gardens also occupied a considerable space, laid out in beds; and dwarf trees, herbs, and flowers, were grown in red earthen pots, exactly like our own, arranged in long rows by the walks and borders.

Besides the orchard and gardens, some of the large villas had a park or paradise, with its fish-ponds and preserves for game, as well as poultry-yards for keeping hens and geese, stalls for fattening cattle, wild goats, gazelles, and other animals originally from the desert, whose meat was reckoned among the dainties of the table. It was in these extensive preserves that the rich amused themselves with the chase; and they also enclosed a considerable space in the desert itself with net-fences, into which the animals were driven, and shot with arrows, or hunted with dogs.

Gardens are frequently represented in the tombs of Thebes and other parts of Egypt, many of which are remarkable for their extent. The one here introduced is shown to have been surrounded by an embattled wall, with a canal of water passing in front of it, connected with the river. Between the canal and the wall, and parallel to them both, was a shady avenue of various trees; and about the centre was the entrance, through a lofty door, whose lintel and jambs were decorated with hieroglyphic inscriptions, containing the name of the owner of the grounds, who in this instance was the king himself. In the gateway were rooms for the porter, and other persons employed about the garden, and, probably, the receiving room for visiters,

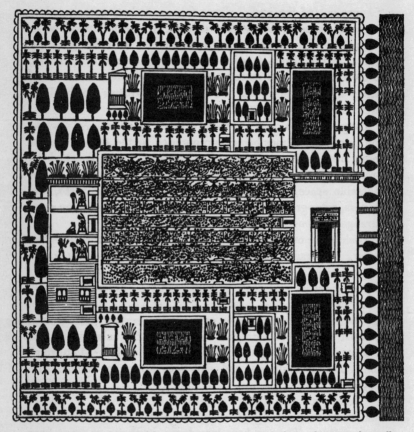

A large garden, with the vineyard and other separate enclosures, tanks of water, and a small
house.   *From the Work of Prof. Rosellini.*

43.

whose abrupt admission might be unwelcome; and at the back
a gate opened into the vineyard. The vines were trained on a
trellis-work, supported by transverse rafters resting on pillars;
and a wall, extending round it, separated this part from the rest
of the garden. At the upper end were suites of rooms on three
different stories, looking upon green trees, and affording a pleasant retreat in the heat of summer. On the outside of the vineyard wall were planted rows of palms, which occurred again

with the *dôm* and other trees, along the whole length of the exterior wall : four tanks of water, bordered by a grass plot, where
geese were kept, and the delicate flower of the lotus was encouraged to grow, served for the irrigation of the grounds ; and
small *kiosks* or summer-houses, shaded with trees, stood near the
water, and overlooked beds of flowers. The spaces containing
the tanks, and the adjoining portions of the garden, were each
enclosed by their respective walls, and a small subdivision on
either side, between the large and small tanks, seems to have
been reserved for the growth of particular trees, which either
required peculiar care, or bore a fruit of superior quality.

In all cases, whether the orchard stood apart from, or was
united with, the rest of the garden, it was supplied, like the other
portions of it, with abundance of water, preserved in spacious
reservoirs, on either side of which stood a row of palms, or an
avenue of shady sycamores. Sometimes the orchard and vine-

Egyptian mode of representing a tank of water with a row of palms on either side.
44.   *Thebes.*

45.

The vineyard and orchard contiguous.

Tombs near the Pyramids.

yard were not separated by any wall, and figs * and other trees
were planted within the same limits as the vines. But if not
connected with it, the vineyard was close to the orchard, and
their mode of training the vines on wooden rafters, supported
by rows of columns, which divided the vineyard into numerous
avenues, was both tasteful and convenient.

The columns were frequently coloured, but many were simple
wooden pillars, supporting, with their forked summits, the poles
that lay over them. Some vines were allowed to grow as
standing bushes, and, being kept low, did not require any support; others were formed into a series of bowers; and from

46. Plucking grapes in a vineyard; the vines trained in bowers. *Thebes.*

the form of the hieroglyphic, signifying vineyard, we may con-

47. Figurative hieroglyphic signifying vineyard.

clude that the most usual method of training them was in bowers,
or in avenues formed by rafters and columns. But they do not

* *Comp.* Luke xiii. 6, " A certain man had a fig-tree planted in his vineyard ;"
and 1 Kings, iv. 25, " Every man under his vine and under his fig-tree."

appear to have attached them to other trees, as the Romans often did to the elm and poplar, and as the modern Italians do to the white mulberry; nor have the Egyptians of the present day adopted this European custom.

When the vineyard was enclosed within its own wall of circuit, it frequently had a reservoir of water attached to it, as well as

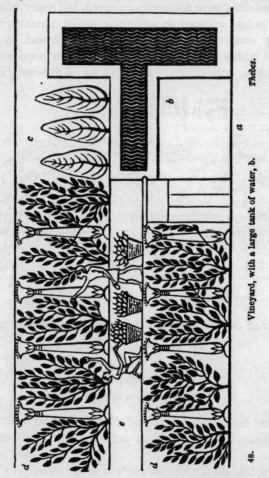

Vineyard, with a large tank of water, b.   Thebes.

48.

the building which contained the winepress;* but the various modes of arranging the vineyard, as well as the other parts of the garden, depended, of course, on the taste of each individual, or the nature of the ground. Great care was taken to preserve the clusters from the intrusion of birds; and boys were constantly employed, about the season of the vintage, to frighten them with a sling and the sound of the voice.

49.   Frightening away the birds with a sling.   *Thebes.*

When the grapes were gathered the bunches were carefully put into deep wicker baskets, which men carried, either on their head or shoulders, or slung upon a yoke, to the winepress; but when intended for eating, they were put, like other fruits, into flat open baskets, and generally covered with leaves of the palm,

50.   Fig. 1. Basket containing grapes covered with leaves, from the sculptures.
           Fig. 2. Modern basket used for the same purpose.

vine, or other trees. These flat baskets were of wicker-work, and similar to those of the present day, used at Cairo for

* *Comp.* Isaiah v. 1, 2, "And he fenced it (the vineyard), and gathered out the stones thereof, and planted it with the choicest vine, and built a tower in the midst of it, and also made a winepress therein;" and Matthew xxi. 33, " planted a vineyard . . . . and digged a winepress in it."

the same purpose, which are made of osiers or common twigs.
Monkies appear to have been trained to assist in gathering the
fruit, and the Egyptians represent them in the sculptures handing

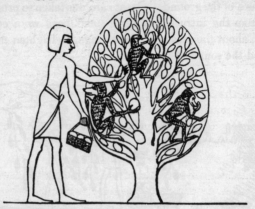

51.   Monkies assisting in gathering fruit.   *Beni-Hassan.*

down figs from the sycamore-trees to the gardeners below : but,
as might be expected, these animals amply repaid themselves for
the trouble imposed upon them, and the artist has not failed to
show that they consulted their own wishes as well as those of
their employers.

Many animals were tamed in Egypt for various purposes, as
the lion, leopard, gazelle, baboon, crocodile, and others; and in
the Jimma country, which lies to the south of Abyssinia, monkies
are still taught several useful accomplishments. Among them
is that of officiating as torch-bearers at a supper party; and
seated in a row, on a raised bench, they hold the lights until the
departure of the guests, and patiently await their own repast as
a reward for their services. Sometimes the party is alarmed by
an unruly monkey throwing his lighted torch into the midst of
the unsuspecting guests; but fortunately the ladies there do not
wear muslin dresses; and the stick and " no supper " remind
the offender of his present and future duties.

After the vintage was over, they allowed the kids to browse
upon the vines which grew as standing bushes (*comp. Hor.* ii. *Sat.*

52.　　　Kids allowed to browse upon the vines.　　　*Beni-Hassan.*

v. 43); and the season of the year when the grapes ripened in
Egypt was the month Epiphi, towards the end of June, or the
commencement of July. Some have pretended to doubt that the
vine was commonly cultivated, or even grown, in Egypt; but the
frequent notice of it, and of Egyptian wine, in the sculptures,
and the authority of ancient writers, sufficiently answer those
objections; and the regrets of the Israelites on leaving the vines
of Egypt prove them to have been very abundant, since even
people in the condition of slaves could procure the fruit (Numb.
xx. 5, *comp.* Gen. xl. 11).

The winepress was of different kinds. The most simple consisted merely of a bag, in which the grapes were put, and squeezed,
by means of two poles turning in contrary directions: a vase
being placed below to receive the falling juice. Another press,

53.　　　　　　　Winepress.　　　　　　　*Beni-Hassan.*

nearly on the same principle, consisted of a bag supported in a
frame, having two upright sides, connected by beams at their
summit. In this the bag was retained in a horizontal position,
one end fixed, the other passing through a hole in the opposite

side, and was twisted by means of a rod turned with the hand ;
the juice, as in the former, being received into a vase beneath ;
and within the frame stood the superintendent, who regulated the
quantity of pressure, and gave the signal to stop.

Sometimes a liquid was heated on the fire, and, having been
well stirred, was poured into the sack containing the grapes,
during the process of pressure ; but whether this was solely with
a view of obtaining a greater quantity of juice, by moistening the
husks, or was applied for any other purpose, it is difficult to determine : the fact, however, of its being stirred while on the fire
suffices to show it was not simple water ; and the trituration
of the fruit, while it was poured upon it, may suggest its use in
extracting the colouring matter for red wine.

The two Egyptian hand-presses were used in all parts of the
country, but principally in Lower Egypt, the grapes in the
Thebaïd being generally pressed by the feet.   The footpress was
also used in the lower country ; and we even find the two
methods of pressing the grapes represented in the same sculptures ; it is not therefore impossible that, after having been sub-
jected to the foot, they may have undergone a second pressure in

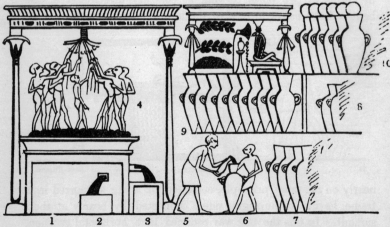

54.   Large footpress; the amphoræ; and the asp, or Agathodæmon, the protecting deity of the
store-room, fig. 11.   *Thebes.*

the twisted bag. This does not appear to have been the case in the Thebaïd, where the *footpress* is always represented alone ; and the juice was allowed to run off by a pipe directly to an open tank (*comp.* Is. lxiii. 3, Nehem. xiii. 15, Judg. ix. 27, Virg. Georg. ii. 7).

Some of the large presses were highly ornamented, and consisted of at least two distinct parts.; the lower portion or vat, and the trough, where the men, with naked feet, trod the fruit, supporting themselves by ropes suspended from the roof ; though, from their great height, some may have had an intermediate reservoir, which received the juice in its passage to the pipe, answering to the strainer, or *colum*, of the Romans.

After the fermentation was over, the juice was taken out in small vases, with a long spout, and poured into earthenware jars, which corresponded to the *cadi* or *amphoræ* of the Romans.

fig. 1.　　　*a*　*b*　*c*　*d*　*e*　　*fig.* 2.

55.　　　　The new wine poured into jars. *f.* Jars closed.

They appear also to have added something to it after or previous to the fermentation ; and an instance occurs in the sculptures of a man pouring a liquid from a small cup into the lower reservoir. When the *must* was considered in a proper state, the amphoræ were closed with a lid, resembling an inverted saucer, covered with liquid clay, pitch, gypsum, mortar, or other composition, which was stamped with a seal : they were then removed from the winehouse, and placed upright in the cellar.

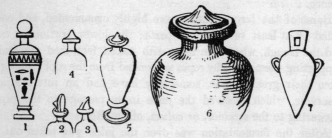

56. Wine-jars with Covers. On *fig.* 1 is Êrp, " wine." *Thebes.*

Previous to pouring in the wine they generally put a certain quantity of resin into the *amphoræ*, which coated the inside of those porous jars, preserved the wine, and was even supposed to improve its flavour ; a notion, or rather an acquired taste, owing, probably, to their having at first used skins·instead of jars : and the flavour imparted by the resin, which was necessary to preserve the skins, having become, from long habit, a favourite peculiarity of the wine, it was afterwards added from choice, after they had adopted the use of earthenware. And this custom, formerly so general in Egypt, Italy, and Greece, is still preserved throughout the islands of the Archipelago. In Egypt, a resinous substance is always found at the bottom of amphoræ which have served for holding wine; it is perfectly preserved, brittle, and, when burnt, smells like a very fine quality of pitch. The Romans, according to Pliny, employed the Brutian pitch, or resin of the picea pine, in preference to all others, for this purpose : and if, "in Spain, they used that of the pinaster, it was little esteemed on account of its bitterness and oppressive smell." In the East, the terebinthus was considered to afford the best resin, superior even to the mastic of the lentiscus ; and the resins of Judæa and Syria only yielded in quality to that of Cyprus.

The mode of arranging amphoræ in an Egyptian cellar was

similar to that adopted by the Greeks and Romans. They stood
upright in successive rows, the inner-
most set resting against the wall, with
their pointed ends firmly fixed in the
ground ; and each jar was secured
by means of a stone ring fitting round
its pointed base, or was raised on a
wooden stand.   Others appear occasionally to have been placed in upper
rooms, as the amphoræ in a Roman
apotheca.

57.   Vase supported by a stone ring.

The Egyptians had several different kinds of wine, some of
which have been commended by ancient authors for their excellent qualities. That of Mareotis was the most esteemed, and in
the greatest quantity. Its superiority over other Egyptian wines
may readily be accounted for, when we consider the nature of
the soil in that district ; being principally composed of gravel,
which, lying beyond the reach of the alluvial deposit, was free
from the rich and tenacious mud usually met with in the valley
of the Nile, so little suited for grapes of delicate quality ; and
from the extensive remains of vineyards still found on the
western borders of the Arsinoïte nome, or Fyoom, we may conclude that the ancient Egyptians were fully aware of the advantages of land, situated beyond the limits of the inundation, for
planting the vine. According to Athenæus, " the Mareotic
grape was remarkable for its sweetness," and the wine is thus
described by him : " Its colour is white, its quality excellent, and
it is sweet and light with a fragrant *bouquet;* it is by no means
astringent, nor does it affect the head." But it was not for its
flavour alone that this wine was esteemed, and Strabo ascribes to
it the additional merit of keeping to a great age. " Still, however," says Athenæus, " it is inferior to the Teniotic, a wine which
receives its name from a place called Tenia, where it is produced. Its colour is pale and white, and there is such a degree
of richness in it, that, when mixed with water, it seems gradually
to be diluted, much in the same way as Attic honey when a

liquid is poured into it; and besides the agreeable flavour of
the wine, its fragrance is so delightful as to render it perfectly
aromatic, and it has the property of being slightly astringent.
There are many other vineyards in the valley of the Nile, whose
wines are in great repute, and these differ both in colour and
taste : but that which is produced about Anthylla is preferred to
all the rest." Some of the wine made in the Thebaïd was particularly light, especially about Coptos, and " so wholesome,"
says the same author, " that invalids might take it without inconvenience, even during a fever." The Sebennytic was likewise one of the choice Egyptian wines ; and, as Pliny says, was
made of three different grapes ; one of which was a sort of
Thasian. The Thasian grape he afterwards describes as excelling
all others in Egypt for its sweetness, and remarkable for its
medicinal properties.

The Mendesian is also mentioned by Clemens, with rather a
sweet flavour: and another singular wine, called by Pliny
ecbolada (εκϐολας), was also the produce of Egypt ; but, from
its peculiar powers, we may suppose that men alone drank it, or
at least that it was forbidden to newly married brides. And,
considering how prevalent the custom was amongst the ancients
of altering the qualities of wines, by drugs and divers processes,
we may readily conceive the possibility of the effects ascribed to
them ; and thus it happened that opposite properties were frequently attributed to the same kind.

Wines were much used by them for medicinal purposes, and
many were held in such repute as to be considered specifics in
certain complaints ; but the medical men of the day were prudent
in their mode of prescribing them ; and as imagination has on
many occasions effected the cure, and given celebrity to a medicine,
those least known were wisely preferred, and each extolled the
virtues of some foreign wine. In the earliest times, Egypt was renowned for drugs, and foreigners had recourse to that country for
wines as well as herbs ; yet Apollodorus, the physician, in a treatise
on wines, addressed to Ptolemy, king of Egypt, recommended those
of Pontus as more beneficial than any of his own country, and

particularly praised the Peparethian, produced in an island of the Ægean Sea ; but he was disposed to consider it less valuable as a medicine, when its good qualities could not be discovered in six years.

The wines of Alexandria and Coptos are also cited among the best of Egyptian growth ; and the latter was so light as not to affect even those in delicate health.

In offerings to the Egyptian deities wine frequently occurs, and several different kinds are noticed in the sacred sculptures ; but it is probable that many of the Egyptian wines are not introduced in those subjects, and that, as with the Romans, and other people, all were not admitted at their sacrifices. According to Herodotus, their sacrifices commenced with a libation of wine, and some was sprinkled on the ground where the victim lay ; yet at Heliopolis, if Plutarch may be credited, it was forbidden to take it into the temple, and the priests of the god worshipped in that city were required to abstain from its use. "Those of other deities," adds the same author, " were less scrupulous," but still they used wine very sparingly, and the quantity allowed them for their daily consumption was regulated by law ; nor could they indulge in it at all times, and the use of it was strictly prohibited during their more solemn purifications, and in times of abstinence. The number of wines, mentioned in the lists of offerings presented to the deities in the tombs or temples, varies in different places. Each appears with its peculiar name attached to it ; but they seldom exceed three or four kinds, and among them I have observed, at Thebes, that of the " northern country," which was, perhaps, from Mareotis, Anthylla, or the nome of Sebennytus.

Private individuals were under no particular restrictions with regard to its use, and it was not forbidden to women. In this they differed widely from the Romans : for in early times no female at Rome enjoyed the privilege, and it was unlawful for women, or, indeed, for young men below the age of thirty, to drink wine, except at sacrifices. Even at a later time the Romans considered it disgraceful for a woman to drink wine ; and they sometimes saluted a female relation, whom they suspected, in order to discover if she had secretly indulged in its use. It was afterwards allowed them on the plea of health, and no better method could have been devised for removing the restriction.

That Egyptian women were not forbidden the use of wine, nor the enjoyment of other luxuries, is evident from the frescoes which represent their feasts; and the painters, in illustrating this fact, have sometimes sacrificed their gallantry to a love of

58.   A servant called to support her mistress.   *Thebes.*

caricature. Some call the servants to support them as they sit, others with difficulty prevent themselves from falling on those behind them; a basin is brought too late by a reluctant servant

59.   A party of Egyptian ladies.   *Thebes.*

and the faded flower, which is ready to drop from their heated hands, is intended to be characteristic of their own sensations.

That the consumption of wine in Egypt was very great is evident from the sculptures, and from the accounts of ancient authors, some of whom have censured the Egyptians for their excesses; and so much did the quantity used exceed that made in the country, that, in the time of Herodotus, twice every year a large importation was received from Phœnicia and Greece.

Notwithstanding all the injunctions or exhortations of the priests in favour of temperance, the Egyptians of both sexes appear from the sculptures to have committed occasional excesses, and men were sometimes unable to walk from a feast, and were carried home by servants. These scenes, however, do not

60.   Men carried home from a drinking p.   *Beni Hassan.*

appear to refer to members of the higher, but of the lower, classes, some of whom indulged in extravagant buffoonery, dancing in a ludicrous manner, or standing on their heads, and frequently in amusements which terminated in a fight.

At the tables of the rich, stimulants were sometimes introduced, to excite the palate before drinking, and Athenæus mentions cabbages as one of the vegetables used by the Egyptians for this purpose.

Throughout the upper and lower country, wine was the favourite beverage of the wealthy: they had also very excellent beer, called *zythus*, which Diodorus, though wholly unaccustomed to it, and a native of a wine country, affirms was scarcely inferior to the juice of the grape. Strabo and other ancient authors have likewise mentioned it under the name of zythus; and though Herodotus pretends that it was merely used as a substitute for wine in the lowlands, where corn was principally cultivated, it is more reasonable to conclude it was drunk by the peasants in all parts of Egypt, though less in those districts where vines were abundant. Native wines of a choice kind, whether made in the vicinity or brought from another province, were confined to the rich; and we learn from Strabo that this was the case even at Alexandria, where wine could be obtained in greater quantity than in any other part of Egypt, owing to the proximity of the Mareotic district; and the common people were there content with beer and the poor wine of the coast of Libya.

Egyptian beer was made from barley; but, as hops were unknown, they were obliged to have recourse to other plants, in order to give it a grateful flavour; and the lupin, the skirret (*Sium sisarum*), and the root of an Assyrian plant, were used by them for that purpose.

The vicinity of Pelusium was the most noted for its beer, and the Pelusiac zythus is mentioned by more than one author. The account given by Athenæus of Egyptian beer is that it was very strong, and had so exhilarating an effect that they danced, and sang, and committed the same excesses as those who were intoxicated with the strongest wines; an observation confirmed by the authority of Aristotle, whose opinion on the subject has at least the merit of being amusing. For we must smile at the philosopher's method of distinguishing persons suffering under the influence of wine and beer, however disposed he would have been to accuse us of ignorance in not having yet discovered how invariably the former in that state "lie upon their face, and the latter on their backs."

Besides beer, the Egyptians had what Pliny calls factitious, or artificial, wine, extracted from various fruits, as figs, *myxas*, pomegranates, as well as herbs, some of which were selected for their medicinal properties. The Greeks and Latins comprehended every kind of beverage made by the process of fermentation under the same general name, and beer was designated as

barley-*wine;* but, by the use of the name zythos, they show that
the Egyptians distinguished it by its own peculiar appellation.
Palm-wine was also made in Egypt, and used in the process of
embalming.

The palm-wine now made in Egypt and the Oases is simply
from an incision in the heart of the tree, immediately below the
base of the upper branches, and a jar is attached to the part to
catch the juice which exudes from it. But a palm thus tapped is
rendered perfectly useless as a fruit-bearing tree, and generally
dies in consequence ; and it is reasonable to suppose that so great
a sacrifice is seldom made except when date-trees are to be felled,
or when they grow in great abundance. The modern name of
this beverage in Egypt is *lowbgeh;* in flavour it resembles a
very new light wine, and may be drunk in great quantity when
taken from the tree ; but, as soon as the fermentation has commenced, its intoxicating qualities have a powerful and speedy
effect.

Among the various fruit-trees cultivated by the ancient
Egyptians, palms, of course, held the first rank, as well from their
abundance as from their great utility. The fruit constituted a
principal part of their food, both in the month of August, when
it was gathered fresh from the trees, and at other seasons of the
year, when it was used in a preserved state. They had two
different modes of keeping the dates ; one was by the simple
process of drying them, the other was by making them into a
conserve, like the *agweh* of the present day ; and of this, which
was eaten either cooked or as a simple sweetmeat, I have found
some cakes, as well as the dried dates, in the sepulchres of
Thebes.

Pliny makes a just remark respecting the localities where the
palm prospers, and the constant irrigation it requires ; and though
every one in the East knows the tree will not grow except where
water is abundant, we still read of " palm-trees of the desert," as
if it delighted in an arid district. Wherever it is found it is a
sure indication of water ; and if it may be said to flourish in a
sandy soil, this is only in situations where its roots can obtain

a certain quantity of moisture. The numerous purposes for which its branches and other parts might be applied rendered the cultivation of this valuable and productive tree a matter of primary importance, for no portion of it is without its peculiar use. The trunk serves for beams, either entire, or split in half; of the *gereét*, or branches, are made wicker baskets, bedsteads, coops, and ceilings of rooms, answering every purpose for which laths or any thin woodwork are required; the leaves are converted into mats, brooms, and baskets; of the fibrous tegument at the base of the branches, strong ropes and mats are made, and even the thick ends of the *gereét* are beaten flat and formed into brooms. Besides the *lowbgeh* of the tree, brandy, wine, and vinegar are made from the fruit; and the quantity of saccharine matter in the dates might be used in default of sugar or honey.

In Upper Egypt another tree, called the *Dôm*, or Theban palm, was also much cultivated, and its wood, more solid and compact than the date-tree, is found to answer as well for rafts, and other purposes connected with water, as for beams and rafters.

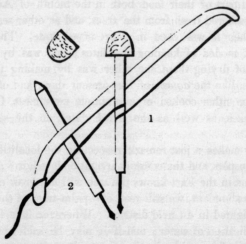

61.   Fig. 3. *Dôm* nut, which is the head of the drill.   *Found at Thebes.*

The fruit is a large rounded nut, with a fibrous exterior envelope, which has a flavour very similar to our gingerbread ; and from its extreme hardness this nut was used for the hollow socket of their drills, or centre-bits, as well as for beads and other purposes. Of the leaves of the *dôm* were made baskets, sacks, mats, fans, fly-flaps, brushes, and light sandals ; and they served as a general substitute for those of the date-tree, and for the rushes, *halfeh* or *poa* grass, the cyperus, osiers, and other materials employed for the same purposes in Egypt.

Next to the palms, the principal trees of the garden were the fig, sycamore, pomegranate, olive, peach, almond, persea, *nebk* or *sidr*, *mokhayt* or *myxa*, *kharoób* or locust-tree ; and of those that bore no fruit the most remarkable were the two tamarisks, the cassia fistula, senna, palma christi or castor-berry tree, myrtle, various kinds of " acanthus " or acacia, and some others still found in the deserts between the Nile and the Red Sea. So fond were the Egyptians of trees and flowers, and of rearing numerous and rare plants, that they even made them part of the tribute exacted from foreign countries ; and such, according to Athenæus, " was the care they bestowed on their culture, that those flowers which elsewhere were only sparingly produced, even in their proper season, grew profusely at all times in Egypt ; so that neither roses, nor violets, nor any others, were wanting there, even in the middle of winter." The tables in their sitting-rooms were always decked with bouquets, and they had even artificial flowers, which received the name of " Ægyptian." The lotus was the favourite for wreaths and chaplets ; they also employed the leaves or blossoms of other plants, as the chrysanthemum, *acinon*, acacia, *strychnus*, *persoluta*, anemone, convolvulus, olive, myrtle, *amaricus*, xeranthemum, bay-tree, and others ; and when Agesilaus visited Egypt he was so delighted with the chaplets of papyrus sent him by the Egyptian king, that he took some home with him on his return to Sparta. But it is singular that, while the lotus is so often represented, no instance occurs on the monuments of the Indian lotus, or *Nelumbium*, though the Roman-Egyptian sculptures point it out as a peculiar plant of Egypt, placing it about the figure of the god Nile; and it is stated by Latin writers to have been common in the country.

In the furniture of their houses the Egyptians displayed considerable taste; and there, as elsewhere, they studiously avoided too much regularity, justly considering that its monotonous effect fatigued the eye. They preferred variety both in the arrangement of the rooms and in the character of their furniture, and neither the windows, doors, nor wings of the house, exactly corresponded with each other. An Egyptian would therefore have been more pleased with the form of our Elizabethan, than of the box-shaped rooms of later times.

In their mode of sitting on chairs they resembled the modern Europeans rather than Asiatics, neither using, like the latter, soft *divans*, nor sitting cross-legged on carpets. Nor did they recline at meals, as the Romans, on a *triclinium*, though couches and ottomans formed part of the furniture of an Egyptian as of an English drawing-room. When Joseph entertained his brethren, he ordered them to *sit* according to their ages. And if they sometimes sat cross-legged on the ground, on mats and carpets, or knelt on one or both knees, these were rather the customs for certain occasions, and of the poorer classes. To sit on their heels was also customary as a token of respect in the presence of a

62.   Positions, when seated on the ground.   Fig. 1. Cross-legged.

superior, as in modern Egypt; and when a priest bore a shrine before the deity he assumed this position of humility; a still greater respect being shown by prostration, or by kneeling and

kissing the ground. But the house of a wealthy person was always
furnished with chairs and couches. Stools and low seats were
also used, the seat being only from 8 to 14 inches high, and of

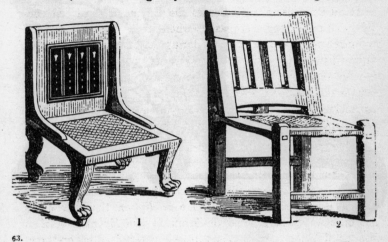

63.

Chairs.   *British Museum.*

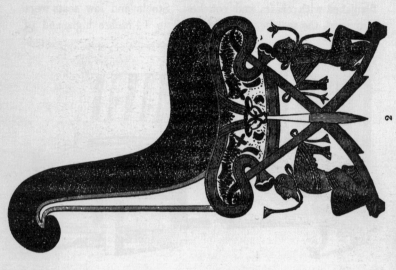

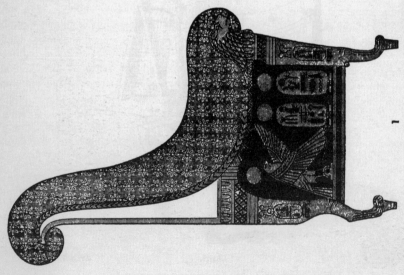

Fauteuils painted in the Tomb of Remeses III.

Thebes.

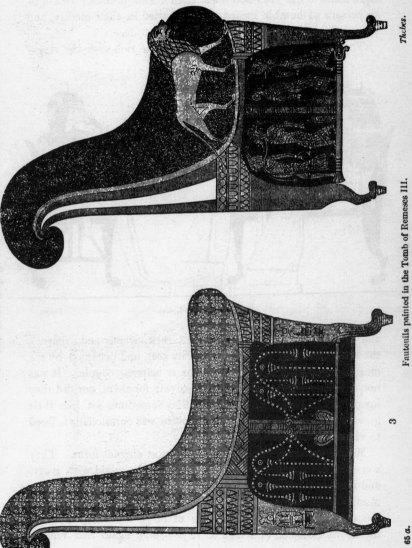

Fauteuils painted in the Tomb of Remeses III.

Thebes.

3

65 a.

wood, or interlaced with thongs; these however may be considered
equivalent to our rush-bottomed chairs, and probably belonged
to persons of humble means. They varied in their quality, and
some were inlaid with ivory and various woods.

Those most common in the houses of the rich were the single

66.   Double and Single Chairs.   *Thebes.*

and double chair (answering to the Greek *thronos* and *diphros*),
the latter sometimes kept as a family seat, and occupied by the
master and mistress of the house, or a married couple. It was
not, however, always reserved exclusively for them, nor did they
invariably occupy the same seat; they sometimes sat like their
guests on separate chairs, and a *diphros* was occasionally offered
to visiters, both men and women.

Many of the fauteuils were of the most elegant form. They
were made of ebony and other rare woods, inlaid with ivory,
and very similar to some now used in Europe. The legs were
mostly in imitation of those of an animal; and lions' heads, or
the entire body, formed the arms of large fauteuils, as in the
throne of Solomon (1 Kings x. 19). Some again had folding

legs, like our camp-stools; the seat was often slightly concave; and those in the royal palace were ornamented with the figures of captives, or emblems of his dominion over Egypt and other countries. The back was light and strong, and consisted of a single set of upright and cross bars, or of a frame receding gradually and terminating at its summit in a graceful curve, supported from without by perpendicular bars; and over this was thrown a handsome pillow of coloured cotton, painted leather, or gold and silver tissue, like the beds at the feast of Ahasuerus, mentioned in Esther; or like the feathered cushions covered with stuffs and embroidered with silk and threads of gold in the palace of Scaurus. (*Woodcuts* 65 and 65 *a*.)

Seats on the principle of our camp-stools seem to have been much

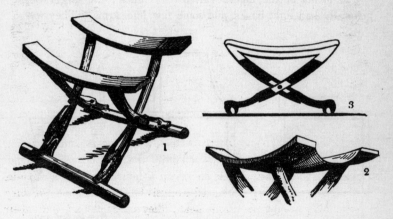

67.   Fig. 1. A stool in the British Museum, on the principle of our camp-stools.
        2. Shows the manner in which the leather seat was fastened.
        3. A similar one from the sculptures, with its cushion.

in vogue. They were furnished with a cushion, or were covered with the skin of a leopard, or some other animal, which was removed when the seat was folded up; and it was not unusual to make even head-stools, or wooden pillows, on the same principle. They were also adorned in various ways, bound with metal plates, and inlaid with ivory or foreign woods ; and the wood of common chairs was often painted to resemble that of a rarer and more valuable kind.

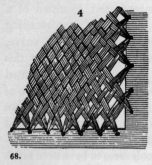

4

68.

The seats of chairs were frequently of leather, painted with flowers and fancy devices ; or of interlaced work made of string or thongs, carefully and neatly arranged, which, like our Indian cane chairs, were particularly adapted for a hot climate ; but over this they occasionally placed a leather cushion, painted in the manner already mentioned.

The forms of the chairs varied very much ; the larger ones generally had light backs, and some few had arms. They were

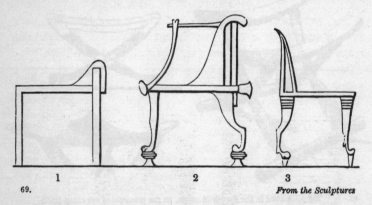

1　　　　　2　　　　　3

69.　　　　　　　　　　　　　　　　*From the Sculptures*

mostly about the height of those now used in Europe, the seat nearly in a line with the bend of the knee ; but some were very low, and others offered that variety of position which we seek in the kangaroo chairs of our own drawing-room (*Woodcut* 70, *fig.* 3). The ordinary fashion of the legs was in imitation of those of some wild animal, as the lion or the goat, but more usually the former, the foot raised and supported on a short pin ; and, what is remarkable, the skill of their cabinet-makers, even before the time of Joseph, had already done away with the necessity of uniting the legs with bars. Stools, however, and more rarely

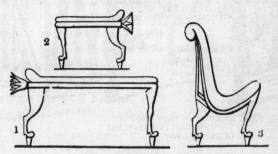

70

Fig. 1. A διφρος or double chair, without a back.
    2. A single chair, of similar construction.
    3. A kangaroo chair.

Sculptures.

chairs, were occasionally made with these strengthening members, as is still the case in our own country; but the drawing-room fauteuil and couch were not disfigured by so unseemly and so unskilful a support.

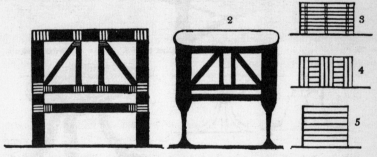

71.   Fig. 1. Stools.   2. With a cushion.   3, 4, 5. With solid sides.   *Thebes.*

The stools used in the saloon were of the same style and elegance as the chairs, frequently differing from them only in the absence of a back; and those of more delicate workmanship were made of ebony, and inlaid, as already stated, with ivory

VOL. I.

72.   Fig. 1. Stool of ebony inlaid with ivory.   *British Museum.*
                2. Shows the inlaid parts of the legs.
                3. Of ordinary construction, in the same collection.

73.   A stool with leather cushion.   *British Museum.*

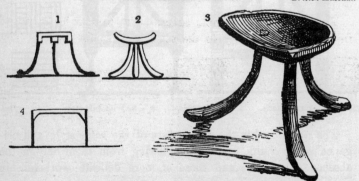

74.   Figs. 1, 2. Three-legged stools, from the Sculptures.
                3. Wooden stool, *in the British Museum.*
                4, and 1, are probably of metal.

or rare woods.   Some of an ordinary kind had solid sides, and
were generally very low ; and others, with three legs, not unlike
those used by the peasants of England, belonged to persons of
inferior rank.

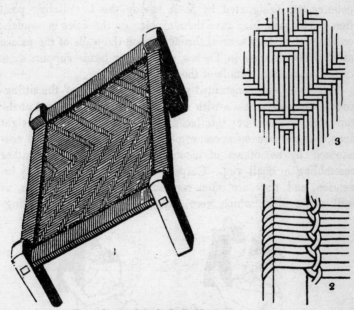

75.   Fig. 1. Low stool, in the Berlin Museum.
                   2, 3. Mode of fastening, and the pattern of the seat.

The ottomans were simple square sofas, without backs, raised
from the ground nearly to the same level as the chairs.   The

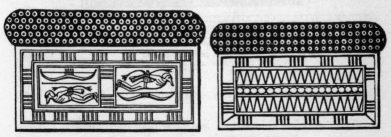

76.   Ottomans, from the tomb of Remeses III.   *Thetes.*

upper part was of leather, or a cotton stuff, richly coloured, like the cushions of the fauteuils ; the base was of wood, painted with various devices ; and those in the royal palace were ornamented with the figures of captives, the conquest of whose country was designated by their having this humiliating position. The same idea gave them a place on the soles of sandals, on the footstools of a royal throne, and on the walls of the palace at Medeenet Haboo, in Thebes, where their heads support some of the ornamental details of the building.

Footstools also constituted part of the furniture of the sitting-room ; they were made with solid or open sides, covered at the top with leather or interlaced work, and varied in height according to circumstances, some being of the usual size now adopted by us, others of inconsiderable thickness, and rather resembling a small rug. Carpets, indeed, were a very early invention, and they are often represented sitting upon them, as well as on mats, which were commonly used in their sitting-

77.   Fig. 1. A low seat, perhaps a carpet.
           2. Either similar to fig. 1, or of wood.
           3. A mat.

rooms, as at the present day, and remnants of them have been found in the Theban tombs.

Their couches evinced no less taste than the fauteuils. They were of wood, with one end raised, and receding in a graceful curve; and the feet, as in many of the chairs already described, were fashioned to resemble those of some wild animal.

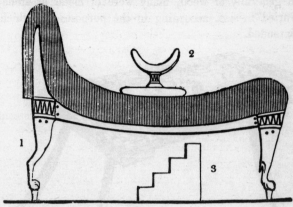

78.   Fig. 1. A couch.
                    2. Pillow or head stool.
                    3. Steps for ascending a lofty couch. (*Tomb of Remeses III.*) *Thebes.*

Egyptian tables were round, square, or oblong; the former were generally used during their repasts, and consisted of a circular flat summit, supported, like the *monopodium* of the Romans, on a single shaft, or leg, in the centre, or by the figure of a

79.   Fig. 1. Table, probably of stone or wood, from the sculptures.
                    2. Stone table supported by the figure of a captive.
                    3. Probably of metal, from the sculptures.

man, intended to represent a captive. Large tables had usually three or four legs, but some were made with solid sides; and though generally of wood, many were of metal or stone; and they varied in size, according to the purposes for which they were intended.

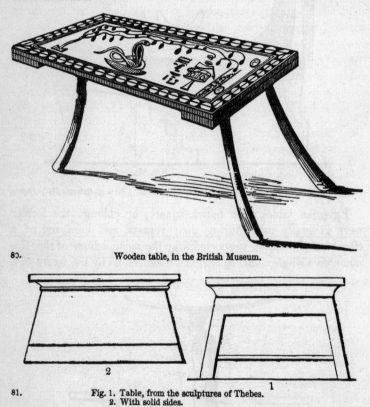

80.   Wooden table, in the British Museum.

81.   Fig. 1. Table, from the sculptures of Thebes.
               2. With solid sides.

Of the furniture of their bed-rooms we know little or nothing: but that they universally employed the wooden pillow above alluded to is evident, though Porphyry would lead us to suppose its use was confined to the priests, when, in noticing their mode of life, he mentions a half cylinder of well polished wood "sufficing to support their head," as an instance of their simplicity

and self-denial. For the rich they were made of oriental alabaster, with an elegant grooved
or fluted shaft, ornamented with
hieroglyphics, carved in intaglio,
of sycamore, tamarisk, and other
woods of the country; the poorer
classes being contented with a
cheaper sort, of pottery or stone.
Porphyry mentions a kind of
wicker bedstead of *palm branches*,
hence called *baïs*, evidently the species of framework called

82.   Wooden pillow.

1

83.   Fig. 1. Wooden pillow of unusual form.
          2. Another found by me at Thebes, and now in the British Museum. The
          base was lost.

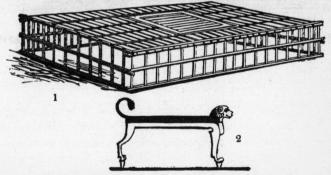

1

2

84.   Fig. 1. *Kaffass* bedstead of palm sticks used by the modern Egyptians.
          2. Ancient bier on which the bodies were placed after death.

kaffass, still employed by the modern Egyptians as a support to the *diwans* of sitting rooms, and to their beds.   Wooden, and perhaps also bronze, bedsteads (like the iron one of Og, King of Bashan), were used by the wealthier classes of the ancient Egyptians ; and it is at least probable that the couches they slept upon were as elegant as those on which their bodies reposed after death ; and the more so, as these last, in their general style, are very similar to the furniture of the sitting-room.

[B. Modern *shadóof,* or pole and bucket, used for raising water, in Upper and Lower Egypt.

c.   Pavilion of Remeses III. at Medeenet Haboo.   *Thebes*

CHAPTER II.

RECEPTION OF GUESTS — MUSIC — VARIOUS INSTRUMENTS — SACRED
MUSIC — DANCE.

In their entertainments they appear to have omitted nothing
which could promote festivity and the amusement of the guests.
Music,* songs, dancing,† buffoonery, feats of agility, or games of
chance, were generally introduced ; and they welcomed them with
all the luxuries which the cellar and the table could afford.

The party, when invited to dinner, met about midday,‡ and
they arrived successively in their chariots, in palanquins borne
by their servants, or on foot. Sometimes their attendants
screened them from the sun by holding up a shield, (as is still
done in Southern Africa,) or by some other contrivance ; but
the chariot of the king, § or of a princess, ‖ was often fur-

---

* Comp. Isaiah v. 12, "The harp and the viol, the tabret and pipe, and wine,
are at their feasts."

† Comp. the feast given on the arrival of the prodigal son : " Bring hither the
fatted calf, and kill it ; and let us eat and be merry :" and his brother, when he
drew nigh to the house, " heard music and dancing."   Luke xv. 23, 25.

‡ Joseph said, " These men shall dine with me at noon."   Gen. xliii. 16.

§ Woodcut 86.   ‖ *See* a Chariot in Chapter vi.

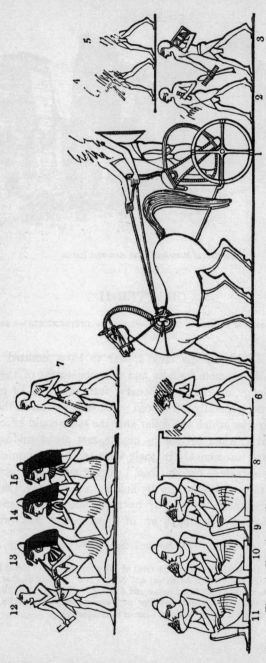

85.   Fig. 1. An Egyptian gentleman driving up in his curricle to the house.   2, 3, 4, 5, 6, and 7, are his footmen.
9, 10, 11. The guests assembled within.   12, 13, 14, 15. The musicians,
8. The door of the house.   *Thebes.*

86.   Chariot with Umbrella.   *Thebes.*

Military chief carried in a sort of palanquin, an attendant bearing a parasol behind him.
87.   *Beni Hassan.*

nished with a large parasol; and the flabella borne behind the king, which belonged exclusively to royalty, answered the same purpose. They were composed of feathers, and were not very unlike those carried on state occasions behind the Pope in modern Rome. Parasols or umbrellas were also used in Assyria, Persia, and other Eastern countries.

When a visitor came in his car, he was attended by a number of servants, some of whom carried a stool, to enable him to alight, and others his writing tablet, or whatever he might want during his stay at the house. In the wood-cut (No. 85) the guests are assembled in a sitting room within, and are entertained with music during the interval preceding the announcement of dinner; for, like the Greeks, they considered it a want of good breeding to sit down to table immediately on arriving, and, as Bdelycleon, in Aristophanes, recommended his father Philocleon to do, they praised the beauty of the rooms and the furniture, taking care to show particular interest in those objects which were intended for admiration. As usual in all countries, some of the party arrived earlier than others; and the consequence, or affectation of fashion, in the person who now drives up in his curricle, is shown by his coming some time after the rest of the company; one of his footmen runs forward to knock at the door, others, close behind the chariot, are ready to take the reins, and to perform their accustomed duties; and the one holding his sandals in his hand, that he may run with greater ease, illustrates a custom, still common in Egypt, among the Arabs and peasants of the country, who find the power of the foot greater when freed from the encumbrance of a shoe.

To those who arrived from a journey, or who desired it, water was brought * for their feet, previous to entering the festive chamber. They also washed their hands before dinner, the water being brought in the same manner as at the present day; and

* Joseph ordered his servants to fetch water for his brethren, that they might wash their feet before they ate. Gen. xliii. 24. *Comp.* also xviii. 4, and xxiv. 32; 1 Sam. xxv. 46. It was always a custom of the East, as with the Greeks and Romans. *Comp.* Luke vii. 44, 46.

ewers, not unlike those used by the modern Egyptians, are represented, with the basins belonging to them, in the paintings of a
Theban tomb.   In the houses of the rich they were of gold,

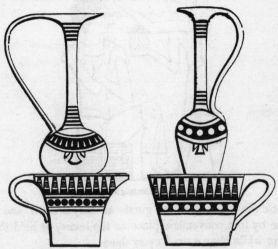

88.   Golden ewers and basins in the tomb of Remeses III.   *Thebes.*

or other costly materials.   Herodotus mentions the golden
foot-pan, in which Amasis and his guests used to wash their
feet.   The Greeks had the same custom of bringing water to the
guests, numerous instances of which we find in Homer; as when
Telemachus and the son of Nestor were received at the house of
Menelaus, and when Asphalion poured it upon the hands of his
master, and the same guests, on another occasion.   Virgil also
describes the servants bringing water for this purpose, when
Æneas was entertained by Dido.   Nor was the ceremony thought
superfluous, or declined, even though they had previously bathed
and been anointed with oil.

   It is also probable that, like the Greeks, the Egyptians
anointed themselves before they left home ; but still it was customary for a servant to attend every guest, as he seated himself,
and to anoint his head ; which was one of the principal tokens
of welcome.   The ointment was sweet-scented, and was con-

tained in an alabaster, or in an elegant glass or porcelain vase, some of which have been found in the tombs of Thebes.*   Ser-

89.   A servant anointing a guest.   *Thebes.*

vants took the sandals of the guests as they arrived, and either put them by in a convenient place in the house, or held them on their arm while they waited upon them.

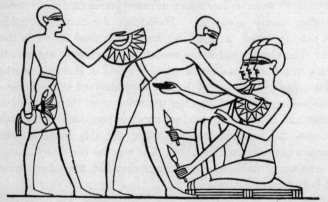

90.   Servants bringing necklaces of flowers.   *Thebes.*

After the ceremony of anointing was over, and, in some cases,

* Mary, when she washed Jesus' feet, brought an alabaster box of ointment. Luke vii. 37.   Matt. xxvi. 7.

at the time of entering the saloon, a lotus flower was presented
to each guest, who held it in his hand during the entertainment.
Servants then brought necklaces of flowers, composed chiefly of
the lotus; a garland was also put round the head, and a single
lotus bud, or a full-blown flower, was so attached as to hang over
the forehead. Many of them, made up into wreaths and other
devices, were suspended upon stands in the room ready for immediate use; and servants were constantly employed to bring
other fresh flowers from the garden, in order to supply the
guests as their bouquets faded.

The stands that served for holding the flowers and garlands
were similar to those of the amphoræ and vases, some of which
have been found in the tombs of Thebes; and the same kind of
stand was introduced into a lady's dressing-room, or the bath, for
the purpose of holding clothes and other articles of the toilet.
They varied in size according to circumstances, some being low
and broad at the top, others higher, with a small summit, merely
large enough to contain a single cup, or a small bottle. Others,

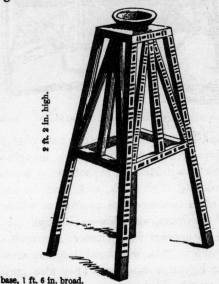

2 ft. 2 in. high.

base, 1 ft. 6 in. broad.

91.   Wooden stand, 8 in. square at the summit, holding a small cup.   *British Museum.*

though much smaller than the common stands, were broader in proportion to their height, and answered as small tables, or as the supports of cases containing bottles; and one of these last, preserved in the Berlin Museum, is supposed to have belonged to a medical man, or to the toilet of a Theban lady.

The vases are six in number, varying slightly in form and size; five of alabaster, and the remaining one of serpentine, each standing in its own cell or compartment.

92.   A case containing bottles supported on a stand.   *Berlin Museum.*

The Greeks and Romans had the same custom of presenting guests with flowers or garlands, which were brought in at the beginning of their entertainments, or before the second course. They not only adorned their *heads*, *necks*, and *breasts*, like the Egyptians, but often bestrewed the couches on which they lay, and all parts of the room, with flowers; though the head was chiefly regarded, as appears from Horace, Anacreon, Ovid, and other ancient authors. The wine-bowl, too, was crowned with flowers, as at an Egyptian banquet. They also perfumed the apartment with myrrh, frankincense, and other choice odours, which they obtained from Syria; and if the sculptures do not give any direct representation of this practice among the Egyptians, we know it to have been adopted and deemed indispensable among them; and a striking instance is recorded by Plutarch, at the reception of Agesilaus by Tachos. A sumptuous dinner was prepared for the Spartan prince, consisting, as usual, of beef, goose, and other Egyptian dishes: he was crowned with garlands of papyrus, and received with every token of welcome; but when he refused " the sweetmeats, confections, and perfumes," the Egyptians held him in great contempt, as a person unaccustomed to, and unworthy of, the manners of civilized society.

The Greeks, and other ancient people, usually put on a particular garment at festive meetings, generally of a white colour; but it does not appear to have been customary with the Egyptians to make any great alteration in their attire, though they evidently abstained from dresses of a gloomy hue.

The guests being seated, and having received these tokens of welcome, wine was offered them by the servants. To the ladies it was generally brought in a small vase, which, when emptied into the drinking-cup, was handed to an under servant, or slave, who followed; but to the men it was frequently pre-

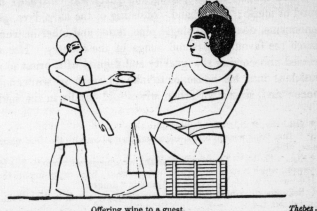

93.   Offering wine to a guest.   *Thebes*.

sented in a one-handled goblet, without being poured into any cup, and sometimes in a large or small vase of gold, silver, or other materials.

Herodotus and Hellanicus both say that they drank wine out of brass or bronze goblets; and, indeed, the former affirms that this was the only kind of drinking-cup known to the Egyptians; but Joseph* had one of silver, and the sculptures represent them of glass, and porcelain, as well as of gold, silver, and bronze. Those who could not afford the more costly kind were satisfied with a cheaper quality, and many were contented with cups of common earthenware; but the wealthy Egyptians used vases of glass, porcelain, and the precious metals, for numerous purposes, both in their houses and in the temples of the gods.

The practice of introducing wine at the commencement† of an entertainment, or before dinner had been served up, was not peculiar to this people; and the Chinese, to the present day, offer it at their parties to all the guests, as they arrive, in the same manner as the ancient Egyptians. They also drank wine during the repast,‡ perhaps to the health of one another, or of an absent friend, like the Romans; and no doubt the master of the house, or "the ruler of the feast," § recommended a choice wine, and pledged them to the cup.

While dinner was preparing, the party was enlivened by the sound of music; and a band, consisting of the harp, lyre, *guitar*, tambourine, double and single pipe, flute, and other instruments, played the favourite airs and songs of the country. Nor was it deemed unbecoming the gravity and dignity of a priest to admit musicians into his house, or to take pleasure in witnessing the dance; and, seated with their wives and family in the midst of

* Gen. xliv. 2, 5, " My cup, the silver cup."
† " That drink wine in bowls, and anoint themselves with the chief ointments." Amos, vi. 6.
‡ Gen. xliii. 34. " They drank wine and were merry with him." The Hebrew is שכרן, which is to be merry from strong drink. Sikr, שבר, implies the same in Hebrew and Arabic. *Sakrán*, in Arabic is " drunken."
§ Rex convivii, arbiter bibendi, or συμποσιαρχος, chosen by lot. John ii. 9; Hor. Od. lib. i. 4.

their friends, the highest functionaries of the sacerdotal order enjoyed the lively scene. In the same manner, at a Greek entertainment, diversions of all kinds were introduced; and Xenophon and Plato inform us that Socrates, the wisest of men, amused his friends with music, jugglers, mimics, buffoons, and whatever could be desired for exciting cheerfulness and mirth.

Though impossible for us now to form any notion of the character or style of Egyptian music, we may be allowed to conjecture that it was studied on scientific principles; and, whatever defects existed in the skill of ordinary performers, who gained their livelihood by playing in public, or for the entertainment of a private party, music was looked upon as an important science, and diligently studied by the priests themselves. According to Diodorus it was not customary to make music part of their education, being deemed useless and even injurious, as tending to render the minds of men effeminate; but this remark can only apply to the custom of studying it as an amusement. Plato, who was well acquainted with the usages of the Egyptians, says that they considered music of the greatest consequence, from its beneficial effects upon the mind of youth; and according to Strabo, the children of the Egyptians were taught letters, the songs appointed by law, and a certain kind of music, established by government.

That the Egyptians were particularly fond of music, is abundantly proved by the paintings in their tombs of the earliest times; and we even find they introduced figures performing on the favourite instruments of the country, among the devices with which they adorned fancy boxes or trinkets. The skill of the Egyptians, in the use of musical instruments, is also noticed by Athenæus, who says that both the Greeks and barbarians were taught by refugees from Egypt, and that the Alexandrians were the most scientific and skilful players on pipes and other instruments.

In the infancy of music, as Dr. Burney observes, "no other instruments were known than those of percussion, and it was, therefore, little more than metrical." Pipes of various kinds and the flute were afterwards invented; at first very rude, and made of reeds, which grew in the rivers and lakes, and some of these have been found in the Egyptian tombs. To discover, we can scarcely say to invent, such simple instruments, required a very slight effort. But it was long before music and musical instruments attained to any degree of excellence; and the simple instruments of early times being in time succeeded by others of a more complicated kind, the many-stringed harp, lyre, and other instruments, added to the power and variety of musical sounds.

To contrive a method of obtaining perfect melody from a smaller number of strings, by shortening them on a neck during the performance, like our modern violin, was, unquestionably, a more difficult task than could be accomplished in the infancy of music, and great advances must have been already made in the science before this could be attained, or before the idea would suggest itself to the mind. With this principle, however, the Egyptians were well acquainted; and the sculptures unquestionably prove it, in the frequent use of the three-stringed guitar.

A harp or lyre, having a number of strings, imitating various sounds, and disposed in the order of notes, might be invented even in an early stage of the art; but a people who had not attentively studied the nature of musical sounds would necessarily remain ignorant of the method of procuring the same tones from a limited number of strings; nor are our means simplified till they become perfectly understood. It is, then, evident, not only from the great fondness for music evinced by the early Egyptians, but from the nature of the very instruments they used, that the art was studied with great attention, and that they extended the same minute and serious investigation to this as to other sciences.

The fabulous account of its origin, mentioned by Diodorus, shows music to have been sanctioned, and even cultivated, by the priests themselves, who invariably pretended to have derived from the gods the knowledge of the sciences they encouraged. Hermes or Mercury was, therefore, reputed to be the first discoverer of the harmony and principle of voices or sounds, and the inventor of the lyre.

Harps, pipe, and flute, from an ancient tomb near the Pyramids.

From his limiting the number of its chords to three, the historian evidently confounds the lyre with the Egyptian guitar; yet this traditional story serves to attest the remote antiquity of stringed instruments, and proves the great respect paid to music by the Egyptian priests, who thought it not unworthy of a deity to be its patron and inventor.

It is sufficiently evident, from the sculptures of the ancient Egyptians, that their hired musicians were acquainted with the triple symphony: the harmony of instruments; of voices; and of voices and instruments. Their band was variously com-

1   2

95.   The harp and double pipe.   *Thebes.*

posed, consisting either of two harps, with the single pipe and flute; of the harp and double pipe, frequently with the addition of the guitar; of a fourteen-stringed harp, a guitar, lyre, double pipe, and tambourine; of two harps, sometimes of different sizes, one of seven, the other of four, strings; of two harps of eight chords, and a seven-stringed lyre; of the guitar and the square or oblong tambourine; of the lyre, harp, guitar, double pipe, and a sort of harp with four strings, which was held upon the shoulder; of the harp, guitar, double pipe, lyre, and square

96.   The harp, guitar, and double pipe.   *Thebes.*

97.   Harp and a smaller one of four chords.   *Thebes.*

tambourine ;* of the harp, two guitars, and the double pipe ;† of
the harp, two flutes, and a guitar ;‡ of two harps and a flute ; of a
seventeen-stringed lyre, the double-pipe, and a harp of fourteen
chords ; of the harp, and two guitars ; or of two seven-stringed

* Woodcut 98.   † Woodcut 101.
             ‡ *See* Sacred Music.

98.

Harp, guitar, double pipe, lyre, and square tambourine.   Thebes.

1   2   3   4   5   6

99.   Men and women singing to the harp, lyre, and double pipe.   *Thebes.*

3   2   1

100.   Harp and two guitars.   *Thebes.*

harps and an instrument held in the hand, not unlike an eastern
fan,* to which were probably attached small bells, or pieces
of metal that emitted a jingling sound when shaken, like the
crescent crowned *bells* of our modern bands.   There were many
other combinations of these various instruments; and in the Bac-

* Woodcut 103, fig. 3.

Two guitars, a harp, and double pipe, and a woman beating time with her hands.

Thebes.

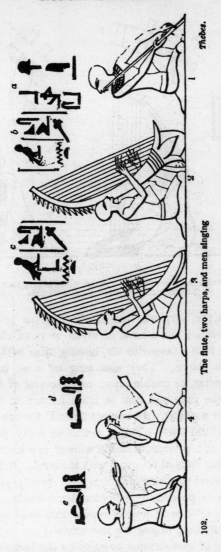

The flute, two harps, and men singing

102.

chic festival of Ptolemy Philadelphus, described by Athenæus, more than 600 musicians were employed in the chorus, among whom were 300 performers on the *cithara*.

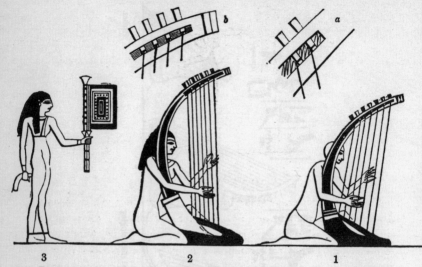

103. Two harps, and another instrument, which perhaps emitted a jingling sound. *a* and *b* show
how the strings were wound round the pegs.   *Beni Hassan.*

Sometimes the harp was played alone, or as an accompaniment to the voice; and a band of seven or more choristers frequently sang to it a favourite air, beating time with their hands
between each stanza. They also sang to other instruments,*
as the lyre, guitar, or double pipe; or to several of them played
together, as the flute and one or more harps; or to these last
with a lyre, or a guitar. It was not unusual for one man or one
woman to perform a solo; and a chorus of many persons occasionally sang at a private assembly without any instrument, two
or three beating time at intervals with the hand. Sometimes the
band of choristers consisted of more than twenty persons, only
two of whom responded by clapping their hands; and in one
instance I have seen a female represented holding what was
perhaps another kind of jingling instrument.†

The custom of beating time by clapping the hands between the
stanzas is still usual in Egypt.

* Woodcuts 99, 100, 101, and 102.   † Woodcut 104.

104.   An unusual kind of instrument.   *Thebes.*

On some occasions women beat the tambourine and *darabooka* drum, without the addition of any other instrument ; dancing or singing to the sound ; and bearing palm branches or green twigs in their hands, they proceeded to the tomb of a deceased friend, accompanied by this species of music. The same custom may still be traced in the Friday visit to the cemetery, and in some other funeral ceremonies among the Moslem peasants of modern Egypt.

If it was not customary for the higher classes of Egyptians to

    7   6   5   4   3   2   1
105.   Women beating tambourines, and the *darabooka* drum (fig. 1).   *Thebes.*

learn music for the purpose of playing in society, and if few amateur performers could be found among persons of rank, still some general knowledge of the art must have been acquired by a people so alive to its charms ; and the attention paid to it by the priests regulated the taste, and prevented the introduction of a vitiated style.   Those who played at the houses of the rich, as well as the ambulant musicians of the streets, were of the lower classes, and made this employment the means of obtaining their livelihood ; and in many instances both the minstrels and the choristers were blind.*

It was not so necessary an accomplishment for the higher classes of Egyptians as of the Greeks, who, as Cicero says, " considered the arts of singing and playing upon musical instruments a very principal part of learning ; whence it is related of Epaminondas, who, in my judgment, was the first of all the Greeks, that he played very well upon the flute.   And, some time before, Themistocles, upon refusing the harp at an entertainment, passed for an uninstructed and ill-bred person.   Hence Greece became celebrated for skilful musicians ; and as all persons there learned music, those who attained to no proficiency in it were thought uneducated and unaccomplished."   Cornelius Nepos also states that Epaminondas "played the harp and flute, and perfectly understood the art of dancing, with other liberal sciences," which, " though trivial things in the opinion of the Romans, were reckoned highly commendable in Greece."

The Israelites also delighted in music and the dance ; and persons of rank deemed them a necessary part of their education. Like the Egyptians with whom they had so long resided, the Jews carefully distinguished sacred from profane music.   They introduced it at public and private rejoicings, at funerals, and in religious services ; but the character of the airs, like the words of their songs, varied according to the occasion ; and they had canticles of mirth, of praise, of thanksgiving, and of lamentation. Some were *epithalamia,* or songs composed to celebrate mar-

* As in woodcut 106.

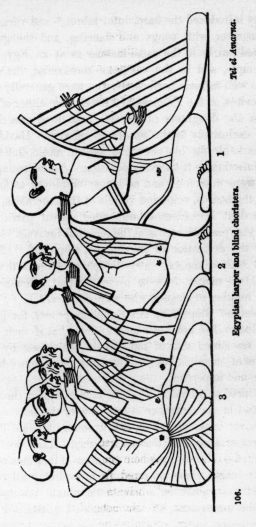

Egyptian harper and blind choristers.

riages; others to commemorate a victory, or the accession of a prince; to return thanks to the Deity, or to celebrate his praises; to lament a general calamity, or a private affliction; and others, again, were peculiar to their festive meetings. On these occasions they introduced the harp, lute, tabret,* and various instruments, together with songs and dancing, and the guests were entertained nearly in the same manner as at an Egyptian feast. In the temple, and in the religious ceremonies, the Jews had female as well as male performers, who were generally daughters of the Levites, as the Pallaces of Thebes were either of the royal family, or the daughters of priests; and these musicians were attached exclusively to the service of religion. David was not only remarkable for his taste and skill in music, but took a delight in introducing it on every occasion. "And seeing that the Levites were numerous, and no longer employed as formerly in carrying the boards, veils, and vessels of the tabernacle, its abode being fixed at Jerusalem, he appointed a great part of them to sing and play on instruments, at the religious festivals." Solomon, again, at the dedication of the temple, employed "120 priests, to sound with trumpets;" and Josephus pretends that no less than 200,000 musicians were present at that ceremony, besides the same number of singers, who were Levites.

The method adopted by the Egyptian priests, for preserving their melodies, has not been ascertained; but if their system of notation resembled that of the Greeks, which was by disposing the letters of the alphabet in different ways, it must have been cumbrous and imperfect.

When hired to attend at a private entertainment, the musicians either stood in the centre, or at one side, of the festive chamber, and some sat cross-legged on the ground, like the Turks and other Eastern people of the present day. They were usually accompanied on these occasions by dancers, either men or women, sometimes both; whose art consisted in assuming all the graceful or ludicrous gestures, which could obtain the applause, or tend to the amusement, of the assembled guests. For music

---

* Comp. Luke, xv. 25, "He heard music and dancing;" and Gen. xxxi. 27, where Laban complains that Jacob did not allow him to celebrate his departure with a festive meeting, "with mirth and with songs, with tabret and with harp." This last, however, in the Hebrew, is kinoor, כנור, which is rather a lyre. It was known in the days of Seth, Gen. iv. 21, and of Job, xxi. 12.

and dancing were considered as essential at their entertainments, as among the Greeks; but it is by no means certain that these diversions counteracted the effect of wine, as Plutarch imagines; a sprightly air is more likely to have invited another glass; and sobriety at a feast was not one of the objects of the lively Egyptians.

Some of their songs, it is true, bore a plaintive character, but not so the generality of those introduced at their festive meetings. That called Maneros is said by Herodotus to be the same as the Linus of the Greeks, "which was known in Phœnicia, Cyprus, and other places;" and was peculiarly adapted to mournful occasions. Plutarch, however, asserts that it was suited to festivities and the pleasures of the table, and that, "amidst the diversions of a sociable party, the Egyptians made the room resound with the song of Maneros." We may, therefore, conclude that the Egyptians had two songs, bearing a name resembling Maneros, which have been confounded together by Greek writers; and that one of these bore a lugubrious, the other a lively, character.

The airs and words were of course made to suit the occasion, either of rejoicing and festivity, of solemnity, or of lamentation; and all their agricultural and other occupations had, as at the present day, their appropriate songs.

At the religious ceremonies and processions, certain musicians attached to the priestly order, and organised for this special purpose, were employed; who were considered to belong exclusively to the service of the temple, as each military band of their army to its respective corps.

When an individual died, it was usual for the women to issue forth from the house, and throwing dust and mud upon their heads, to utter cries of lamentation as they wandered through the streets of the town, or amidst the cottages of the village. They sang a doleful dirge in token of their grief; they, by turns, expressed their regret for the loss of their relative or friend, and their praises of his virtues; and this was frequently done to the time and measure of a plaintive, though not inharmonious, air.

Sometimes the tambourine was introduced, and the "mournful song" was accompanied by its monotonous sound. On these occasions, the services of hired performers were uncalled for; though during the period of seventy days, while the body was in the hands of the embalmers, mourners* were employed, who sang the same plaintive dirge to the memory of the deceased; a custom prevalent also among the Jews, when preparing for a funeral.†

At their musical *soirées*, men or women played the harp, lyre, *guitar*, and the single or double pipe, but the flute appears to have been confined to men; and the tambourine and *darabooka* drum were generally appropriated to the other sex.

The *darabooka* drum is rarely met with in the paintings of Thebes, being only used on certain occasions, and chiefly, as at the present day, by the peasant women, and the boatmen of the Nile. It was evidently the same as the modern one, which is made of parchment, strained and glued over a funnel-shaped case

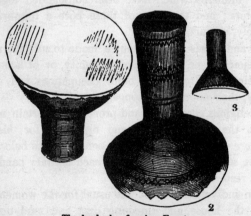

107.   The darabooka of modern Egypt.

of pottery, which is a hollow cylinder, with a truncated cone attached to it. It is beaten with the hand, and when relaxed, the parchment is braced by exposing it a few moments to the sun, or the warmth of a fire. It is generally supported by a band

* Exod. l. 3; Herod. ii. 86.   † Matt. ix. 23; Jer. xvi. 5, 7.

round the neck of the performer, who, with the fingers of the right hand, plays the air, and with the left grasps the lower edge of the head, in order to beat the bass, as in the tambourine; which we find from the sculptures was played in the same manner by the ancient Egyptians.

They had also cymbals, and cylindrical maces (*crotala*, or clappers), two of which were struck together, and probably emitted a sharp metallic sound. The cymbals were of mixed metal, apparently brass, or a compound of brass and silver, and of a form exactly resembling those of modern times, though smaller, being only seven, or five inches and a half in diameter. The handle was also of brass, bound with leather, string, or any similar substance, and being inserted in a small hole at the sum-

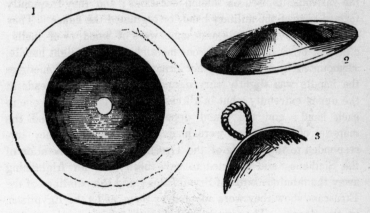

108.   Egyptian cymbals, 5¼ inches in diameter.   *British Museum.*

mit, was secured by bending back the two ends. The same kind of instrument is used by the modern inhabitants of the country; and from them have been borrowed the very small cymbals played with the finger and thumb, which supply the place of castanets in the *almeh* dance. These were the origin of the Spanish castanet, having been introduced into that country by the Moors, and afterwards altered in form, and made of chestnut (castaña) and other wood instead of metal.

The cymbals of modern Egypt are chiefly used by the attendants of shekhs' tombs, who travel through the country at certain periods of the year, to exact charitable donations from the credulous, or the devout, among the Moslems, by the promise of some blessing from the indulgent saint.   Drums and some other noisy instruments, which are used at marriages and on other occasions, accompany the cymbals, but these last are more peculiarly appropriated to the service of the shekhs, and the external ceremonies of religion, as among the ancient Egyptians; and a female, whose coffin contained a pair of cymbals, was described in the hieroglyphics of the exterior as the minstrel of a deity.

The cylindrical maces, or clappers, were also admitted among the instruments used on solemn occasions; and they frequently formed part of the military band, or regulated the dance.   They varied slightly in form; and some were of wood, or of shells; others of brass, or some sonorous metal, having a straight handle, surmounted by a head, or other ornamental device.   Sometimes the handle was slightly curved, and double, with two heads at the upper extremity; but in all cases the performer held one in each hand; and the sound depended on their size, and the material of which they were made.   When of wood they corresponded to the *crotala* of the Greeks, a supposed invention of the Sicilians; and reported to have been used for frightening away the fabulous birds of Stymphalus; and the paintings of the Etruscans show they were adopted by them, as by the Egyptians, in the dance.   They were probably the same as the round-headed pegs, resembling large nails, seen in the hands of some dancing figures in the paintings of Herculaneum; and Herodotus describes the crotala played as an accompaniment to the flute by the votaries of the Egyptian Diana, on their way to her temple at Bubastis.

Though the Egyptians were fond of buffoonery and gesticulation, they do not seem to have had any public show which can be said to resemble a theatre.   The stage is allowed to have been purely a Greek invention; and to dramatic entertainments,

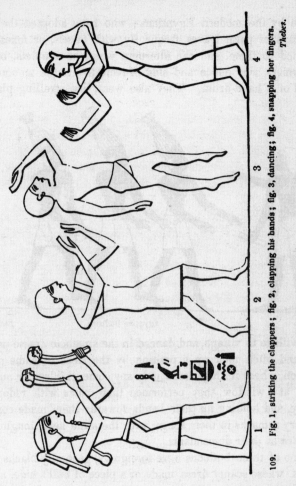

109.   Fig. 1, striking the clappers; fig. 2, clapping his hands; fig. 3, dancing; fig. 4, snapping her fingers.
Thebes.

which were originally of two kinds, comedy and tragedy, were added the ancient Italian pantomime. The Egyptian common people had certain jocose songs, accompanied with mimic and extravagant gestures, containing appropriate and laughable remarks on the bystanders; extempore sallies of wit, like the Fescennine verses of ancient Italy, which were also peculiar to the country people. Their object was to provoke a retort from him they addressed, or to supply one if unanswered; a custom still continued by the modern Egyptians; who have adopted the high foolscaps of palm leaves, frequently with tassels, or foxes' tails attached to them, and the alternate verse, or couplets, of two performers, who dance and sing in recitative to the monotonous sound of a hand-drum. They also went, like strolling players,

110.   Egyptian Buffoons.   *Thebes.*

from village to village, and danced in the streets to amuse passers by; and often took up a position by the steps of some grand mansion, where if they could only spy some children or nursery maids at a window, they performed their parts with redoubled energy, and holding up their hands towards them made complimentary remarks in their songs, with the same keen longing for *bakshish* as their descendants.

Some of these buffoons were foreigners, generally blacks from Africa, whose scanty dress, made of a piece of bull's hide, added not a little to their grotesque appearance; purposely increased by a small addition resembling a tail. (*Woodcut* 111.) They also had tags, like beads, suspended from their elbows; which were often put on by Egyptian performers on festive occasions; as they are still by the people of Ethiopia and Kordofan in their dances; and they are shown by the vases to have been adopted by the Greeks in bacchanalian and other ceremonies. The tail was also given to Greek fauns.

Men dancing in the street to the sound of the drum.

111.

In their military bands some of the instruments differed from those of ordinary musicians, but the sculptures have not recorded all the various kinds used in the Egyptian army. The principal ones appear to have been the trumpet and drum: the former used to marshal the troops, summon them to the charge, and direct them in their evolutions; the latter to regulate and enliven their march.

The trumpet, like that of the Israelites, was about one foot and a half long, of very simple form, apparently of brass; and when sounded, it was held with both hands, and either used singly, or as part of the military band, with the drum and other instruments.

1   2   3   4   5
112.   A military band.   Thebes.

The trumpet was particularly, though not exclusively, appro priated to martial purposes. It was straight, like the Roman tuba, or our common trumpet, and was used in Egypt at the earliest times. In Greece it was also known before the Trojan war; it was reputed to have been the invention of Minerva, or of Tyrrhenus, a son of Hercules; and in later times it was generally adopted, both as a martial instrument, and by the am- bulant musicians of the streets. In some parts of Egypt a preju- dice existed against the trumpet; and the people of Busiris

and Lycopolis would never use it, because the sound resembled
the braying of an ass, which, being the
emblem of Typhon, gave them very unpleasant sensations, by reminding them of
the Evil Being.   The same kind of notion
prevents the Moslems using bells, which,
if they do not actually bring bad spirits
into the house, keep away good ones ; and
many seem to think that dogs are also in
league with the powers of darkness.

   The Israelites had trumpets for warlike,
as well as sacred purposes, for festivals
and rejoicings ; and the office of sounding
113.   The trumpet.   *Thebes.*

them was not only honourable, but was committed solely to the
priests.   Some were of silver, which were suited to all occasions ;
others were animals' horns (like the original *cornu* of the Romans),
and these are stated to have been employed at the siege of
Jericho.   The Greeks had six kinds of trumpets ; the Romans
four,—the tuba, cornu, buccina, and lituus, and, in ancient times,
the *concha*, so called from having been originally a shell—which
were the only instruments employed by
them for military purposes, and in this
they differed from the Greeks and
Egyptians.

   The only drum represented in the
sculptures is a long drum, very similar
to one of the *tomtoms* of India.   It was
about two feet or two feet and a half in
length, and was beaten with the hand,
like the Roman tympanum.   The case
was of wood or copper, covered at either
end with parchment or leather, braced
by cords extending diagonally over the
exterior of the cylinder, and when played,
it was slung by a band round the neck
of the drummer, who during the march
114.   The drum.   *Thebes.*

carried it in a vertical position at his back. Like the trumpet,

115.   Mode of slinging the drum behind
them, when on a march.

it was chiefly employed in the army; and the evidence of the sculptures is confirmed by Clement of Alexandria, who says the drum was used by the Egyptians in going to war.* It was also common at the earliest period of which we have any account from the sculptures of Thebes, or about the sixteenth century before our era.

When a body of troops marched to the beat of drum, the drummer was often stationed in the centre or the rear, and sometimes immediately behind the standard bearers; the trumpeter's post being generally at the head of the regiment, except when summoning them to form or advance to the charge; but the drummers were not always alone, or confined to the rear and centre; and when forming part of the band, they marched in the van, or, with the other musicians, were drawn up on one side while the troops defiled.

Besides the long drum, the Egyptians had another, not very unlike our own, both in form and size, which was much broader in proportion to its length than the *tomtom* just mentioned, being two feet and a half high, and two feet broad. It was beaten with two wooden sticks; but as there is no representation of the mode of using it, we are unable to decide whether it was suspended horizontally and struck at both ends, as the drum of the same kind still used at Cairo, or at one end only, like our own; though, from the curve of the sticks, I am inclined to think it was slung and beaten as the *tamboor* of modern Egypt. Sometimes the sticks were straight, and consisted of two parts, the handle and a thin round rod, at whose end a small knob pro-

* Clemens Alex. Stromat. ii. 164.

jected, for the purpose of fastening the leather pad with which
the drum was struck; they were about a foot in length, and,

judging from the form of the handle of one in the Berlin Museum, we may conclude they belonged, like those above mentioned, to a drum beaten at both ends. Each extremity of the
drum was covered with red leather, braced with catgut strings
passing through small holes in its broad margin, and extending
in direct lines over the copper body, which, from its convexity,
was similar in shape to a cask.

In order to tighten the strings, and thereby to brace the drum,
a piece of catgut extended round each end, near the edge of the
leather; and crossing the strings at right angles, and being
twisted round each separately, braced them all in proportion as
it was drawn tight: but this was only done when the leather and
the strings had become relaxed by constant use; and as this
piece of catgut was applied to either end, they had the means of
doubling the power of tension on every string.

117.   Fig. 1. The drum.   2. shows how the strings were braced.   3. The sticks.
                                                         Found at Thebes.

Besides the ordinary forms of Egyptian instruments, several
were constructed according to a particular taste or accidental
caprice. Some were of the most simple kind, others of very

118.   Harpers painted in the tomb of Remeses III.,

costly materials, and many were richly ornamented with brilliant colours and fancy figures ; particularly the harps and lyres.
The harps varied greatly in form, size, and the number of their

known as Bruce's, or the Harper's tomb.   *Thebes.*

strings ; they are represented in the ancient paintings with four,
six, seven, eight, nine, ten, eleven, twelve, fourteen, seventeen,
twenty, twenty-one, and twenty-two chords : that in the Paris

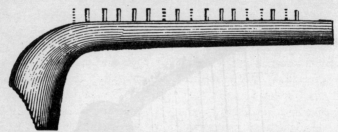

119.   Head of a harp brought by me from Thebes, and now in the British Museum.

collection appears also to have had twenty-one; and the head of
another I found at Thebes was made for seventeen strings. They
were frequently very large, even exceeding the height of a man,
tastefully painted with the lotus and other flowers, or with fancy
devices; and those of the royal minstrels were fitted up in the
most splendid manner, adorned with the head or bust of the
monarch himself: like those in Bruce's tomb at Thebes.

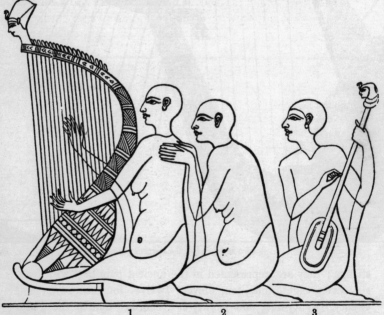

                    1   2   3
120. A richly painted harp on a stand, a man beating time with his hands, and a player on the guitar.

The oldest harps found in the sculptures are in a tomb, near the pyramids of Geezeh, upwards of four thousand years old. They are more rude in shape than those usually represented; and though it is impossible to ascertain the precise number of their chords,[*] they do not appear to have exceeded seven or eight, and are fastened in a different manner from ordinary Egyptian harps. These date long before the Shepherd invasion, and the fact of the Egyptians being already sufficiently advanced to combine the harmony of various instruments with the voice shows they were not indebted for music to that Asiatic race. The combination of harps and lyres of great compass with the flute, single and double pipes, guitars, and tambourines, prove the proficiency to which they had arrived; and even in the reign of Amosis, the first king of the 18th dynasty, about 1570 B.C., nine hundred years before Terpander's time, the ordinary musicians of Egypt used harps of fourteen, and lyres of seventeen strings.

The Greeks were indebted to Asia for their stringed instruments, and even for the cithara (κιθάρα), which was originally styled "Asiatic," and was introduced from Lesbos. It had only seven chords, till Timotheus of Miletus added four others, about 400 B.C.; and Terpander, who lived 200 years after Homer, was the first to lay down any laws for this instrument, some time before they were devised for the flute or pipe. The harp, indeed, seems always to have been unknown to the Greeks.

The strings of Egyptian harps were of catgut, as of the lyres still used in Nubia. Some harps stood on the ground while played, having an even, broad, base; others were placed on a stool, or raised upon a stand, or limb, attached to the lower part.[†] Men and women often used harps of the same compass, and even the smallest, of four strings, were played by men;[‡] but the largest were mostly appropriated to the latter, who stood during the performance. These large harps had a flat base, so as to stand without support, like those in Bruce's tomb;[§] and a lighter kind was also squared for the same purpose,[||] but, when played, was frequently inclined towards the performer, who supported

---

[*] Woodcut 94.   [†] Woodcuts 96, 97, 121, 122.   [‡] Woodcuts 96, 97, 103.
     [§] Woodcuts 118, 118 a, and 99.   [||] Woodcut 101.

121.   Minstrel standing, while playing the harp.   *Dendera.*

122.   Harp raised on a stand, or support.   *Thebes.*

the instrument in the most convenient position.* Many harps were of wood, covered with bull's hide, † or with leather, sometimes of a green or red colour, and painted with various devices, vestiges of which may be traced in that of the Paris collection ; ‡ and small ones were sometimes made, like many Greek lyres, of tortoise shell. (*Woodcuts* 96, 97.)

The Egyptians had no means of shortening the harp strings during the performance, by any contrivance resembling our modern pedals, so as to introduce occasional sharps and flats; they could, therefore, only play in one key, until they tuned the instrument afresh, by turning the pegs. Indeed it was not more necessary in their harp than in the lyre, since the former was always combined with other instruments, except when used as a mere accompaniment to the voice. But they seem occasionally to have supplied this deficiency by a double set of pegs ; and their great skill in music during so many centuries would necessarily suggest some means of obtaining half notes.

The Egyptian harps have another imperfection, for which it is not easy to account,—the absence of a pole, and consequently of a support to the bar, or upper limb, in which the pegs were fixed ; and it is difficult to conceive how, without it, the chords could have been properly tightened, or the bar sufficiently strong to resist the effect of their tension ; particularly in those of triangular form. The pole is not only wanting in those of the paintings, but in all that have been found in the tombs ; and even in that of the Paris Collection, which, having twenty-one strings, was one of the highest power they had, since they are seldom represented on the monuments with more than two octaves. This last, however, may hold an intermediate place between a harp and the many triangular stringed instruments of the Egyptians.

The harp was thought to be especially suited for the service of religion ; and it was used on many occasions to celebrate the praises of the gods. It was even represented in the hands of the deities themselves, as well as the tambourine and the sacred sistrum.

* Woodcuts 95, 98, 100.   † Woodcuts 97, fig. 2, 98, 100, 101.
‡ Woodcut 123.

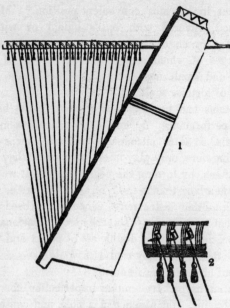

123.   Harp of the Paris Collection.

The Egyptian lyre was not less varied in form, and the number of its chords, than the harp, and they ornamented it in many ways, as their taste suggested; some with the head of an animal carved in wood, as the horse, ibex, or gazelle; while others were of more simple shape.

Mercury has always obtained the credit of its invention, both among the Egyptians and the Greeks; and Apollodorus gravely explains how it came into his head: "The Nile," he says, "after having overflowed the whole land of Egypt, returned once more within its banks, leaving on the shore a great number of dead animals of various kinds, and among the rest a tortoise. Its flesh was quite dried up by the hot Egyptian sun, so that nothing remained within the shell but nerves and cartilages; and these, being braced and contracted by the heat, had become sonorous. Mercury, walking by the river side, happened to strike his foot against this shell, and was so pleased with the sound produced, that the idea of a lyre presented itself to his imagination. He therefore constructed the instrument in the form of a tortoise, and strung it with the sinews of dead animals."

124.   Lyre ornamented with the head of an animal.   *Thebes .*

Many Egyptian lyres were of considerable power, having 5, 7, 10, and 18 strings. They were usually supported between the elbow and the side; and the mode of playing them was with the hand, or sometimes with the plectrum, which was made of bone, ivory, or wood, and was often attached to one limb of the lyre by a string.

The Greeks also adopted both methods, but more generally used the plectrum; and in the frescoes of Herculaneum are lyres of 3, 6, 9, and 11 strings played with it; of 4, 5, 6, 7, and 10 with the hands; and of 9 and 11 strings played with the plectrum and fingers at the same time.

The strings were fastened at the upper end to a cross bar connecting the two limbs or sides, and at the lower end they were attached to a raised ledge or hollow sounding board, about the

125.   Lyres played with and without the plectrum.   *Thebes.*

centre of the body of the instrument, which was entirely of wood.
In the Berlin and Leyden museums are lyres of this kind, which,
with the exception of the strings, are perfectly preserved.   That

126.   Lyre in the Berlin Museum.

in the former collection has the two limbs terminating in horses' heads; and in form and principle, and in the alternate long and short chords, resembles some of those represented in the paintings;* though the board to which the strings are fastened is nearer the bottom of the instrument, and the number of chords is 13 instead of 10.

We have thus an opportunity of comparing real Egyptian lyres with those represented at Thebes in the reign of Amunoph, and other kings, who reigned more than three thousand years ago.

The body of the Berlin lyre is about ten inches high, and fourteen and a half broad, and the total height of the instrument is two feet. That of Leyden is smaller, and less ornamented; but it is equally well preserved, and highly interesting from a hieratic inscription written in ink upon the front. It had no extra sounding board; its hollow body sufficiently answered this purpose; and the strings passed over a moveable bridge, and were secured at the bottom by a small metal ring or staple. Both these lyres were entirely of wood; and one of the limbs, like many represented in the paintings, was longer than the opposite one, so that the instrument might be tuned by sliding the strings upwards along the bar, as well as round it, which was the usual method, and is continued to the present day in the *Kisírka* of modern Nubia.

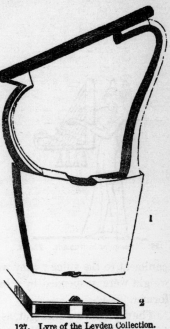

127.   Lyre of the Leyden Collection.
Fig. 2 shows the lower end.

In Greece the lyre had at first only four chords, till the addi-

* Woodcuts 98, 125.

tional three were introduced by Amphion, who seems to have
borrowed his knowledge of music from Lydia ; and was, as
usual, reputed to have been taught by Mercury.   Terpander
(670 B.C.) added several more notes ; and the lyres represented
at Herculaneum have 3, 4, 5, 6, 7, 8, 9, 10, and 11 chords.

Numerous other instruments, resembling harps or lyres in
principle, were common in Egypt, which varied so much in
form, compass, and sound, that they were considered quite distinct from them, and had each its own name.   They have been
found in the tombs, or are represented in the paintings of Thebes
and other places.   Those of a triangular shape were held under
the arm while played, and, like the rest, were used as an accom-

128.   Triangular instrument. *Thebes.*   129.   Another, held under the arm. *Dakkeh.*

paniment to the voice ; they were mostly light, but when of any
weight were suspended by a band over the shoulder of the performer.

The strings were of catgut, as in the harps ; and those of *woodcut*
130, *fig*. 1, were so well preserved that, when found at Thebes,
in 1823, they sounded on being touched, though buried two or three
thousand years.   It was an instrument of great compass, having
twenty strings wound round a rod at the lower end, which was

probably turned in order to tighten them ; and the frame was of wood, covered with leather, on which could be traced a few

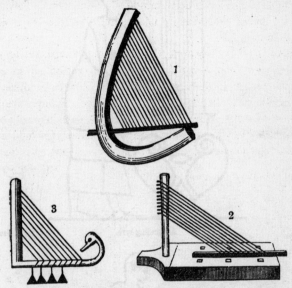

130.

Fig. 1 found at Thebes in 1823.

hieroglyphics. That in fig. 2, given by Professor Rosellini, has the peculiarity of being tuned by pegs; but its ten strings are fastened to a rod in the centre of its sounding-board, as in other instruments.

Another, which may be called a standing-lyre, was of great height. It consisted of a round body, probably of wood and metal, in the form of a vase, from which two upright limbs rose, supporting the transverse bar to which the upper ends of its eight strings were fastened; and the minstrel sang to it, as he touched the chords with his two hands.

A still more jingling instrument was used as an accompaniment to the lyre. It consisted of several bars, probably of wire, attached to a frame, or some sounding body; which were struck by a rod held in both hands by the performer. (*Woodcut* 132.)

More common was a light instrument of four strings, which

131.   A standing lyre.   *Tel el Amarna.*

132.   An instrument played as an accompaniment to the lyre.   *Tel el Amarna.*

was carried on the shoulder while played, and was mostly used
by women, who chanted to it as the Jews did "to the sound

133.   A light kind of instrument borne on the shoulder.   *Thebes.*

of the (*nabl*) viol" (Amos, vi. 5). Some of these have been
found in the tombs of Thebes, and the most perfect one is that
in the British Museum, which is 41 inches long, the neck 22,
and the breadth of the body 4 inches. Its exact form, the pegs,
the rod to which the chords were fastened, and even the parchment covering its wooden body and serving as a sounding-board,

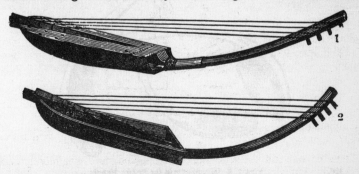

134.   Instrument differing from the harp, lyre, and guitar.   *British Museum.*

still remain, and all it wants are the four strings. The mode of fastening the strings to the rod is not quite evident, and they seem to have passed through the parchment to the rod lying beneath it, which has notches at intervals to receive them. It is of hard wood, apparently acacia; and sufficient remains of one of the strings to show they were of catgut.

Similar in principle to this was a small instrument of five chords, having a hollow wooden body, over which was stretched a covering of parchment, or of thin wood; and the strings extended in the same manner from a rod in the centre, to the pegs at the end of the neck.

135.   The instrument restored.

Three have been found in the tombs; one of which is in the Berlin, and two in the British Museum; the former with the five pegs entire, and the body composed of three pieces of sycamore

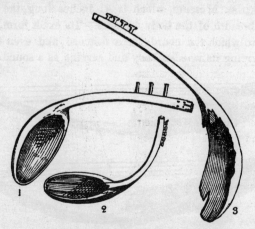

136.   Figs. 1. 3. Instruments *in the British Museum.*
                  Fig. 2. *In the Berlin Museum.*

wood. Their whole length is 2 feet, the neck about 1 foot 3 inches, in the under side of which are the five pegs, placed in a direct line, one after the other. At the opposite end of the body are two holes for fastening the rod that secured the strings.

Besides harps and lyres, the Egyptians had a sort of guitar with three chords, which have been strangely supposed to correspond to the three seasons of the Egyptian year: and here again Thoth or Mercury has received the credit of the invention; for the instrument having only three strings, and yet equalling the power of those of great compass, was considered by the Egyptians worthy of the God; whose intervention on this and similar occasions is, in fact, only an allegorical mode of expressing the intellectual gifts communicated from the Divinity to man.

The guitar consisted of two parts: a long flat neck, or handle, and a hollow oval body, either wholly of wood, or covered with parchment, having the upper surface perforated with holes to allow the sound to escape. Over this body, and the whole length of the handle, were stretched three strings of catgut, secured at the upper extremity either by the same number of pegs, or by passing through an aperture in the handle; they were then bound round it, and tied in a knot. It does not appear to have had any bridge, but the chords were fastened at the lower end to a triangular piece of wood or ivory, which raised them to a sufficient height; and they were sometimes elevated at the upper extremity of the handle by means of a small crossbar, immediately below each

137.   Female playing the guitar.   *Thebes.*

of the apertures where the strings were passed through and tightened.* This answered the same purpose as the depressed

* Woodcuts 96, 98, 101, 138, 139.

end of our modern guitar; and, indeed, since the neck was in a
straight line with the body of the instrument, some contrivance
of the kind was absolutely required.

The length of the handle was from twice, to thrice, that
of the body; and the whole instrument measured about 4
feet, the breadth of the body being equal to half its length.
It was struck with the plectrum, which was attached by a
string to the neck, and the performers usually stood as they
played. It was considered equally suited to men or women;
and some danced while they touched its strings, supporting it on
the right arm. It was sometimes slung by a band round the
neck, like the modern Spanish guitar, to which it also corresponded in being an accompaniment to the voice, though this did
not prevent its being part of a band with other instruments.*

138. Dancing while playing the guitar.   *Thebes.*   139. Supported by a strap.   *Thebes.*

It is from an ancient instrument of this kind, sometimes called
kithára (κιθάρα), that the modern name guitar (*chitarra*) has
been derived; though the cithara of the Greeks and Romans, in
early times, at least, was a lyre. The Egyptian guitar may be

* Woodcuts 96, 98, 100, 101.

called a lute, but it does not appear to correspond to the three-
stringed lyre of Greece.

An instrument of an oval form, with a circular or cylindrical
handle, was found at Thebes, not altogether unlike the guitar;
but, owing to the imperfect state
of its preservation, nothing could
be ascertained respecting the pegs,
or the mode of tightening the
chords. The wooden body was
faced with leather, the handle extending down it to the lower
end, and part of the string remained which attached the plectrum. Three small holes indicated
the place where the chords were secured, and two others, a short distance above, appear to have been
intended for fastening some kind of bridge.

140.   An instrument like the guitar found
at Thebes.

Wire strings were not used by the Egyptians in any of their
instruments, catgut being alone employed, and the twang of this
in the warlike bow doubtless led to its adoption in the peaceful
lyre, owing to the accidental discovery of its musical sound; for
men hunted animals, and killed each other, with the bow and
arrow, long before they recited verses, or indulged in music. It
is, therefore, not surprising that the Arabs, a nation of hunters,
were the inventors of the *monochordium*, an instrument of the most
imperfect kind (except when the skill of a Paganini is employed
to command its tones); for, with all the accumulated practice of
ages, the modern Cairenes have not succeeded in making their
one-stringed *rahab* a tolerable accompaniment to the voice. No
doubt the instrument was very ancient; for, being used by the
reciters of poems, it evidently belonged to the early bards, the
first musicians of every country; and the wild Montenegrins
still sing their primitive war and love songs to the sound of the
one-stringed *gûsla*, handed down to them from the "wizards" of
the ancient Slavonians.

If we are surprised at the number of stringed instruments of the Egyptians (and many more are of course unknown to us), and if we wonder what sort of tones, and what variety of sounds, could be obtained from them, what shall we think of those mentioned by the Greeks, who seem to have adopted every one they could obtain from other countries? Some, as the phorminx, barbiton, and other lyres, are known; the first of which, according to Clemens, was not very different from the cithara; but the bare recital of the names of the rest is bewildering.

There were the *nablum, sambuca*,* pandurum, magadis, trigon (one of the three-cornered instruments) Phœnicica, pêctis, scindapsus, enneachordon (" of nine strings "), the square shaped psithyra or ascarum, heptagona (septangles) psaltery, spadix, pariambus, clepsiambus, jambyce, epigoneum, and many more; and even most Jewish instruments are uncertain, as the *kitharus* or harp, "the ten stringed" ashûr, the triangular *sambukê*, or *sabka*, the *nabl* or viol, the *kinnóor* or lyre of six or nine strings, and the *psanterin* or psaltery. And though the last is said to have had twelve notes, and to have been played with the fingers, and the *ashur*, or ten stringed viol, to have been played with the bow (or rather plectrum), we have no definite idea of their appearance; so that the Egyptian paintings give by far the best insight into the instruments used in those early times.

The flute was of great antiquity; for in a tomb near the Great Pyramid, built more than four thousand years ago, is a concert of vocal and instrumental music, where two harps, a pipe, a flute, and several voices are introduced.†

In Greece it was at first very simple, "with few holes," which were limited to four, until Diodorus of Thebes, in Bœotia, added others, and made a lateral opening for the mouth. It was originally of reed; afterwards of bone or ivory, and covered with bronze. But even this improved instrument was very small; and I have seen part of one, measuring 5½ inches in length and

---

* Described by Athenæus as a " ship with a ladder placed over it ;" by Suidas, as a triangular instrument.
† Woodcut 94.

¼ an inch in diameter, broken off at the fifth hole; the first of the five holes being distant only 1¼ inch from that of the mouth.

The Egyptian flute was of great length; for, reaching the ground when the' performer was seated, it could not be less than 2 feet 3 inches; and some were so long that, when playing, he was obliged to extend his arms below his waist, to touch the holes.* Those who played it generally sat on the ground; and in every instance I have met with they are men.

It was made of reed, of wood, of bone, or of ivory; and from the word *sêbi*, written over the instrument in the hieroglyphics, which is the same as its Coptic name, we may suppose it was originally the leg-bone of some animal. The Latin *tibia* has the same

Flute-player. The flute is of great length.
141.   *Thebes.*

meaning; and flutes are said to have been made in Bœotia of those hollow bones. The Egyptians probably had several kinds of flutes, some suited to mournful, others to festive, occasions, like the Greeks; and it is evident they used them both at banquets and religious ceremonies. But no Egyptian deity is represented playing the flute; and the gods and goddesses may have felt the same aversion to it as Minerva, when she perceived "the deformed appearance of her mouth,"—an allegory signifying, according to Aristotle, that it "interfered with mental reflection," and had most immoral effects, which in these ignorant days we are unable to perceive.

The pipe was of equal antiquity with the flute,† and belonged also to male performers; but, as it is seldom represented at concerts, and all those discovered are of common reed, it appears not to have been in great repute. In most countries it has been the instrument of the peasantry; but if the pipe "made of the straw of barley" was the invention of Osiris, it does not speak well for the musical talents of that deity. It was a

* Woodcuts 94, 141.   † Woodcut 94

straight tube, without any increase at the mouthpiece, and when
played was held with both hands. Its length did not exceed a
foot and a half : two in the British Museum are 9 and 15 inches
long, and those in the Collection at Leyden vary from 7 to 15
inches. Some have three, others four, holes, as is the case with
fourteen of those at Leyden ; and one at the British Museum had
a small mouthpiece of reed or thick straw, inserted into the hollow
of the pipe, the upper end so compressed as to leave a very
small aperture for the admission of the breath.

(9 inches long)

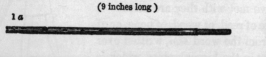

142.   Reed pipes, of Mr. Salt's Collection, now in the British Museum.

The double pipe was quite as common in Egypt, as in Greece.
It consisted of two tubes, one played by the right, the other by
the left hand, the latter giving a deep sound for the base, the
right a sharp tone for the tenor. The double *zummára* of the
modern Egyptians is a rude imitation of it, but its piping harshness and monotonous drone exclude it even from their imperfect
bands ; and it is only used by the boatmen of the Nile, and by the
peasants, who seem to think it a suitable accompaniment to the tedious camel's pace. Fortunately this national instrument delights

143.   Woman dancing, while playing the double pipe.   *Thebes.*

its admirers out of doors, like the bagpipes of the Abbruzzi and other countries, which, at a little distance, it so much resembles.

The double, like the single pipe, was at first of reed, and afterwards of wood and other materials; and it was introduced both on solemn and festive occasions among the Egyptians, as among the Greeks. Men, but more frequently women, performed upon it, occasionally dancing as they played; and, from its repeated occurrence in the sculptures of Thebes, it was evidently preferred to the single pipe.

The tambourine was a favourite instrument in religious ceremonies and at private banquets. It was played by men and women, but more usually by the latter, who often danced and sang to its sound; and it was used as an accompaniment to other instruments.* It was of three kinds; one circular, like our own; another square or oblong; and the third consisted of two squares, separated by a bar; all of which were beaten by the hand;† but there is no appearance of balls, or moveable pieces of metal attached to the frame, as in the Greek and modern tambourine. The *taph*, "timbrel," or "tabret" of the Jews was the same instrument,‡ and was of very early use among them, as well as the harp, even before they "went down into Egypt;" and the Jewish, like the Egyptian, women, danced to its sound.

Nearly all their instruments were admitted by the Egyptians into their *sacred music*, as the harp, lyre, flute, double pipe, tambourine, cymbals, and guitar; and neither the trumpet, drum, nor clappers, were excluded from the religious processions in which the military were engaged. The harp, lyre, and tambourine performed a part in the services of the temple; and two goddesses in the frieze at Dendera are represented playing the harp and tambourine, in honour of Athor, the Egyptian Venus. The priests, bearing sacred emblems, often walked in procession to the sound of the flute; and, excepting those of Osiris at Abydus, the sacred rites of an Egyptian deity did not forbid the introduction of the harp and flute, or the voice of singers.

---

* Woodcuts 98, 121.   † Woodcuts 105, 151.
‡ Gen. xxi. 27; Exod. xv. 20; Job xxi. 12; Judges xi. 34; 1 Sam. xviii. 6.

The harp, indeed, was considered particularly suited to religious purposes; the title "minstrels of Amun" applied to some harpers, and the two performers before the god in the tomb of Remeses III., show the honour in which it was held; and it was played either alone, or in combination with other instruments. The minstrel often chanted as he touched its strings; and the harp, guitar, and two flutes joined in a sacred air, while the high priest offered incense to the deity. The *crotala*, or clappers, were also used with the flute during pilgrimages and processions to the shrine of a god, accompanied by choristers who chanted hymns in his honour.

144.   Sacred musicians, and a priest offering incense.   *Leyden Museum.*

The Jews, in like manner, regarded music as indispensable for religious rites; their favourite instruments were the harp, lute or psaltery, and ten-stringed *ashur*, the tabret, trumpet, cornet, cymbals, and others;* and many "singing men and

---

* Psalm xxxiii. 2; lxxxi. 2. 1 Chron. xvi. 5; and xxv. 1. 2 Sam. vi. 5. Exod. xv. 20, &c.

singing women" attended in the processions to the Jewish sanctuary.*

The sistrum was the sacred instrument *par excellence*, and belonged as peculiarly to the service of the temple, as the small tinkling bell to that of a Roman Catholic chapel. Some pretend it was used to frighten away Typhon, and the rattling noise of its moveable bars was sometimes increased by the addition of several loose rings. It had generally three, rarely four, bars; and the whole instrument was from 8 to 16 or 18 inches in length, entirely of brass or bronze. It was sometimes inlaid with silver, or gilt, or otherwise ornamented; and, being held upright, was shaken, the rings moving to and fro upon the bars. These last were frequently made to imitate the sacred asp, or were simply bent at each end to secure them. Plutarch mentions a cat with a human face on the top of the instrument, and at the upper part of the handle, beneath the bars, the face of Isis on one side, and of Nepthys on the other.

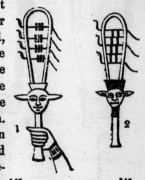

145.　　　　　　146.

Fig. 1. The sistrum of four bars.
　　　2. Of unusual form.

Thebes.

The British Museum possesses an excellent specimen of the sistrum, well preserved, and of the best period of Egyptian art. It is 1 foot 4 inches high, and had three moveable bars, which have been unfortunately lost. On the upper part are represented the goddess Pasht, or Bubastis, the sacred vulture, and other emblems; and on the side below is the figure of a female, holding in each hand one of these instruments.

The handle is cylindrical, and surmounted by the double face of Athor, wearing an "asp-formed crown," on whose summit appears to have been the cat, now scarcely traced in the remains of its feet. It is entirely of bronze; the handle, which is hollow, and closed by a moveable cover of the same metal, is

* Psalm lxviii. 25; 2 Sam. xix. 35.

supposed to have held something appertaining to the sistrum;
and the lead, still remaining within the head, is a portion of that
used in soldering it.

Two others, in the same collection, are highly preserved, but
of a late time, and another is of still more recent date; they
have four bars, and are of very small size.

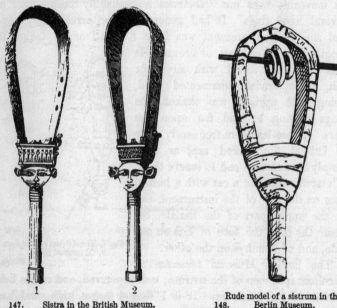

147.   Sistra in the British Museum.   148.   Rude model of a sistrum in the
                                                        Berlin Museum.

One of the Berlin sistra is 8, the other 9 inches in height: the
former has four bars, and on the upper or circular part lies a cat,
crowned with the disc or sun.   The other has three bars: the
handle is composed of a figure, supposed to be of Typhon, surmounted by the heads of Athor; and on the summit are the horns,
globe, and feathers of the same goddess.   They are both destitute
of rings; but the rude Egyptian model of another, in the same
collection, has three rings upon its single bar, agreeing in this
respect, if not in the number of the bars, with those represented
in the sculptures.   They are not of early date.

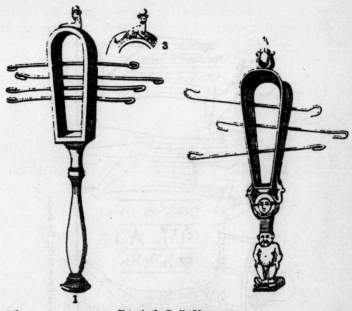

149.　　　　　Sistra in the Berlin Museum.　　　　150.

It was so great a privilege to hold the sacred sistrum in the temple, that it was given to queens, and to those noble ladies who had the distinguished title of "women of Amun," and were devoted to the service of the deity; and the Jews seem, in like manner, to have intrusted the principal sacred offices held by women to the daughters of priests, and of persons of rank.

The χνουη, an instrument said by Eustathius to have been used by the Greeks, at sacrifices, to assemble the congregation, was reputed to have been of Egyptian origin; but it has not been met with in the sculptures. It was a species of trumpet, of a round shape, and was said to have been the invention of Osiris.

The dance consisted mostly of a succession of figures, in which the performers endeavoured to exhibit a great variety of gesture: men and women danced at the same time, or in separate parties, but the latter were generally preferred, from their superior grace and elegance. Some danced to slow airs, adapted

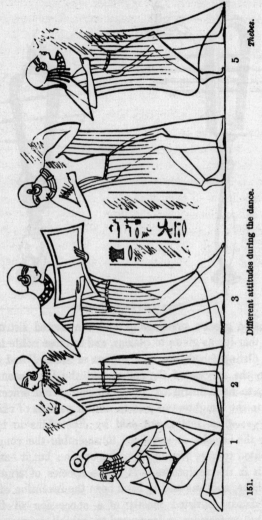

151.   Different attitudes during the dance.   Thebes.

to the style of their movement : the attitudes they assumed frequently partook of a grace not unworthy of the Greeks;* and

* Woodcut 151.

others preferred a lively step, regulated by an appropriate tune. Men sometimes danced with great spirit, bounding from the ground more in the manner of Europeans than of an Eastern people : on which occasions the music was not always composed of many instruments, but consisted only of *crotala* or maces, a man clapping his hands, and a woman snapping her fingers to the time.*

Graceful attitudes and gesticulation were the general style of their dance ; but, as in other countries, the taste of the performance varied according to the rank of the person by whom they were employed, or their own skill ; and the dance at the house of a priest differed from that among the uncouth peasantry, or the lower classes of townsmen.

It was not customary for the upper orders of Egyptians to indulge in this amusement, either in public or private assemblies, and none appear to have practised it but the lower ranks of society, and those who gained their livelihood by attending festive meetings. The Greeks, however, though they employed women who professed music and dancing, to entertain the guests, looked upon the dance as a recreation in which all classes might indulge, and an accomplishment becoming a gentleman ; and it was also a Jewish custom for young ladies to dance at private entertainments,† as it still is at Damascus and other Eastern towns.

The Romans, on the contrary, were far from considering it worthy of a man of rank, or of a sensible person ; and Cicero says, " No man who is sober dances, unless he is out of his mind, either *when alone*, or in any decent society ; for dancing is the companion of wanton conviviality, dissoluteness, and luxury." Nor did the Greeks indulge in it to excess ; and effeminate dances, or extraordinary gesticulation, were deemed indecent in men of character and wisdom. Indeed, Herodotus tells a story of Hippoclides, the Athenian, who had been preferred before all the nobles of Greece, as a husband for the daughter of Clisthenes, king of Argos, having been rejected on account of his extravagant gestures in the dance.

* Woodcut 109.   † Matth. xiv. 6.

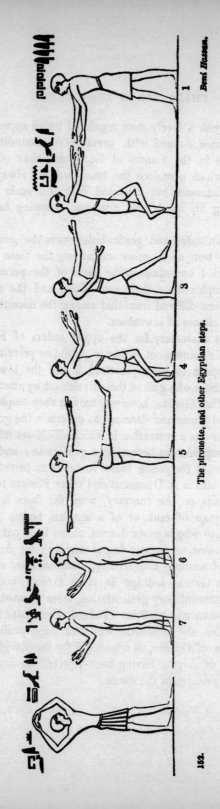

Beni Hassan.

The pirouette, and other Egyptian steps.

152.

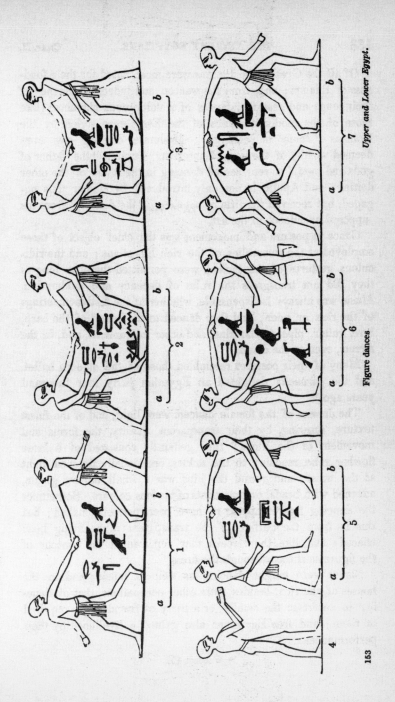

Figure dances.

Upper and Lower Egypt.

Of all the Greeks, the Ionians were most noted for their fondness of this art; and, from the wanton and indecent tendency of their songs and gestures, dances of a voluptuous character (like those of the modern Alméhs of the East) were styled by the Romans "Ionic movements." Moderate dancing was even deemed worthy of the gods themselves. Jupiter, "the father of gods and men," is represented dancing in the midst of the other deities; and Apollo is not only introduced by Homer thus engaged, but received the title of ορχηστης, "the dancer," from his supposed excellence in the art.

Grace in posture and movement was the chief object of those employed at the assemblies of the rich Egyptians; and the ridiculous gestures of the buffoon were permitted there, so long as they did not transgress the rules of decency and moderation. Music was always indispensable, whether at the festive meetings of the rich or poor; and they danced to the sound of the harp, lyre, guitar, pipe, tambourine, and other instruments, and, in the streets, even to the drum.

Many of their postures resembled those of the modern ballet, and the *pirouette* delighted an Egyptian party four thousand years ago.*

The dresses of the female dancers were light, and of the finest texture, showing, by their transparent quality, the forms and movement of the limbs: they generally consisted of a loose flowing robe, reaching to the ankles, occasionally fastened tight at the waist; and round the hips was a small narrow girdle, adorned with beads, or ornaments of various colours. Sometimes the dancing figures appear to have been perfectly naked; but this is from the outline of the transparent robe having been effaced; and, like the Greeks, they represented the contour of the figure as if seen through the dress.

Slaves were taught dancing as well as music; and in the houses of the rich, besides their other occupations, that of dancing to entertain the family, or a party of friends, was required of them; and free Egyptians also gained a livelihood by their performances.

* Woodcut 152.

Some danced by pairs, holding each other's hands; others went through a succession of steps alone ;* and sometimes a man performed a *solo* to the sound of music, or the clapping of hands.†

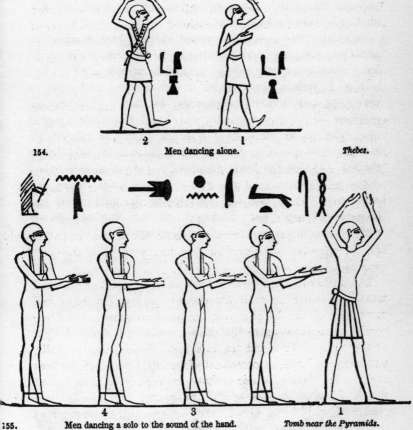

154.   Men dancing alone.   *Thebes.*

155.   Men dancing a solo to the sound of the hand.   *Tomb near the Pyramids.*

The dances of the lower orders generally had a tendency towards a species of pantomime ; and the rude peasantry were more delighted with ludicrous and extravagant dexterity, than with gestures which displayed elegance and grace.

Besides the pirouette and the steps above mentioned, a

* Woodcut 154.   † Woodcut 155.

favourite figure dance was universally adopted throughout the country, in which the two partners, who were usually men, advanced towards each other, or stood face to face upon one leg, and, having performed a series of movements, retired again in opposite directions, continuing to hold by one hand, and concluding by turning each other round.*

In another they struck the ground with the heel, standing on one foot, changing, perhaps, alternately from the right to the left; which is not very unlike a step of the present day.†

The Egyptians also danced at the temples in honour of the gods, and in some processions, as they approached the precincts of the sacred courts; and though this custom may at first sight appear inconsistent with the gravity of religion, we may recollect with what feelings David himself danced ‡ before the ark, and that the Jews considered it part of their religious duties to approach the Deity with the dance, § with tabret, and with harp. Their mode of worshipping the golden calf also consisted of songs and dancing; and this was immediately derived from the ceremonies of the Egyptians.

---

* Woodcut 153.   † Woodcut 154.   ‡ 1 Chron. xv. 29.   2 Sam. vi. 14.
§ Psalm cxlix. 3, " Let them praise his name in the dance." Exod. xv. 20.

D.   The palace-temple of Remeses the Great, generally called the Memnonium, at Thebes, during the inundation.

E.   The two Colossi of Thebes before the temple built by Amunoph III., with the ruins of
Luxor in the distance, during the inundation.

CHAPTER III.

AMUSEMENT OF THE GUESTS — VASES — ORNAMENTS OF THE HOUSE — PRE-
PARATION FOR DINNER — THE KITCHEN — MODE OF EATING — SPOONS —
WASHING BEFORE MEALS — FIGURE OF A DEAD MAN BROUGHT IN — GAMES
WITHIN, AND OUT OF, DOORS — WRESTLING — BOAT-FIGHTS — BULL-FIGHTS.

WHILE the party was amused with music and dancing, and the
late arrivals were successively announced, refreshments continued to be handed round, and every attention was shown to the
assembled guests. Wine was offered to each new comer, and
chaplets of flowers were brought by men servants to the gentlemen, and by women or white slaves to the ladies, as they took
their seats.* An upper servant, or slave, had the office of handing the wine, and a black woman sometimes followed, in an inferior
capacity, to receive an empty cup when the wine had been poured
into the goblet. The same black slave also carried the fruits
and other refreshments; and the peculiar mode of holding a
plate with the hand reversed, so generally adopted by women
from Africa, is characteristically shown in the Theban paintings.†

* Woodcut 157; *figs.* 4, 5, 8, 9, 12, 21.   † Woodcut 158.

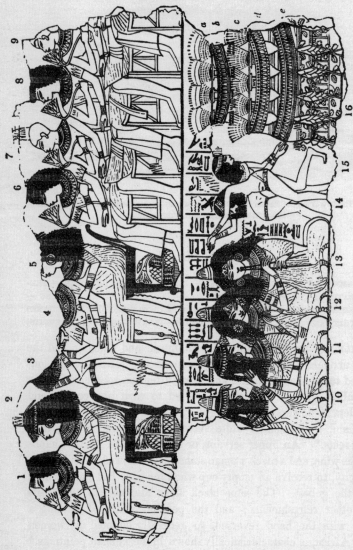

156.   A party of guests, entertained with music and the dance.

Figs. 1, 2, 4, 5, 6, 7, 8, 9. Men and Women seated together at the feast.
3. A servant offering a cup of wine.
10, 11, 12. Women singing and clapping their hands to the sound of the double pipe, 13.   14, 15. Dancing women.
16. Vases on stands, stopped with heads of wheat, and decked with garlands.

From Thebes, and now in the British Museum.

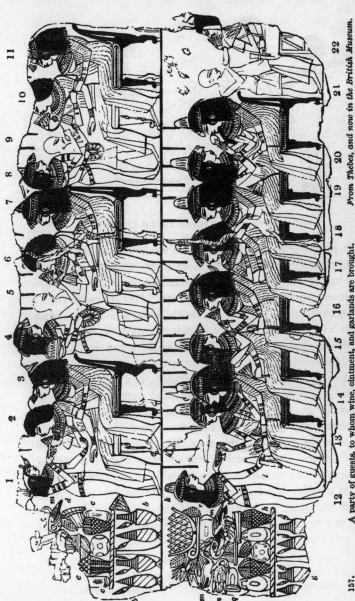

157.   A party of guests, to whom wine, ointment, and garlands are brought.

From Thebes, and now in the British Museum.

Fig. 1. A maid-servant presenting a cup of wine to a gentleman and lady, seated on chairs with cushions, probably of leather.
  4. Another holding a vase of ointment and a garland.
  5. presents a lotus flower; and 9, a necklace or garland, which he is going to tie round the neck of the guest, 10.
 12. A female attendant offering wine to a guest; in her left hand is a napkin, *l*, for wiping the mouth after drinking.
    The tables, *a*, *f*, have cakes of bread, *c r*; meat, *d*, *q*; geese, *n*; and other birds, *m*; figs, *e*, *k*; grapes in baskets, *h*; flowers *p*; and other things prepared for the feast: and beneath them are glass bottles of wine, *b*, *g*.

1   2   3

158.   A black and white slave waiting upon a lady at a party   *Thebes.*

To each person after drinking a napkin was presented for wiping the mouth,* answering to the *máhrama* of the modern Egyptians ; and the bearer of it uttered a complimentary sentiment, when she offered it and received back the goblet : as, " May it benefit you !" and no oriental at the present day drinks water without receiving a similar wish. But it was not considered rude to refuse wine when offered, even though it had been poured out ;† and a teetotaller might continue smelling a lotus without any affront. Men and women either sat together, or separately, in a different part of the room ; but no rigid mistrust prevented strangers, as well as members of the family, being received into the same society ; which shows how greatly the Egyptians were advanced in the habits of social life. In this they, like the Romans, differed widely from the Greeks, and might say with Cornelius Nepos, " Which of us is ashamed to bring his wife to an entertainment ? and what mistress of a family can be shown who does not inhabit the chief and most frequented part of the house ? Whereas in Greece she never appears at any entertainments, except those to which relations alone are invited, and constantly lives in the women's apartments at the upper part of the house, into which

* Woodcut 157 ; *figs.* 12, 21.   † Woodcut 157 ; *fig.* 13.

no man has admission, unless he be a near relation." Nor were married people afraid of sitting together, and no idea of their having had too much of each other's company made it necessary to divide them. In short, they were the most Darby and Joan people possible, and they shared the same chair at home, at a party, and even in their tomb, where sculpture grouped them together.

The master and mistress of the house accordingly sat side by side on a large fauteuil, and each guest as he arrived walked up to receive their welcome. The musicians and dancers hired for the occasion also did obeisance to them, before they began their part. To the leg of the fauteuil was tied a favourite monkey, a dog, a gazelle, or some other pet; and a young child was permitted to sit on the ground at the side of its mother, or on its father's knee.

In the mean time the conversation became animated, especially in those parts of the room where the ladies sat together, and the numerous subjects that occurred to them were fluently discussed. Among these the question of dress was not forgotten, and the patterns, or the value of trinkets, were examined with propor-

159.   Ladies at a party talking about their earrings.   *Thebes.*

tionate interest. The maker of an earring, and the shop where it was purchased, were anxiously inquired; each compared the work-

VOL. I.

manship, the style, and the materials of those she wore, coveted her neighbour's, or preferred her own ; and women of every class vied with each other in the display of " jewels of silver and jewels of gold," in the texture of their " raiment," the neatness of their sandals, and the arrangement or beauty of their plaited hair.

It was considered a pretty compliment to offer each other a flower from their own bouquet, and all the vivacity of the Egyptians was called forth as they sat together. The hosts omitted nothing that could make their party pass off pleasantly, and keep up agreeable conversation, which was with them the great charm of accomplished society, as with the Greeks, who thought it " more requisite and becoming to gratify the company by cheerful conversation, than with variety of dishes." The guests, too, neglected no opportunity of showing how much they enjoyed themselves ; and as they drew each other's attention to the many knick-knacks that adorned the rooms, paid a well-turned compliment to the taste of the owner of the house. They admired the vases, the carved boxes of wood or ivory, and the light tables on which many a curious trinket was displayed ; and commended the elegance and comfort of the luxurious fauteuils, the rich cushions and coverings of the couches and ottomans, the carpets and the other furniture. Some, who were invited to see the sleeping apartments, found in the ornaments on the toilet-tables, and in the general arrangements, fresh subjects for admiration ; and their return to the guest-chamber gave an opportunity of declaring that good taste prevailed throughout the whole house. On one occasion, while some of the delighted guests were in these raptures of admiration, and others were busied with the chitchat, perhaps the politics, or the scandal, of the day, an awkward youth, either from inadvertence, or a little too much wine, reclined against a wooden column placed in the centre of the room to support some temporary ornament, and threw it down upon those who sat beneath it.*

---

* I regret having lost the copy of this amusing subject. It was in a tomb at Thebes.

The confusion was great: the women screamed; and some, with uplifted hands, endeavoured to protect their heads and escape from its fall. No one, however, seems to have been hurt; and the harmony of the party being restored, the incident afforded fresh matter for conversation; to be related in full detail to their friends, when they returned home.

The vases were very numerous, and varied in shape, size, and materials; being of hard stone, alabaster, glass, ivory, bone, porcelain, bronze, brass, silver, or gold; and those of the poorer classes were of glazed pottery, or common earthenware. Many of their ornamental vases, as well as those in ordinary use, were of the most elegant shape, which would do honour to the Greeks, the Egyptians frequently displaying in these objects of private *luxe* the taste of a highly refined people; and so strong a resemblance did they bear to the productions of the best epochs of ancient Greece, both in their shape and in the fancy devices upon them, that some might even suppose them borrowed from Greek patterns. But they were purely Egyptian, and had been universally adopted in the valley of the Nile, long before the graceful forms we admire were known in Greece; a fact invariably acknowledged by those who are acquainted with the remote age of Egyptian monuments, and of the paintings that represent them.

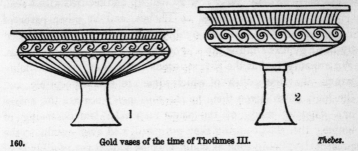

160.   Gold vases of the time of Thothmes III.   *Thebes.*

For some of the most elegant date in the early age of the third Thothmes, who lived between fourteen and fifteen hundred years before our era; and we not only admire their forms, but the richness of the materials of which they were made, their colour, as well as the hieroglyphics, showing them to have been of gold and silver, or of this last, inlaid with the more precious metal.

Those of bronze, alabaster, glass, porcelain, and even of ordinary pottery, were also deserving of admiration, from the beauty of their shapes, the designs which ornamented them, and the superior quality of the material; and gold and silver cups were often beautifully engraved, and studded with precious stones. Among these we readily distinguish the green emerald, the purple amethyst, and other gems; and when an animal's head adorned their handles, the eyes were frequently composed of them, except when enamel, or some coloured composition, was employed as a substitute.

That the Egyptians made great use of precious stones for their vases, and for women's necklaces, rings, bracelets, and other ornamental purposes, is evident from the paintings at Thebes,

and from the numerous articles of jewellery discovered in the tombs; and they appear sometimes to have been sent to Egypt in bags, similar to those containing the gold dust brought by the conquered nations tributary to the Egyptians, which were tied up and secured with a seal.

161. Bags, generally containing gold dust, tied up and sealed. *Thebes*.

Many bronze vases found at Thebes, and in other parts of Egypt, are of very excellent quality, and prove the skill possessed by the Egyptians in the art of working and compounding metals. We are surprised at the rich sonorous tones they emit on being struck, the fine polish of which some are still susceptible, and the high finish given them by the workmen: nor are the knives and daggers, made of the same materials, less deserving of notice; the elastic spring they possessed, and even retain to the present day, being such as could only be looked for in a blade of steel. The exact proportions of the copper and alloys, in all the different specimens preserved in the museums of Europe, have not yet been ascertained; but it would be curious to know

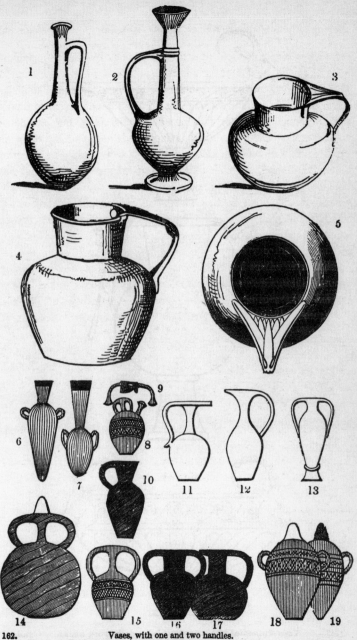

162. Vases, with one and two handles.
Figs. 1, 2. Earthenware vases found at Thebes. 3. Bronze vase. 4. Bronze vase.
5. The same seen from above, showing the top of the handle.
6 to 19. From the paintings of Thebes.

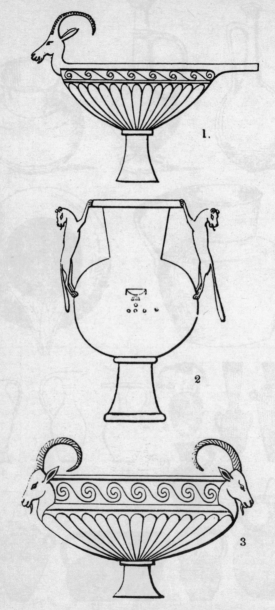

163.   Vases ornamented with one and two heads, or the whole animal.   *Thebes.*
Fig. 2 has the word "gold" upon it.

161.

1   Vases richly ornamented with animals' heads, and figures of captives.

2   *Thebes.*

their composition, particularly the interesting dagger of the Berlin collection, which is as remarkable for the elasticity of its blade, as for the neatness and perfection of its finish. Many contain 10 or 20 parts tin, to 90 and 80 copper.

Some vases had one, others two handles; some were ornamented with the heads of wild animals, as the ibex, oryx, or gazelle; others had a head on either side, a fox, a cat, or something similar; and many were ornamented with horses' heads, a whole quadruped, a goose's head, figures of captives, or fancy devices. They were occasionally grotesque, and monstrous; especially when introduced among the offerings brought by the conquered people of the north, which may be Asiatic rather than Egyptian; and one of them (fig. 1) appears to have for its cover the head of the Assyrian god represented in the Nimroud sculptures, supposed to be a vulture, a bird whose name, *nisr*, recalls that of "Nisroch, the god" of Nebuchadnezzar. They were either made of porcelain, or an enamel on gold, and were re-

165.

Fig. 1. Vase, with the head of a bird as a cover.
2. With head of a Typhonian monster.
3. A golden vase, without handles.   *Thebes.*

They are of the time of the 18th and 19th dynasties.

markable for the brilliancy of their colours. The head of a
Typhonian monster also served for the cover of some of these
vases, as it often did for the support of a mirror (contrasted
daily with the beauty of an Egyptian lady) ; but both this, and
the head of the bird, are of early time, being found on vases
brought as part of the tribute from Asia to the kings of the
18th and 19th dynasties. The Typhonian head bears some
analogy to that of Medusa. It is thought to be of the Syrian god
Baal; whose name was sometimes associated with that of Seth,
or Typhon, the Evil Being.

There was also a *rhyton*, or drinking-cup, in the form of a
cock's head, represented among the tribute of the people of Kûfa
brought to Thothmes III.

These very highly ornamented vases, with a confused mixture of
flower and scroll patterns, appear to have been mostly brought
from Asia; and it is remarkable that the Nineveh ornaments have
much the same kind of character. They are occasionally as
devoid of taste as the wine bottles and flower-pots of an English
cellar and conservatory; but many of those brought by the
people of Rotŭn have all the beauty of form found in those of
Greece.

Some had a single handle fixed to one side, and were in shape
not unlike our cream jugs,* ornamented with the heads of oxen,
or fancy devices; others were of bronze, bound with gold, having
handles of the same metal. Several vases had simple handles or
rings on either side; others were destitute of these, and of every
exterior ornament; some again were furnished with a single ring
attached to a neat bar,† or with a small knob, projecting from the
side ;‡ and many of those used in the service of the temple, highly
ornamented with figures of deities in relief,§ had a moveable
curved handle, on the principle of, though more elegant in form
than that of their common culinary utensils.‖ They were of
bronze, ornamented with figures, in relief, or engraved upon

* Woodcut 166, *figs.* 1, 2.   † Woodcut 167, *figs.* 1, 2.
‡ Woodcut 167, *figs.* 3, 4, 5.   § Woodcut 168, *fig.* 1.
‖ Woodcut 168 *fig.* 3.

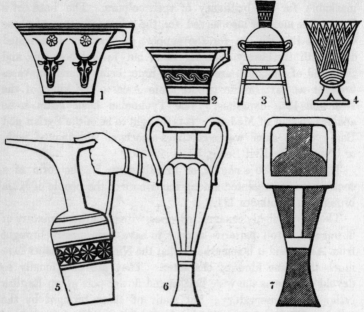

166.   *From the Paintings of Thebes.*
    Figs. 1 and 2. Vases of an early period.   3. Vase on a stand.
    4. Drinking-cup of porcelain.   7. Bronze vase, bound with gold.

them; and one of those found by Mr. Salt showed, by the
elastic spring of its cover, and the nicety with which this fitted
the mouth of the vase, the great skill of the Egyptian workmen.*

Another, of much larger dimensions, and of a different form,
brought by me from Thebes, and presented to the British
Museum, is also of bronze, with two large handles fastened on
with pins; and, though it resembles some of the caldrons represented by the paintings in an Egyptian kitchen, its lightness
seems to show that it was rather intended as a basin, or for a
similar purpose.†

Vases, surmounted with a human head forming the cover,

    * Woodcut 172.   † Woodcut 169.

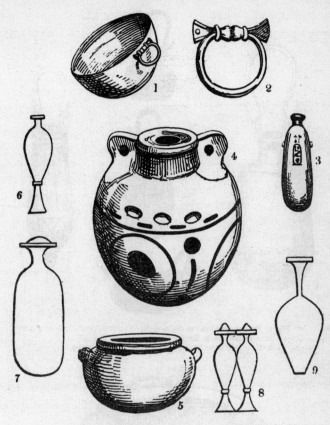

167. Fig. 1. Bronze vase brought by me from Thebes, now in the British Museum.
    2. Showing how the handle is fixed.
    3. Alabaster vase from Thebes, of the time of Neco.
    4. Vase at Berlin of cut glass.   5. Stone vase.
    6 to 9. From the sculptures of Thebes.

appear to have been frequently used for keeping gold and other precious objects, as in certain small side chambers of Medeenet Haboo, which were the treasury of King Remeses III. And if this Remeses was really the same as the wealthy Rhampsinitus of Herodotus, these chambers may have been the very treasury he mentions, where the thieves displayed so much dexterity.

Bottles, small vases, and pots used for holding ointment, or

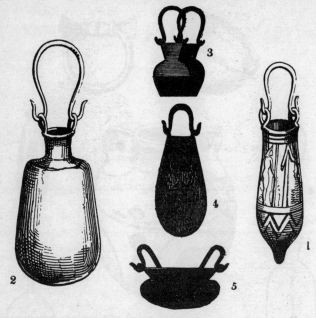

168.   Fig. 1. Bronze vase used in the temple.
            2. A larger one in the Berlin Museum.
            3, 4, 5. Culinary utensils in the sculptures at Thebes.

169.   Large bronze vase brought by me from Thebes.

other purposes connected with the toilet, were of alabaster, glass, porcelain, and hard stone, as granite, basalt, porphyry, serpentine, or breccia; some were of ivory, bone, and other materials, according to the choice or means of individuals; and the porous

170.

Fig. 1. Alabaster vase in my possession, from Thebes.
    2. Porcelain vase in Mr. Salt's Collection.

Fig. 1. Alabaster vase, containing sweet scented ointment, in the Museum of Alnwick Castle.
    2. Hieroglyphics on a vase, presenting the name of a queen, the sister of Thothmes III.
    3. The stopper.   4 and 9. Porcelain vases, from the paintings of Thebes.
    5. Porcelain cup, in my possession, from Thebes.
    6. Small ivory vase, in my possession, containing a dark-coloured ointment, from Thebes.
    7. Alabaster vase, with its lid (8), in the Museum of Alnwick Castle.

171.

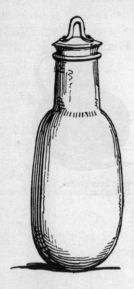

172. Bronze vase of Mr. Salt's Collection.   173. Glass bottle.   *Thebes.*

earthenware jars and water-bottles of Coptos, like the modern
ones of Ballas and Kéneh in the same neighbourhood, were
highly prized, even by foreigners.

Small boxes, made of wood or ivory, were also numerous ; and,
like the vases, of many different forms ; and some, which contained cosmetics of divers kinds, served to deck the dressing
table, or a lady's boudoir. They were carved in various ways,
and loaded with ornamental devices in relief; sometimes representing the favourite lotus flower, with its buds and stalks, a
goose, gazelle, fox, or other animal. Many were of considerable
length, terminating in a hollow shell, not unlike a spoon in
shape and depth, covered with a lid turning on a pin ; and to
this, which may properly be styled the box, the remaining part
was merely an accessory, intended for ornament, or serving as a
handle.

They were generally of sycamore wood, sometimes of tamarisk,* or of acacia ; and occasionally ivory, and inlaid work, were

* Woodcuts 174, 175.

substituted for wood. To many, a handle of less disproportionate
length was attached, representing the usual lotus flower, a figure,
a Typhonian monster, an animal, a bird, a fish, or a reptile ; and

174. Box with a long handle.   175. Box in the Berlin Museum,
     Mr. Salt's Collection.   showing the lid open.

the box itself, whether covered with a lid or open, was in character with the remaining part. Some shallow ones were probably intended to contain small portions of ointment, taken from
a large vase at the time it was wanted, or for other purposes

176.   Wooden boxes, or saucers without covers.   *Mr. Salt's Collection.*

connected with the toilet, where greater depth was not required;
and in many instances they rather resembled spoons than boxes.

Many were made in the form of a royal oval, with and without

177.   Other open boxes, whose form is taken from the oval of a king's name.
                    Alnwick Castle, and Leyden Museum.

a handle ;* and the body of a wooden fish was scooped out, and
closed with a cover imitating the scales, to deceive the eye by the

178. Box in the form of a fish, with turning lid. *Mr. Salt's Collection.*

appearance of a solid mass. Sometimes a goose was represented,
ready for table,† or swimming on the water,‡ and pluming itself ;
the head being the handle of a box formed of its hollow body ;

179 Box with and without its cover. *Museum of Alnwick Castle.*

180. Boxes in form of geese. *Mr. Salt's Collection and Leyden Museum.*

some consisted of an open part or cup, attached to a covered box ;§
others of different shapes offered the usual variety of fancy devices,
and some were without covers, which may come under the de-

* Woodcut 177. † Woodcut 179. ‡ Woodcut 180, *fig.* 2.
§ Woodcut 181.

nomination of saucers. Others bore the precise form and character of a box, being deeper and more capacious; and these
were probably used for holding trinkets, or occasionally as reposi-
tories for the small pots of ointment, or scented oils, and bottles
containing the collyrium, which women applied to their eyes.

181.   One part open, and one covered.   *Mr. Salt's Collection.*

182.   Box with the lid turning, as usual, on a pin.   *Mr. Salt's Collection.*

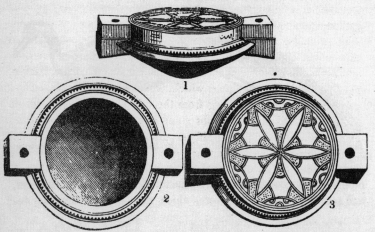

183.   A box with and without its lid.   *Mr. Salt's Collection.*

Some were divided into separate compartments, covered by a common lid, either sliding in a groove,* or turning on a pin at one end; and many of still larger dimensions sufficed to contain a mirror, combs, and perhaps even some articles of dress.

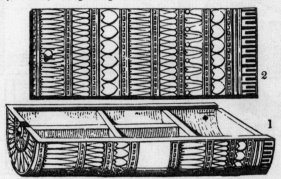

184.　　　Fig. 1. A box, with devices carved in relief, divided into cells.
　　　　　　2. The lid, which slides into a groove.　　*Mr. Salt's Collection.*

These boxes were frequently of costly materials, veneered with rare woods, or made of ebony, inlaid with ivory, painted with various devices, or stained to imitate materials of a valuable nature; and the mode of fastening the lid, and the curious substitute for a hinge given to some of them, show the former was entirely removed, and that the box remained open, while used. The principle of this will be better understood by reference to woodcut 185, where fig. 1 represents a side section of the box, and fig. 2 the inside of the lid. At the upper part of the back c, fig. 3, a small hole E is cut, which, when the box is closed, receives the nut D, projecting from the cross-bar B, on the inside of the lid; and the two knobs F and G, one on the lid, the other on the front of the box itself, serve not only for ornament but for fastening it, a band being wound round them, and secured with a seal.

Knobs of ebony, or other hard wood, were very common. They were turned with great care, and inlaid with ivory and silver; an instance of which is given in fig. 5.

* Woodcut 184.

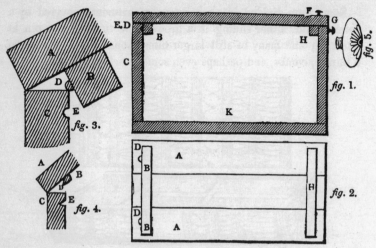

185.   Fig. 1. Section of the box. A, the lid. K, the bottom. C, D, the two sides.
         2. The inside of the lid. B, H, cross-bars nailed inside the lid. *Found at Thebes.*

Some boxes were made with a pointed summit, divided into
two parts, one of which alone opened, turning on small pivots at
the base, and the two ends of the box resembled in form the
gable ends, as the top, the shelving roof, of a house.*   The sides
were, as usual, secured by glue and nails, generally of wood,
and dovetailed, a method of joining adopted in Egypt at the
most remote period ; but the description of these belongs more
properly to cabinet work, as those employed for holding the
combs, and similar objects, to the toilet.

Some vases have been found in boxes, made of wicker-work,
closed with stoppers of wood, reed, or other materials, supposed
to belong either to a lady's toilet or to a medical man ; one of
which, now in the Berlin Museum, has been already noticed.†

Bottles of terra cotta are also met with, in very great abundance, of the most varied forms and dimensions, made for every
kind of purpose of which they were susceptible ; and I have
seen one which appears to have belonged to a painter, and

---

* See the boxes in Chap. vii. in the department of the Carpenters.
† Page 80, Woodcut 92.

to have been intended for holding water to moisten the colours;
the form and position of the handle suggesting that it was held
on the thumb of the left hand, while the person wrote or painted
with his right.

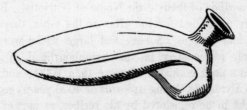

186.   Terra-cotta bottle, perhaps used by painters for holding water, and carried on the
thumb.   *Mr. Salt's Collection.*

Besides vases and bottles of stone, and of the materials above
mentioned, the Egyptians made them of leather or prepared
skin; and some of these were imported into Egypt from foreign
countries. As with the Greeks and Romans, skins were often
used for carrying wine; but leathern bottles are never seen at an
Egyptian party, either for drawing wine from the amphora, or
for handing it to table.

Bottles and narrow-mouthed vases, placed in the sitting-room,
and holding water, were frequently closed with some light substance, through which the warm air could pass, as it rose, during
the cooling process, being submitted to a current of air, to increase the evaporation: leaves were often employed for this
purpose, as at the present day, those of a fragrant kind being
probably selected; and the same prejudice against leaving a vase
uncovered evidently existed among the ancient, as among the
modern, inhabitants of Egypt.*

While the guests were entertained with music and the dance,
dinner was prepared; but as it consisted of a considerable number of dishes, and the meat was killed for the occasion, as at the
present day in Eastern and tropical climates, some time elapsed
before it was put upon table. An ox, kid, wild goat, gazelle, or
an oryx, and a quantity of geese, ducks, teal, quails, and other

* Woodcut 156, *figs. a, b, c, d, e.*

birds, were generally selected ; but mutton was excluded from
a Theban table.   Plutarch even states that " no Egyptians
would eat the flesh of sheep, except the Lycopolites," who did so
out of compliment to the wolves they venerated ; and Strabo confines the sacrifice of them to the Nome of Nitriotis.   But, though
sheep were not killed for the altar or the table, they abounded
in Egypt, and even at Thebes ; and large flocks were kept for
their wool, particularly in the neighbourhood of Memphis.
Sometimes a flock consisted of more than 2000 ; and in a tomb
below the Pyramids, dating upwards of 4000 years ago, 974 rams
are brought to be registered by his scribes, as part of the stock
of the deceased ; implying an equal number of ewes, independent
of lambs.*

Beef and goose constituted the principal part of the animal
food throughout Egypt ; and by a prudent foresight, in a country
possessing neither extensive pasture lands, nor great abundance of
cattle, the cow was held sacred, and consequently forbidden to be
eaten.   Thus the risk of exhausting the stock was prevented, and
a constant supply of oxen was kept up for the table and for
agricultural purposes.   A similar fear of diminishing the number
of sheep, so valuable for their wool, led to a preference for
such meats as beef and goose ; though they were much less light
and wholesome than mutton.   In Abyssinia it is a sin to eat
geese or ducks ; and modern experience teaches that in Egypt,
and similar climates, beef and goose are not eligible food, except
in the winter months.

A considerable quantity of meat was served up at those repasts,
to which strangers were invited, as among people of the East at
the present day; whose *azooma*, or feast, prides itself in the
quantity and variety of dishes, in the unsparing profusion of
viands, and, whenever wine is permitted, in the freedom of the
bowl.   An endless succession of vegetables was also required on
all occasions ; and, when dining in private, dishes composed chiefly
of them, were in greater request than joints, even at the tables of

* See the seventh woodcut in Chapter viii.

the rich ; and consequently the Israelites, who, by their long re-
sidence there, had acquired similar habits, regretted them equally
with the meat and fish * of Egypt.

Their mode of dining was very similar to that now adopted in
Cairo, and throughout the East ; each person sitting round a
table, and dipping his bread into a dish placed in the centre,
removed on a sign made by the host, and succeeded by others,
whose rotation depends on established rule, and whose number
is predetermined according to the size of the party, or the quality
of the guests.

Among the lower orders, vegetables constituted a very great
part of their ordinary food, and they gladly availed themselves
of the variety and abundance of esculent roots growing spontaneously, in the lands irrigated by the rising Nile, as soon as its
waters had subsided ; some of which were eaten in a crude state, and
others roasted in the ashes, boiled, or stewed : their chief aliment,
and that of their children, consisting of milk and cheese, roots,
leguminous, cucurbitaceous, and other plants, and the ordinary
fruits of the country.   Herodotus describes the food of the workmen, who built the Pyramids, to have been the " *raphanus*,
onions, and garlic ;" the first of which, now called *figl*, is like a
turnip-radish in flavour ; but he has omitted one more vegetable,
lentils, which were always, as at the present day, the chief article
of their diet ; and which Strabo very properly adds to the number.

The nummulite rock, in the vicinity of those monuments, frequently presents a conglomerate of testacea imbedded in it,
which, in some positions, resemble small seeds ; and Strabo
imagines they were the petrified residue of the lentils brought
there by the workmen, from their having been the ordinary food
of the labouring classes, and of all the lower orders of Egyptians.

Much attention was bestowed on the culture of this useful
pulse, and certain varieties became remarkable for their excellence,
the lentils of Pelusium being esteemed both in Egypt and in
foreign countries.

* Numbers xi. 4, 5.

In few countries were vegetables more numerous than in Egypt; as is proved by ancient writers, the sculptures, and the number of persons who sold them; and at the time of the Arab invasion, when Alexandria was taken by Amer, the lieutenant of the caliph Omer, no less than 4000 persons were engaged in selling vegetables in that city.

The lotus, the papyrus, and other similar productions of the land, during and after the inundation, were, for the poor, one of the greatest blessings nature ever provided for any people; and, like the acorn in northern climates, constituted perhaps the sole aliment of the peasantry, at the early period when Egypt was first colonised. The fertility of the soil, however, soon afforded a more valuable produce to the inhabitants; and long before they had made any great advances in civilisation, corn and leguminous plants were grown to a great extent throughout the country. The palm was another important gift bestowed upon them: it flourished spontaneously in the valley of the Nile, and, if it was unable to grow in the sands of the arid desert, yet wherever water sufficed for its nourishment, this useful tree produced an abundance of dates, a wholesome and nutritious fruit, which might be regarded as an universal benefit, being within the reach of all classes of people, and neither requiring expense in the cultivation, nor interfering with the time demanded for other agricultural occupations.

Among the vegetables above mentioned, is one which requires some observations. Juvenal says that they were forbidden to eat the onion, and it is reported to have been excluded from an Egyptian table. But even if, as Plutarch supposes, onions were prohibited to the priests, who "abstained from most kinds of pulse; they were not excluded from the altars of the gods, either in the tombs or temples; and a priest is frequently seen holding them in his hand, or covering an altar with a bundle of their leaves and roots. They were introduced at private as well as public festivals; and brought to table with gourds, cucumbers, and other vegetables; and the Israelites, when they left the country, regretted "the onions" as well as the cucumbers, the water-melons,* the leeks, the garlic, and the meat they " did eat" in Egypt.†

The onions of Egypt were mild, and of an excellent flavour. They were eaten crude as well as cooked, by persons both of the higher and the lower classes; but it is difficult to say if they introduced them to table like the cabbage, as a *hors-d'œuvre*, to stimulate the appetite, which Socrates recommends in the Banquet of Xenophon. On this occasion, some curious reasons for their use are brought forward, by different members of the party. Nicerates observes that onions relish well with wine, and cites Homer in support of his remark; Callias affirms that they inspire courage in the hour of battle; and Charmidas suggests their utility "in deceiving a jealous wife, who, finding her husband return with his breath smelling of onions, would be induced to believe he had not saluted any one while from home."

In slaughtering for the table, it was customary to take the ox, or whatever animal had been chosen for the occasion, into a court-yard near the house; to tie its four legs together, and then

1　　　　　　2　　　　　　3

187. A butcher killing and cutting up an ibex or wild goat: the other two sharpening their knives on a *steel*.　　　　　*Thebes.*

to throw it upon the ground; in which position it was held by one or more persons, while the butcher, sharpening his broad

---

* *Abtikhim, comp.* Arabic *batikh,* " water-melon."

† Exod. xvi. 3; Numb. xi. 5.

knife upon a *steel* attached to his apron, proceeded to cut the throat, as near as possible from one ear to the other; sometimes continuing the opening downwards.* The blood was frequently received into a vase or basin for the purposes of cookery,† which was repeatedly forbidden to the Israelites by the Mosaic law;‡ and the reason of the explicit manner of the prohibition is readily explained, from the necessity of preventing their adopting a custom they had so recently witnessed in Egypt. Nor is it less strictly denounced by the Mohammedan religion; and all Moslems look upon this ancient Egyptian, and modern European, custom with unqualified horror and disgust. But black-puddings were popular in Egypt.

The head was then taken off, and they proceeded to skin the animal, beginning with the leg and neck. The first joint removed was the right foreleg or shoulder; the other parts following in succession, according to custom or convenience; and the same rotation was observed, in cutting up the victims offered in sacrifice to the gods. Servants carried the joints to the kitchen on wooden trays, and the cook having selected the parts suited for boiling, roasting, and other modes of dressing, prepared them for the fire by washing, and any other preliminary process he thought necessary. In large kitchens, the *chef*, or head cook, had several persons under him; who were required to make ready and boil the water of the caldron, to put the joints on spits or skewers, to cut up or mince the meat, to prepare the vegetables, and to fulfil various other duties assigned to them.

The very peculiar mode of cutting up the meat frequently prevents our ascertaining the exact part they intend to represent in the sculptures; the chief joints, however, appear to be the head, shoulder, and leg, with the ribs, tail, or rump, the heart, and kidneys; and they occur in the same manner on the altars of the temple, and the tables of a private house. One is remarkable,

---

* The Israelites sometimes cut off the head at once. Deut. xxi. v. 4, 6.
† Woodcut 191, *fig.* 2.
‡ Deut. xv. 23. "Only thou shalt not eat the blood thereof: thou shalt pour it upon the ground as water." And c. xii. 16, 23; "be sure that thou eat not the blood, for the blood is the life." Gen. ix. 4, and Levit. xvii. 10, 11, 14, &c.

not only from being totally unlike any of our European joints,
but from its exact resemblance to that commonly seen at table in
modern Egypt: it is part of the leg, consisting of the flesh
covering the bone, whose two extremities project slightly beyond
it; and the accompanying drawing from the sculptures, and a
sketch of the same joint from a modern table in Upper Egypt,
show how the mode of cutting it has been preserved by traditional custom to the present day.

188.   Peculiar joint of meat at an ancient and modern Egyptian table.

The head was left with the skin and horns; and was sometimes
given away to a poor person, as a reward for holding the walking
sticks of those guests who came on foot; but it was frequently

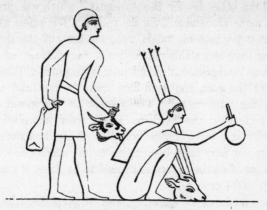

189.   One head given to a poor man.   *Thebes.*

taken to the kitchen with the other joints; and, notwithstanding
the positive assertion of Herodotus, we find that even in the
temples themselves it was admitted at a sacrifice, and placed with
other offerings on the altars of the gods.

The historian would lead us to suppose that a strict religious
scruple prevented the Egyptians of all classes from eating this
part, as he affirms, " that no Egyptian will taste the head of any
species of animal," in consequence of certain imprecations
having been uttered upon it at the time it was sacrificed; but as
he is speaking of heifers slaughtered for the service of the gods,
we may conclude that the prohibition did not extend to those
killed for table, nor even to all those offered for sacrifice in the
temple; and as with the scapegoat of the Jews, that important
ceremony was perhaps confined to certain occasions, and to
chosen animals, without extending to every victim which was
slain.

The formula of the imprecation was probably very similar with
the Jews and Egyptians. Herodotus says the latter pray the
gods " that if any misfortune was about to happen to those who
offered, or to the other inhabitants of Egypt, it might fall upon
that head :" and with the former it was customary for the priest
to take two goats and cast lots upon them, " one lot for the
Lord, and the other lot for the scapegoat," which was presented
alive " to make atonement " for the people. The priest was then
required to " lay both his hands upon the head of the live goat,
and confess over him all the iniquities of the children of Israel,
and all their transgressions in all their sins, putting them upon
the head of the goat, and send him away by the hand of a fit
man into the wilderness." The remark of Herodotus should
then be confined to the head, on which their imprecation was
pronounced; and being looked upon by every Egyptian as an
abomination, it may have been taken to the market and sold to
foreigners, or if no foreigners happened to be there, it may have
been given to the crocodiles.

The same mode of slaughtering, and of preparing the joints,
extended to all the large animals; but geese, and other wild and

tame fowl, were served up entire, or, at least, only deprived
of their feet and pinion joints.
Fish were also brought to table
whole, whether boiled or fried,
the tails and fins being removed.
For the service of religion, they
were generally prepared in the
same manner as for private feasts;
sometimes, however, an ox was
brought entire to the altar, and
birds were often placed among

190.   An ox and a bird placed entire on
the altar.

the offerings, without even having the feathers taken off.

In Lower Egypt, or, as Herodotus styles it, " the corn country,"
they were in the habit of drying and salting birds of various
kinds, as quails, ducks, and others ;* and fish were prepared by
them in the same manner both in Upper and Lower Egypt.†

Some joints were boiled, others roasted : two modes of dressing
their food to which Herodotus appears to confine the Egyptians,
at least in the lower country ; but the various modes of artificial
cookery which Menes introduced, and which offended the simple
habits of King Tnephachthus, had long since taught them to make
" savoury meats," such as prevented Isaac's distinguishing the
flesh of kids from venison.

For though the early Greeks were contented with roast meats,
and, as Athenæus observes, the heroes of Homer seldom " boil
their meat, or dress it with sauces," the Egyptians were far more
advanced in the habits of civilisation in those remote times.

The Egyptians never committed the same excesses as the
Romans under the Empire ; but they gave way to habits of in-
temperance and luxury after the Persian conquest, and the
accession of the Ptolemies ; so that writers who mention them
at that period, describe the Egyptians as a profligate and luxurious
people, addicted to an immoderate love of the table, and to every

* See Fowlers, in chap. viii.   † See Fishermen, chap. viii.

excess in drinking. They even used excitants for this purpose,
and *hors d'œuvres* were provided to stimulate the appetite ; crude
cabbage, provoking the desire for wine, and promoting the con-
tinuation of excess.

As is the custom in Egypt, and other hot climates, at the present day, they cooked the meat as soon as killed ; with the same
view of having it tender, which makes northern people keep it
until decomposition is beginning ; and this explains the order of
Joseph to "slay and make ready" for his brethren to dine with
him the same day at noon. As soon, therefore, as this had been done,
and the joints were all ready, the kitchen presented an animated
scene, and the cooks were busy in their different departments.
One regulated the heat of the fire, raising it with a poker, or
blowing it with bellows, worked by the feet ;* another superintended the cooking of the meat, skimming the water with
a spoon, or stirring it with a large fork ;† while a third pounded
salt, pepper, or other ingredients, in a large mortar, which were
added from time to time during this process.   Liquids of various
kinds also stood ready for use, which were sometimes drawn off
by means of siphons ;‡ and those things they wished to raise
beyond the reach of rats, or other intruders, were placed upon
trays, and pulled up by ropes running through rings in the ceiling,
answering the purposes of a safe.§

Other servants took charge of the pastry, which the bakers or
confectioners had made for the dinner table ; and this department, which may be considered as attached to the kitchen, appears even more varied than that of the cook.   Some sifted and
mixed the flour,‖ others kneaded the paste with their hands,¶ and
formed it into rolls, which were then prepared for baking, and,
being placed on a long tray or board, were carried on a man's

---

* *See* chap. ix.   † Woodcut 191, *figs.* 4 and 5.
  ‡ This part of the picture is very much damaged, but sufficient remains to
show them using the siphons ; which occur again, perfectly preserved, in a tomb
at Thebes. *See* chap. ix.
  § At *h* and *f* in woodcut 191.
  ‖ Woodcut 191*a*, *figs.* 13 and 14.   ¶ *Fig.* 15.

An Egyptian kitchen, from the tomb of Remeses III., at Thebes.

Fig. 1. Killing and preparing the joints, which are placed at a, b, c.
2. Catching the blood for the purposes of cookery, which is removed in a bowl by fig. 3.
4 and 5. Employed in boiling meat, and stirring the fire.
7. Preparing the meat for the caldron, which fig. 6 is taking to the fire
8. Pounding some ingredients for the cook.
f, h. Apparently siphons.
i, j. Ropes passing through rings, and supporting different things, as a sort of safe.
s. Probably plates.
u, v. Tables.

191.

191 *a*. Kneading the dough with their feet.

Fig. 1, 2. Kneading the dough with their feet.   3, 4. Carrying it to the confectioner (5), who rolls out the paste, which is afterwards made into cakes of various
forms, *d, e, f, g, h*.   6, 7. Making a sort of maccaroni (*l, m, η*), on a pan over the fire, *m*.   9. Cooking lentils, which are in the baskets, *p, p*.
8. Preparing the oven.   11, 12. Making cakes of bread sprinkled with seeds.   15, 16. Kneading paste with the hands.

Cooks and Confectioners.   In the Tomb of Remeses III. at Thebes.

At *h*, the dough is probably left to ferment in a basket, as is now done at Cairo.

head * to the oven.† Certain seeds were previously sprinkled upon the upper surface of each roll,‡ and, judging from those still used in Egypt for the same purpose, they were chiefly the *nigella sativa*, or *kamóon aswed*, the *simsim*,§ and the caraway. Pliny also mentions this custom, and says that seeds of cummin were put upon cakes of bread in Egypt, and that condiments were mixed with them.

Sometimes they kneaded the paste with their feet,‖ having placed it in a large wooden bowl upon the ground; it was then in a more liquid state than when mixed by the hand, and was carried in vases to the pastrycook, who formed it into a sort of maccaroni, upon a shallow metal pan over the fire. Two persons were engaged in this process; one stirring it with a wooden spatula, and the other taking it off when cooked, with two pointed sticks,¶ who arranged it in a proper place, where the rest of the pastry was kept. This last was of various kinds, apparently made up with fruit, or other ingredients, with which the dough, spread out with the hand, was sometimes mixed; and it assumed the shape of a three-cornered cake, a recumbent ox, a leaf, a crocodile's head, a heart, or other form,** according to the fancy of the confectioner. That his department was connected with the kitchen†† is again shown, by the presence of a man in the corner of the picture, engaged in cooking lentils for a soup or porridge; ‡‡ his companion §§ brings a bundle of faggots for the fire, and the lentils themselves are seen standing near him in wicker baskets.‖‖

---

* As at the present day. *Comp.* Pharaoh's chief baker, with "three white baskets on his *head.*" Gen. xl. 16, and Herod. ii. 35. "Men carry loads on their *heads,* women on their shoulders." But it was not the general custom.

† Woodcut 191a, *figs.* 19 and *x.*

‡ *Figs.* 11 and *z.* Called *oĭk* by the Egyptians.　　§ Sesamum Orientale, Linn.

‖ Herod. ii. 36, and *figs.* 1 and 2.　　　　　　　¶ *Figs.* 6 and 7, and *l.*

** *Figs. d, f, g, h, i, k. f* and *g* appear to have the fruit apart from the pastry. Cakes of the form of *f* have been found in a tomb at Thebes, but without any fruit or other addition.

†† The chief baker (שר האפים) of Pharaoh carried in the uppermost basket "all manner of bake-meats," not only "bread," but "all kind of food." כל מאכל Gen. xl. 17. Anciently, the cook and baker were the same with the Romans.

‡‡ *Fig.* 9.　　　　　　§§ *Fig.* 10.　　　　　　‖‖ At *p.*

The large caldrons containing the meat for boiling, having
been taken from the dresser,* where they were placed for the
convenience of putting in the joints, stood over a wood fire upon
the hearth, supported on stones, or on a metal frame or tripod.†
Some of smaller dimensions, probably containing the stewed
meat, stood over a pan ‡ containing charcoal, precisely similar

192.   Cooking geese and different joints of meat.   *Tomb near the Pyramids.*
Figs. *a a.* Joints in caldrons, on the dresser *b.*   *c.* A table.
1. Preparing a goose for the cook (2), who puts them into the boiler *d.*
3. Roasting a goose over a fire (*e*) of peculiar construction.
4. Cutting up the meat.   *l.* Joints on a table.
g. Stewed meat over a pan of fire, or *magoor.*

to the *magoor,* used in modern Egypt ;§ and geese, or joints of
meat, were roasted over a fire of a peculiar construction, intended
solely for this purpose ;‖ the cook passing over them a fan,¶
which served for bellows. In heating water, or boiling meat,
faggots of wood were principally employed; but for the roast
meat charcoal, as in the modern kitchens of Cairo; and the
sculptures represent servants bringing this last in mats, of the same
form as those of the present day. They sometimes used round

* At *b.*   † Woodcut 192, at *d.*   ‡ At *c.*   § At *g,*
                ‖ At *e.*   ¶ At *f.*

balls for cooking, probably a composition of charcoal, and other ingredients, which a servant is represented taking out of a basket, and putting on the stove, while another blows the fire with a fan.

That dinner was served up at midday, may be inferred from the invitation given by Joseph to his brethren; but it is probable that, like the Romans, they also ate supper in the evening, as is still the custom in the East. The table was much the same as that of the present day in Egypt: a small stool, supporting a round tray, on which the dishes are placed; but it differed from this in having its circular summit fixed on a pillar, or leg, which was often in the form of a man, generally a captive, who supported the slab upon his head; the whole being of stone, or some hard wood. On this the dishes were placed, together with loaves of bread, some of which were not unlike those of the present day in Egypt, flat and round as our crumpets. Others had the form of rolls or cakes, sprinkled with seeds.

It was not generally covered with any linen, but, like the Greek table, was washed with a sponge, or napkin, after the dishes were removed, and polished by the servants, when the company had retired; though an instance sometimes occurs of a napkin spread on it, at least on those which bore offerings in honour of the dead. One or two guests generally sat at a table, though from the mention of persons seated in rows according to rank, it has been supposed the tables were occasionally of a long shape, as may have been the case when the brethren of Joseph " sat before him, the first born according to his birth-right, and the youngest according to his youth," Joseph eating alone at another table where " they set on for him by himself." But even if round, they might still sit according to rank; one place being always the post of honour, even at the present day, at the round table of Egypt.

In the houses of the rich, bread was made of wheat; the poorer classes being contented with cakes of barley, or of *doora* (holcus sorghum), which last is still so commonly used by them; for Herodotus is as wrong in saying that they thought it " the greatest disgrace to live on wheat and barley," as that " no one drank out of any but bronze (or brazen) cups." The drinking cups of the Egyptians not only varied in their materials, but also in their forms. Some were plain and unornamented; others, though of small dimensions, were made after the models of larger vases; many were like our own cups without handles; and others may come under the denomination of beakers, and saucers. Of these the former were frequently made of alabaster, with a round base, so that they could not stand when filled, and were held in the hand, or, when empty, were turned downwards upon their rim : and the saucers, which were of glazed pottery, had sometimes lotus blossoms, or fish, represented on their concave surface.

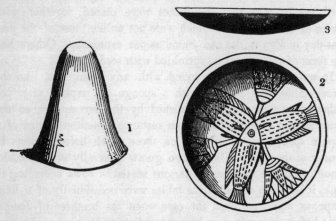

193.   Drinking cups.
Fig. 1. An alabaster beaker, in the Museum of Alnwick Castle.
2. A saucer or cup of blue glazed pottery, in the Berlin Collection.
3. Side view of the same.

The tables, as at a Roman repast, were occasionally brought in, and removed, with the dishes on them; sometimes each joint was served up separately, and the fruit, deposited in a plate or trencher, succeeded the meat at the close of dinner; but in less fashionable circles, particularly of the olden time, fruit was brought in baskets, which stood beside the table. The dishes consisted of fish; meat boiled, roasted, and dressed in various ways; game,

poultry, and a profusion of vegetables and fruit, particularly figs
and grapes, during the season; and a soup, or " pottage of

194.   The table brought in with the dishes upon it.   *Tomb near the Pyramids.*

lentils," as with the modern Egyptians, was not an unusual dish.
Of figs and grapes they were particularly fond, which is shown
by their constant introduction, even among the choice offerings
presented to the gods; and figs of the sycamore must have been
highly esteemed, since they were
selected as the heavenly fruit, given
by the goddess Netpe to those who
were judged worthy of admission to
the regions of eternal happiness.
Fresh dates during the season, and
in a dried state at other periods of
the year, were also brought to table,
as well as a preserve of the fruit,
made into a cake of the same form
as the tamarinds now brought from
the interior of Africa, and sold in
the Cairo market.

195.   A cake of preserved dates, found
by me at Thebes. At *a* is a date stone.

The guests sat on the ground, or on stools and chairs, and, having neither knives and forks, nor any substitute for them answering to the chopsticks of the Chinese, they ate with their fingers,
like the modern Asiatics, and invariably with the right hand;

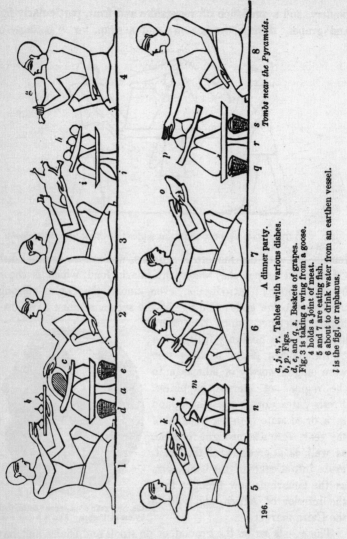

A dinner party.

a, j, n, r. Tables with various dishes.
b, p. Figs.
d, e, and *g, s.* Baskets of grapes.
Fig. 3 is taking a wing from a goose.
4 holds a joint of meat.
5 and 7 are eating fish.
6 about to drink water from an earthen vessel.
l is the figl, or raphanus.

Tombs near the Pyramids.

196.

nor did the Jews * and Etruscans, though they had forks for other purposes, use any at table.

* 1 Sam. ii. 14.

Spoons were introduced when required for soup, or other liquids; and, perhaps, even a knife was employed on some occasions, to facilitate the carving of a large joint, which is sometimes done in the East at the present day.

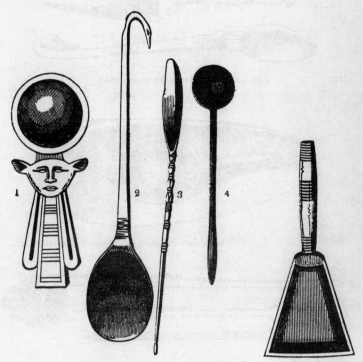

197. Fig. 1. Ivory spoon, about 4 inches long, in the Berlin   198.   Of wood, in Mr.
                Museum, found with the vases of wood-cut 181.   Salt's Collection.
        2. Bronze spoon, in my possession, 8 inches in length.
        3, 4. Bronze spoons, found by Mr. Burton, at Thebes.

The Egyptian spoons were of various forms and sizes. They were principally of ivory, bone, wood, or bronze, and other metals; and in some the handle terminated in a hook, by which, if required, they were suspended to a nail.* Many were ornamented with the lotus flower; the handles of others were made to repre-

* Woodcut 197, *fig.* 2.

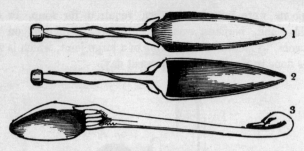

199.   Figs. 1, 2. Front and back of a wooden spoon.
              3. Ivory spoon.   *Mr. Salt's Collection.*

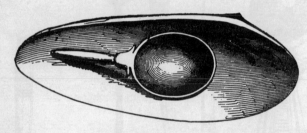

200.   Alabaster shell and spoon.   *Museum of Alnwick Castle.*

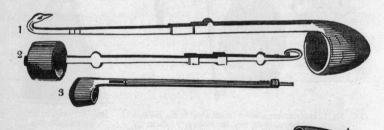

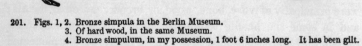

201.   Figs. 1, 2. Bronze simpula in the Berlin Museum.
          3. Of hard wood, in the same Museum.
          4. Bronze simpulum, in my possession, 1 foot 6 inches long.   It has been gilt.

sent an animal, or a human figure; some were of very arbitrary
shape; and a smaller kind, of round form, probably intended for

taking ointment out of a vase, and transferring it to a shell or cup for immediate use, are occasionally discovered in the tombs of Thebes. One in the Museum of Alnwick Castle is a perfect specimen of these spoons, and is rendered more interesting from having been found with the shell, its companion at the toilet-table.*

Simpula, or ladles, were also common, and many have been found at Thebes. They were of bronze, frequently gilt, and the curved summit of the handle, terminating in a goose's head, a favourite Egyptian ornament, served to suspend them at the side of a vessel, after having been used for taking a liquid from it; and, judging from a painting on a vase in the Naples Museum, where a priest is represented pouring a libation from a vase with the simpulum, we may conclude this to have been the principal purpose to which they were applied. The length of some was eighteen inches, and the lower part or ladle nearly three inches deep, and two and a half inches in diameter; but many were much smaller.

Some simpula were made with a joint, or hinge, in the centre of the handle, so that the upper half either folded over the other, or slided down behind it; the extremity of each being furnished with a bar which held them together, at the same time that it allowed the upper one to pass freely up and down (*figs*. 1, 2). Two of these are preserved in the Berlin Museum. There is also a ladle of hard wood, found with a case of bottles. It is very small; the lower part, which may properly be called the handle, being barely more than five inches long, of very delicate workmanship; and the sliding rod, which fits into a groove in the centre of the handle, is about the thickness of a needle (*fig*. 3).

Small strainers, or cullenders, of bronze have also been found at Thebes, about five inches in diameter; and several other utensils.

The Egyptians washed after, as well as before, dinner; an invariable custom throughout the East, as among the Greeks,

* Woodcut 200.

Romans, Hebrews,* and others; and Herodotus speaks of a golden basin, belonging to Amasis, which was used by the King, and "the guests who were in the habit of eating at his table."

An absorbent seems also to have been adopted for scouring the hands; and a powder of ground lupins, the *doqáq* of modern Egypt, is no doubt an old invention, handed down to the present inhabitants.

Soap was not unknown to the ancients, and a small quantity has been found at Pompeii. Pliny, who mentions it as an invention of the Gauls, says it was made of fat and ashes; and Aretæus, the physician of Cappadocia, tells us, that the Greeks borrowed their knowledge of its medicinal properties from the Romans. But there is no evidence of soap having been used by the Egyptians; and if by accident they discovered something of the kind, while engaged with mixtures of natron or potash, and other ingredients, it is probable that it was only an absorbent, without oil or grease, and on a par with steatite, or the argillaceous earths, with which, no doubt, they were long acquainted.

The Egyptians, a scrupulously religious people, were never remiss in expressing their gratitude for the blessings they enjoyed, and in returning thanks to the gods for that peculiar protection they were thought to extend to them and to their country, above all the nations of the earth. They therefore never sat down to meals without saying grace; and Josephus says that when the seventy-two elders were invited by Ptolemy Philadelphus to sup at the palace, Nicanor requested Eleazer to say grace for his countrymen, instead of those Egyptians, to whom that duty was committed on other occasions.

It was also a custom of the Egyptians, during or after their repasts, to introduce a wooden image of Osiris, from one foot and a half to three feet in height, in the form of a human mummy, standing erect, or lying on a bier, and to show it to each of the guests, warning him of his mortality, and the transitory nature of human pleasures. He was reminded that some day he would

* The Pharisees "marvelled that he had not first washed before dinner." Luke xi. 38.

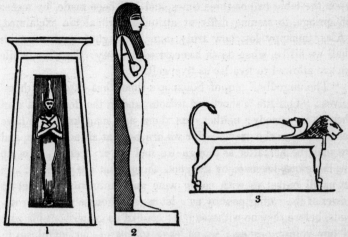

202.   Figure of a mummy in the form of Osiris, brought to an Egyptian table,
and shown to the guests.

be like that figure; that men ought "to love one another, and
avoid those evils which tend to make them consider life too long,
when in reality it is too short;" and while enjoying the blessings
of this world, to bear in mind that their existence was precarious,
and that death, which all ought to be prepared to meet, must
eventually close their earthly career.   Thus, while the guests
were permitted, and even encouraged, to indulge in conviviality,
the pleasures of the table, and the mirth so congenial to their
lively disposition, they were exhorted to put a certain degree of
restraint upon their conduct; and though this sentiment was
perverted by other people, and used as an incentive to present
excesses, it was perfectly consistent with the ideas of the Egyptians to be reminded that this life was only a lodging, or "inn"
on their way, and that their existence here was the preparation
for a future state.

Widely different was the exhortation of Trimalchio, thus given
by Petronius: "To us, who were drinking, and admiring the splendour of the entertainment, a silver model of a man was brought
by a servant, so contrived that its joints and moveable vertebræ
could be bent in any direction.   After it had been produced

upon the table two or three times, and had been made, by means of springs, to assume different attitudes, Trimalchio exclaimed, 'Alas, unhappy lot, how truly man is nought! similar to this shall we all be, when death has carried us away : therefore, while we are allowed to live let us live well.' "

" The ungodly," too, of Solomon's time, thus expressed themselves : " Our life is short and tedious, and in the death of a man there is no remedy ; neither was there any man known to have returned from the grave.   For we are born at all adventure, and we shall be hereafter as though we had never been, ... come on, therefore, let us enjoy the good things that are present, ... let us fill ourselves with costly wine and ointments ; and let no flower of the spring pass by us ; let us crown ourselves with rose-buds, before they be withered ; let none of us go without his part of our voluptuousness ; let us leave tokens of our joyfulness in every place." *

But even if the Egyptians, like other men, neglected a good warning, the original object of it was praiseworthy ; and Plutarch expressly states that it was intended to convey a moral lesson. The idea of death had nothing revolting to them ; and so little did the Egyptians object to have it brought before them, that they even introduced the mummy of a deceased relative at their parties, and placed it at table, as one of the guests ; a fact which is recorded by Lucian, in his " Essay on Grief," and of which he declares himself to have been an eyewitness.

After dinner, music and singing were resumed ; hired men and women displayed feats of agility ; swinging each other round by the hand ; throwing up and catching the ball ; or flinging themselves round backwards head-over-heels, in imitation of a wheel ; which was usually a performance of women.   They also stood on each other's backs, and made a somerset from that position ; and a necklace, or other reward, was given to the most successful tumbler.

The most usual games within doors were odd and even, *mora*,

---

* Book of Wisdom, ii. 1, et seq. *Comp.* Is. xxii. 13, and lvi. 12. Eccles. ii. 24. Luke xii. 19, and 1 Cor. xv. 32.

203.   Tumblers. *Fig.* 1, one of four holding the rewards.   *Beni Hassan.*

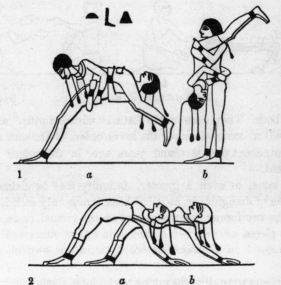

204.   Women tumbling, and performing feats of agility.   *Beni Hassan.*

and draughts; for the first of which (called by the Romans "ludere par et impar") they used bones, nuts, beans, almonds, or shells; and any indefinite number was held between the two hands.

The game of mora was common in ancient as well as modern Italy, and was played by two persons, who each simultaneously threw out the fingers of one hand, while one party guessed the

205.

Fig. 1. Playing at *mora*.
2. At odd and even.

Thebes.

206.   Games of draughts and *mora*.   *Beni Hassan.*

sum of both. They were said in Latin, "micare digitis," and this
game, still so common among the lower orders of Italians, existed
in Egypt, about four thousand years ago, in the reigns of the
Osirtasens.

The same, or even a greater, antiquity may be claimed for
the game of draughts, or, as it has been erroneously called, chess.
As in the two former, the players sat on the ground, or on chairs,
and the pieces, or men, being ranged in line at either end of the
tables, moved on a chequered board, as in our own chess and
draughts.

The pieces were all of the same size and form, though they varied
on different boards, some being small, others large with round
summits: some were surmounted by human heads; and many
were of a lighter and neater shape, like small nine-pins, probably
the most fashionable kind, since they were used in the palace of
king Remeses. These last seem to have been about one inch
and a half high, standing on a circular base of half an inch
in diameter; but some are only one inch and a quarter in

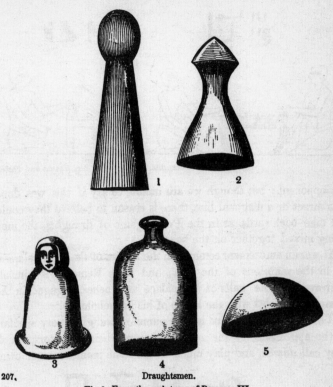

207.

Draughtsmen.

Fig. 1. From the sculptures of Remeses III.
2. Of wood, and 4, 5, of ivory, in my possession.
3. Of glazed pottery, from Thebes.

height, and little more than half an inch broad at the lower end. Others have been found, of ivory, one inch and six-eighths high, and one and an eighth in diameter, with a small knob at the top, exactly like those represented at Beni Hassan, and the tombs near the Pyramids (*fig.* 4).

They were about equal in size upon the same board, one set black, the other white or red; or one with round, the other with flat heads, standing on opposite sides;* and each player, raising it with the finger and thumb, advanced his piece towards those of

* Woodcuts 206, *fig.* 1, and 208, *fig.* 1.

208.   Game of draughts.   *Beni Hassan and Thebes.*

his opponent; but though we are unable to say if this was done
in a direct or a diagonal line, there is reason to believe they could
not take backwards as in the Polish game of draughts, the men
being mixed together on the board.*

It was an amusement common in the houses of the lower classes,
as in the mansions of the rich; and king Remeses is himself
portrayed on the walls of his palace at Thebes, engaged in the
game of draughts with the ladies of his household.

The modern Egyptians have a game of draughts, very similar,
in the appearance of the men, to that of their ancestors, which
they call *dámeh*, and play much in the same manner as our own.

209.   A game perhaps similar to the Greek *kollabismos*.   *Beni Hassan.*

* As in woodcut 208, *fig.* 1.

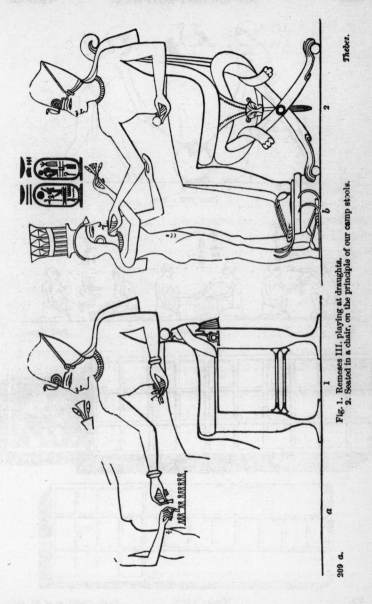

Fig. 1. Remeses III. playing at draughts.
2. Seated in a chair, on the principle of our camp stools.

Thebes.

209 a.

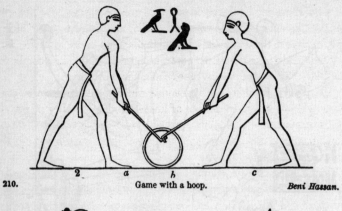

210.   Game with a hoop.   *Beni Hassan.*

211.   Other games.   *Beni Hassan.*

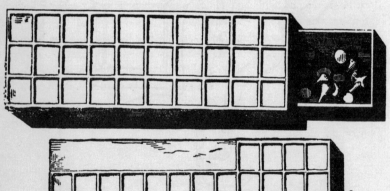

212.   Wooden boards.   *In the Collection of Dr. Abbott.*

Analogous to the game of odd and even was one, in which two of the players held a number of shells, or dice, in their closed hands, over a third person who knelt between them, with his face towards the ground, and who was obliged to guess the combined number ere he could be released from this position.

Another game consisted in endeavouring to snatch from each other a small hoop, by means of hooked rods, probably of metal; and the success of a player seems to have depended on extricating his own from an adversary's rod, and then snatching up the hoop, before he had time to stop it.

There were also two games, of which the boards, with the men, are in the possession of Dr. Abbott. One is eleven inches long by three and a half, and has ten spaces or squares in three rows; the other twelve squares at the upper end (or four squares in three rows) and a long line of eight squares below, forming an approach to the upper part, like the arrangement of German tactics. The men in the drawer of the board are of two shapes, one set ten, the other nine in number.

Other games are represented in the paintings, but not in a manner to render them intelligible; and many, which were doubtless common in Egypt, are omitted both in the tombs, and in the writings of ancient authors.

The dice discovered at Thebes, and other places, may not be of a Pharaonic period, but, from the simplicity of their form, we may suppose them similar to those of the earliest age, in which too the conventional number of six sides had probably always been adopted. They were marked with small circles, representing units, generally with a dot in the centre; and were of bone or ivory, varying slightly in size.

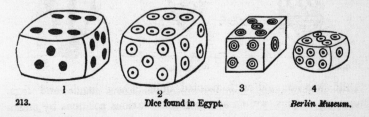

1   2   3   4

213.   Dice found in Egypt.   *Berlin Museum.*

Plutarch shows that dice were a very early invention in Egypt, and acknowledged to be so by the Egyptians themselves, since they were introduced into one of their oldest mythological fables; Mercury being represented playing at dice with the Moon, previous to the birth of Osiris, and winning from her the five days of the epact, which were added to complete the 365 days of the year.

It is probable that several games of chance were known to the Egyptians, besides dice and *mora*, and, as with the Romans, that many a doubtful mind sought relief in the promise of success, by having recourse to fortuitous combinations of various kinds; and the custom of drawing, or casting lots, was common, at least as early as the period of the Hebrew Exodus.

The games and amusements of children were such as tended to promote health by the exercise of the body, and to divert the mind by laughable entertainments. Throwing and catching the ball, running, leaping, and similar feats, were encouraged, as soon as their age enabled them to indulge in them; and a young

214.   Wooden dolls.

child was amused with painted dolls, whose hands and legs, moving on pins, were made to assume various positions by means of strings. Some of these were of rude form, without legs, or with an imperfect representation of a single arm on one side. Some had numerous beads, in imitation of hair, hanging from the doubtful place of the head; others exhibited a nearer approach to the form of a man; and some, made with considerable attention to proportion, were small models of the human figure. They were coloured according to fancy; and the most shapeless had usually the most gaudy appearance, being intended to catch the eye of an infant. Sometimes a man was figured washing, or kneading dough, who was made to work by pulling a string; and a typhonian monster, or a crocodile, amused a child by its grimaces, or the motion of its opening mouth. In the toy of the crocodile, we have sufficient evidence that the notion of this

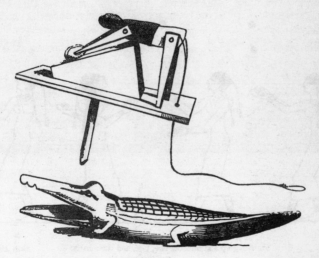

215.   Children's toys.   *Leyden Museum.*

animal " not moving its lower jaw, and being the only creature which brings the upper one down to the lower," is erroneous. Like other animals, it moves the lower jaw *only*; but when seizing its prey, it throws up its head, which gives an appearance of motion in the upper jaw, and has led to the mistake.

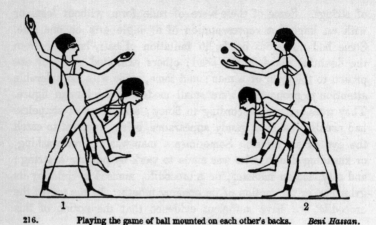

216.   Playing the game of ball mounted on each other's backs.   *Beni Hassan.*

217.   Throwing up and catching one, two, and three balls.   *Beni Hassan.*

The game of ball was of course generally played out of doors. It was not confined to children, nor to one sex, though the mere amusement of throwing and catching it appears to have been considered more particularly adapted to women. They had different modes of playing. Sometimes a person unsuccessful in catching the ball was obliged to suffer another to ride on her

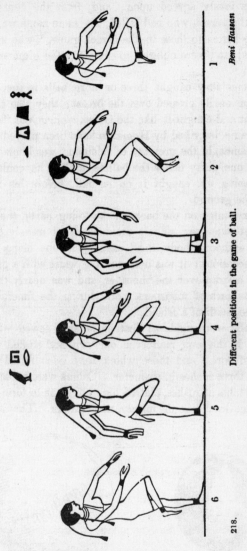

Beni Hassan.

Different positions in the game of ball.

218.

back, who continued to enjoy this post until she also missed it:
the ball being thrown by an opposite player, mounted in the
same manner, and placed at a certain distance, according to the

space previously agreed upon; and, from the beast-of-burden office of the person who had failed, the same name was probably applied to her as to those in the Greek game, " who were called ovoι (asses), and were obliged to submit to the commands of the victor."

Sometimes they caught three or more balls in succession, the hands occasionally crossed over the breast; they also threw it up to a height and caught it, like the Greek ουρανια, our "sky ball;" and the game described by Homer to have been played by Halius and Laodamus, in the presence of Alcinöus, was known to them; in which one party threw the ball as high as he could, and the other, leaping up, caught it on its fall, before his feet again touched the ground.

When mounted on the backs of the losing party, the Egyptian women sat sidewise. Their dress consisted merely of a short petticoat, without a body, the loose upper robe being laid aside on these occasions : it was bound at the waist with a girdle, supported by a strap over the shoulder, and was nearly the same as the undress garb of mourners, worn during the funeral lamentation on the death of a friend.

The balls were made of leather or skin, sewed with string, crosswise, in the same manner as our own, and stuffed with bran, or husks of corn; and those which have been found at Thebes are about three inches in diameter. Others were made of string, or of the stalks of rushes, platted together so as to form a circular mass, and covered, like the former, with leather. They appear also

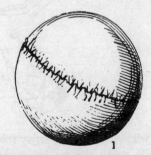

2

1

219.   Fig. 1. Leather ball, three inches in diameter.
            2. Of painted earthenware.   *From Mr. Salt's Collection.*

to have had a smaller kind of ball, probably of the same materials, and covered, like many of our own, with slips of leather of a rhomboidal shape, sewed together longitudinally, and meeting in a common point at both ends, each alternate slip being of a different colour; but these have only been met with in pottery.

In one of their performances of strength and dexterity, two men stood together side by side, and, placing one arm for-

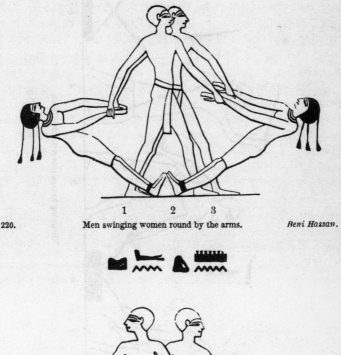

	1	2	3	

220.   Men swinging women round by the arms.   *Beni Hassan.*

	1		2	

221.   Rising from the ground.   *Beni Hassan.*

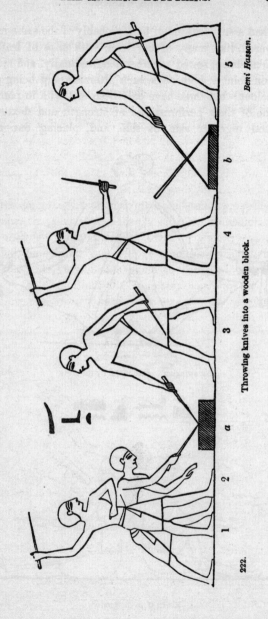

222.   Throwing knives into a wooden block.   Beni Hassan.

ward and the other behind them, held the hands of two women, who reclined backwards, in opposite directions, with their whole weight pressed against each other's feet, and in this position were whirled round ; the hands of the men who held them being occasionally crossed, in order more effectually to guarantee the steadiness of the centre, on which they turned.

Sometimes two men, seated back to back on the ground, at a given signal tried who should rise first from that position, without touching the ground with the hand. And in this, too, there was probably the trial who should first make good his seat upon the ground, from a standing position.

Another game consisted in throwing a knife, or pointed weapon, into a block of wood, in which each player was required to strike his adversary's, or more probably to fix his own in the centre, or at the circumference, of a ring painted on the wood ; and his success depended on being able to ring his weapon most frequently, or approach most closely to the line.

Conjuring appears also to have been known to them, at least thimble-rig, or the game of cups, under which a ball was put,

223.   Conjurors, or thimble-rig.   *From the work of Professor Rosellini.*

while the opposite party guessed under which of four it was concealed.

The Egyptian grandees frequently admitted dwarfs, and deformed persons, into their household ; originally, perhaps, from a

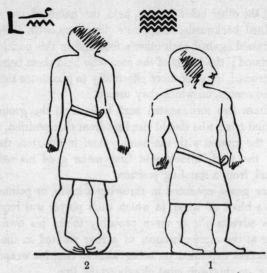

224.   Dwarfs and deformed persons in the service of the Egyptian grandees.
Beni Hassan.
The stone is broken in that part where the hands should be.

humane motive, or from some superstitious regard for men who
bore the external character of one of their principal gods, Pthah-
Sokari-Osiris, the misshapen Deity of Memphis; but, whatever
may have given rise to the custom, it is a singular fact, that
already as early as the age of Osirtasen, or about 4000 years ago,
the same fancy of attaching these persons to their suite existed
among the Egyptians, as at Rome, and even in modern Europe,
till a late period.

The games of the lower orders, and of those who sought to
invigorate the body by active exercises, consisted of feats of
agility and strength. Wrestling was a favourite amusement;
and the paintings at Beni Hassan present all the varied attitudes
and modes of attack and defence of which it is susceptible. And,
in order to enable the spectator more readily to perceive the position of the limbs of each combatant, the artist has availed himself
of a dark and light colour, and even ventured to introduce alternately a black and red figure. The subject covers a whole wall;

Beni Hassan.

225.

Fig. 1. A man holding his girdle.
2. The other binding on his girdle.

Some of the positions of wrestlers.

Fig. 3, 4. Advancing to the attack.
13, 14. Continuing the attack on the ground.

but the selection of a few groups will suffice to convey an idea of the principal positions of the combatants. (*Woodcut* 225.)

It is probable that, like the Greeks, they anointed the body with oil, when preparing for these exercises, and they were entirely naked, with the exception of a girdle, apparently of leathern thongs.

The two combatants generally approached each other, holding their arms in an inclined position before the body; and each endeavoured to seize his adversary in the manner best suited to his mode of attack. It was allowable to take hold of any part of the body, the head, neck, or legs; and the struggle was frequently continued on the ground, after one or both had fallen; a mode of wrestling common also to the Greeks.

They also fought with the single stick, the hand being apparently protected by a basket, or guard projecting over the knuckles; and on the left arm they wore a straight piece of wood, bound on with straps, serving as a shield to ward off their adversary's blow. They do not, however, appear to have used the *cestus*, nor to have known the art of boxing; though in one group, at Beni Hassan, the combatants appear to strike each other. Nor is there an instance, in any of these contests, of the

226.   Singlestick.   *From the work of Professor Rosellini.*

Greek sign of acknowledging defeat, which was by holding up a finger in token of submission; and it was probably done by the

Egyptians with a word. It is also doubtful if throwing the discus, or quoit, was an Egyptian game; but there appears to be one instance of it, in a king's tomb of the 19th dynasty.

One of their feats of strength, or dexterity, was lifting weights; and bags full of sand were raised with one hand from the ground

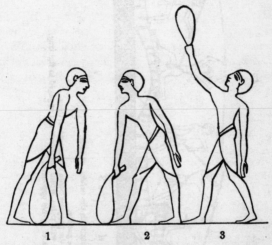

1   2   3

227.   Raising weights.   *From the work of Professor Rosellini.*

and carried with a straight arm over the head, and held in that position.

Mock fights were also an amusement, particularly among those of the military class, who were trained to the fatigues of war, by these manly recreations. One party attacked a temporary fort, and brought up the battering ram, under cover of the testudo; another defended the walls and endeavoured to repel the enemy; others, in two parties of equal numbers, engaged in single stick, or the more usual *nebóot*, a pole wielded with both hands; and the pugnacious spirit of the people is frequently alluded to in the scenes portrayed by their artists.

The use of the *nebóot* seems to have been as common among the ancient, as among the modern, Egyptians; and the quarrels of villages were often decided or increased, as at present, by this

208

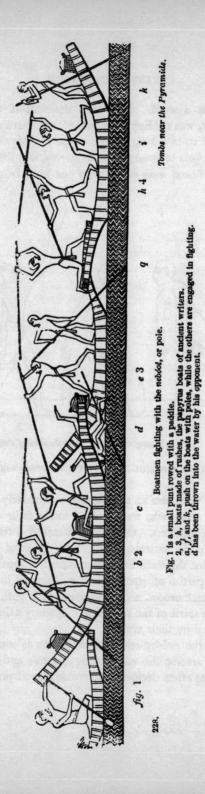

228.

fig. 1

a   b 2   c   d   e 3   q   h 4   i   k

Boatmen fighting with the *nebbot*, or pole.

Fig. 1 is a small punt rowed with a paddle.
2, 3, h, boats made of rushes, the papyrus boats of ancient writers.
a, f, and k, push on the boats with poles, while the others are engaged in fighting.
d has been thrown into the water by his opponent.

Tombs near the Pyramids.

efficient weapon. Crews of boats are also represented attacking each other with the earnestness of real strife. Some are desperately wounded, and, being felled by their more skilful opponents, are thrown headlong into the water; and the truth of Herodotus's assertion, that the heads of the Egyptians were harder than those of other people, seems fully justified by the scenes described by their own draughtsmen. It is fortunate that their successors have inherited this peculiarity, in order to bear the violence of the Turks, and their own combats.

Many singular encounters with sticks are mentioned by ancient authors; among which may be noticed one at Papremis, the city of Mars, described by Herodotus. When the votaries of the deity presented themselves at the gates of the temple, their entrance was obstructed by an opposing party; and all being armed with sticks, they commenced a rude combat, which ended, not merely in the infliction of a few severe wounds, but even, as the historian affirms, in the death of many persons on either side.

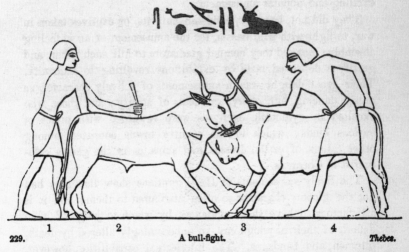

229.   A bull-fight.   Thebes.

Bull-fights were also among their sports; which were sometimes exhibited in the *dromos*, or avenue, leading to the temples, as at Memphis before the temple of Vulcan; and prizes were

VOL. I.

awarded to the owner of the victorious combatant. Great care
was taken in training them for this purpose; Strabo says as
much as is usually bestowed on horses; and herdsmen were not

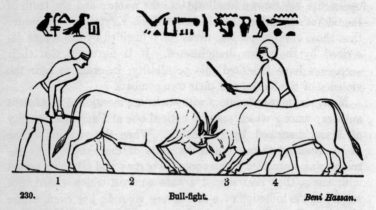

230.   Bull-fight.   *Beni Hassan.*

loth to allow, or encourage, an occasional fight for the love of the
exciting and popular amusement.

They did not, however, condemn culprits, or captives taken in
war, to fight with wild beasts, for the amusement of an unfeeling
assembly; nor did they compel gladiators to kill each other, and
gratify a depraved taste by exhibitions revolting to humanity.
Their great delight was in amusements of a lively character, as
music, dancing, buffoonery, and feats of agility; and those who
excelled in gymnastic exercises were rewarded with prizes of
various kinds; which in the country towns consisted, among
other things, of cattle, dresses, and skins, as in the games celebrated in Chemmis.

The lively amusements of the Egyptians show that they had
not the gloomy character so often attributed to them; and it is
satisfactory to have these evidences by which to judge of it, in
default of their physiognomy, so unbecomingly altered by death,
bitumen, and bandages. The intellectual capabilities, however,
of individuals may yet be subject to the decision of the phreno-
logist; and if they have escaped the ordeal of the *supposed*
spontaneous rotation of a pendulum under a glass bell, their

333

handwriting is still open to the criticisms of the wise, who discover by it the most minute secrets of character; and some of the old scribes may even now be amenable to this kind of scrutiny. But they are fortunately out of reach of the surprise, that some in modern days exhibit, at the exact likeness of themselves, believed to be presented to them from their own handwriting by a few clever generalities; forgetting that the sick man, in each malady he reads of in a book of medicine, discovers his own symptoms, and fancies they correspond with his own particular case. For though a certain neatness, or precision, carelessness, or other habit, may be discovered by handwriting, to describe from it all the minutiæ of character is only feeding the love of the marvellous, so much on the increase in these days, when a reaction of credulity bids fair to make nothing too extravagant for our modern *gobe-mouches.*

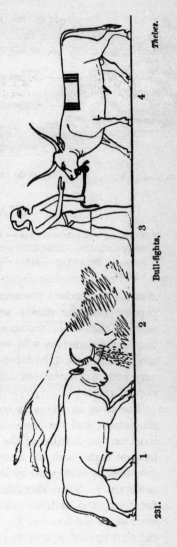

Thebes.   Bull-fights,   231.

View of the Ruins and Vicinity of Philæ.

CHAPTER IV.

THE CHASE — WILD ANIMALS — DOGS — BIRDS — FISHING — CHASE OF THE
HIPPOPOTAMUS — CROCODILE — ITS EGGS — THE TROCHILUS — LIST OF THE
ANIMALS OF EGYPT — BIRDS — PLANTS — EMBLEMS — OFFERINGS — CERE-
MONIES.

AMONG the various pastimes of the Egyptians, none was more
popular than the chase; and the wealthy aristocracy omitted
nothing that could promote their favourite amusement. They
hunted the numerous wild animals in the desert; they had them
caught with nets, to be turned out on some future day; and some
very keen sportsmen took long journeys to spots noted for abundance of game.

The taste, as far as it could be indulged, was general with
all classes; and the peasants hunted down the wild beasts that
lived on the borders of the desert, and invaded the flocks and
fields at night, with the same alacrity as the priestly and military
grandees, or other wealthy land owners, chased the game in their
preserves. Some shot them with arrows, others laid traps
for them, and various methods were devised for securing the
enemies of the farm-yard. Watchers and dogs were always on
the alert against wolves and jackals, the poachers of their flocks
and poultry; and when the peasants heard the melancholy howls
and yelping bark of the large packs of jackals, collecting every
evening in anticipation of a foray among the geese, they waited

for their well-known passage through a ravine, on the desert's edge, or longed that some, in spite of Anubis, might fall into their traps.

The hyæna, an enemy of flocks and herds, a gourmand in the flesh of the peasant's very useful donkey, and, when none of these could be had, a very destructive devourer of the crops, was especially hateful; and the agricultural heart rejoiced when a hyæna, caught in a trap, was brought home muzzled, as a harmless spectacle to the children of the village, and a triumph among the neighbours.

232.   Hyæna caught in a trap.   *Thebes.*

When a grand chase took place in the domain of some grandee, or in the extensive tracts of the desert, a retinue of huntsmen, beaters, and others in his service attended, to manage the hounds, to carry the game-baskets and hunting poles, to set the nets, and to make other preparations for a good day's sport. Some took a fresh supply of arrows, a spare bow, and various requisites for remedying accidents; some were merely beaters, others were to assist in securing the large animals caught by the *lasso*, others had to mark or turn the game, and some carried a stock of provisions for the chasseur and his friends. These last were borne upon the usual wooden yoke, across the shoulders, and consisted of a skin of water, and jars of good wine placed in wicker baskets, with bread, meats, and other eatables. The skin used for holding water was precisely the same as that of the present day, being of a goat, or a gazelle, stripped from the body by a longitudinal opening at the throat; the legs serving as handles, to which ropes for slinging them were attached; and a soft pendent tube of leather, sewed to the throat, in the place of the head, formed the mouth of the water skin, which was secured by a thong fastened round it.

Sometimes a portion of the desert, of considerable extent, was enclosed by nets, into which the animals were driven by beaters; and the place chosen for fixing them was, if possible, across narrow valleys, or torrent beds, lying between some rocky hills. Here a sportsman on horseback, or in a chariot, could waylay them, or get within reach with a bow; for many animals, particularly gazelles, when closely pressed by dogs, fear to take a steep ascent, and are easily overtaken, or shot as they double back.

The spots thus enclosed were usually in the vicinity of the water brooks, to which they were in the habit of repairing in the morning and evening: and having awaited the time when they went to drink, and ascertained it by their recent tracks on the accustomed path, the hunters disposed the nets, occupied proper positions for observing them unseen, and gradually closed in upon them. Such are the scenes partially portrayed in the Egyptian paintings, where long nets are represented surrounding the space they hunted in; and the hyænas, jackals, and various wild beasts unconnected with the sport, are intended to show that they have been accidentally enclosed, within the same line of nets with the antelopes and other animals.

In the same way Æneas and Dido repaired to a wood at break of day, after the attendants had surrounded it with a temporary fence, to enclose the game.

The long net was furnished with several ropes, and was supported on forked poles, varying in length, to correspond with the inequalities of the ground, and was so contrived as to enclose any space, by crossing hills, valleys, or streams, and encircling woods, or whatever might present itself; smaller nets for stopping gaps were also used; and a circular snare, set round with wooden or metal nails, and attached by a rope to a log of wood, which

was used for catching deer, resembled one still made by the
Arabs.

The dresses of the attendants and huntsmen were generally
of a suppressed colour, " lest they should be seen at a distance
by the animals," tight fitting, and reaching only a short way
down the thigh; and the horses of the chariots were divested of
the feathers, and showy ornaments, used on other occasions.

233.   Carrying young animals.   *Tomb near the Pyramids.*

Besides the portions of the open desert and the valleys, which
were enclosed for hunting, the parks and covers on their own
domains in the valley of the Nile, though of comparatively
limited dimensions, offered ample space and opportunity for indulging in the chase; and a quantity of game was kept there;
principally the wild goat, oryx, and gazelle.

They had also fishponds, and spacious poultry-yards set apart
for keeping geese, and other wild fowl, which they fattened for
the table.

It was the duty of the huntsmen, or the gamekeepers, to superintend the preserves; and at proper periods of the year wild
fawns were obtained, to increase the herds of gazelles and other
animals, which always formed part of the stock of a wealthy
Egyptian.

Being fed within pastures enclosed with fences, they were not

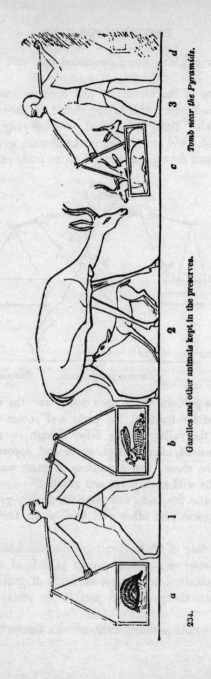

234.

Tomb near the Pyramids.

Gazelles and other animals kept in the preserves.

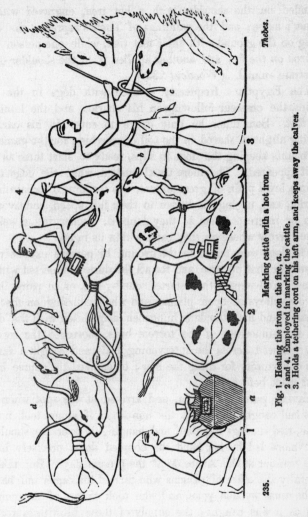

Thebes.

Marking cattle with a hot iron.

Fig. 1. Heating the iron on the fire, *a*.
2 and 4. Employed in marking the cattle.
3. Holds a tethering cord on his left arm, and keeps away the calves.

235.

marked in any particular way like the cattle, which, being let
loose, in open meadows, and frequently allowed to mix with the
herds of the neighbours, required some distinguishing sign by
which they might be recognised. These last were, therefore,

branded on the shoulder with a hot iron, engraved with the owner's name; and the paintings of Thebes represent the cattle lying on the ground with their feet tied, while one person heats an iron on the fire, and another applies it to the shoulder of the prostrate animal. (*Woodcut* 235.)

The Egyptians frequently coursed with dogs in the open plains, the chasseur following in his chariot, and the huntsmen on foot. Sometimes he only drove to cover in his car, and having alighted, shared in the toil of searching for the game, his attendants keeping the dogs in slips, ready to start them as soon as it appeared. The more usual custom, when the dogs threw off in a level plain of great extent, was for him to remain in his chariot, and, urging his horses to their full speed, endeavour to turn or intercept them as they doubled, discharging a well directed arrow whenever they came within its range.

The dogs were taken to the ground by persons expressly employed for that purpose, and for all the duties connected with the kennel; and were either started one by one, or in pairs, in the narrow valleys or open plains: and when coursing on foot, the chasseur and his attendant huntsmen, acquainted with the direction and sinuosities of the torrent beds, shortened the road, as they followed across the intervening hills, and sought a favourable opportunity for using the bow; or enjoyed the course in the level space before them.

Having pursued on foot, and arrived at the spot where the dogs had caught their prey, the huntsman, if alone, took up the game, tied its legs together, and hanging it over his shoulders, once more led by his hand the coupled dogs, precisely in the same manner as the Arabs do at the present day. But this was generally the office of persons who carried the cages and baskets on the usual wooden yoke, and who took charge of the game as soon as it was caught; the supply of these substitutes for our game cart being in proportion to the proposed range of the chase, and the number of head they expected to kill. Sometimes an ibex, oryx, or wild ox, being closely pressed by the hounds, faced round and kept them at bay, with its formidable horns, and

236.   A huntsman carrying home the game, with his coupled dogs.   *Thebes.*

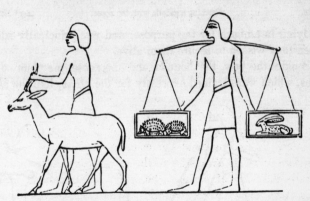

237.   Bringing home the game: a gazelle, porcupines, and hare.   *Beni Hassan.*

the spear of the huntsman, as he came up, was required to decide
the success of the chase.

It frequently happened, when the chasseur had many attendants, and the district to be hunted was extensive, that they divided

into parties, each taking one or more dogs, and starting them on whatever animal broke cover; sometimes they went without hounds, merely having a small dog for searching the bushes, or laid in wait for the larger and more formidable animals, and attacked them with the lance.

The noose, or *lasso*, was also employed to catch the wild ox, the antelope, and other animals; but this could only be thrown

238.   Catching a gazelle with the noose.   *Beni Hassan.*

by lying in ambush for the purpose, and was principally adopted when they wished to secure them alive.

Besides the bow, the hounds, and the noose, they hunted with lions, which were trained expressly for the chase, like the *cheeta*,

239.   Catching a wild ox with the noose or *lasso*.   *Beni Hassan.*

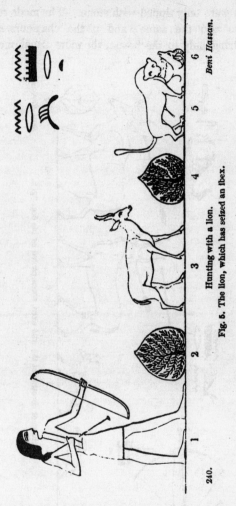

240. Hunting with a lion.
Fig. 5. The lion, which has seized an Ibex.
Beni Hassan.

or hunting leopard of India, being brought up from cubs in a
tame state; and many Egyptian monarchs were accompanied in
battle by a favourite lion. But there is no instance of hawking.

The bow used for the chase was very similar to that employed
in war; the arrows were generally the same, with metal heads,

though some were only tipped with stone. The mode of drawing the bow was also the same; and if the chasseurs sometimes pulled the string only to the breast, the more usual method was

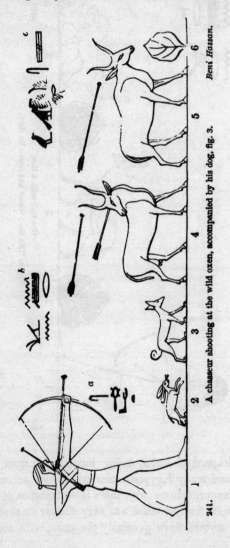

241. A chasseur shooting at the wild oxen, accompanied by his dog, fig. 3. *Beni Hassan.*

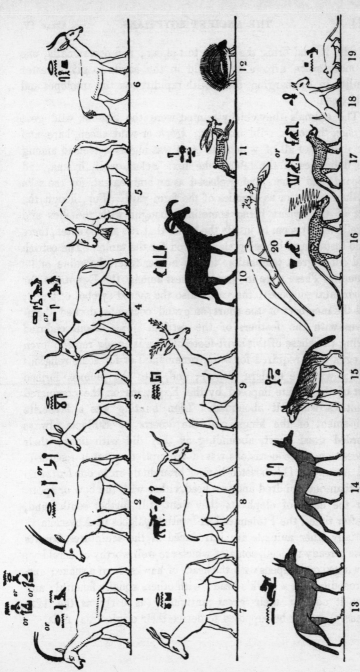

242.

Animals from the sculptures. 5, 15, 20, from *Thebes*; the rest from *Beni Hassan*.

1. The ibex. 2. The oryx. 3, 4. Wild oxen. 5. Humped or Indian ox. 6. Gazelle. 7. Probably the antilope addax. 8. Goat. 9. Stag. 10. The kebsh. 11. Hare. 12. Porcupine. 13. Wolf. 14. Fox. 15. Hyæna. 16, 17. Species of leopard. 18. Cat. 19. Rat. 20. Ichneumon. 10 is coloured red in the paintings: it is the *kebsh*, which is of a sandy colour.

to raise it, and bring the arrow to the ear; and occasionally, one or more spare arrows were held in the hand, to give greater facility in discharging them with rapidity, on the antelopes and wild oxen.

The animals they chiefly hunted were the gazelle, wild goat or *ibex*, the oryx, wild ox, stag, *kebsh* or wild sheep, hare, and porcupine; of all of which the meat was highly esteemed among the delicacies of the table; the fox, jackal, wolf, hyæna, and leopard, and others, being chased as an amusement, for the sake of their skins, or as enemies of the farm-yard. For though the fact of the hyæna being sometimes bought with the ibex and gazelle might seem to justify the belief that it was also eaten, there is no instance of its being slaughtered for the table. The ostrich held out a great temptation to the hunter from the value of its plumes. These were in great request among the Egyptians for ornamental purposes; they were also the sacred symbol of truth; and the members of the court on grand occasions decked themselves with the feathers of the ostrich. The labour endured during the chase of this swift-footed bird was amply repaid; even its eggs were required for some ornamental or for some religious use (as with the modern Copts); and, with the plumes, formed part of the tribute imposed by the Egyptians on the conquered countries where it abounded. Lion hunting was a favourite amusement of the kings, and the deserts of Ethiopia always afforded good sport, abounding as they did with lions; their success on those occasions was a triumph they often recorded; and Amunoph III. boasted having brought down in one *battue* no less than one hundred and two head, either with the bow or spear. For the chase of elephants they went still further south; and, in after times, the Ptolemies had hunting palaces in Abyssinia.

Many other animals are introduced in the sculptures, besides those already noticed, some of which are well worthy of heraldry; as winged quadrupeds with the heads of hawks, or of a snake; and a crocodile with a hawk's head; with others equally fanciful; and were it not for their great antiquity (as early as the 12th dynasty), might be supposed to derive their origin from Asia.

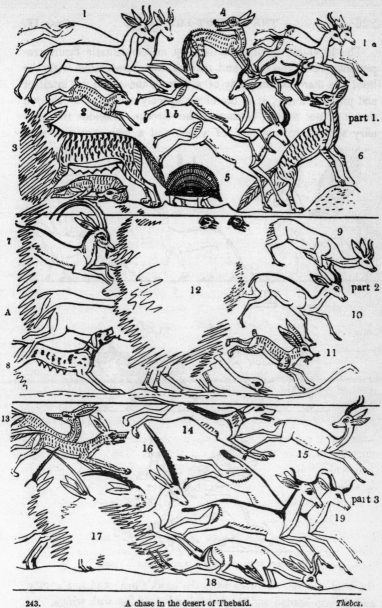

243. A chase in the desert of Thebaïd. *Thebes.*

To the left of A was the chasseur in his chariot shooting with the bow, *now defaced.*
Figs. 1, 9, 15, 18. Gazelles. 2, 11. Hares. 3. Female hyæna, with its young. 4, 13. Foxes.
  5. Porcupine. 6. Hyæna arrived at the top of a hill, and looking towards the chasseur.
  7. The ibex. 8, 14. Hounds. 12. Ostriches (*defaced*). 16. The oryx. 19. Wild oxen.

The Egyptian sphinx was usually an emblematic figure, representative of the king, and may be considered, when with the head of a man and the body of a lion, as the union of intellect and physical force; it is therefore scarcely necessary to observe that it is not female, as that of the Greeks. Besides the ordinary sphinx, compounded of a lion and a man, was one with

244.   Monsters, in the paintings of Beni Hassan and Thebes.

the head of a ram, another with the hawk's head and lion's body, and the asp-headed and the hawk-headed sphinx with wings.

The wild animals now most noted in Egypt, either in the Valley of the Nile, or in the desert, are the gazelle, ibex, *kebsh*, hare, fox, jackal, wolf, hyæna, *jerbóa*, hedgehog, and ichneumon.

The *oryx** is a native of Ethiopia, as is the spotted hyæna or *marafeén*; which last is once represented in the Egyptian sculptures. The oryx has long annulated horns, tapering to a sharp point, and nearly straight, with a slight curve or inclination backwards. It frequently occurs in the sculptures, being among the animals tamed by the Egyptians, and kept in great numbers in their preserves.

The *beïsa* is very like the oryx, except in the black marks upon its face, and a few other points; and the *addax*, another antelope, inhabiting Upper Ethiopia, differs principally from the oryx in its horns, which have a waving or spiral form. It appears to be represented in the sculptures of Beni Hassan.†

The wild ox, which is also of the genus *antilope*, the *defassa* of modern zoologists, though not a native of Egypt, is found in the African desert, and I believe in Eastern Ethiopia; it is of a reddish sandy and grey colour, with a black tuft terminating its tail, and stands about four feet high at the shoulder. At Beni Hassan‡ it is made too much to resemble a common ox, but it is more correctly represented in the Theban sculptures.§

The stag with branching horns,‖ figured at Beni Hassan, is also unknown in the Valley of the Nile; but it is still seen in the vicinity of the Natron Lakes, as about Tunis, though not in the desert between the river and the Red Sea.

The *ibex*,¶ which is common in the Eastern desert, is very similar to the bouquetin of the Alps, and is called in Arabic *Beddan*, or *Táytal*. The former appellation is exclusively applied to the male, which is readily distinguished by a beard and large knotted horns, curving backwards over its body; the female having short erect horns, scarcely larger than those of the gazelle, and being of a much smaller and lighter structure.

The *kebsh*, or wild sheep, is found in the Eastern desert,

---

* Woodcut 242, *fig.* 2.   † Woodcut 242, *fig.* 7.
  ‡ Woodcut 241, *figs.* 4 and 5.   § Woodcut 243. *fig.* 19.
  ‖ Woodcut 242, *fig.* 9.   ¶ Woodcut 242, *fig.* 1; 243, *fig.* 7.

principally in the ranges of primitive mountains, which, commencing about latitude 28° 40′, at the back of the limestone hills of the Valley of the Nile, extend thence into Ethiopia and Abyssinia. The female kebsh is between two and three feet high at the shoulder, and its total length from the tail to the end of the nose is a little more than four feet: but the male is larger, and is provided with stronger horns, which are about five inches in diameter at the roots, and are curved backwards on each side of the neck. The whole body is covered with hair, like many of the Ethiopian sheep, and the throat and thighs of the fore legs are furnished with a long pendent mane; a peculiarity not omitted in the sculptures, and which suffices to prove the identity of the kebsh, wherever its figure is represented. (*Woodcut* 242, *fig.* 10.)

The porcupine is no longer a native of Egypt; nor is the leopard met with on this side of Upper Ethiopia. Bears are altogether unknown, and, if they occur twice in the paintings of the Theban tombs, they are only brought by foreigners, together with the productions of their country, which were deemed rare and curious to the Egyptians.

The wolf is common, and, as Herodotus says, " scarcely larger than a fox;" and the tombs in the mountain above Lycopolis, the modern O'Sioot, contain the mummies of wolves, which were the sacred animals of the place.

The Egyptian hare is a native of the Valley of the Nile, as well as of the two deserts; and is remarkable for the length of its ears, which the Egyptians have not failed to indicate in their sculptures. It is a smaller species than those of Europe; which accords with Denon's remark on the comparative size of animals common to Egypt and Europe, that the former are always smaller than our own.

The *wabber* or *hyrax*, though a native of the eastern desert of Egypt, is not represented in the sculptures; but this is probably owing to its habits, and to their hunting principally in the valleys of the secondary mountains; the wabber only venturing a short distance from its burrow in the evening, and living in the primitive ranges where the *sealeh* or acacia grows. It was probably the *saphan* of the Bible, as Bruce has remarked, and that enterprising traveller is perfectly correct in placing it among ruminating animals. The hedgehog was always common, as at present, in the Valley of the Nile.

The lion is now unknown to the north of Upper Ethiopia: there, however, it is common, as well as the leopard, and other carnivorous beasts; and the abundance of sheep in those districts amply supplies them with food, and has the happy tendency of rendering them less dangerous to man. In ancient times, however, the lion inhabited the deserts of Egypt, and Athenæus mentions one killed by the Emperor Adrian, while hunting near Alexandria. They are even said, in former times, to have been found in Syria, and in Greece.

Among the animals confined to the Valley of the Nile, and its immediate vicinity, may be mentioned the ichneumon, which lives principally in Lower Egypt and the Fyoom, and which, from its enmity to serpents, was looked upon by the Egyptians with great respect. Its dexterity in attacking the snake is truly surprising. It seizes the enemy at the back of the neck, as soon as it perceives it rising to the attack, one firm bite sufficing to destroy it; and when wounded by the venomous fangs of its opponent, it is said by the Arabs to have recourse to some herb, which checks the effect of the deadly poison.

The ichneumon is easily tamed, and is sometimes seen in the houses of Cairo, where, in its hostility to rats, it performs all the duties of a cat; but, from its indiscriminate fondness for eggs, poultry, and many other requisites for the kitchen, it is generally reckoned troublesome, and I have often found reason to complain of those I kept.

Eggs are its favourite food, and it is said to have been greatly venerated by those who held the crocodile in abhorrence, in consequence of its destroying the eggs of that hateful animal: but it is now rarely met with in places where the crocodile abounds; and at all periods its principal recommendation was its hostility to serpents. It is frequently seen in the paintings, where its habits are distinctly alluded to by the Egyptian artists, who represent it in search of eggs, among the bushes, and the usual resorts of the feathered tribe.

The wild cat, the *felis chaus* of Linnæus, is common in the vicinity of the Pyramids and Heliopolis, but it does not occur among the pictured animals of ancient Egypt. Nor is the *jerbóa*, so frequently met with both in the upper and lower country, represented in the sculptures.

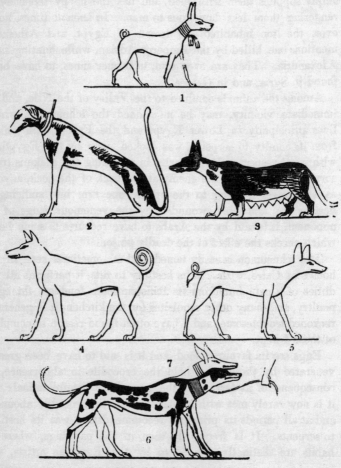

245.   Various kinds of dogs, from the sculptures.

The giraffe was not a native of Egypt, but of Ethiopia, and is only introduced in subjects which relate to that country, where it is brought with apes, rare woods, and other native productions, as part of the tribute annually paid to the Pharaohs.

The Egyptians had several breeds of dogs, some solely used for the chase, others admitted into the parlour, or as companions of their walks; and some, as at the present day, were chosen for their peculiar ugliness. The most common kinds were a sort of fox-dog, and a hound; they had also a short-legged dog, not unlike our turnspit, which was a great favourite, especially in the reigns of the Osirtasens; and, as in later days, the choice of a king, or some noted personage, brought a particular breed into fashion.

Mummies of the fox-dog are common in Upper Egypt; and this was doubtless the parent stock of the modern red wild dog of Egypt, so common in Cairo, and other parts of the lower country.

Pigs, though an abomination to the Egyptians, formed part of a farmer's stock; but, attentive to the habits of animals, they allowed them to range and feed out of doors, under the care of a herdsman; knowing that cleanliness is as beneficial for, as the confinement in a sty is contrary to, the nature of a pig.

Their cattle were of different kinds; the most common being the short and long horned varieties, and the Indian or humped ox; and the two last, though no longer natives of Egypt, are common in Abyssinia and Upper Ethiopia. The buffalo, which abounds in Abyssinia and in modern Egypt, is never represented on the monuments.

Horses and asses were abundant, and the latter were employed as beasts of burden, for treading out corn (particularly in Lower Egypt) and for many other purposes. Like those of the present day, they were small, active, and capable of bearing great fatigue; and, as these hardy animals were maintained at a very trifling expense, their numbers in the agricultural districts were very great, and one individual had as many as seven hundred and sixty employed on different parts of his estate.

246.   Some of the birds of Egypt.   Beni Hassan and the Tombs near the Pyramids.
       Figs. 18, 19, 20. Bats.   21. The locust.   From Thebes.

Some of the birds of Egypt.

Egyptian horses were greatly esteemed ; they were even exported to the neighbouring countries, and Solomon bought them at a hundred and fifty shekels of silver, from the merchants who traded with Egypt by the Syrian Desert.

It is remarkable that the camel, though known in Egypt as early at least as the time of Abraham (being among the presents given by Pharaoh to the Patriarch), has never been met with, even in the latest paintings or hieroglyphics. Yet this does not prove it was even rare in the country ; since the same would apply to fowls and pigeons, of which no instance occurs on the monuments among the stock of the farmyard. Cocks and hens, however, as well as horses, appear to have come originally from Asia.

The birds of Egypt were very numerous, especially wild fowl, which abounded on the lakes and marsh-land of the Delta ; they also frequented the large pieces of water on the estates of the rich landed proprietors, in all parts of the country.

Large flights of quails afforded excellent sport at certain seasons, and the bustard and other birds, found on the edge of the desert, were highly prized for the table.

Many are represented by the Egyptian sculptors; some sacred, others that served for food ; and in the tombs of Thebes and Beni Hassan, the Egyptians have not omitted to notice bats, and even some of the insects that abound in the Valley of the Nile ; and the well-known locust, the butterfly, and the beetle are introduced in the fowling and fishing scenes, and in sacred subjects. (*Woodcuts* 246, 249, 250, 251.)

Fowling was one of the great amusements of all classes. Those who followed this sport for their livelihood used nets and traps ; but the amateur sportsman pursued his game in the thickets, and felled them with the throw-stick, priding himself on his dexterity in its use. The bow was not employed for this purpose, nor was the sling adopted, except by gardeners and peasants, to frighten the birds from the vineyards and fields. The throw-stick was made of heavy wood, and flat, so as to offer little resistance to the air in its flight ; and the distance to which

248.   A sportsman using the throw-stick.   *Thebes.*
Figs. 2 and 3. His sister and daughter.   4. A decoy bird.   5, 5. Birds struck with the stick.

an expert arm could throw it was considerable; though they
always endeavoured to approach the birds as near as possible,
under cover of the bushes and reeds.   It was from one foot and
a quarter to two feet in length, and about one and a half inch in
breadth, slightly curved at the upper end; but in no instance had
it the round shape and flight of the Australian *boomerang.*

On their fowling excursions, they usually proceeded with a
party of friends and attendants, sometimes accompanied by the
members of their family, and even by their young children, to the

jungles and thickets of the marsh-lands, or to the lakes of their own grounds, which, especially during the inundation, abounded with wild fowl; and seated in punts made of the papyrus, they glided, without disturbing the birds, amidst the lofty reeds that grew in the water, and masked their approach. This sort of boat was either towed, pushed by a pole, or propelled by paddles, and the Egyptians fancied that persons who used it were secure from the attacks of crocodiles.

The attendants collected the game as it fell, and one of them was always ready to hand a fresh stick to the chasseur, as soon as he had thrown. They frequently took with them a decoy-bird; and in order to keep it to its post, a female was selected, whose nest, containing eggs, was deposited in the boat.

249. Sportsman using the throw-stick. *British Museum.*
Fig. 2 keeps the boat steady by holding the stalks of a lotus. 4. A cat se izing the game in
the thicket. 5. A decoy-bird.

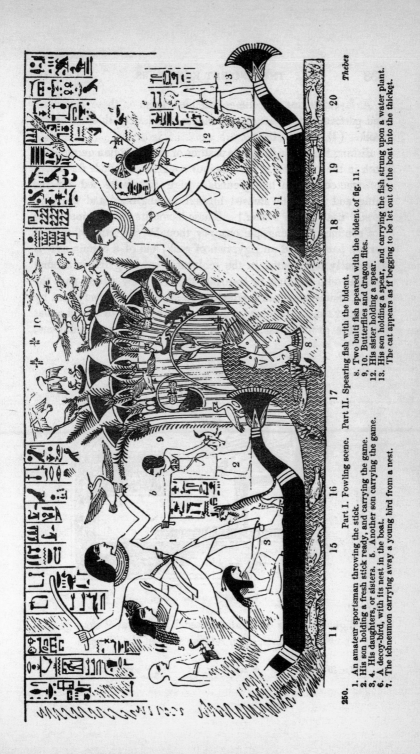

250.

Part I. Fowling scene. Part II. Spearing fish with the bident.

1. An amateur sportsman throwing the stick.
2. His son holding a fresh stick ready, and carrying the game.
3, 4. His daughters, or sisters.   5. Another son carrying the game.
6. A decoy-bird, with its nest in the boat.
7. The ichneumon carrying away a young bird from a nest.
8. Two bulti fish speared with the bident of fig. 11.
9, 10. Butterflies and dragon flies.
12. His sister holding a spear.
13. His son holding a spear, and carrying the fish strung upon a water plant.
    The cat appears as if begging to be let out of the boat into the thicket.

Thebes

A favourite cat sometimes attended them on these occasions, and performed the part of a retriever, amidst the thickets on the bank. (*Woodcut* 249, *fig.* 4.)

Fishing was also a favourite pastime of the Egyptian gentleman; both in the Nile and in the spacious "sluices, or ponds for fish,"* constructed within his grounds, where they were fed for the table, and where he amused himself by angling,† and the dexterous use of the *bident*.‡ These favourite occupations were not confined to young persons, nor thought unworthy of men of serious habits; and an Egyptian of rank, and of a certain age, is frequently represented in the sculptures catching fish in a canal or lake, with the line, or spearing them as they glided past the bank. Sometimes the angler posted himself in a shady spot by the water's edge, and, having ordered his servants to spread a mat upon the ground, sat upon it as he threw his line; and some,

251.   An Egyptian gentleman fishing.   *Thebes.*

with higher notions of comfort, used a chair; as " stout gentlemen" now do in punts, upon retired parts of the Thames.

* Isaiah xix. 10.   † Isaiah xix. 8.   ‡ Woodcut 250, *fig.* 11.

The rod was short, and apparently of one piece; the line usually single, though instances occur of a double line, each with its own hook, which was of bronze. In all cases they adopted a ground bait, as is still the custom in Egypt, without any float; and though several winged insects are represented in the paintings hovering over the water, it does not appear that they ever put them to the hook; and still less that they had devised any method similar to our artificial-fly fishing; which is still as unknown to the unsophisticated modern Egyptians as to their fish.

To spear them with the bident was thought the most sportsmanlike way of killing fish. In throwing it they sometimes stood on the bank, but generally used the papyrus punt, gliding smoothly over the water of a lake in their grounds, without disturbing the fish as they lay beneath the broad leaves of the lotus. Those who were very keen sportsmen even made parties to the lowlands of the Delta; as they did at other times, for shooting, to the highlands of the desert.

The bident was a spear with two barbed points, which was either thrust at the fish with one or both hands as they passed by, or was darted to a short distance; a long line fastened to it preventing its being lost, and serving to recover it with the fish when struck. It was occasionally furnished with feathers like an arrow, and sometimes a common spear was used for the purpose; but in most cases it was provided with a line, the end of which was held by the left hand, or wound upon a reel. This mode of fishing is still adopted in many countries; and the fish-spears of the South Sea islanders have two, three, and four points, and are thrown nearly in the same manner as the bident of the ancient Egyptians. Their attendants, or their children, assisted in securing the fish, which, when taken off the barbed point of the spear, were tied together by the stalk of a rush passed through the gills. (*Woodcut* 250, *fig.* 13.)

The chase of the hippopotamus was a favourite amusement of the sportsman; for it then frequented Lower Egypt, though now confined to Upper Ethiopia. Like the crocodile, it was looked upon as an enemy, from the ravages it committed at night in the fields; and was also killed for its hide, of which they made shields, whips, javelins, and helmets.

252.   *Thebes.*
Attendant carrying a whip, or *corbág.*

The whips, known by the name of *corbág* (*corbaj*), are still very generally used in Egypt and Ethiopia, in riding the dromedary, or for chastising a delinquent peasant; for which purposes it was applied by the ancient Egyptians; and an attendant sometimes followed the steward of an estate, with this implement of punishment in his hand.

The mode of attacking and securing the hippopotamus appears, from the sculptures of Thebes, to have been very similar to that now adopted about Sennar; where, like the ancient Egyptians, they prefer chasing it in the river, to an open attack on shore: and the modern Ethiopians are contented to frighten it from the corn-fields by the sound of drums and other noisy instruments.

It was entangled by a running noose, at the extremity of a long rope wound upon a reel, at the same time that it was struck by a spear. This weapon consisted of a broad flat blade, furnished with a deep tooth, or barb, at the side; having a strong line of considerable length attached to its upper end, and running over the notched summit of a wooden shaft, which was inserted into the head, or blade, like a common javelin. It was thrown in the same manner; but, on striking, the shaft fell, and the iron head alone remained in the body of the animal; which, on receiving a wound, plunged into deep water, the line having been immediately let out. When fatigued by exertion, the hippopotamus was dragged to the boat, from which it again plunged, and the same was repeated till it became perfectly exhausted; frequently receiving additional wounds, and being entangled by other nooses, which the attendants held in readiness, as it was brought within their reach.

253.　　　　Spear used in the chase of the hippopotamus.　　　*Thebes.*

The line attached to the blade was also wound upon a reel, generally carried by some of the attendants, which was of very simple construction, consisting of a half ring of metal, as a handle, and the bar turning in it, on which the line was wound.

Neither the hippopotamus nor the crocodile were used as food by the ancient Egyptians; but the people of Apollinopolis ate the crocodile, upon a certain occasion, in order to show their abhorrence of Typho, the evil genius, of whom it was an emblem. "They had also a solemn hunt of this animal upon a particular day, set apart for the purpose, at which time they killed as many of them as they could, and afterwards threw their dead bodies before the temple of their god, assigning this reason for

254.　A reel held by an attendant.　*Beni Hassan*

their practice, that it was in the shape of a crocodile Typho eluded the pursuit of Orus."

In some parts of Egypt it was sacred, "while in other places they made war upon it; and those who lived about Thebes and the Lake Mœris (in the Arsinoïte nome) held it in great veneration."

It was there treated with the most marked respect, and kept at a considerable expense; it was fed and attended with the most scrupulous care; geese, fish, and various meats were dressed purposely for it; they ornamented its head with ear-rings, its feet with bracelets, and its neck with necklaces of gold and artificial stones; it was rendered perfectly tame by kind treatment; and after death its body was embalmed in a most sumptuous manner. This was particularly the case in the Theban, Ombite, and Arsinoïte nomes; and at a place now called Maabdeh, opposite the modern town of Manfaloot, are extensive grottoes, cut far into the limestone mountain, where numerous crocodile mummies have been found, perfectly preserved, and evidently embalmed with great care.

The people of Apollinopolis, Tentyris, Heracleopolis, and other places, on the contrary, held the crocodile in abhorrence, and lost no opportunity of destroying it; and the Tentyrites were so expert, from long habit, in catching, and even in overcoming this powerful animal in the water, that they were known to follow it into the Nile, and bring it by force to the shore. Pliny and others mention the wonderful feats performed by them, not only in their own country, but in the presence of the Roman people: and Strabo says that on the occasion of some crocodiles being exhibited at Rome, the Tentyrites, who were present, fully confirmed the truth of the report of their power over those animals; for, having put them into a spacious tank of water, with a shelving bank artificially constructed at one side, the men boldly entered the water, and, entangling them in a net, dragged them to the bank, and back again into the water; which was witnessed by numerous spectators.

The crocodile is in fact a timid animal, flying on the approach of man; and little danger need be apprehended from it, except by

any one incautiously standing on a sloping bank of sand near the
river, when it can approach unseen. Egypt produces two varieties,
distinguished by the number and position of the scales on the
neck, and by one being black, the other of a greener colour.
They do not exceed eighteen or twenty feet, though travellers
have mentioned some of awful size. The story of the " *trochilus* "
entering its mouth as it sleeps on the sandbanks, and relieving it
of the leeches in its throat, would be " remarkable, if true " that
any leeches existed in the Nile; but the friendly offices of this
winged toothpick may have originated in the habits of the small
" *running bird*," a species of *charadrius*, or dottrel, so common
there; which, by its shrill cry on the approach of man, warns
the crocodile (quite unintentionally) of its danger.   And its
proximity to the crocodile is readily explained by its seeking the
flies and other insects, that are attracted to the sleeping beast.

255.   The Trochilus, or Charadrius melanocephalus, Linn.

The eggs of the crocodile are remarkably small; only three
inches long, by two in breadth (or diameter); being less than
those of a goose. They are equally thick at each end. They
are laid in the sand, till hatched by the warmth of the sun; and
the small crocodile, curled up with its tail to its nose, awaits the
time for breaking the shell. But the ichneumon is far more
dangerous to the eggs, than the trochilus is useful to their
parents; and its destruction of the unhatched young obtained for
it great veneration in those places where the crocodile was not
held sacred.

There were various modes of catching it.   One was " to fasten
a piece of pork to a hook, and throw it into the middle of the
stream, as a bait; then, standing near the water's edge, they beat
a young pig, and the crocodile, being enticed to the spot by its
cries, found the bait on its way, and, swallowing it, was caught
by the hook.   It was then pulled ashore, and its eyes being
quickly covered up with mud, it was easily overcome."

It is singular that the wild boar is never represented among
the animals of Egypt, though a native of the country, and still
frequenting the Fyoom and the Delta.   It is even eaten at the
present day, in spite of the religious prejudices of the Moslems,
by some of the people about Damietta.   Even if it never inhabited Upper Egypt, it ought to be figured in some of the fowling
and hunting scenes, which relate to the marsh lands of the Delta;
and the fabled chase of it by Typho shows it was known in Egypt
at the earliest times.   Nor is the wild ass met with in the paintings either of Upper or Lower Egypt, though it is common in the
deserts of the Thebaïd; and other animals have already been
shown to be wanting in the sculptures.   We are, therefore, more
reconciled, by these omissions, to the absence of several from the
monuments, which appear in all probability to have existed in
the country.

And here it may not be out of place to give a list of the different animals, birds, reptiles, fish, and plants; noticing at the
same time those that were sacred, and adding an account of the
emblems connected with the religion.

256.   257.   a.   b.   c.   d.

The name of "Egypt."

Div. I.—VERTEBRATA.
Class I.—MAMMALIA.

Name.	If sacred.	To what Deity.	In what Place (particularly).	Where mentioned.	Where found embalmed.
Orders 1 and 2.					
BIMANA AND QUADRUMANA.					
Cynocephalus Ape	Sacred	Thoth	Hermopolis	The sculptures. Strabo, xvii. Horapollo, i. 15, 16. Juvenal, Sat. xv. 4. Sculptures	Thebes and Hermopolis.
Green Monkey of Ethiopia, or *Cercopithecus*?	Sacred	Thoth?	At Thebes?		Thebes.
Order 3.					
CARNARIA.					
Bat	Not sacred			Sculptures.	
Hedgehog	Not sacred			Represented in ornaments.	
Shrew-mouse, or *Mygale*	Sacred	Buto or Latona	Athribis, Butos	Strabo, xv. Herodot. ii. 59.	Thebes.
Bear	Not sacred		Not found in Egypt.	Herodot. ii. 67; and sculptures.	
Weasel	Not sacred			Plutarch de Is. s. 74.	
Otter	Not sacred		Not found in Egypt.	Herodotus, ii. 72.	
Dog	Sacred	Anubis?	Cynopolis	Plut, Plato, &c.	Thebes, El Hareïb, &c.
Wolf	Sacred	Anubis?	Lycopolis	Strabo, xvii. Plut. s. 72; and sculptures	Lycopolis.
Fox	Sacred?	Anubis?	Lycopolis?		

Name.	If sacred.	To what Deity.	In what Place (particularly).	Where mentioned.	Where found embalmed.
CARNARIA—*continued.*					
Jackal .	Sacred	Anubis	Lycopolis?	Sculptures. Clem. Alex. Orat. Adhort. p. 17. Strabo, xvii.; and sculptures.	Lycopolis.
Ichneumon .	Sacred	.	Heracleopolis	In sculptures.	
Hyæna vulgaris .	Not sacred.				
Spotted Hyæna, or *Crocuta*	Not sacred.				
Cat .	Sacred	{ Pasht or Bubastis	Bubastis	{ Cicero, Diodor., &c.; and sculptures.	} Thebes, &c.
Lion .	Sacred	{ Gom or Hercules	Leontopolis	{ Strabo, xvii. Diodor. i. 84. Porphyr. de Abst. iv. 9.	
Panther .	Not sacred			Sculptures.	
Leopard .	Not sacred				
Felis Chaus .	Not sacred.				
Order 5.					
RODENTIA.					
Mouse .	Not sacred			Sculptures. Plin. x. 65.	Thebes.
Rat .	Not sacred.				Thebes.
Dipus, or *Jerboa*	Not sacred.				
Porcupine .	Not sacred			Sculptures.	
Hare .	{ Not sacred. An emblem			Sculptures. Horapollo.	
Order 7.					
PACHYDERMATA.					
Elephant .	Not sacred			Sculptures.	
Hippopotamus .	{ Sacred Emblem of Typho	Mars	} Papremis	Herodot. ii. 71. Diodor., &c.	Thebes?

Pig	Emblem of Typho	•		Plut., Ælian, Herodot., &c. Plut. de Is. s. 8.	At Thebes?
Wild Boar	Not sacred	•			
Hyrax (Arab. *Wabber*)	Not sacred.				
Horse	Not sacred.	•		Sculptures, &c.	
Ass	Sacred to, or emblem of } Typho	•		Plutarch.	
Order 8.					
RUMINANTIA.					
Camel	Not sacred	•		*Vide suprà*, p. 234.	
Stag, or *Cervus Elaphus*	Not sacred	•		*Vide suprà*, p. 227.	
Camelopardalis, or Giraffe	Not sacred? perhaps an emblem			{ Sculptures at Hermonthis, &c.	
Gazelle	Not sacred?	•		•	
Antilope Addax?		•		•	
— *Defassa*		•			
Oryx Beisa	Not sacred	•		Sculptures.	
Oryx and Leucoryx	An emblem	of Pthah-Sokari-Osiris.	{ Thebes, &c.	Plin. ii. 40. Sculptures.	
Goat	Sacred	Mendes ?	{ Mendesian nome ?	{ Clem. Orat. Adhort. p. 17; and Strabo, xvii. Diodor. i. 84.	} Thebes, &c.
Ibex	Not sacred	•		Sculptures.	
Sheep, Ram	Sacred	•	{ Thebes and Saïs	{ Clem. Alex. Oratio Adhort., p. 17. Strabo, xvii. p. 559 and 552	
Kebsh, or *Ovis Tragelaphus*	Not sacred	•		Sculptures.	

Name.	If sacred.	To what Deity.	In what Place (particularly).	Where mentioned.	Where found embalmed.
RUMINANTIA—*continued.*					
Cow	Sacred	Athor		Sculptures	Thebes, &c.
The Sacred Bulls { Apis	Sacred	{ A God, and the type of Osiris	} Memphis	{ Plut. Herodot. Diodor. i. 84 and 21.	
Mnevis	Sacred	{ The Sun, or Apollo	} Heliopolis	{ Diodor. i. 84 and 21. Plut. s. 33.	
Basis, Bacchis	Sacred		Hermonthis	{ Macrob. Sat. i. 26. Strabo, xvii. Ælian, xii. 11.	
Onuphis	Sacred			Not represented.	
Buffalo	Not sacred			Sculptures.	
Indian or humped Ethiopian Ox	Not sacred ?				
Order 9.					
CETACEA.					
Dolphin	Not sacred			Strabo, xvii. Plin. & Seneca.	
FABULOUS ANIMALS.					
Sphinx { with Man's head, Hawk's head, Ram's head.				Sculptures. Clemens, &c.	
Other monsters				Sculptures.	

The principal Birds are—

Class II.—Aves.

Name.	Sacred to what Deity.	In what Place.	Where mentioned.	Where found embalmed.
Order 1.				
ACCIPITRES, or RAPTORES.				
Vultur Nubicus, or *Barbarus* (Arab. the *Nisser*)	Sacred to Eileithyia	At Eileithyias	Sculptures	Thebes.
V. percnopterus, Pharaoh's Hen (Arab. *Rákham*)	?	.	Sculptures.	
Eagle (Arab. *Okáb* or *Ogáb*)	Sacred?	In Thebes?	Strabo, xvii. Diodor. i. 87.	
Falco Aroeris? the sacred Hawk of Re	Sacred to Re, and other Deities	Heliopolis, and other towns	Diodor., Strabo, and others; and the sculptures	Thebes, &c.
F. tenunculoides, or small brown Hawk	?	.	Sculptures	Thebes.
Falco milvus (*F. cinereo-ferugineus*, Forsk., *F. arda* of Savigny), the Kite	Not sacred?	.	Sculptures	
Horned Owl, or *Bubo maximus*	Not sacred?	.	Sculptures	Thebes.
White Owl, or *Strix flammea*	?	.	Sculptures	Thebes.
Small Owl, or *Strix passerina*, Minerva's Owl	?	.	Sculptures.	

Name.	Sacred to what Deity.	In what Place.	Where mentioned.	Where found embalmed.
Order 2,				
INSESSORES, or PASSERINE.				
Lanius excubitor, Butcher Bird.	Not sacred .		Sculptures ?	
Motacilla, alba and *flava,* Wag-tail }	Not sacred .		Sculptures	Thebes.
Swallow	Not sacred .	·	Sculptures .	
Sparrow	Not sacred .	·	Horapollo, ii. 115.	
Raven, or *Corvus corax* .	Not sacred .	·	Sculptures.	
C. cornix, the Royston Crow	Not sacred .	·	Sculptures. Horapollo.	
Upupa epops . . .	Not sacred .		Sculptures. Horapollo.	
Turdus viscivorus, Thrush .	Not sacred .	·	Sculptures ?	
Alauda cristata, Crested Lark	Not sacred .	·	Sculptures ?	
Alauda arenaria, Sand Lark	Not sacred .	·	Sculptures ?	
Hirundo rustica, Swallow .	Not sacred .	·	Sculptures ?	
Alcedo Ispida, Kingfisher .	Not sacred .	·	Sculptures ?	
Alcedo Rutteis, id. of the Nile	Not sacred .	·	Sculptures ?	
Fringilla, several species .	Not sacred .	·	Sculptures ?	
Order 3.				
RASORES, or GALLINACEÆ,				
Fowls, Cocks . . .	White and saffron-coloured cocks sacrificed to Anubis	·	Plut. de Is. s. 61.	
Columba turtur, Turtle-dove .	Not sacred .	·	Sculptures.	
Columba domestica, Pigeon .	Not sacred .	·	Sculptures.	
Pterocles melanogaster (Arab. Gutta), Sand-grouse	Not sacred .	·	Sculptures ?	
Quail, *Perdix Coturnix* . .	Not sacred .	·	Sculptures.	
Ostrich, or *Struthio Camelus* .	Not sacred .	·	Sculptures.	
Otis Hebara, Ruffed Bustard .	Not sacred .	·	Sculptures ?	

Order 4.
GRALLATORIÆ.

Species		Locality	Authority	Localities
Charadrius Œdicnemus (*Trochilus?*), or *Me-lanocephalus*	Not sacred ·	·	Sculptures?	
—— *armatus*, Spurwinged	Not sacred?	·	Herodot. ii. 68.	
Plover · *cristatus*, Peewit	Not sacred ·	·	Sculptures?	
Ardea cinerea, Grey Heron	Not sacred?	·	Sculptures.	
Ardea garzetta, Little Egret, perhaps the *Benno*, which was	sacred to Osiris	·	Sculptures.	
Ardea minuta, small Bittern				
Ciconia alba, White Stork				
Grus cinerea, Common Crane, and some other species	Not sacred ·	·	Sculptures.	
Tantalus, or *Numenius Ibis*, or *Ibis religiosa*, Cuv.	Sacred to Thoth	Hermopolis ·	{ Herodot., Plato, &c.; and sculptures · · · }	{ Thebes, Memphis, Hermophis, Hermopolis, Abydus, &c. }
Ibis falcinellus, small Ibis	Not sacred ·	·	Sculptures?	
Plataleu leucorodia, Spoonbill	Not sacred ·	·	Sculptures.	
Scolopax gallinago, Snipe				
Fulica atra, Common Coot				
Phœnicopterus ruber, Flamingo				

Order 5.
NATATORES, or PALMIPEDES.

Species		Locality	Authority	Localities
Goose, or *Anser Ægyptius*, the *Chenalopex*, or *Vulpanser*	Emblem of Seb.	·	Herodot. ii. 72. Sculptures	Thebes.
Anas, various species of Ducks	Not sacred ·	·	Sculptures.	
Anas creca, Teal				
Pelicanus Onocrotulus	Not sacred? ·	·	Horapollo. Sculptures.	
Recurvirostra avosetta, Avoset	Not sacred ·	·	Sculptures.	

Name.	Sacred to what Deity.	In what Place.	Where mentioned.	Where found embalmed.
FABULOUS AND UNKNOWN BIRDS.				
Phœnix (perhaps the *Benno* ?	sacred to Osiris	.	Sculptures.	
The " Pure Soul " of the King (a bird with man's head and arms)	.	.	Sculptures.	
Emblem of the Soul .	.	.	Sculptures.	
Vulture with a Snake's head .	.	.	Sculptures.	
Hawk with Man's and Ram's head .	.	.	Sculptures.	
Class III.—Reptiles.				
CHELONIA. Order 1.				
Tortoise .	{ A tortoise head-ed God .	.	Sculptures.	
SAURIA. Order 2.				
Crocodile .	Sacred to Savak	The Arsinoïte nome and its capital, Crocodilopolis. Lake Mœris, Thebes, &c.	Herodot. Strabo, xvii. Diodor. i. 48. Sculptures, &c.	Thebes, Maabdeh, &c.

Waran el bahr, *Monitor of the Nile, Lacerta Nilotica* .	Not sacred?		Thebes.
Waran el ard, *Land Monitor, Lac. scincus* .	Not sacred?		
The *Dthobb,* or *Lac. Caudiverbera* .	Not sacred?		
Lac. Gecko, or *Boorse,* and many other of the Lizard tribe .	Not sacred?		
OPHIDIA. Order 3.			
Asp, *Coluber Haje,* or *Naja, Haje* .	Sacred to Neph and Ranno	Sculptures. Plut. s. 74, &c.	Thebes.
The common Snake of Egypt .	Not sacred?	Sculptures. {Herodot., and sculptures, &c.}	Thebes.
The *Coluber,* or *Vipera Cerastes,* the horned Snake .	Not sacred to Amun?	Thebes	
The small spotted Viper of Egypt, *Echis pavo?* .	Not sacred.		
Order 4.			
BATRACHIANS.			
Frog .	Emblem of Pthah?	Sculptures. Horapollo.	Thebes.
Toad .	Not sacred?		
FABULOUS REPTILES.			
Snakes { with Human head, Hawk's head, Lion's head. }		Sculptures.	

The Fish are noticed elsewhere; I shall therefore content myself with the names of those which were held sacred.

Class IV.—FISHES.

Name.	Sacred to what Deity.	In what Place.	Where mentioned.	Where found embalmed.
Oxyrhinchus . . .	Sacred . .	At Oxyrhinchus, &c.	Plut., Strabo. Sculptures	Several fish found embalmed at Thebes.
Phagrus, the Eel. .	Sacred . .	Among the Syenitæ, and at Phagrorio-polis	Clemens, Orat. Adhort. p. 17. Athenæus, Deipn. vii. Sculptures.	
Lepidotus . . .	Sacred . .	In most parts of Egypt.	Plut, &c. Sculptures.	
Latus . . .	Sacred . .	At Latopolis.	Strabo, xvii. Sculptures?	
Mæotes . . .	Sacred . .	At Elephantine .	Clemens Alex. Orat. Adhort. p. 17. Sculptures?	

Of the second division of the animal kingdom, the Mollusca, containing shellfish, nothing is known which connects any of them with the religion of Egypt: and of the third, or Articulata, the only one which appears to have been sacred to, or emblematic of, any Deity, is the Scorpion, in the third class, or ARACHNIDES.

Div. III.—ARTICULATA.

Class III.—ARACHNIDES.

Name.	Sacred to what Deity.	In what Place.	Where mentioned.	Where found embalmed.
Scorpion . . .	Emblem of the Goddess Selk .		Sculptures.	

Class IV.—Insects.

Name.	Sacred to what Deity.	In what Place.	Where mentioned.	Where found embalmed.
COLEOPTERA. Scarabæus, and probably different genera and species of Beetles . . .	Sacred to the Sun and to Pthah, and adopted as an emblem of the world, and sometimes also of Hor-Hat.	·	Horapollo. Sculptures,&c. (The modern Nubians, confounding those who venerated it with the scarabæus itself, have called it a *Káfer*, "infidel.")	Thebes.
HYMENOPTERA. Bees . . . Wasps . . . Ichneumons . . .	Not sacred? . .	·	Sculptures.	
DIPTERA. Flies . . .	Not sacred	·	Sculptures, and in pottery.	Thebes.

Locusts, butterflies, moths, and other insects, are represented in the sculptures ; but none appear to claim the honour of being sacred.

Some fabulous insects may also be cited, as well as fabulous quadrupeds, which were chiefly emblems appropriated to particular gods, or representative of certain ideas connected with religion, the most remarkable of which were scarabæi with the heads of hawks, rams, and cows. Of these, many are found made of pottery, stone, and other materials, and the sculptures represent the beetle with a human head. Such changes did not render them less fit emblems of the gods: the Scarabæus of the Sun appears with the head of a ram as well as a hawk ; and the god Pthah was sometimes figured with the body of a scarabæus, and the head and legs of his usual human form.

Among the Vegetables of Egypt, the following were sacred, or connected with religion:—

Name.	Sacred to what Deity.	In what Place.	Where mentioned.	Where found embalmed.
The Persea	Sacred to Athor . .	•	Sculptures.	
Peach?	(Supposed to be sacred to Harpocrates.)	•	Plut. de Is. s. 68.	
Pomegranate, Vine, and Acanthus	Used for sacred purposes	•	Athen. xv. 680. Sculp.	
Sycomore Fig . . .	Sacred to Netpe . .	•	Sculptures.	
Tamarisk	Sacred to Osiris . .	•	Plut. s. 15, 21. Sculp.	
Lotus. Perhaps the modern name Nufar may be related to Nofr, the epithet "good" attached to the god	(Emblem of the God Nofr Atmoo?, and connected with Har-pocrates.)	•	{Sculptures and Ancient Authors.	
Garlick		•		
Onion	Not sacred . . .	•	{Plin. xix. 6; Juvenal, Sat. xv.	
Leek		•		
Palm-branch . . .	{Symbol of Astrology, and type of a year.}	•	{Clem. Strom. 6; Hora-pollo, &c.	
Melilotus? . . .		•	Plut. s. 38.	
Papyrus		•	Sculptures & Anc. Auth.	
Ivy?		•	Plut. s. 37. Diodor. i. 17.	
Periploca Secamone? .	Sacred? to Osiris . .	•	Sculptures?	

Many of these were conspicuous among the offerings made to the gods.

The most remarkable emblems, independent of the types of the deities, were the signs of, 1, Life; 2, 3, of Goodness; 4, of Power (or of Purity); 5, of Majesty and Dominion (the flail and crook of Osiris); 6, of Authority; 7, 8, 9, 10, of Royalty; 11, of Stability; which were principally connected with the gods and kings.

1   2   3   4   5   6   7   8   9   10   11
258.   Emblems of Life, Goodness, Purity, Royalty, and Stability.

Many others belonged to religious ceremonies; a long list of which may be seen in the chamber of Osiris at Philæ, and in the coronation ceremony at Medeenet Haboo.

The sign of Life (*tau*, or crux ansata) is held by the gods in one hand, and the sceptre of Power (or Purity) generally in the other. The lotus was always a favourite symbol; the palm branch was the sign of "the year;" and a frog with the young palm leaf, as it springs from the date stone, rising from its back, was the type of man in embryo. The eye of Osiris was sometimes a representation of "Egypt," (*see page* 244;) and was placed at the head of their boats; and numerous other emblems occur

259.

in the sacred subjects represented on the monuments. Among flowers, two frequently occur, the papyrus head and another water plant, which were the emblems of Lower and Upper Egypt.

Flowers were presented in different ways; either loosely, tied together by the stalks,* or in carefully formed bouquets, without any other gifts.   Sometimes those of a particular kind were offered alone; the most esteemed being the lotus, papyrus, convolvulus, and other favourite productions of the garden: and a bouquet of peculiar form was occasionally presented,† or two smaller ones, carried in each of the donor's hands.‡

* Woodcut 260.   † Woodcut 260, *fig.* 12.   ‡ Woodcut 260, *fig.* 13.

260.   **Various flowers from the sculptures.**   *Thebes.*

In fig. 8 is an attempt at perspective. The upper part (*a*) appears to be the papyrus; *b* is a lotus; and *c* probably the melilotus. From fig. 1 *a*, it would seem that one bell-formed flower is a convolvulus; though 1 *b*, 4, 6, 7, and 9 *a*, may be the papyrus; and the shafts of columns with that kind of capital have an indication of the triangular form of its stalk. 3. The lotus. 2, 11, 12, 13. Different bouquets. 10. A flower from an ornamental cornice. 5. Perhaps the same as 4. *See* Flowers in Chapter VI.

Chaplets and wreaths of flowers were also laid upon the altars, and offered to the deities, whose statues were frequently crowned with them.   In the selection of them, as of herbs and roots, those most grateful, or useful, to man, were chosen as most acceptable to the gods; and it was probably the utility, rather than the flavour, that induced them to show a marked preference for the onion, the *Raphanus*, and cucurbitaceous plants, which so generally found a place amongst the offerings.

Of fruits, the sycamore, fig, and grapes were the most esteemed for the service of the altar. They were presented on baskets or trays, frequently covered with leaves to keep them fresh ; and sometimes the former were represented placed in such a manner, on an open basket, as to resemble the hieroglyphic signifying " *wife*."*

Ointment often formed part of a large donation, and always entered into the list of those things which constituted a complete set of offerings. It was placed before the deity in vases of alabaster or other materials ; the name of the god to whom it was vowed being frequently engraved upon the vase that contained it. Sometimes the king, or priest, took out a certain portion to anoint the statue of the deity, which was done with the little finger of the right hand.

261.

Ointment was presented in different ways, according to the ceremony performed in honour of the gods; and the various kinds of sweet-scented ointments used by the Egyptians were liberally offered at every shrine. According to Clemens, the *psagdæ* of Egypt were among the most noted; and Pliny and Athenæus both bear testimony to the variety of Egyptian ointments, as well as the importance attached to them; which is confirmed by the sculptures, and even by the vases discovered in the tombs.

* Woodcut 284, *figs.* 1, 2, 3, 4.

Rich vestments, necklaces, bracelets, jewellery of various kinds, and other ornaments, vases of gold, silver, and porcelain, bags of gold, and numerous gifts of the most costly description, were also presented to the gods. They constituted the riches of the treasury of the temples; and the spoils taken from conquered nations were deposited there by a victorious monarch, as a votive gift for the success of his arms, or as a token of gratitude for favours already received. Tables of the precious metals, and rare woods, were among the offerings; and an accurate catalogue of his votive presents was engraved on the walls of the temple, to commemorate the piety of the donor, and the wealth of the sanctuary. They do not, however, properly come under the denomination of offerings to the gods, but are rather dedications to their temples; and it was in presenting them that some of the grand processions took place.

But it was not only customary to deposit the necklaces and other "precious gifts" collectively in the temple; the kings frequently offered each singly to the gods, decorating their statues with them, and placing them on their altars.

They also presented numerous emblems, connected with the vows they had made, the favours they desired, or the thanksgivings they returned to the gods: among which the most usual were a small figure of Truth; the symbol of the assemblies

262.   "He gives Truth (or Justice) to his father." (fig. 1); the cow of Athor (2); the hawk-headed necklace of Sokari (3); a cynocephalus (4); parts of dress? (5); ointment (6); gold and silver in bags, or in rings (7 a and b); three feathers, or heads of reeds, the emblem of a field (8); a scribe's tablet and ink-stand (9 a and b); a garland or wreath (10); and an emblem of pyramidal form, perhaps a particular kind of "white" cake (11).

Thanksgivings for the birth of a child, escape from danger, or other marks of divine favour, were offered by individuals through the medium of the priests. The same was also done in private; and secret as well as public vows were made in the hope of future

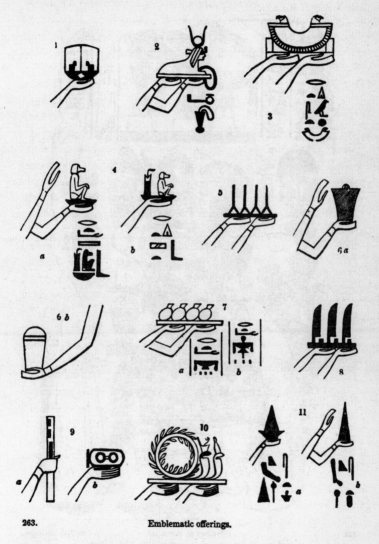

263.   Emblematic offerings.

favours. The quality of these oblations depended on the god
to whom presented, or the occupation of the donor; a shepherd

264.   Offerings on the Altar.   *British Museum.*

1, 2, 3. Vases of ointment, &c., on stands crowned with lotus flowers.
4. Bouquets of lotus and other flowers presented by the son of the deceased.
5. Table of offerings; the most remarkable of which are cakes, grapes, figs, fore leg and head of a victim, two hearts, a goose, lotus flowers, and cucumbers or gourds.
6. Four vases on stands, with their mouths closed with ears of corn; over them is a wreath of leaves.
7. The person of the tomb seated.

bringing from his flocks, a husbandman from his fields, and others according to their means; provided the offering was not forbidden by the rites of the deity.

Though the Egyptians considered certain oblations suited to particular gods, others inadmissible to their temples, and some more peculiarly adapted to prescribed periods of the year, the greater part of the deities were invoked with the same offerings; the most usual of which were fruit, flowers, vegetables, ointment, incense, grain, wine, milk, beer, oil, cakes, and the sacrifice of animals and birds. These last were either offered whole, with the feathers, or plucked and trussed; and when presented alone, they were some-

265.　Stands for bearing offerings.

times placed upon a portable stand, furnished with spikes, over which the bird was laid.

The bronze instruments with long curved spikes, found in the Etruscan tombs, were probably intended for a similar purpose; though they were once thought to be for torturing Christian martyrs.

Even oxen and other animals were sometimes offered entire, though generally after the head had been taken off; and it does not appear that this depended on any particular ceremony.

In slaying a victim, the Egyptians suffered the blood to flow upon the ground, or over the altar, if placed upon it; and the mode of cutting it up appears to have been the same as when killed for the table. The head was first taken off; and, after the skin had been removed, they generally cut off the right leg and shoulder, and the other legs and parts in succession; which, if required for the table, were placed on trays, and carried to the kitchen, or if intended for sacrifice, were deposited on the altar, with fruit, cakes, and other offerings.

The joints, and parts, most readily distinguished in the sculptures, are the head, the fore leg (fig. 1), with the shoulder (which was styled *sapt*, " the chosen part ;") the upper joint of the hind

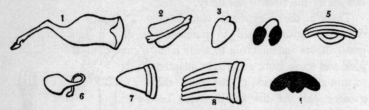

266.   Different joints placed on the altars or the tables.   *Thebes*

leg (2), the kidneys (4), the ribs (5 and 8), the heart (3), and the rump (6) ; and those most commonly seen on the altars are the head, the leg, and the ribs. When the Egyptians offered a holocaust, they commenced with a libation of wine, a preliminary ceremony common, according to Herodotus, to all their sacrifices ; and, after it had been poured upon the altar, the victim was slain. They first removed the head and skin (a statement, as I have already shown, fully confirmed by the sculptures) ; they then took out the stomach, leaving only the entrails and the fat ; after which the thighs, the upper part of the haunches, the shoulders, and the neck, were cut off in succession. Then, filling the body with cakes of pure flour, honey, dried raisins, figs, incense, myrrh, and other odoriferous substances, they burnt it on the fire, pouring over it a considerable quantity of oil. The portions which were not consumed were afterwards given to the votaries, who were present on the occasion, no part of the offering being left ; and it was during the ceremony of burning the sacrifice at the fête of Isis, that they beat themselves in honour of Osiris.

The ordinary subjects, in the interior of the temples, represent the king presenting offerings to the deities worshipped there ; the most remarkable of which are the sacrifices already mentioned, incense, libation, and several emblematic figures or devices connected with religion. He sometimes made an appropriate offering to the presiding deity of the sanctuary, and to each of the contemplar gods, as Diodorus says Osymandyas was represented to have done; the memorial of which act of piety was preserved in the sculptures of his tomb.

Incense was presented to all the gods, and introduced on every grand occasion when a *complete* oblation was made. For they sometimes merely offered a libation of wine, oil, and other liquids, or a single gift, a necklace, a bouquet of flowers, or whatever they had vowed. Incense was also presented alone, though more usually accompanied by a libation of wine. It consisted of various ingredients, according to circumstances; and in offerings to the sun, Plutarch says that resin, myrrh, and a mixture of sixteen ingredients, called *kuphi*, were adapted to different times of the day.

In offering incense, the king held in one hand the censer, and with the other threw balls or pastiles of incense into the flame.

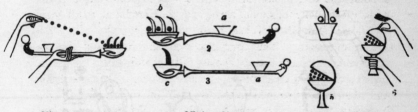

267.   Offering of incense.

Then, addressing the God, before whose statue he stood, with a suitable prayer, to invoke his aid and favour, he begged him to accept the incense he presented : in return for which the deity granted him " a long, pure, and happy life," with other favours accorded by the gods to men.

A libation of wine was frequently offered, together with incense; or two censers of incense, with several oxen, birds, and other consecrated gifts. And that it was customary to present several of the same kind is shown by the ordinary formula of presentation, which says, " I give you a thousand (*i.e.* many) cakes, a thousand vases of wine, a thousand head of oxen, a thousand geese, a thousand vestments, a thousand censers of

268. Offering of incense
and a libation.

incense, a thousand libations, a thousand boxes of ointment."
The cakes were of various kinds. Many were round, oval, or
triangular; and others had the edges folded over, like the
fateereh of the present day. They also assumed the shape of
leaves, or the form of an animal, a crocodile's head, or some
capricious figure; and it was frequently customary to sprinkle
them (particularly the round and oval cakes) with seeds.

Wine was presented in two cups. It was not then a libation,
but merely an offering of wine; and since the pouring out of wine
upon the altar was a preliminary ceremony, as Herodotus observes, common to all their sacrifices, we find that the king is
often represented making a libation upon an altar covered with
offerings of cakes, flowers, and the joints of a victim killed for the
occasion.

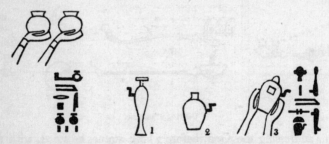

269. Wine HPII offered in two cups.   270. Vases used for libations.

Two kinds of vases were principally used for libations; but
that used on grand occasions, and carried in procession by the
Prophet, or by the king, was of long shape, with the usual spout
(fig. 1).

The various kinds of wine were indicated by the names af-
fixed to them. White and red wines, those of the Upper and
Lower Country, grape juice or wine of the vineyard (one of the
most delicious beverages of a hot climate,
and one which is commonly used in Spain
and other countries at the present day),
were the most noted.

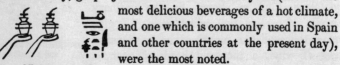

271. Offering
of milk, ⲉⲡⲱϯ.

Beer and milk, as well as oils of various

kinds, for which Egypt was famous, were also common among the offerings.

No people had greater delight in ceremonies and religious pomp than the Egyptians; and grand processions constantly took place, to commemorate some legendary tale connected with superstition. Nor was this tendency of the Egyptian mind neglected by the priesthood; whose influence was greatly increased by the importance of the post they held on those occasions: there was no ceremony in which they did not participate; and even military regulations were subject to their influence.

One of the most important ceremonies was " the procession of

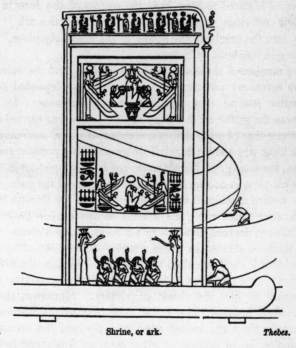

271a.   Shrine, or ark.   *Thebes.*

shrines," which is mentioned in the Rosetta Stone, and is frequently represented on the walls of the temples. The shrines were of two kinds: the one a sort of canopy; the other an ark or sacred boat, which may be termed the great shrine. This was carried with grand pomp by the priests, a certain number being selected for that duty, who, supporting it on their shoulders by means of long staves, passing through metal rings at the side of the sledge on which it stood, brought it into the temple, where it was placed upon a stand or table, in order that the prescribed ceremonies might be performed before it.

The stand was also carried in the procession by another set of priests, following the shrine, by means of similar staves; a method usually adopted for transporting large statues, and sacred emblems, too heavy or too important to be borne by one person. The same is stated to have been the custom of the Jews in some of their religious processions, as in carrying the ark " to its place, into the oracle of the house, to the most holy place," when the temple was built by Solomon.

The number of shrines in these processions, and the splendour of the ceremony performed on the occasion, depended on the particular festival they intended to commemorate. In many instances the shrine of the deity of the temple was carried alone, sometimes that of other deities accompanied it, and sometimes that of the king was added; a privilege granted as a peculiar mark of esteem, for some great benefit conferred by him upon his country, or for his piety in having beautified the temples of the gods. Such is the motive mentioned in the description of the Rosetta Stone; which, after enumerating the benefits conferred upon the country by Ptolemy, decrees, as a return for them, " that a statue of the king shall be erected in every temple, in the most conspicuous place; that it shall be called the statue of Ptolemy, the defender of Egypt; and that near it shall be placed the presiding deity, presenting to him the shield of victory. Moreover, that the priests shall minister three times every day to the statues, and prepare for them the sacred dress, and perform the accustomed ceremonies, as in honour of other gods at feasts and festivals. That there shall be erected an image, and *golden shrine*, of King Ptolemy, in the most honourable of the temples, to be set up in the sanctuary among the other shrines; and that on the great festivals, when the *procession of shrines* takes place, that of the god Epiphanes shall accompany them; ten royal golden crowns being deposited upon the shrine, with an asp attached to each; and the (double) crown *Pshent*, which he wore at his coronation, placed in the midst." (*See the Pshent, in Woodcut* 258, *fig.* 10.)

It was also usual to carry this statue of the principal Deity, in whose honour the procession took place, together with that of the king, and the figures of his ancestors, borne in the same manner on men's shoulders; like the Gods of Babylon mentioned by Jeremiah.

Diodorus speaks of an Ethiopian festival of Jupiter, when his statue was carried in procession, probably to commemorate the supposed refuge of the gods in that country; which may have been a memorial of the flight of the Egyptians with their gods, at the time of the Shepherd invasion, mentioned by Josephus on the authority of Manetho. Diodorus also says, " Homer derived from Egypt his story of the embraces of Jupiter and Juno, and their travelling into Ethiopia, because the Egyptians every year carry Jupiter's shrine over the river into Africa, and a few days after bring it back again, as if the gods had returned out of Ethiopia. The fiction of their nuptials was taken from the solemnization of these festivals; at which time both their shrines, adorned with all sorts of flowers, are carried by the priests to the top of a mountain."

The usual number of priests, who performed the duty of bearers, was generally twelve or sixteen, to each shrine. They were accompanied by another of a superior grade, distinguished by a lock of hair pendent on one side of his head, and clad in a leopard skin, the peculiar badge of his rank, who, walking near them, gave directions respecting the procession, its position in the temple, and whatever else was required during the ceremony; which agrees well with the remark of Herodotus, that " each deity had many priests, and one high priest." Sometimes two priests of the same peculiar grade attended, both during the

procession, and after the shrine had been deposited in the temple.
These were the Pontiffs, or highest order of priests: they had
the title of " Sem," and enjoyed the privilege of offering sacrifices on all grand occasions.

When the shrine reached the temple, it was received with
every demonstration of respect by the officiating priest, who was
appointed to do duty upon the day of the festival; and if the
king happened to be there, it was his privilege to perform the
appointed ceremonies.   These consisted of sacrifices and prayers;
and the shrine was decked with fresh-gathered flowers and rich
garlands.   An endless profusion of offerings was placed before
it, on several separate altars; and the king, frequently accompanied by his queen, who held a sistrum in one hand, and in the
other a bouquet of flowers made up into the particular form required for these religious ceremonies, presented incense and
libation. This part of the ceremony being finished, the king
proceeded to the presence of the god (represented by his statue),
from whom he was supposed to receive a blessing, typified by the
sacred *tau*, the sign of Life. Sometimes the principal contemplar deity was also present, usually the second member of the
triad of the place; and it is probable that the position of the

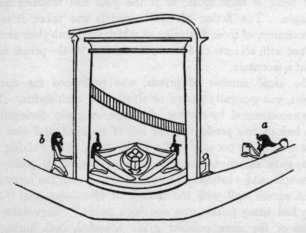

272. One of the sacred boats or arks, with two figures resembling Cherubim. *a* and
b represent the king; the former under the shape of a sphinx.

statue was near to the shrine, alluded to in the inscription of the Rosetta Stone.

Some of the sacred boats, or arks, contained the emblems of life and stability, which, when the veil was drawn aside, were partially seen; others, the figure of the Divine Spirit, Nef, or Nou; and some presented the sacred beetle of the sun, overshadowed by the wings of two figures of the goddess Thmei or Truth, which call to mind the cherubim of the Jews. (*Woodcut* 272.)

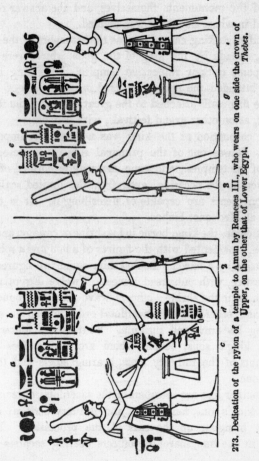

273. Dedication of the pylon of a temple to Amun by Remeses III., who wears on one side the crown of Upper, on the other that of Lower Egypt.

The dedication of the whole or part of a temple was, as may be reasonably supposed, one of the most remarkable solemnities, at which the king presided. And if the actual celebration of the rites practised on the occasion, the laying of the foundation stone, or other ceremonies connected with it, are not represented on the monuments, the importance attached to it is shown by the conspicuous manner in which it is recorded in the sculptures, the ostentation with which it is announced in the dedicatory inscriptions of the monuments themselves, and the answer returned by the god in whose honour it was erected.

Another striking ceremony was the transport of the dedicatory offerings made by the king to the gods, which were carried in great pomp to their respective temples. The king and all the priests attended the procession, clad in their robes of ceremony: and the flag-staffs attached to the great towers of the façade were decked, as on other grand festivals, with banners.

The coronation of the king was a peculiarly imposing ceremony. It was one of the principal subjects represented in the court of the temples; and some idea may be formed of the pomp displayed on the occasion, even from the limited scale on which the monuments are capable of describing it. It is thus represented at Medeenet Haboo.

First comes the king, borne in his shrine or canopy, and seated on a throne, ornamented with the figures of a lion and a sphinx, which is preceded by a hawk. Behind him stand two figures of Truth and Justice, with outspread wings. Twelve Egyptian princes, his sons, bear the shrine; officers wave flabella around the monarch; and others, of the sacerdotal order, attend on either side, carrying his arms and insignia. Four others follow; then six of the king's sons, behind whom are two scribes and eight attendants of the military class, bearing stools and the steps of the throne.

In another line are members of the sacerdotal order, four others of the king's sons, fan-bearers, and military scribes; a guard of soldiers bringing up the rear of the procession. Before the shrine, in one line, march six officers bearing sceptres and other insignia; in another a scribe reads aloud the contents of a scroll he holds unfolded in his hand, preceded by two of the king's sons, and two distinguished persons of the military and priestly orders.   The rear of both these lines is closed by a pontiff, who, turning round towards the shrine, burns incense before the monarch; and a band of music, composed of the trumpet, drum, double-pipe, and other instruments, with choristers, forms the van of the procession.

The king, alighted from his throne, officiates as priest before the statue of Amun-Khem, or Amun-Re *generator;* and, still wearing his helmet, he presents libations and incense before the altar, which is loaded with flowers, and other suitable offerings. The statue of the god, attended by officers bearing flabella, is carried on a palanquin, covered with rich drapery, by twenty-two priests; behind it follow others, bringing the table and the altar of the deity.   Before the statue is the sacred bull, followed by the king on foot, wearing the cap of the " Lower country." Apart from the procession itself stands the queen, as a spectator of the ceremony; and before her, a scribe reads a scroll he has unfolded.   A priest turns round to offer incense to the white bull; and another, clapping his hands, brings up the rear of a long procession of *hieraphori*, carrying standards, images, and other sacred emblems; and the foremost bear the statue of the king's ancestors.

This part of the picture refers to the *coronation* of the king, who, in the hieroglyphics, is said to have " put on the crown of the Upper and Lower countries;" which the birds, flying to the four sides of the world, are to announce to the gods of the south, north, east, and west.

In the next compartment, the president of the assembly reads a long invocation, the contents of which are contained in the hieroglyphic inscription above; and the six ears of corn which the king, once more wearing his helmet, has cut with a golden sickle, are held out by a priest towards the deity.   The white bull and images of the king's ancestors are deposited in his temple, in the presence of Amun-Khem, the queen still witnessing the ceremony, which is concluded by an offering of incense and libation, made by Remeses to the statue of the god.

Clemens gives an account of an Egyptian procession; which, as it throws some light on similar ceremonies, and is of interest from having some points of resemblance with the one before us, I here transcribe.

"In the solemn pomps of Egypt the singer generally goes first, bearing one of the symbols of music. They say it is his duty to carry two of the books of Hermes; one of which contains hymns of the gods, the other precepts relating to the life of the king. The singer is followed by the Horoscopus, bearing in his hand the measure of time (hour-glass) and the palm (branch), the symbols of astrology (astronomy), whose duty it is to be versed in (or recite) the four books of Hermes, which treat of that science. Of these, one describes the position of the fixed stars, another the conjunctions (eclipses) and illuminations of the sun and moon, and the others their risings. Next comes the Hierogrammat (or sacred scribe), having feathers on his head, and in his hands a book (papyrus), with a ruler (palette) in which is ink, and a reed for writing. It is his duty to understand what are called hieroglyphics, the description of the world, geography, the course of the sun, moon, and planets, the condition of the land of Egypt and the Nile, the nature of the instruments or sacred ornaments, and the places appointed for them, as well as weights and measures, and the things used in holy rites. Then follows the *Stolistes*, or 'dresser,' bearing the cubit of justice and the cup of libation. He knows all subjects relating to education, and the choice of calves for victims, which are comprehended in ten books. These treat of the honours paid to the gods, and of the Egyptian religion, including sacrifice, first fruits, hymns, prayers, processions, holydays, and the like. Last of all comes the prophet, who carries in his bosom a water jar, followed by persons bearing loaves of bread. He presides over all sacred things, and is obliged to know the contents of the ten books called sacerdotal, relating to the gods, the laws, and all the discipline of the priests."

One of the principal solemnities connected with the coronation was the anointing of the king, and his receiving the emblems of majesty from the gods. The sculptures represent the deities themselves officiating on this as on other similar occasions, in order to convey to the Egyptian people, who beheld these records, a more exalted notion of the special favours bestowed on their monarch.

We, however, who at this distant period are less interested in the direct intercourse between the Pharaohs and the gods, may be satisfied with a more simple interpretation of such subjects, and conclude that it was the priests who performed the ceremony, and bestowed upon the prince the title of " the anointed of the gods."

With the Egyptians, as with the Jews, the investiture to any sacred office, as that of king or priest, was confirmed by this external sign ; and as the Jewish lawgiver mentions the ceremony of pouring oil upon the head of the high priest *after* he had put on his entire dress, with the mitre and crown, the Egyptians represent the anointing of their priests and kings *after* they were attired in their full robes, with the cap and crown upon their head.   Some of the sculptures introduce a priest pouring oil over the monarch, in the presence of Thoth, Hor-Hat, Seth, and Nilus ; which may be considered a representation of the ceremony, before the statues of those gods.   The functionary who officiated was the high priest, or prophet, clad in a leopard skin ; the same who attended on all occasions which required him to assist, or assume the duties of, the monarch in the temple.

There was also the ceremony of anointing the statues of the gods, which was done with the little finger of the right hand ; and another, of pouring from two vases, alternate emblems of life and purity, over the king, in token of purification, previous to his admittance into the presence of the god of the temple. This was performed by Thoth on one side, and the hawk-headed Hor-Hat on the other; sometimes by Hor-Hat and Seth, or by two hawk-headed deities, or by one of these last and the god Nilus.   The deities Seth and Horus are also represented placing the crown of the two countries upon the head of the king, saying "Put this cap upon your head like your father Amun-Re:" and the palm branches they hold in their hands allude to the long series of years they grant him to rule over his country. The emblems of Dominion and Majesty, the crook and flagellum of Osiris, have been already given him, and the asp-formed fillet is bound upon his head.

Another mode of investing the sovereign with the diadem is figured on the apex of some obelisks, and on other monuments, where the god, in whose honour they were raised, puts the crown

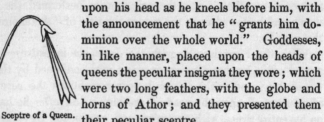

upon his head as he kneels before him, with the announcement that he "grants him dominion over the whole world." Goddesses, in like manner, placed upon the heads of queens the peculiar insignia they wore; which were two long feathers, with the globe and horns of Athor; and they presented them their peculiar sceptre.

274.   Sceptre of a Queen.

The custom of anointing was not confined to the appointment of kings and priests to the sacred offices they held: it was the ordinary token of welcome to guests in every party at the house of a friend; and in Egypt, no less than in Judæa, the metaphorical expression, "anointed with the oil of gladness," was fully understood, and applied to the ordinary occurrences of life. It was not confined to the living; the dead were made to participate in it, as if sensible of the token of esteem thus bestowed upon them; and a grateful survivor, in giving an affectionate token of gratitude to a regretted friend, neglected not this last unction of his mortal remains. Even the head of the bandaged mummy, and the case which contained it, were anointed with oils and the most precious ointments.

Another ceremony, represented in the temples, was the blessing bestowed by the gods on the king, at the moment of his assuming the reins of government. They laid their hands upon him; and, presenting him with the symbol of life, they promised that his reign should be long and glorious, and that he should enjoy tranquillity, with certain victory over his enemies. If about to undertake an expedition against foreign nations, they gave him the falchion of victory, to secure the defeat of the people whose country he was about to invade, saying, "Take this weapon, and smite with it the heads of the impure Gentiles."

To show the special favour he enjoyed from heaven, the gods were even represented admitting him into their company and communing with him; and sometimes Thoth, with other deities, taking him by the hand, led him into the presence of the great Triad, or of the presiding divinity, of the temple. He was welcomed with suitable expressions of approbation; and on this, as on other occasions, the sacred *tau*, or sign of life, was presented to him,—a symbol which, with the sceptre of purity, was usually placed in the hands of the gods. These two were deemed the greatest gifts bestowed by the deity on man.

The origin of the *tau* I cannot precisely determine; but this curious fact is connected with it in later times,—that the early Christians of Egypt adopted it in lieu of the cross, which was afterwards substituted for it, prefixing it to inscriptions in the same manner as the cross in later times; and numerous inscriptions headed by the *tau* are preserved to the present day in early Christian sepulchres at the Great Oasis.

275.   Tau, or Sign of Life.

The triumph of the king was a grand solemnity. Flattering to the national pride of the Egyptians, it awakened those feelings of enthusiasm which the celebration of victory naturally inspires, and led them to commemorate it with the greatest pomp. When the victorious monarch, returning to Egypt after a glorious campaign, approached the cities which lay on his way, from the confines of the country to the capital, the inhabitants flocked to meet him, and with welcome acclamations greeted his arrival and the success of his arms. The priests and chief people of each place advanced with garlands and bouquets of flowers; the principal person present addressed him in an appropriate speech; and as the troops defiled through the streets, or passed without the walls, the people followed with acclamations, uttering earnest thanksgivings to the gods, the protectors of Egypt, and praying them for ever to continue the same marks of favour to their monarch and their nation.

Arrived at the capital, they went immediately to the temple, where they returned thanks to the gods, and performed the customary sacrifices on this important occasion. The whole army attended, and the order of march continued the same as on entering the city. A corps of Egyptians, consisting of chariots and infantry, led the van in close column, followed by the allies of the different nations, who had shared the dangers of the field and the honour of victory. In the centre marched the body guards, the king's sons, the military scribes, the royal arm-bearers, and the staff corps, in the midst of whom was the monarch himself, mounted in a splendid car, attended by his fan-bearers on foot, bearing over him the state flabella. Next followed other regiments of infantry, with their respective banners; and the rear was closed by a body of chariots. The prisoners, tied together with ropes, were conducted by some of the king's sons, or by the chief officers of the staff, at the side of the royal car. The king himself frequently held the cord which bound them, as he drove slowly in the procession; and two or more chiefs were sometimes suspended beneath the axle of his chariot, contrary to the usual humane principles of the Egyptians, who seem to have refrained from unnecessary cruelty to their captives, extending this feeling so far as to rescue, even in the heat of battle, a defenceless enemy from a watery grave.

Having reached the precincts of the temple, the guards and royal attendants selected to be the representatives of the whole army entered the courts, the rest of the troops, too numerous for admission, being drawn up before the entrance; and the king, alighting from his car, prepared to lead his captives to the shrine of the god. Military bands played the favourite airs of the country; and the numerous standards of the different regiments, the banners floating in the wind, the bright lustre of arms, the immense concourse of people, and the grandeur of the lofty towers of the temple, decked with their bright-coloured flags streaming above the cornice, presented an imposing scene. But the most striking feature of this pompous ceremony was the brilliant cortége of the monarch, who was either borne in his chair of state by the principal officers of state under a rich canopy, or walked on foot, overshadowed with rich flabella and fans of waving plumes. As he approached the inner gateway, a long procession of priests advanced to meet him, dressed in their robes of office; censers full of incense were burnt before him; and a sacred scribe read from a papyrus roll the glorious deeds of the victorious monarch, and the tokens he had received of the divine favour. They then accompanied him into the presence of the presiding deity of the place; and having performed sacrifice, and offered suitable thanksgivings, he dedicated the spoil of the conquered enemy, and expressed his gratitude for the privilege of laying before the feet of the god, the giver of victory, those prisoners he had brought to the vestibule of the divine abode.

In the mean time, the troops without the sacred precincts were summoned by sound of trumpet, to attend the sacrifice prepared by the priests, in the name of the whole army, for the benefits they had received from the gods, the success of their arms, and their own preservation in the hour of danger. Each regiment marched up by turn to the altar, temporarily raised for the occasion, to the sound of the drum, the soldiers carrying in their hand a twig of olive, with the arms of their respective corps; but the heavy-armed soldier laid aside his shield on this occasion, as if to show the security he enjoyed in the presence of the deity. An ox was then killed; and wine, incense, and the customary offerings of cakes, fruit, vegetables, joints of meat, and birds, were presented to the god. Every soldier deposited the twig of olive he carried at the altar; and as the trumpet summoned them, so also it gave the signal for each regiment to withdraw, and cede its place to another. The ceremony being

over, the king went in state to his palace, accompanied by the
troops; and having distributed rewards to them, and eulogised
their conduct in the field, he gave his orders to the commanders
of the different corps, and they withdrew to their cantonments, or
to the duties to which they were appointed.

Of the fixed festivals, one of the most remarkable was the celebration of the grand assemblies, or panegyries, held in the great
halls of the principal temples, at which the king presided in
person. That they were of the greatest importance is abundantly
proved by the frequent mention of them in the sculptures; and
that the post of president of the assemblies was the highest possible honour may be inferred, as well from its being enjoyed by
the sovereign alone of all men, as from its being assigned to the

deity himself in these legends: " Phrah
(Pharaoh), lord of the panegyries, like
Re," or " like his father Pthah;" which
so frequently occur on the monuments of
Thebes and Memphis.

Their celebration was fixed to certain
periods of the year; as were the festivals
of the new moons, and those recorded in
the great calendar, sculptured on the exterior of the S.W. wall of Medeenet Haboo, which took place during several successive days of each month, and were even
repeated in honour of different deities every day during some
months, and attended by the king in person.

Another important religious ceremony is often alluded to in
the sculptures, which appears to be connected with the assemblies
just mentioned. In this the king is represented running, with a
vase or some emblem in one hand, and the flagellum of Osiris, a
type of majesty, in the other, as if hastening to enter the hall
where the panegyries were held; and two figures of him are
frequently introduced, one crowned with the cap of the Upper,
the other with that of the Lower country, as they stand beneath
a canopy indicative of the hall of assembly. The same deities,

who usually preside on the anointing of the king, present him with the sign of life, and bear before him the palm branch, on which the years of the assemblies are noted. Before him stands the goddess Milt, bearing on her head the water-plants, her emblem; and around are numerous emblems appropriated to this subject. The monarch sometimes runs into the presence of the god bearing two vases, which appears to be the commencement of, or connected with, this ceremony; and the whole may be the anniversary of the foundation of the temple, or of the sovereign's reign. An ox (or cow) is in some instances represented running with the king, on the same occasion.

The birthdays of the kings were celebrated with great pomp. They were looked upon as holy; no business was done upon them; and all classes indulged in the festivities suitable to the occasion. Every Egyptian attached much importance to the day, and even to the hour of his birth; and it is probable that, as in Persia, each individual kept his birthday with great rejoicings, welcoming his friends with all the amusements of society, and a more than usual profusion of the delicacies of the table.

They had many other public holydays, when the court of the king and all public offices were closed. This was sometimes owing to a superstitious belief of their being unlucky; and such was the prejudice against the "third day of the Epact, the birthday of Typho, that the sovereign neither transacted any business upon it, nor even suffered himself to take any refreshment till the evening." Other fasts were also observed by the king and the priesthood, out of respect to certain solemn purifications they deemed it their duty to undergo for the service of religion.

Among the ordinary rites the most noted, because the most frequent, were the daily sacrifices offered in the temple by the sovereign pontiff. It was customary for him to attend there early every morning, after he had examined and settled his epistolary correspondence relative to the affairs of state; and the service began by the high priest reading a prayer for the welfare of the monarch, in the presence of the people.

Of the anniversary festivals one of the most remarkable was

the Niloa, or invocation of the blessings of the inundation, offered
to the tutelary deity of the Nile. According to Heliodorus, it
was one of the principal festivals of the Egyptians. It took
place about the summer solstice, when the river began to rise;
and the anxiety with which they looked forward to a plentiful
inundation induced them to celebrate it with more than usual
honour. Libanius asserts that these rites were deemed of so
much importance by the Egyptians, that unless they were performed at the proper season, and in a becoming manner, by the
persons appointed to this duty, they felt persuaded that the Nile
would refuse to rise and inundate the land. Their full belief in
the efficacy of the ceremony, secured its annual performance on a
grand scale. Men and women assembled from all parts of the
country in the towns of their respective nomes, grand festivities
were proclaimed, and all the enjoyments of the table were united
with the solemnity of a holy festival. Music, the dance, and appropriate hymns, marked the respect they felt for the deity;
and a wooden statue of the river god was carried by the priests
through the villages in solemn procession, that all might appear
to be honoured by his presence, while invoking the blessings
he was about to confer.

Another festival, particularly welcomed by the Egyptian peasants, and looked upon as a day of great rejoicing, was (if it may
be so called) the harvest home, or the close of the labours of the
year, and the preparation of the land for its future crops by the
inundation; when, as Diodorus tells us, the husbandmen indulged
in recreations of every kind, and showed their gratitude for the
benefits the deity had conferred upon them by the blessings of
the inundation. This, and other festivals of the peasantry, I
shall notice in treating of the agriculture of Egypt.*

Games were also celebrated in honour of certain gods, in
which wrestling and other gymnastic exercises were practised.

The investiture of a chief was a ceremony of considerable importance, when the post conferred was connected with any high dignity

* In chap. vi.

about the person of the monarch, in the army, or the priesthood. It took place in the presence of the sovereign seated on his throne; and two priests, having arrayed the candidate in a long loose vesture, placed necklaces round his neck. One of these ceremonies frequently occurs in the monuments, which was sometimes performed immediately after a victory; in which case we may conclude that the honour was granted in return for distinguished services in the field: and as the individual, on all occasions, holds the flabella, crook, and other insignia of the office of fan-bearer, it appears to have been either the appointment to that post, or to some high command in the army.

A similar mode of investiture appears to have been adopted in all appointments to the high offices of state, both of a civil and military kind. In this, as in many customs detailed in the sculptures, we find an interesting illustration of a ceremony mentioned in the Bible, which describes Pharaoh taking a ring from his hand and putting it on Joseph's hand, arraying him in vestures of fine linen, and putting a gold chain about his neck.

In a tomb, opened at Thebes by Mr. Hoskins, another instance occurs of this investiture to the post of fan-bearer; in which the two attendants, or inferior priests, are engaged in clothing him with the robes of his new office. One puts on the necklace, the other arranges his dress, a fillet being already bound round his head; and he appears to wear *gloves* upon his uplifted hands. In the next part of the same picture (for, as is often the case, it presents two actions and two periods of time) the individual holding the insignia of fan-bearer, and followed by the two priests, presents himself before the king, who holds forth his hand to him to touch, or perhaps to kiss.

The office of fan-bearer to the king was a highly honourable post, which none but the royal princes, or the sons of the first nobility, were permitted to hold. These constituted a principal part of his staff; and in the field they either attended on the monarch to receive his orders, or were despatched to take the command of a division; some having the rank of generals of cavalry, others of heavy infantry or archers, according to the service to which they belonged. They had the privilege of presenting the prisoners to the king, after the victory had been gained, announcing at the same time the amount of the enemy's slain, and the booty that had been taken; and those, whose turn it was to attend upon the king's person, as soon as the enemy had been vanquished, resigned their command to the next in rank, and returned to their post of fan-bearers. The office was divided into two grades,—the one serving on the right, the other on the left, hand of the king; the most honourable post being given to those of the highest rank, or to those most esteemed for their services. A certain number were always on duty; and they were required to attend during the grand solemnities of the temple, and on every occasion when the monarch went out in state, or transacted public business at home.

At Medeenet Haboo is a remarkable instance of the ceremony of carrying the sacred boat of Pthah-Sokari-Osiris, which may represent the funeral of Osiris. It is frequently introduced in the sculptures; and in one of the tombs of Thebes this solemnity occurs, which, though on a smaller scale than on the walls of Medeenet Haboo, offers some interesting peculiarities. First comes the boat, carried as usual by several priests, superintended by the pontiff, clad in a leopard skin; after which two *hieraphori*, each bearing a long staff, surmounted by a hawk; then a man beating the tambourine, behind whom is a flower with the stalk bound round with ivy (or the periploca, which so much resembles it). These are followed by two *hieraphori* (or bearers of holy emblems), carrying each a staff with a jackal on the top, and another carrying a flower; behind whom is a priest turning round to offer incense to the emblem of Nofre-Atmoo. The latter is placed horizontally upon six columns, between each of which stands a human figure, with uplifted arms, either in the act of adoration, or aiding to support the sacred emblem; and behind it is an image of the king kneeling; the whole borne on the usual staves by several priests, attended by a pontiff in his leopard-skin dress. In this ceremony, as in some of the tales related of Osiris, we may trace those analogies which led the

Greeks to suggest the resemblance between that deity and their Bacchus; as the tambourine, the ivy-bound flower or thyrsus, and the leopard skin, which last recalls the leopards that drew his car. The spotted skin of the nebris, or fawn, may also be traced in that suspended near Osiris in the region of Amenti.

At Medeenet Haboo the procession is on a more splendid scale: the ark of Sokari is borne by sixteen priests, accompanied by two pontiffs, one clad in the usual leopard skin; and Remeses himself officiates on the occasion. The king also performs the singular ceremony of holding a rope at its centre, the two ends being supported by four priests, eight of his sons, and four other chiefs; before whom two priests turn round to offer incense, while a sacred scribe reads the contents of a papyrus he holds in his hands. These are preceded by one of the *hieraphori* bearing the hawk on a staff decked with banners (the standard of the king, or of Horus), and by the emblem of Nofre-Atmoo, borne by eighteen priests, the figures standing between the columns, over which it is laid, being of kings, and the columns themselves being surmounted by the heads of hawks.

In the same ceremony at Medeenet Haboo, it appears that the king, when holding the rope, has the cubit in his hand, and, when following the ark, the cup of libation; which calls to mind the office of the Stolistes mentioned by Clemens, " having in his hand the cubit of justice, and the cup of libation;" and he, in like manner, is preceded by the sacred scribe.

The mode of carrying the sacred arks on poles borne by priests, or by the nobles of the land, was extended to the statues of the gods, and other sacred objects belonging to the temples. The former, as Macrobius states, were frequently placed in a case or canopy; and the same writer is correct in stating that the chief people of the nome assisted in this service, even the sons of the king being proud of so honourable an employment. What he afterwards says of their " being carried forward according to divine inspiration, whithersoever the deity urges them, and not by their own will," cannot fail to call to mind the supposed dictation of a secret influence, by which the bearers of the dead, in the funeral processions of modern Egypt, pretend to be actuated. To such an extent do they carry this superstitious belief of their ancestors, that I have seen them in their solemn march suddenly stop, and then run violently through the streets, at the risk of throwing the body off the bier, pretending that they were obliged, by the irresistible will of the deceased, to visit a certain mosk, or seek the blessing of a particular saint.

Few other processions of any great importance are represented in the sculptures; nor can it be expected that the monuments would give more than a small proportion of the numerous festivals, or ceremonies, which took place in the country.

Many of the religious festivals were indicative of some peculiar attribute or supposed property of the deity in whose honour they were celebrated. One, mentioned by Herodotus, was emblematic of the generative principle, and the same that appears to be alluded to by Plutarch under the name of Paamylia, which he says bore a resemblance to one of the Greek ceremonies. The assertion, however, of these writers, that such figures belonged to Osiris, is contradicted by the sculptures, which show them to have been emblematic of the god Khem, or Pan; and this is confirmed by another observation of the latter writer, that the leaf of the fig-tree represented the deity of that festival, as well as the land of Egypt. The tree does indeed represent Egypt, and always occurs on the altar of Khem; but it is not in any way connected with Osiris, and the statues mentioned by Plutarch evidently refer to the Egyptian Pan.

According to Herodotus, the only two festivals, in which it was lawful to sacrifice pigs, were those of the Moon and Bacchus (or Osiris): the reason of which restriction he attributes to a sacred reason, which he does not think it right to mention. " In sacrificing a pig to the Moon, they killed it; and when they had put together the end of the tail, the spleen, and the caul, and covered them with all the fat from the inside of the animal, they burnt them; the rest of the victim being eaten on the day of the full Moon, which was the same on which the sacrifice was offered, for on no other day were they allowed to eat the flesh of the pig. Poor people who had barely the means of subsistence made a paste figure of a pig, which being baked, they offered as a sacrifice." The same kind of substitute was, doubtless, made for other victims, by those who could not afford to purchase them: and some of the small glass and clay figures of animals found in the tombs, have probably served for this purpose. " On the fête of Bacchus, every one immolated a pig before the door of his house, at the hour of dinner; he then gave it back to the person of whom it had been bought." " The Egyptians," adds the historian, " celebrate the rest of this fête nearly in the same manner as the Greeks, with the exception of the sacrifice of pigs."

The procession on this occasion was headed, as usual, by music, a flute-player, according to Herodotus, leading the van; and the first sacred emblem they carried was a *hydria*, or water-pitcher. A festival was also held on the 17th of Athyr, and three succeeding days, in honour of Osiris, during which they exposed to view a gilded ox, the emblem of that deity; and commemorated what they called the " *loss of Osiris*." Another followed in honour of the same deity, after an interval of six months, or 179 days, " upon the 19th of Pachon; when they marched in procession towards the sea-side, whither, likewise, the priest and other proper officers carried the sacred chest, inclosing a small boat or vessel of gold, into which they first poured some fresh water, and then all present cried out with a loud voice, ' Osiris is found.' This ceremony being ended, they threw a little fresh mould, together with rich odours and spices, into the water, mixing the whole mass together, and working it up into a little image in the shape of a crescent. The image was afterwards dressed and adorned with a proper habit; and the whole was intended to intimate that they looked upon these gods as the essence and power of Earth and Water."

Another festival in honour of Osiris was held " on the new Moon of the month Phamenoth, which fell in the beginning of spring, called the entrance of Osiris into the Moon;" and on the 11th of Tybi (or the beginning of January) was celebrated the fête of Isis's return from Phœnicia, when cakes, having a hippopotamus bound stamped upon them, were offered in her honour, to commemorate the victory over Typho. A certain rite was also performed in connection with the fabulous history of Osiris, in which it was customary to throw a cord in the midst of the assembly and then chop it to pieces; the supposed purport of which was to record the desertion of Thueris, the concubine of Typho, and her delivery from a serpent, which the soldiers killed with their swords as it pursued her in her flight to join the army of Horus.

Among the ceremonies connected with Osiris, the fête of Apis holds a conspicuous place.

For Osiris was also worshipped under the form of Apis, the Sacred Bull of Memphis, or as a human figure with a bull's head, accompanied by the name "Apis-Osiris." According to Plutarch, " Apis was a fair and beautiful image of the Soul of Osiris ;" and the same author tells us that " Mnevis, the Sacred Ox of Heliopolis, was also dedicated to Osiris, and honoured by the Egyptians with a reverence next to that paid to Apis, whose sire some pretend him to be." This agrees with the statement of Diodorus, who says, Apis and Mnevis were both sacred to Osiris, and worshipped as gods throughout the whole of Egypt; and Plutarch suggests that, from these well-known representations of Osiris, the people of Elis and Argos derived the idea of Bacchus with an ox's head; Bacchus being reputed to be the same as Osiris. Herodotus, in describing him, says, "Apis, also called Epaphus, is a young bull, whose mother can have no other offspring, and who is reported by the Egyptians to conceive from lightning sent rom heaven, and thus to produce the god Apis. He is known by certain marks: his hair is black; on his forehead is a white triangular spot, on his back an eagle, and a beetle under his tongue, and the hair of his tail is double." Ovid represents him of various colours. Strabo says his forehead and some parts of his body are of a white colour, the rest being black; " by which signs they fix upon a new one to succeed the other, when he dies;" and Plutarch thinks that, "on account of the great resemblance they imagine between Osiris and the Moon, his more bright and shining parts being shadowed and obscured by those that are of a darker hue, they call the Apis the living image of Osiris, and suppose him begotten by a ray of generative light, flowing from the moon, and fixing upon his mother, at a time when she was strongly disposed for it."

Pliny speaks of Apis "having a white spot in the form of a crescent upon his right side, and a lump under his tongue in the form of a beetle." Ammianus Marcellinus says the white crescent on his right side was the principal sign, and Ælian mentions twenty-nine marks, by which he was recognized, each referable to some mystic signification. But he pretends that the Egyptians did not allow those given by Herodotus and Aristagoras. Some suppose him entirely black; and others contend that certain marks, as the predominating black colour, and the beetle on his tongue, show him to be consecrated to the sun, as the crescent to the moon. Ammianus and others say that "Apis was sacred to the Moon, Mnevis to the Sun;" and most authors describe the latter of a black colour.

It is difficult to decide if Herodotus is correct respecting the peculiar marks of Apis. There is, however, evidence from the bronzes, found in Egypt, that the vulture (not eagle) on his

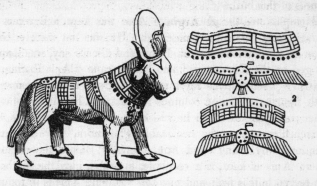

277.   *In the possession of Miss Rogers.*
     1. Bronze figure of Apis.   2. The marks on his back.

back was one of his characteristics, supplied, no doubt, like many others, by the priests themselves; who probably put him to much inconvenience, and pain too, to make the marks and hairs conform to his description.

To Apis belonged all the clean oxen, chosen for sacrifice; the necessary requisite for which, according to Herodotus, was, that they should be entirely free from black spots, or even a single black hair; though, as I shall have occasion to remark in treating of the sacrifices, this statement of the historian is far from accurate. It may also be doubted if the name Epaphus, by which he says Apis was called by the Greeks in their language, was of Greek origin.

He is called in the hieroglyphic legends Hapi; and the bull, the demonstrative and figurative sign following his name, is accompanied by the *crux ansata*, or emblem of life. It has

278.   Hieroglyphical name of Apis.

seldom any ornament on its head; but the figure of Apis-(or Hapi-)Osiris generally wears the globe of the sun, and the Asp, the symbol of divine majesty; which are also given to the bronze figures of this bull.

Memphis was the place where Apis was kept, and where his worship was particularly observed. He was not merely looked upon as an emblem, but, as Pliny and Cicero say, was deemed "a god by the Egyptians:" and Strabo calls "Apis the same as Osiris." Psammaticus there erected a grand court (ornamented with figures in lieu of columns 12 cubits in height, forming an inner peristyle), in which he was kept when exhibited in public. Attached to it were the two stables ("delubra," or "thalami"), mentioned by Pliny: and Strabo says, "Before the enclosure where Apis is kept, is a vestibule, in which also the mother of the sacred bull is fed; and into this vestibule Apis is introduced, in order to be shown to strangers. After being brought out for a little while, he is again taken back; at other times he is only seen through a window." "The temple of Apis is close to that of Vulcan; which last is remarkable for its architectural beauty, its extent, and the richness of its decoration."

The festival in honour of Apis lasted seven days; on which occasion a large concourse of people assembled at Memphis. The priests then led the sacred bull in solemn procession, all people coming forward from their houses to welcome him as he passed; and Pliny and Solinus affirm, that children who smelt his breath were thought to be thereby gifted with the power of predicting future events.

Diodorus derives the worship of Apis from the belief of "the soul of Osiris having migrated into this animal, who was thus supposed to manifest himself to man through successive ages; though some report that the members of Osiris, when killed by Typho, having been deposited in a wooden ox, enveloped in byssine cloths, gave the name to the city of Busiris, and established its worship there."

When the Apis died, certain priests, chosen for this duty, went in quest of another, who was known from the signs mentioned in the sacred books. As soon as he was found, they took him to the city of the Nile, preparatory to his removal to Memphis, where he was kept 40 days; during which period women alone were permitted to see him. These 40 days being completed, he was placed in a boat, with a golden cabin prepared to receive him, and he was conducted in state upon the Nile to Memphis.

Pliny and Ammianus, however, declare that they led the bull Apis to the fountain of the priests, and drowned him with much ceremony, as soon as the time prescribed in the sacred books was fulfilled. This Plutarch limits to 25 years ("the square of five, and the same number as the letters of the Egyptian alphabet"), beyond which it was forbidden that he should live; and having put him to death, they sought another to succeed him. His body was embalmed, and a grand funeral procession took place at Memphis, when his coffin, "placed on a sledge, was followed by the priests," "dressed in the spotted skins of fawns (leopards), bearing the thyrsus in their hands, uttering the same cries, and making the same gesticulations as the votaries of Bacchus during the ceremonies in honour of that god."

When the Apis died a natural death, his obsequies were celebrated on the most magnificent scale; and to such extravagance was this carried, that those who had the office of taking charge of him were often ruined by the heavy expenses entailed upon them. On one occasion, during the reign of the first Ptolemy, upwards of 50 talents were borrowed to defray the necessary cost of his funeral; "and in our time," says Diodorus, "the curators of other sacred animals have expended 100 talents in their burial."

As soon as he was buried, permission was given to the priests to enter the temple of Sarapis, though previously forbidden during the whole festival.

The burial-place of the Apis bulls has lately been discovered by M. Mariette, near Memphis. It consists of an arched gallery hewn in the rock, about 20 feet in height and breadth, and 2000 feet in length (besides a lateral gallery). On each side is a series of chambers, or recesses, which might be called sepulchral *stalls;* every one containing a large sarcophagus of granite, 15 feet by 8, in which the body of a sacred bull was deposited; and when visited by Mr. Harris (in March, 1852) 30 sarcophagi had been already found. One only had an inscription, with the blank oval of a king; but on the walls were several tablets, and fragments of others lay on the ground, containing dedications to Apis, in behalf of some person deceased; one with the name of Amasis, and another of Ptolemaïc time. Mention was also made of the birth, death, and burial of the bulls. They mostly lived 17 to 20 years (25 being the prescribed limit of their life), so that the 30 would only go back to about the beginning of the 26th dynasty. Many more have, therefore, to be discovered.

Before this is a paved road, with lions ranged on each side, about 8 feet high, which forms the approach; and before this again is a temple, supposed to be the Sarapeum, with a sort of vestibule; and at the door-way, between these two, are, on

either side, a crouched lion and a tablet, on one of which king
Nectanebo, followed by a priest of Apis-Osiris (Sarapis?), is
represented making an offering; and in the upper line are eight
deities, with an altar before them—Amunra, Maut, Khons,
Horus, Athor, Mandoo (Month), Khem, and Osiris.　In the
vestibule are statues of 11 divinities, of Greek form (one of whom
is Jupiter), seated in a half circle.　These are of Greek or
Roman time; but near the spot have been found the names of
Amyrtæus, and of some late unknown Egyptian kings; and that
of the second Remeses on the surface of the ground above.

From whatever cause the death of Apis took place, the people
performed a public lamentation, as if Osiris himself had died: and
this mourning lasted until the other Apis, his successor, had been
found.　They then commenced the rejoicings, which were celebrated with an enthusiasm equal to the grief exhibited during the
previous mourning.

Of the discovery of a new Apis, Ælian gives the following
account:—" As soon as a report is circulated that the Egyptian
god has manifested himself, certain of the sacred scribes, well
versed in the mystical marks, known to them by tradition, approach the spot where the divine cow has deposited her calf, and
then (following the ancient ordonnance of Hermes) feed him with
milk during four months, in a house facing the rising sun.　When
this period has passed, the sacred scribes and prophets resort to
the dwelling of Apis, at the time of the new moon, and placing
him in a boat prepared for the purpose, convey him to Memphis,
where he has a convenient and agreeable abode, with pleasure
grounds, and ample space for wholesome exercise.　Female companions of his own species are provided for him, the most beautiful that can be found, kept in apartments, to which he has access
when he wishes.　He drinks out of a well or fountain of clear
water; for it is not thought right to give him the water of the
Nile, which is considered too fattening.

" It would be tedious to relate what pompous processions and
sacred ceremonies the Egyptians perform, on the celebration of
the rising of the Nile, at the fête of the Theophania, in honour

of this god, or what dances, festivities, and joyful assemblies are appointed on the occasion, in the towns and in the country." He then says, " the man from whose herd the divine beast has sprung, is the happiest of mortals, and is looked upon with admiration by all people; " which refutes his previous statement respecting the divine cow: and the assertions of other writers, as well as probability, show that it was not the mother which was *chosen to produce* a calf with particular marks, but that the Apis was selected from its having them. The honour conferred on the cow which bore it was retrospective, being given her *after* the Apis with its proper marks " had been found " by the priests; and this is consistent with the respect paid to the possessor of the favoured herd, in which the sacred bull had been discovered. " Apis," continues the naturalist, " is an excellent interpretation of futurity. He does not employ virgins, or old women, sitting on a tripod, like some other gods, nor require that they should be intoxicated with the sacred potion; but inspires boys, who play around his stable, with a divine impulse, enabling them to pour out predictions in perfect rhythm."

The Egyptians not only paid divine honours to the bull Apis, but, considering him the living image and representative of Osiris, they consulted him as an oracle, and drew from his actions good or bad omens. They were in the habit of offering him any kind of food with the hand: if he took it, the answer was considered favourable; if he refused, it was thought to be a sinister omen. Pliny and Ammianus observe, that he refused what the unfortunate Germanicus presented to him; and the death of that prince, which happened shortly after, was thought to confirm most unequivocally the truth of those presages. The Egyptians also drew omens respecting the welfare of their country, according to the stable in which he happened to be. To these two stables he had free access; and when he spontaneously entered one, it foreboded benefits to Egypt, as the other the reverse; and many other tokens were derived from accidental circumstances connected with this sacred animal.

Pausanias says, that those who wished to consult Apis first

burnt incense on an altar, filling the lamps with oil which were lighted there, and depositing a piece of money on the altar to the right of the statue of the god.   Then placing their mouth near his ear, in order to consult him, they asked whatever question they wished.   This done, they withdrew, covering their two ears until they were outside the sacred precincts of the temple; and there listening to the first expression any one uttered, they drew from it the desired omen.

Children, also, according to Pliny and Solinus, who attended in great numbers during the processions in honour of the divine bull, received the gift of foretelling future events; and the same authors mention a superstitious belief at Memphis, of the influence of Apis upon the Crocodile, during the seven days when his birth was celebrated.   On this occasion, a gold and silver patera was annually thrown into the Nile, at a spot called from its form the "Bottle;" and while this festival was held, no one was in danger of being attacked by crocodiles, though bathing carelessly in the river.   But it could no longer be done with impunity after the sixth hour of the eighth day.   The hostility of that animal to man was then observed invariably to return, as if permitted by the deity to resume its habits.

Apis was usually kept in one or other of the two stables— seldom going out, except into the court attached to them, where strangers came to visit him.   But on certain occasions he was conducted through the town with great pomp.   He was then escorted by numerous guards, who made a way amidst the crowd, and prevented the approach of the profane; and a chorus of children singing hymns in his honour headed the procession.

The greatest attention was paid to the health of Apis; they took care to obtain for him the most wholesome food; and they rejoiced if they could preserve his life to the full extent prescribed by law.   Plutarch also notices his being forbidden to drink the water of the Nile, in consequence of its having a peculiarly fattening property.   "For," he adds, "they endeavour to prevent fatness, as well in Apis, as in themselves; always studious that their bodies may sit as light about their souls as possible, in order that their mortal part may not oppress and weigh down the more divine and immortal."

Many fêtes were held at different seasons of the year; for, as Herodotus observes, far from being contented with one festival, the Egyptians celebrate annually a very great number: of which that of Diana (Pasht), kept at the city of Bubastis, holds the first rank, and is performed with the greatest pomp. Next to it is that of Isis, at Busiris, a city situated in the middle of the Delta, with a very large temple, consecrated to that Goddess, the Ceres of the Greeks. The third in importance is the fête of Minerva (Neith), held at Saïs; the fourth, of the Sun, at Heliopolis; the fifth, of Latona in the city of Buto; and the sixth is that performed at Papremis, in honour of Mars.

In going to celebrate the festival of Diana at Bubastis, it was customary to repair thither by water; and parties of men and women were crowded together on that occasion in numerous boats, without distinction of age or sex. During the whole of the journey, several women played on *crotala* (clappers) and some men on the flute; others accompanying them with the voice and the clapping of hands, as was usual at musical parties in Egypt. Whenever they approached a town, the boats were brought near to it; and while the singing continued, some of the women, in the most abusive manner, scoffed at those on the shore as they passed by.

Arrived at Bubastis, they performed the rites of the festival, oy the sacrifice of a great number of victims; and the quantity of wine consumed on the occasion was said to be more than during all the rest of the year. The number of persons present was reckoned by the inhabitants of the place to be 700,000, without including children; and it is probable that the appearance presented by this concourse of people, the scenes which occurred, and the picturesque groups they presented, were not altogether unlike those witnessed at the modern fêtes of Tanta and Dessook in the Delta, in honour of the Sayd el Beddawee, and Shekh Ibrahim e' Dessookee.

The number stated by the historian is beyond all probability, notwithstanding the population of ancient Egypt; and cannot fail to call to mind the 70,000 pilgrims, reported by the Moslems to be annually present at Mekkeh; whose explanation of the mode adopted, for keeping up that exact number, is very ingenious; every deficiency being supplied by a mysterious complement of angels, obligingly presenting themselves for the purpose; and some contrivance of the kind may have suggested itself to the ancient Egyptians, at the festival of Bubastis.

The fête of Isis was performed with great magnificence. The votaries of the Goddess prepared themselves beforehand by fastings .and prayers, after which they proceeded to sacrifice an ox. When slain, the thighs and upper part of the haunches, the shoulders, and neck were cut off; and the body was filled with unleavened cakes of pure flour, with honey, dried raisins, figs, incense, myrrh, and other odorific substances. It was then burnt, and a quantity of oil was poured on the fire during the process. In the mean time those present scourged themselves in honour of Osiris, uttering lamentations around the burnt offering; and this part of the ceremony being concluded, they partook of the remains of the sacrifice.

This festival was celebrated at Busiris, to commemorate the death of Osiris, who was reported to have been buried there, as well as in other places, and whose tomb gave the name to the city. It was probably on this occasion that the branch of absinthium, mentioned by Pliny, was carried by the priests of Isis; and dogs were made to head the procession, to commemorate the recovery of his body.

Another festival of Isis was held at harvest time, when the Egyptians throughout the country offered the first-fruits of the earth, and with doleful lamentations presented them at her altar. On this occasion she seems to answer to the Ceres of the Greeks, (as has been observed by Herodotus); and the multiplicity of names she bore may account for the different capacities in which she was worshipped, and remove the difficulty any change appears to present in the wife and sister of Osiris. One similarity is observable between this last and the fête celebrated at Busiris

—that the votaries presented their offerings in the guise of mourners ; and the first-fruits had probably a direct reference to Osiris, in connection with one of those allegories which represented him as the beneficent property of the Nile.

The festival of Minerva at Saïs was performed on a particular night, when every one, who intended to be present at the sacrifice, was required to light a number of lamps in the open air around his house. They were small vases filled with salt and oil, on which a wick floated, and being lighted continued to burn all night. They called it the Festival of Burning Lamps. It was not observed at Saïs alone : every Egyptian who could not attend in person was required to observe the ceremony of lighting lamps, in whatever part of the country he happened to be ; and it was considered of the greatest consequence to do honour to the deity, by the proper performance of this rite.

On the sacred lake of Saïs they represented, probably on the same occasion, the allegorical history of Osiris, which the Egyptians deemed the most solemn mystery of their religion, and which Herodotus always mentions with great caution.

The lake of Saïs still exists, near the modern town of Sa-el-Hagar ; and the walls and ruins of the town stand high above the level of the plain.

Those who went to Heliopolis, and to Buto, merely offered sacrifices. At Papremis the rites were much the same as in other places ; but when the Sun went down, a body of priests made certain gestures about the statue of Mars, while others, in greater numbers, armed with sticks, took up a position at the entrance of the temple. A numerous crowd of persons, amounting to upwards of 1000 men, armed with sticks, then presented themselves with a view of performing their vows ; but no sooner did the priests proceed to draw forward the statue, which had been placed in a small wooden gilded shrine, upon a four-wheeled car, than they were opposed by those in the vestibule, who endeavoured to prevent their entrance into the temple. Each party attacked its opponents with sticks ; when an affray ensued, which, as Herodotus observes, must, in spite of all the assertions of the Egyptians to the contrary, have been frequently attended with serious consequences, and even with loss of life.

Another festival, mentioned by Herodotus, is said to have been founded on a mysterious story of King Rhampsinitus, of which he witnessed the celebration.

On that occasion the priests chose one of their number, whom they dressed in a peculiar robe, made for the purpose on the very day of the ceremony, and then conducted, with his eyes bound, to a road leading to the temple of Ceres. Having left him there, they all retired ; and two wolves were said to direct his steps to the temple, a distance of twenty stades (2 to 2¼ miles), and afterwards to reconduct him to the same spot.

On the 19th of the first month was celebrated the fête of Thoth, from whom that month took its name. It was usual for those who attended " to eat honey and eggs, saying to each other, ' *How sweet a thing is truth!* ' " And a similar allegorical custom was observed in Mesoré, the last month of the Egyptian year, when, on " offering the first-fruits of their lentils, they exclaimed ' The tongue is fortune, the tongue is God ! ' "

Most of their fêtes appear to have been celebrated at the new or the full moon, the former being also chosen by the Israelites for the same purpose ; and this, as well as a month being represented in hieroglyphics by a moon, may serve to show that the months of the Egyptians were originally lunar ; as in many countries, to the present day.

The historian of Halicarnassus speaks of an annual ceremony, which the Egyptians informed him was performed at Saïs, in memory of the daughter of Mycerinus.

But this was evidently connected with the rites of Osiris ; and if Herodotus is correct in stating that it was a heifer (and not an ox), it may have been the emblem of Athor, in the capacity she held in the regions of the dead. The honours paid to it on such an occasion could not have referred solely to a princess, whose body was deposited within it : they were evidently intended for the Deity of whom it was the emblem ; and the introduction of Athor, with the mysterious rites of Osiris, may be explained by the fact of her frequently assuming the character of Isis.

Plutarch, who seems to have in view the same ceremony, states the animal exposed to public view on this occasion was an ox, in commemoration of the misfortunes reported to have happened to Osiris. "About this time (the month of Athyr, when the Etesian winds have ceased to blow, and the Nile, returning to its own channel, has left the country everywhere bare and naked), in consequence of the increasing length of the nights, the power of darkness appears to prevail, whilst that of light is diminished and overcome. The priests, therefore, practise certain doleful rites ; one of which is to expose to public view, as a proper representation of the present grief of the goddess (Isis), an ox covered with a pall of the finest black linen, that animal being looked upon as the living image of Osiris. The ceremony is performed four days successively, beginning on the 17th of the above-mentioned month. They represent thereby four things which they mourn :—1. The falling of the Nile and its retiring within its own channel : 2. The ceasing of the northern winds, which are now quite suppressed by the prevailing strength of those from the south : 3. The length of the nights and the decrease of the days : 4. The destitute condition in which the land now appears, naked and desolate, its trees despoiled of their leaves. Thus they commemorate what they call the ' loss of Osiris ;' and on the 19th of the month (Pachons?) another festi· val represents the ' finding of Osiris.' "

Small tablets in the tombs sometimes represent a black bull, bearing the corpse of a man to its final abode in the regions of the dead. The name of this bull is shown by the sculptures in the Oasis to be Apis, the type of Osiris; it is therefore not unreasonable to suppose it, in some way, related to this fable.

There were several festivals in honour of Re, or the Sun. Plutarch states that a sacrifice was performed to him, on the fourth day of every month, as related in the books of the genealogy of Horus, by whom that custom was said to have been instituted ; and so great was the veneration paid to the Sun, that they burnt incense to him three times a day—resin at his " first rising, myrrh when in the meridian, and a mixture called kuphi" at the time of setting.　The principal worship of Re was at Heliopolis, of which he was the presiding deity; and every city had certain holy days peculiarly consecrated to its patron, besides those common to the whole country.

Another festival in honour of the Sun was held on the 30th day of Epiphi, called the birth-day of Horus's eyes, when the Sun and Moon were in the same right line with the earth; and " on the 22d day of Phaophi, after the autumnal equinox, was a similar one, to which, according to Plutarch, they gave the name of ' the nativity of the staves of the Sun:' intimating that the Sun was then removing from the earth; and as its light became weaker and weaker, that it stood in need of a staff to support it.　In reference to which notion," he adds, " about the winter solstice, they lead the sacred Cow seven times in procession around her temple ; calling this the searching after Osiris, that season of the year standing most in need of the Sun's warmth."

Clemens mentions the custom of carrying four golden figures in the festivals of the gods.　They were, two dogs, a hawk, and an ibis, which, like the number four, had a mysterious meaning. The dogs represented the Hemispheres, the hawk the Sun, and the ibis the Moon ; but he does not state if this was usual at all festivals, or confined to those in honour of particular deities.

In their religious solemnities music was permitted, and even required, as acceptable to the gods ; except, if we may believe Strabo, in the temple of Osiris, at Abydus.　It probably differed much from that used on ordinary festive occasions, and was, according to Apuleius, of a lugubrious character.　But this I have already mentioned in treating of the music of the Egyptians.*

* Chapter ii. p. 129.

G. The Pyramids, during the Inundation, from near the Fork of the Delta.

CHAPTER V.

ORIGIN OF THE EGYPTIANS — POPULATION OF EGYPT AND OF THE WORLD OF OLD — HISTORY — THE KING — PRINCES — PRIESTS — THEIR SYSTEM — RELIGION — GODS — TRIADS — DRESSES AND MODE OF LIFE OF THE PRIESTS — SOLDIERS — ARMS — CHARIOTS — SHIPS AND NAVY — ENEMIES OF EGYPT — CONQUESTS.

HAVING mentioned those customs particularly connected with the private life of the Egyptians, I proceed to notice their early history, government, and institutions; as well as the occupations of the different classes of the community.

The origin of the Egyptians is enveloped in the same obscurity as that of most people; but they were undoubtedly from Asia; as is proved by the form of the skull, which is that of a Caucasian race, by their features, hair, and other evidences; and the whole valley of the Nile throughout Ethiopia, all Abyssinia, and the coast to the south, were peopled by Asiatic immigrations. Nor are the Kafirs a Negro race. Pliny is therefore right in saying that the people on the banks of the Nile, south of Syene, were Arabs (or a Semitic race) "who also founded Heliopolis."

At the period of the colonization of Egypt, the aboriginal population was doubtless small, and the change in the peculiarities of the new comers was proportionably slight; little variation being observable in the form of the skull from the Caucasian original. Still there was a change: and a modification in character as well as conformation must occur, in a greater or less degree, whenever a mixture of races has taken place.

I may even venture to suggest that while the present races in

Europe are all traceable to an Asiatic origin, they must there have found at the period of their immigration an indigenous population, which, though small, had its influence upon them. And this conclusion is confirmed by the fact, that while in N. America the people who have become its new inhabitants are (as they always will continue to be) essentially European, the Europeans are decidedly not Asiatics, and differ entirely from them in character, habits, and appearance. The difference between all Europeans and the Asiatics is as palpable, as the identity of the new American race and their European ancestors; and this is readily explained by the Asiatic tribes who peopled Europe having mixed with the indigenous races of our continent, while the Europeans who colonised America have kept themselves distinct from the aborigines. It is not necessary that the primitive Europeans should, as some have thought, be traceable in the Basques, or any other people, and the absorption of all of them is rather to be expected after so many ages.

The Egyptians probably came to the Valley of the Nile as conquerors. Their advance was through Lower Egypt southwards; and the extraordinary notion that they descended, and derived their civilisation, from Ethiopia has long since been exploded. Equally obsolete is the idea that the Delta occupies a tract once covered by the sea, even after Egypt was inhabited; and the argument derived from Homer's "Isle of Pharos" having been a day's sail "from Ægyptus" has failed before the fact of his "Ægyptus" being the name he applies to the Nile, not to the coast of Egypt; which being rock in that part, is exactly the same distance from the Pharos now as at any previous period, though the intermediate channel has been filled up by a causeway that unites it to the shore. The oldest towns, too, on the coast of the Delta occupy the same site, close to the sea, as of old; and whatever may be the accumulation of soil, it is counterbalanced by a sinking of the land, from subterraneous agency, along the whole of the northern coast of Egypt.

Though a country which played a distinguished part in the early history of the world, its extent was very limited; Egypt itself consisting merely of the narrow strip of land between the Mediterranean and the first cataract, about seven degrees and a half of latitude. For, with the exception of the northern part about the Delta, the average width of the valley of the Nile, between the eastern and western hills, is only about seven miles, and that of the cultivable land scarcely more than five and a half, being in the widest part ten and three-quarters, and in the narrowest two miles, including the river. And that portion between Edfoo and Asouan, at the first cataract, is still narrower, barely leaving room for any soil, so that those sixty miles do not enter into the general average.

The extent in square miles of the northernmost district, between the Pyramids and the sea, is considerable; and that of the Delta alone, which forms a portion of it, may be estimated at 1976 square miles; for though it is very narrow about its apex, at the junction of the modern Rosetta and Damietta branches, it gradually widens on approaching the coast, where the base of this somewhat irregular triangle is eighty-one miles. And as much irrigated land stretches on either side E. and W. of the two branches, the northern district, with the intermediate Delta included, will be found to contain about 4500 square miles, or double the whole arable land of Egypt, which may be computed at 2255 square miles, exclusive of the Fyoom, a small province consisting of about 340.

The number of towns and villages reported to have stood on this tract, and in the upper parts of the valley of the Nile, appears incredible; and Herodotus affirms that 20,000 populous *cities* existed in Egypt during the reign of Amasis. Diodorus calculates 18,000 large villages and towns; and states that, under Ptolemy Lagus, they amounted to upwards of 30,000, a number which remained even at the period when he wrote, or about forty-four years before our era. But the population was already greatly reduced, and of the seven millions who once inhabited Egypt, about three only remained in the time of the historian; so that Josephus must overstate it when, in the reign of Vespasian, he still reckons seven millions and a half in the valley of the Nile, besides the population of Alexandria, which amounted to more than 300,000 souls. To such an extent has the population of Egypt diminished, that it now scarcely amounts to two millions; but this decrease is not peculiar to Egypt; and other countries, once more remarkable for their populousness, have undergone a similar change; while others, then scantily peopled, now teem with inhabitants. Indeed, the question suggests itself, whether the world, within historic times at least, has not always had the same amount of population as at the present day? Whatever increase has taken place in some parts of the globe, the total will not surpass that of olden times; and when we compare the populous condition of Assyria, and the neighbouring countries, Persia, India, Asia Minor, Syria, and Scythia, which, till Tartar times, spread its hordes over distant countries, we are led to the conviction that the inhabitants of the small continent of Europe, and the rising population of America, do not exceed the numbers that crowded the ancient world. This, however, is only a question I offer (with great deference) to those who are competent to decide it.

Besides the inhabitants of the country between the first cataract and the sea, Egypt included those of the neighbouring districts under her sway, who greatly increased her power; and in her flourishing days, the Ethiopians, Libyans, and others, united with her, and formed part of her permanent dominions.

The produce of the land was doubtless much greater in the earlier periods of its history than at the present day, owing as well to the superior industry of the people as to a better system of government, and sufficed for the support of a very dense population; yet Egypt, if well cultivated, could now maintain many more inhabitants than at any former period, owing to the increased extent of the irrigated land : and if the ancient Egyptians enclosed those portions of the uninundated edge of the desert which were capable of cultivation, the same expedient might still be resorted to; and a larger proportion of soil now overflowed by the rising Nile offers additional advantages. That the irrigated part of the valley was much less extensive than at present, at least wherever the plain stretches to any distance E. and W., or to the right and left of the river, is evident from the fact of the alluvial deposit constantly encroaching in a horizontal direction upon the gradual slope of the desert; and, as a very perceptible elevation of the river's bed, as well as of the land of Egypt, has always been going on, it requires no argument to prove that a perpendicular rise of the water must cause it to flow to a greater distance over an open space to the E. and W.

Thus the plain of Thebes, in the time of Amunoph III., or about 1400 years before our era, was not more than two thirds of its present breadth; and the statues of that monarch, around which the alluvial mud has accumulated to the height of nearly seven feet, are based on the sand that once extended some distance before them. This at once explains why the ancient Egyptians were constantly obliged to raise mounds round the old towns, to prevent their being overwhelmed by the inundation of the Nile; the increased height of its rise, which took place after a certain number of years, keeping pace with the gradual elevation of the bed of the river. How erroneous, then, is it to suppose that the drifting sands of the encroaching desert threaten the welfare of this country, or have in any way tended to its downfall! and how much more reasonable is it to ascribe the degraded condition, to which Egypt is reduced, to causes of a far more baneful nature,—foreign despotism, the insecurity of property, and the effects of that old age which is the fate of every country, as well as of every individual, to undergo! For though the sand has encroached in a few places on the west side, from the Libyan desert, the general encroachment is vastly in favour of the alluvial deposit of the Nile.

Besides the numerous towns and villages in the plain, many were prudently placed by the ancient Egyptians on the slope of the desert, at a short distance from the irrigated land, in order not to occupy more than was necessary of the soil so valuable for its productions; and frequently with a view of encouraging some degree of cultivation in the desert plain; which, though above the reach of the inundation, might be irrigated by artificial ducts, or by water raised from inland wells. Mounds and ruined walls still mark the sites of those villages, in different parts of Egypt; and in a few instances the remains of magnificent temples, or the authority of ancient authors, attest the existence of large cities in similar situations. Thus Abydus, Athribis, Tentyris, parts of Memphis, and Oxyrhinchus, stood on the edge of the desert; and the town that once occupied the vicinity of Kasr Kharóon, at the western extremity of the Fyoom, was far removed from the fertilising influence of the inundation. This province, formerly the Nome of Crocodilopolis, or Arsinoë, was indebted entirely for its fertility to artificial irrigation; and a supply of water was conducted to it by a canal from the Nile, and kept up all the year in the immense reservoir made there by King Mœris.

The Egyptians seem at first to have had a hierarchical form of government, which lasted a long time, until Menes was chosen king, probably between 2000 and 3000 years before our era. Menes was of This, in Upper Egypt; and at his death, or that of his son, the country was divided into the southern and northern kingdoms, a Thinite and Memphite dynasty ruling at the same time. Other independent kingdoms, or principalities, also started up, and reigned contemporaneously in different parts of Egypt. The Memphite kings of the 3rd and 4th, who built the Pyramids, and Osirtasen I., the leader of the 12th, or 2nd Theban dynasty, were the most noted among them. The latter was the original Sesostris; but his exploits having been, many generations afterwards, eclipsed by those of Remeses the Great, they were transferred together with the name of Sesostris to the later and more glorious conqueror; and Remeses II. became the traditional Sesostris of Egyptian history. Osirtasen, who seems to have ruled all Egypt as lord paramount, ascended the throne about 2080 B.C.; but the contemporaneous kingdoms continued, till a new one arose which led to the subjugation of the country, and to the expulsion of the native princes from Lower, and apparently for a time from Upper Egypt also; when they were obliged to take refuge in Ethiopia. This dominion of the Shepherd kings lasted upwards of half a century. At length about 1530 B.C. Amosis, the leader of the 18th dynasty, having united in his own hands the previously divided power of the kingdom, drove the Shepherds out of the country, and Egypt was thenceforth governed by one king, bearing the title of " Lord of the Upper and Lower Country." Towards the latter end of this dynasty, some " Stranger kings " obtained the sceptre, probably by right of marriage with the royal family of Egypt; (a plea on which the Ethiopian princes and others obtained the crown at different times,) and Egypt again groaned under a hateful tyranny. They even introduced very heretical changes into the religion, they expelled the favourite God Amun from the Pantheon, and introduced a Sun worship unknown in Egypt. Their rule was not of very long duration; and having been expelled, their monuments, as well as every record of them, were purposely defaced.

The kings of the 18th dynasty had extended the dominion of Egypt far into Asia, and the interior of Africa, as the sculptures of the Thothmes, the Amunophs, and others show; but Sethos and his son Remeses II., of the 19th, who reigned from about 1370 to 1270 B.C., advanced them still farther. The conquests of the Egyptians had been pushed into Mesopotamia as early as the reign of Thothmes III., about 1445 B.C.; the strong fortress of Carchemish remained in their hands nearly all the time till the reign of Necho; and whenever the Egyptians boasted, in after ages, of the power of their country, they referred to the glorious era of the 18th and 19th dynasties. Remeses III., of the 20th dynasty, also carried his victorious arms into Asia and Africa, about a century after his namesake; enforcing the tributes, previously levied by Thothmes III. and his successors, from many countries that formed part of the Assyrian empire. But little was done by the kings who followed him, until the time of Sheshonk (Shishak), who pillaged the temple of Jerusalem, and laid Judæa under tribute B.C. 971. The power of the Pharaohs was on the decline; and Assyria, becoming the dominant kingdom, threatened to wrest from Egypt all the possessions she had obtained during a long career of conquest. Tirhaka (Tehrak), who with the Sabacos composed the 25th Ethiopian dynasty, checked the advance of the Assyrians, and forcing Sennacherib to retire from Judæa, restored the influence of Egypt in Syria. The Saïte kings of the 26th dynasty continued to maintain it, though with doubtful success, until the reign of Necho; when it was entirely lost; for soon after Necho had defeated and killed Josiah, king of Judah, the "king of Babylon" "smote" his army "in Carchemish,"* and took from the Egyptians "all that pertained to the king of Egypt," from the boundary torrent† on the Syrian confines "unto the river Euphrates."

No permanent conquests of any extent were henceforth made, "out of his land," by the Egyptian king; and though Apries sent an expedition against Cyprus, defeated the Syrians by sea, besieged and took Gaza and Sidon, and recovered much of the influence in Syria which had been taken from Egypt by Nebuchadnezzar, these were only temporary successes; the prestige of Egyptian power had vanished; it had been found necessary to employ Greek mercenaries in the army; and in the reign of Amasis, another still greater power than Assyria, or Babylon, arose to threaten and complete the downfall of Egypt. In the reign of his son Psammenitus, B.C. 525, Cambyses invaded the country, and Egypt submitted to the arms of Persia.

Several attempts were made by the Egyptians to recover their lost liberty; and at length, the Persian garrison having been over-powered, and the troops sent to reconquer the country having been defeated, the native kings were once more established (B.C. 414). These formed the 28th, 29th, and 30th dynasties; but the last of the Pharaohs, Nectanebo II., was defeated by Ochus, or Arta-xerxes III., B.C. 340, and Egypt again fell beneath the yoke of Persia. Eight years after this, Alexander the Great liberated it from the Persians, and Ptolemy and his successors once more erected it into an independent kingdom, though governed by a foreign dynasty, which lasted until it became a province of the Roman Empire.

Though far better pleased with the rule of the Macedonian

---

* Jerem. xlvi. 2; 2 Chron. xxxv. 20.   † *Nahal,* "rivulet."   2 Kings xxiv. 7.

kings than of the Persians, the Egyptians were never thoroughly satisfied to be subject to foreigners, whose manners and customs were so different from their own; and, however much the Ptolemies courted their goodwill, consulted their prejudices, and flattered the priesthood, they never ceased to be discontented; and occasionally showed their impatience by sudden and ill-judged outbreaks. To the Romans they were equally troublesome; but they had then ceased to be the Egyptians of bygone days; and oppression under the Persians, and loss of independence, had changed their character, and introduced the bad qualities of cunning, deceit, perverseness, and insubordination; which a shrewd and vain people often have recourse to, as their offensive and defensive weapons against an unwelcome master.

Proud of the former greatness of their nation, they could never get over the disgrace of their fallen condition; and so strong was their bias towards their own institutions and ancient form of government, that no foreign king, whose habits differed from their own, could reconcile them to his rule. For no people were more attached to their own country, to their own peculiar institutions, and to their own reputation as a nation; and the sentiments of attachment that their ancestors had always felt for their kings never lost an opportunity of displaying themselves, as was shown by the repeated and almost hopeless efforts they made to expel the Persians, as well as by the delight they manifested in once more re-establishing a native dynasty.

The king was to them the representative of the deity; his name, Phrah (Pharaoh), signifying "the sun," pronounced him the emblem of the god of light, and his royal authority was directly derived from the gods. He was the head of the religion and of the state; he was the judge and lawgiver; and he commanded the army and led it to war. It was his right and his office to preside over the sacrifices, and pour out libations to the gods; and, whenever he was present, he had the privilege of being the officiating high priest.

The sceptre was hereditary; but, in the event of a direct heir failing, the claims for succession were determined by proximity of parentage, or by right of marriage. The king was always either of the military or priestly class, and the princes also belonged to one of them. The army or the priesthood were the two professions followed by all men of rank, the navy not being an exclusive service; and the "long ships of Sesostris" and other kings were commanded by generals and officers taken from the army, as was the custom of the Turks, and some others in modern Europe to a very recent time. The law too was in the hands of the priests; so that there were only two professions. Most of the kings, as might be expected, were of the military class, and during the glorious days of Egyptian history, the younger princes generally adopted the same profession. Many held offices also in the royal household, some of the most honourable of which were fan-bearers on the right of their father, royal scribes, superintendents of the granaries, or of the land, and treasurers of the king; and they were generals of the cavalry, archers, and other corps, or admirals of the fleet.

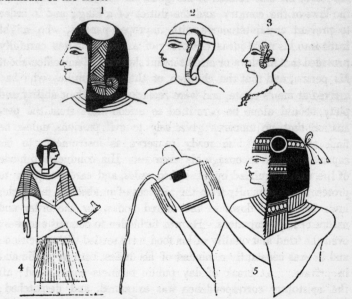

279.   Princes and Children.   *Thebes.*
1. Head-dress of a prince. 2 and 3. Lock of hair worn by children. 4. Dress of a son of
Remeses III. 5. Head-dress of a prince, Remeses.

Princes were distinguished by a badge hanging from the side of the head, which enclosed, or represented, the lock of hair emblematic of a " **son** ;" in imitation of the youthful god " Horus, the son of Isis and Osiris," who was held forth as the model for all princes, and the type of royal virtue.   For though the Egyptians shaved the head, and wore wigs or other coverings to the head, children were permitted to leave certain locks of hair; and if the sons of kings, long before they arrived at the age of manhood, had abandoned this youthful custom, the badge was attached to their head-dress as a mark of their rank as princes; or to show that they had not, during the lifetime of their father, arrived at *kinghood;* on the same principle that a Spanish prince, of whatever age, continues to be styled an " infant."

When the sovereign was a military man, it was his duty, as well as his privilege, on ascending the throne, to be instructed in the mysteries of the religion, and the various offices of a pontiff. He learnt all that related to the gods, the service of the temple, the laws of the country, and the duties of a king; and in order to prevent any intercourse with improper persons, who might instil into his mind ideas unworthy of a prince, it was carefully provided that no slave or hired servant should hold any office about his person, and that the children of the first families, who had arrived at man's estate, and were remarkable for their ability and piety, should alone be permitted to attend him; from the persuasion that no monarch gives way to evil passions, unless he finds those about him ready to serve as instruments to his caprices, and to encourage his excesses.   His conduct and mode of life were regulated by prescribed rules, and care was taken to protect the community from the caprices of an absolute monarch; laws being laid down in the sacred books, for the order and nature of his occupations.   He was forbidden to commit excesses; even the kind and quality of his food were settled with precision; and he was constantly reminded of his duties, both in public and in private.   At break of day public business commenced; all the epistolary correspondence was examined, and despatched; the ablutions for prayer were then performed, and the monarch, having put on his robes of ceremony, and attended by proper officers with the insignia of royalty, repaired to the temple to superintend the customary sacrifices to the gods of the sanctuary. The victims being brought to the altar, it was usual for the high priest to place himself close to the king, while the whole congregation present on the occasion stood round at a short distance from them, and to offer up prayers for the monarch, beseeching the gods to bestow on him " health, victory, power, and all other blessings," and to " establish the kingdom unto him and his children for ever." His qualities were then separately enumerated; and the high priest particularly noticed his piety towards the gods, and his conduct towards men. He lauded his self-command, his justice, his magnanimity, his love of truth, his munificence and generosity, and, above all, his entire freedom from envy and covetousness. He exalted his moderation in awarding the most lenient punishment to those who had transgressed, and his benevolence in requiting with unbounded liberality those who had merited his favours. These and other similar encomiums having been passed on the character of the monarch, the priest proceeded to review the general conduct of kings, and to point out those faults which were the result of ignorance and misplaced confidence. And it is a curious fact, that this ancient people had already adopted the principle, that the king " could do no wrong:" and while he was exonerated from blame, every curse and evil were denounced against his ministers, and those advisers who had given him injurious counsel. The idea, too, of the king " never dying " was contained in their common formula of " life having been given him for ever."

The object of this oration, says Diodorus, was to exhort the sovereign to live in fear of the deity, and to cherish that upright line of conduct and demeanour, which was deemed pleasing to the gods; and they hoped that, by avoiding the bitterness of reproach, and by celebrating the praises of virtue, they might stimulate him to the exercise of those duties which he was expected to fulfil. The king then proceeded to examine the entrails of the victim, and to perform the usual ceremonies of sacrifice: and the hierogrammat, or sacred scribe, read those extracts from the holy writings which recorded the deeds and sayings of the most celebrated men.

These regulations were instituted by a cautious people, when the change took place which introduced the kingly form of government. The law could, if required, be repealed, to protect the country from the arbitrary conduct of a king; and even if he had the means of defying its power, there still remained a mode of avenging its dignity, for the voice of the people could punish the refractory tyrant at his death, by the disgrace of excluding his body from interment in his own tomb. It was, however, rather as a precaution that these laws were set forth: they were seldom enforced, and the indulgence of the Egyptians to their king gave him no excuse for tyranny or injustice. Nor were the rigid regulations respecting his private life vexatiously enforced; and though the quantity of wine he was allowed to drink, and numerous punctilious observances, were laid down in some old statute, he was not expected to regard them to the very letter, provided he benefited society by his general conduct. It was no difficult task for a king to be popular; the Egyptians were prone to look upon him with affection and respect; and if he had done nothing to obtain their approbation as prince, the moment he ascended the throne he was sure to be regarded with favour.

Nor did it require any great effort on his part to conform to the general rules laid down for his conduct: and by consulting the welfare of the country, he easily secured for himself that good will which was due from children to a parent; the whole nation being as anxious for the welfare of the king as for that of their own wives and children, or whatever was most dear to them. To this Diodorus ascribes the duration of the Egyptian state; which not only lasted long, but enjoyed the greatest prosperity, both at home, and in its wars with distant nations, and was enabled by its immense riches, resulting from trade and foreign conquest, to display a magnificence, in its provinces and cities, unequalled by that of any other country.

Love and respect were not merely shown to the sovereign during his lifetime, but were continued to his memory after his

death; and the manner in which his funeral obsequies were celebrated tended to show, that, though their benefactor was no more,
they retained a grateful sense of his goodness, and admiration for
his virtues. And what, says the historian, can convey a greater
testimony of sincerity, free from all colour of dissimulation,
than the cordial acknowledgment of a benefit, when the person
who conferred it no longer lives to witness the honour done to
his memory?

On the death of every Egyptian king, a general mourning was
instituted throughout the country for seventy days,* hymns com-
memorating his virtues were sung, the temples were closed,
sacrifices were no longer offered, and no feasts or festivals were
celebrated during the whole of that period. The people tore
their garments, and, covering their heads with dust and mud,

280. People throwing dust on their heads, in token of grief. *Thebes.*

formed a procession of 200 or 300 persons of both sexes, who
met twice a day in public to sing the funeral dirge. A general
fast was also observed, and they neither allowed themselves to
taste meat nor wheat bread, and abstained, moreover, from wine
and every kind of luxury.

* Gen. l. 3, "The Egyptians mourned for Jacob threescore and ten days," for
"so are fulfilled the days of those which are embalmed."

In the mean time the funeral was prepared, and on the last day the body was placed in state within the vestibule of the tomb, and an account was then given of the life and conduct of the deceased.

The Egyptians are said to have been divided into castes, similar to those of India; but though a marked line of distinction was maintained between the different ranks of society, they appear rather to have been classes than castes, and a man did not necessarily follow the precise occupation of his father. Sons, it is true, usually adopted the same profession or trade as their parent, and the rank of each depended on his occupation; but the children of a priest frequently chose the army for their profession, and those of a military man could belong to the priesthood.

The priests and military men held the highest position in the country after the family of the king, and from them were chosen his ministers and confidential advisers, "the wise counsellors of Pharaoh," * and all the principal officers of state.

The priests consisted of various grades—as the chief priests, or pontiffs; the prophets; judges; sacred scribes; the sphragistæ, who examined the victims for sacrifice; the stolistæ, dressers, or keepers of the sacred robes; the bearers of the shrines, banners, and other holy emblems; the sacred sculptors, draughtsmen, and masons; the embalmers; the keepers of sacred animals; and various officers employed in the processions and other religious ceremonies; under whom were the beadles, and inferior functionaries of the temple. There was also the king's own priest; and the royal scribes were chosen either from the sacerdotal or the military class.

Women were not excluded from certain offices in the temple; there were priestesses of the gods, of the kings and queens, and they had many employments connected with religion. They even attended in some religious processions; as well as at the funeral of a deceased relation; and an inferior class of women

* Isa. xix. 11 ; Diodor. i. 73.

acted as hired mourners on this occasion. The queens, indeed, and other women of high rank, held a very important post in the service of the gods; and an instance occurs of the title "pourer out of libations" being applied to a queen, which was only given to the priests of the altar. They usually accompanied their husbands as they made offerings in the temple, holding two sistra, or

281.   King offering, and the Queen holding two emblems.   *Thebes.*

other emblems, before the statue of the deity. This was the office of those "holy women," whose duties in the temple of the Theban Jupiter led to the strange mistake respecting the "Pellices Jovis," or Pallacides of Amun; but its dignity and importance is sufficiently shown by its having been filled by women of the first families in the country, and by the wives and daughters of the kings. They were of various grades—the highest of them were the queens, princesses, and the wives and daughters of the high priests, who held the sistra; others praised the deity with various instruments; and from being often called "minstrels" of the god, their office seems to have been particularly connected with the sacred music of the temple. The institution may have

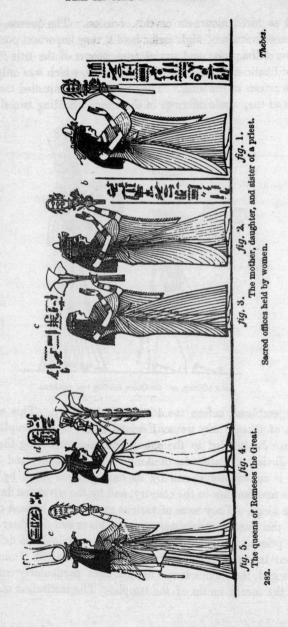

Thebes.

fig. 1.

fig. 2.

fig. 3.

The mother, daughter, and sister of a priest.

Sacred offices held by women.

fig. 4.

The queens of Remeses the Great.

fig. 5.

282.

been a sort of college, or convent; but as married women and even young children might belong to it, they were evidently not immured within the precincts of any place resembling a modern nunnery; and if they were obliged to take certain vows, and attend to the duties attached to their honourable office, nothing prevented their performing all others of a public and social kind. It was not forbidden to strangers naturalized in Egypt to belong to it; and one instance occurs on a papyrus of a "foreign" woman having the same holy office in the service of Amun.

The priests enjoyed great privileges. They were exempt from taxes; they consumed no part of their own income in any of their necessary expenses; and they had one of the three portions into which the land of Egypt was divided, free from all duties. They were provided for from the public stores, out of which they received a stated allowance of corn, and all the other necessaries of life; and we find that when Pharaoh, by the advice of Joseph, took all the land of the Egyptians in lieu of corn, the priests were not obliged to make the same sacrifice of their landed property, nor was the tax of the fifth part of the produce entailed upon it, as on that of the other people.

In the sacerdotal as among the other classes, a great distinction existed between the different grades; and the various orders of priests ranked according to their peculiar office. The chief or high priests held the first and most honourable station; but the one who offered sacrifice and libation in the temple had the highest post. He appears to have been called "the prophet," and his title in the hieroglyphic legends is "*Sem.*" He superintended the sacrifice of the victims, the processions of the sacred boats or arks, the presentation of the offerings at the altar, and at funerals, and the anointing of the king; and the same office was held by the sovereign, when he presented incense and libations to the gods. He was marked by a peculiar dress; a leopard skin fitting over his linen robes; and the same was worn by the king on similar occasions.

The duty of the prophet was to be fully versed in all matters relating to religion, the laws, the worship of the gods, and the

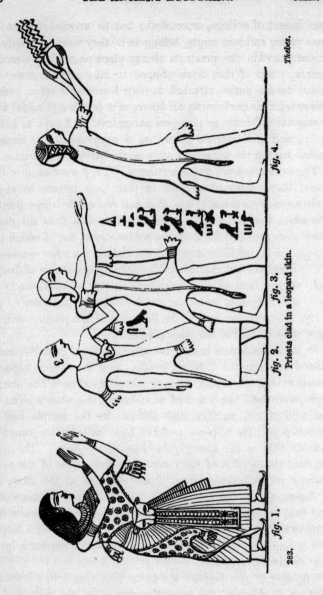

fig. 4.   *fig. 3.*   *fig. 2.*   *fig. 1.*

Priests clad in a leopard skin.

Thebes.

283.

discipline of the whole order of the priesthood; he presided over the temple and the sacred rites, and directed the management of the priestly revenues. In the processions he bore the holy *hydria*, or vase, which the king also carried on similar occasions; and when any new regulations were introduced in matters of religion, the prophets with the chief priests headed the conclave.

It was the great privilege of the priests to be initiated into the mysteries; though they were not all admitted indiscriminately to that honour; and " the Egyptians neither entrusted them to every one, nor degraded the secrets of divine matters by disclosing them to the profane; reserving them for the heir-apparent of the throne, and for *such priests* as excelled in virtue and wisdom." The mysteries were also distinguished into the greater and the less;—the latter preparatory to a fuller revelation of their secrets. This, and the superior knowledge they possessed, gave the priests a great ascendency over the rest of the people; and though all might enjoy the advantages of education, some branches of learning were reserved for particular persons.

Diodorus says, " The children of the priests are taught two different kinds of writing,—what is called the sacred, and the more general; and they pay great attention to geometry and arithmetic. For the river, changing the appearance of the country very materially every year, causes many and various discussions among neighbouring proprietors, about the extent of their property; and it would be difficult for any person to decide upon their claims without geometrical proof, founded on actual observation.

" Of arithmetic they have also frequent need, both in their domestic economy, and in the application of geometrical theorems, besides its utility in the cultivation of astronomical studies; for the orders and motions of the stars are observed at least as industriously by the Egyptians as by any people whatever; and they keep a record of the motions of each for an incredible number of years, the study of this science having been, from the remotest times, an object of national ambition with them. They have also most punctually observed the motions, periods, and stations of the

planets, as well as the powers which they possess with respect to
the nativities of animals, and what good or evil influences they
exert; and they frequently foretel what is to happen to a man
throughout his life, and not uncommonly predict the failure of
crops, or an abundance, and the occurrence of epidemic diseases
among men and beasts : foreseeing also earthquakes and floods,
the appearance of comets, and a variety of other things which
appear impossible to the multitude.

" But the generality of the common people learn only from
their parents, or relations, that which is required for the exercise
of their peculiar occupations; a few only being taught anything
of literature, and those principally the better classes of artificers."

If the priests were anxious to establish a character for learning
and piety, they were not less so in their endeavours to excel in the
propriety of outward demeanour, and to set forth a proper example of humility and self-denial; and if not in their houses, at
least in their mode of living, they were remarkable for simplicity
and abstinence. They committed no excesses either in eating or
drinking; their food was plain, and in a stated quantity, and
wine was used with the strictest regard to moderation. And so
fearful were they lest the body should not " sit light upon the
soul," and excess should cause a tendency to increase " the cor-
poreal man," that they paid a scrupulous attention to the most
trifling particulars of diet; and similar precautions were extended
even to the deified animals : Apis not being allowed to drink the
water of the Nile, since it was thought to possess a fattening property.

They were not only scrupulous about the quantity, but the
quality of their food ; and certain viands were alone allowed to appear at their table. Above all meats, that of swine was particularly
obnoxious ; and fish both of the sea and the Nile was forbidden
them, though so generally eaten by the rest of the Egyptians.
And indeed, on the 9th of the month Thoth, when a religious
ceremony obliged all the people to eat a fried fish before the door
of their houses, the priests were not even then expected to conform to the general custom, and they were contented to substitute

the ceremony of burning theirs at the appointed time. Beans they held in utter abhorrence ; and Herodotus affirms that " beans were never sown in the country, and if they grew spontaneously, they neither formed an article of food, nor even if cooked were ever eaten by the Egyptians." But this aversion, which originated in a supposed sanitary regulation, and which was afterwards so scrupulously adopted by Pythagoras, did not prevent their cultivation ; nor were the people obliged to abstain from them ; and they were allowed to eat them in common with other pulse and vegetables, which abounded in Egypt. Not only beans, but lentils, peas, garlick, leeks, and onions were forbidden to the priests ; who were not permitted to eat them under any pretence. The prohibition, however, regarding them, as well as certain meats, was confined to the sacerdotal order ; and even swine, if we may believe Plutarch, were not forbidden to the other Egyptians at all times : " for those who sacrificed a sow to Typho once a year, at the full moon, afterwards ate its flesh."

It is a remarkable fact that onions, as well as the first fruits of their lentils, were admitted among the offerings placed upon the altars of the gods, together with gourds, figs, garlic, *raphanus* (or *figl*), cakes, beef, goose, or wild fowl, grapes, wine, and the

284.   Fig. 1. A basket of sycamore figs.
         2, 3, 4. Hieroglyphic signifying " wife," apparently taken from it.
         5, 6. Cucurbita Lagenaria, γ, or Karra-toweël.   7. Garlic (?)
         8. Raphanus sativus *var.* edulis, or *figl.*   9. Onions.

head of the victim. Onions were generally bound in a single bundle, seldom presented singly ; and they were sometimes arranged in a hollow circular bunch, which, descending upon the table or altar, enveloped and served as a cover to whatever was placed upon it. And the privilege of presenting them in this

orm appears to have been generally enjoyed by that class of
priests who wore the leopard-skin dress.

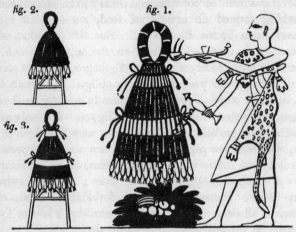

285.   Mode of tying up the onions for some offerings.   *Thebes.*

In general, "the priests abstained from most sorts of pulse,
from mutton, and swine's flesh; and in their more solemn purifications even excluded salt from their meals;" but some vegetables
were considered lawful food, being remarkable for their wholesome nature; and many of the leguminous productions and fruits
of Egypt represented on the tables placed before priests, as part
of the *inferiæ,* or offerings to the dead, must have been acceptable
to them while living.

In their ablutions, as in their diet, they were equally severe,
and they maintained the strictest observance of numerous religious
customs.   They bathed twice a day, and twice during the night;
and some who pretended to a more rigid observance of religious
duties, washed themselves with water which had been tasted by
the ibis, supposed in consequence to bear an unquestionable
evidence of purity; and shaving the head and the whole body
every third day, they spared no pains to promote the cleanliness
of their persons, without indulging in the bath, as a luxury.   A
grand ceremony of purification took place, previous and pre-

paratory to their fasts, many of which lasted from seven to forty-two days, and sometimes even a longer period : during which time they abstained entirely from animal food, from herbs and vegetables, and from all extraordinary indulgences.

These " numerous religious observances," as well as the dependence of all classes upon them for instruction, and the possession of secrets known only to themselves, gave them that influence they so long possessed ; but they had obtained a power, which, while it raised their own class, could not fail to degrade the rest of the people ; who, allowed to substitute superstition for religion, and credulity for belief, were taught to worship the figures of imaginary beings, while they were excluded from a real knowledge of the Deity, and of those truths which constituted " the wisdom of the Egyptians." It was to liberate mankind from the dark superstition, in which the selfish views of the priesthood of those days had kept the world, that Moses received his grand and important mission. Men were by him taught to offer their prayers directly to the Deity, without the necessity of depending on a frail mortal, like themselves, for his pretended intercession with One equally accessible to all ; and they learnt that heaven was not to be purchased by money paid to the cupidity of a privileged class, whose assumed right of pronouncing against a man his exclusion from future happiness was an unwarrantable assumption of divine authority, and an attempt to fabricate a judgment in this world, which alone belonged to the Deity.

Privilege and power the priests certainly did enjoy, when they could reach a man after his death, by refusing him a passport to eternal happiness, and could still force his family to pay them for pretended prayers for their deceased relative ; and nothing could be better devised to enforce obedience to their will. It must, however, be allowed that they deserved credit for setting a good example by their abstinence and moral conduct ; their wisdom was shown by their tact and good policy in giving no occasion for scandal and discontent ; and they did not affect to be superior to the world by disregarding all social ties. Thus while performing the affectionate duties of

fathers and husbands, they still kept up their influence over
society, and ruled a flourishing country, without prostrating
its resources, or checking the industry of the inhabitants; and,
though we may censure an artful piece of priestcraft, we must
remember that it was established long before mankind enjoyed
the advantages of a thorough revelation.

The long duration of their system, and the feeling with which
it was regarded by the people, may also plead some excuse
for it; and while the function of judges and the administra-
tion of the laws gave them unusual power, they had an ap-
parent claim to those offices, from having been the framers
of the codes of morality, and of the laws they superintended.
Instead of setting themselves above the king, and making
him succumb to their power, like the unprincipled Ethiopian
pontiffs, they acknowledged him as the head of the religion
and the state; nor were they above the law; no one of them,
nor even the king himself, could govern according to his own
arbitrary will; his conduct was amenable to an ordeal of his
subjects at his death, the people being allowed to accuse him of
misgovernment, and to prevent his being buried in his tomb on
the day of his funeral.

But though the regulations of the priesthood may have suited
the Egyptians in early times, certain institutions being adapted
to men in particular states of society, they erred in encouraging
a belief in legends they knew to be untrue, instead of puri-
fying and elevating the religious views of the people, and committed the fault of considering their unbending system perfect,
and suited to all times. Abuses therefore crept in; credulity,
already shamefully encouraged, increased to such an extent that
it enslaved the mind, and paralyzed men's reasoning powers;
and the result was that the Egyptians gave way to the grossest
superstitions, which at length excited universal ridicule and
contempt.

The religion of the Egyptians is a subject of too great extent
to be treated fully in a work of limited dimensions: little more
can therefore be given of it than a general outline.

The fundamental doctrine was the unity of the Deity; but this unity was not represented, and He was known by a sentence, or an idea, being, as Jamblichus says, " worshipped in silence." But the attributes of this Being were represented under positive forms; and hence arose a multiplicity of gods, that engendered idolatry, and caused a total misconception of the real nature of the Deity, in the minds of all who were not admitted to a knowledge of the truth through the mysteries. The division of God into his attributes was in this manner. As soon as he was thought to have any reference to his works, or to man, he ceased to be quiescent; he became an agent; and he was no longer the One, but distinguishable and divisible, according to his supposed character, his actions, and his influence on the world. He was then the Creator, the Divine Goodness, (or the abstract idea of Good,) Wisdom, Power, and the like; and as we speak of Him as the Almighty, the Merciful, the Everlasting, so the Egyptians gave to each of his various attributes a particular name. But they did more: they separated them; and to the uninitiated they became distinct gods. As one of these, the Deity was Amun; probably, the divine mind in operation, the bringer to light of the secrets of its *hidden* will; and he had a complete human form, because man was the intellectual animal, and the principal design of the divine will in the creation. As the " Spirit of God" that moved on the face of the *waters*, the Deity was Nef, Nû, or Nûm; over whom the asp, the emblem of royalty and of the good genius, spread itself as a canopy, while he stood in his *boat*. As the Creator he was Pthah; and in this character he was accompanied by the figure of Truth,—a combination of it with the creative power which recalls this sentence in the Epistle of St. James, " Of his own will begat he us with the word of truth." As the principle of generation he was Khem, called " the father of his own father " —the abstract idea of father; as the goddess Maut was that of mother,—who consequently "proceeded from herself;" and other attributes, characters, and offices of the Deity held a rank according to their closer, or more distant, relation to his essence and operations.

In order to specify and convey an impression of these abstract notions to the eyes of men, it was thought necessary to distinguish them by some fixed representation; and the figures of Pthah, Osiris, Amun, Maut, Neith, and other gods or goddesses, were invented as the signs of the various attributes of the Deity. But it did not stop there; and as the subtlety of philosophical speculation entered into the originally simple theory, numerous subdivisions of the divine nature were made; and at length anything which appeared to partake of, or bear analogy to it, was admitted to a share of worship. Hence arose the various grades of deities: and they were known as the gods of the first, second, and third orders. But Herodotus is quite right in saying that the Egyptians gave no divine honours to heroes.

The Egyptian figures of gods were only vicarious forms, not intended to be looked upon as real personages; and no one was expected to believe that a being could exist with the head of an animal joined to a human body; but credulity will always do its work; the uneducated failed to take the same view of them, as the initiated portion of the community; and mere emblems soon assumed the importance of the divine personages to which they belonged. These abuses were the natural consequences of such representations; and experience has often shown how readily the mind may be drawn away from the most spiritual worship to a superstitious veneration for images, whether at first intended merely to fix the attention, or to represent some legendary tale or abstract idea. The religion of the Egyptians was a pantheism rather than a polytheism; and their admitting the sun and moon to divine worship may rather be ascribed to this than to any admixture of Sabæism. The sun was thought to possess much of the divine influence in its vivifying power, and its various other effects; and it was not only one of the grandest works, but was one of the direct *agents*, of the deity. The moon was in another similar capacity; and, as the regulator of *time* and the messenger of heaven, was figured as the Ibis-headed Thoth, the god of letters, and the deity who registered man's actions and the events of his life.

They not only attributed to the sun and moon, and to other

supposed agents, a participation in the divine essence, but even
stones and plants were thought to have some portion of it; and
certain peculiarities were often discovered in the habits or appearance of animals, which were supposed to bear a resemblance to
the divine character. Even a king was sometimes represented
making offerings to another figure of himself in the temples,
signifying that his human did homage to his divine nature.

They also represented the same deity under different names and
characters; Isis, from the number of her titles, was called " My-
riônymus," or "with ten thousand names." A god or goddess
was also worshipped as residing in some particular place, or
as gifted with some peculiar quality; like the Minerva Polias,
and various Minervas, the several Venuses, the Jupiters, and
others; and modern custom has made a variety of Madonnas
from the one Virgin.

Among other remarkable theories of the Egyptians, was the
union of certain attributes into triads; the third number of which
proceeded from the other two; and in every city one of these
combinations was the triad of the place. The first members were
not always of the first order of gods, nor was it necessary they
should be; and an attribute of the deity might be combined with
some abstract idea to form a result.

This notion had been held by them at the earliest periods of
the Egyptian monarchy; it is, therefore, an anachronism to
derive this, and other Egyptian doctrines, from the peninsula of
India, in which part of the country the Hindoos did not settle
till long after the age of the 18th dynasty, when they gradually
dispossessed, and confined to certain districts, those original populations, who are supposed to be of Scythian origin; and if there
is any connexion between the two religions of Egypt and India,
this must be ascribed to the period before the two races left
Central Asia.

Certain innovations were introduced in early days into the
religion of Egypt, but they were partial, and such as might
be expected from the progress of superstition; and if instances
occur of sudden and positive changes, there is reason to believe

they were brought about by the influence of strangers; as the banishment of Amun from the Pantheon for a short time, through the usurpation of the Stranger kings, towards the end of the 18th dynasty.

The expulsion of Seth, or Evil, seems also to have been the result of foreign influence. The children of Seb and Netpe (Saturn and Rhea) were Osiris, Seth, Aroeris, Isis, and Nepthys. Osiris and Seth (or Typho) were brothers; the former represented " good," the latter " evil." In early times they were both adored as gods throughout Upper and Lower Egypt, and were considered part of the same divine system. For Evil had not yet been confounded with sin or wickedness; and this last was figured as Apôp (Apophis) " the giant," who, in the form of the " great serpent," the enemy of gods and of mankind, was pierced by the spear of Horus, Atmoo, and other deities. Osiris and Seth were even placed synonymously in the names of some kings at the same period, and on the same monument; the latter was figured instructing the monarch in the use of the bow, being a cause of evil; and Seth's pouring from a vase, in conjunction with Horus, the emblems of life and power over the newly-crowned king, was intended to show that good and evil affected the world equally, as a necessary condition of human existence.

As soon as the change was resolved upon, the name and figure of the square-eared Seth were everywhere hammered out; he was branded as the enemy of Osiris; not merely opposed as a necessary consequence, but as if it were from his own agency, as Ariman to Ormusd, or the Manichæan Satan to God. The exact period when he was " expelled from Egypt" is uncertain. It may have been at the time of the 22nd dynasty; and if Seshonk (Shishak), and the other kings of that dynasty, were Assyrians, as Mr. Birch supposes, the reason of it may be readily explained.

The conflict of *wickedness* and *goodness* was not, however, a novel theory with the Egyptians, as is shown by the most ancient representations of the snake-giant Apôp, the symbol of sin; nor was the peculiar office of Osiris a late introduction, after Seth (or Typho) had been banished from the Pantheon. The unphilosophical innovation was, in Seth being converted from *evil* into *sin*, and made the *enemy*, instead of the *necessary antagonistic companion*, of good.

The peculiar character of Osiris, his coming upon earth for the benefit of mankind, with the titles of "manifester of good and truth," his being put to death by the malice of the evil one; his burial and resurrection, and his becoming the judge of the dead, are the most interesting features of the Egyptian religion. This was the great mystery; and this myth and his worship were of the earliest times, and universal in Egypt. He was to every Egyptian the great judge of the dead; and it is evident that Moses abstained from making any very pointed allusion to the future state of man, because it would have recalled the well-known Judge of the dead, and all the funeral ceremonies of Egypt, and have brought back the thoughts of the "mixed multitude," and of all whose minds were not entirely uncontaminated by Egyptian habits, to the very superstitions from which it was his object to purify them. Osiris was to every Egyptian the great deity of a future state; and though different gods enjoyed particular honours in their respective cities, the importance of Osiris was admitted throughout the country.

Certain cities and districts were appropriated to certain gods, who were the chief deities of the place; and while Amun had his principal temple at Thebes, Memphis was the great city of Pthah, as Heliopolis of Re or the Sun, and other cities of other divinities; no two neighbouring districts, or chief cities, being given to the same god. But although Amun was the great god of Thebes, as Pthah was of Memphis, it is not to be supposed that their separate worship originated in two parts of Egypt, or that the religions of the Upper and Lower country were once distinct, and afterwards united into one. They were members of the same Pantheon.

"A balance of power," as of honour, was thus established for the principal gods; minor deities being satisfied with towns of minor importance. Other divinities shared the honours of the sanctuary; and different triads, or single gods, were admitted to a post in the various temples of Egypt: thus Pthah had a suitable position in a Theban adytum; Amun, and Nef, or the triads of Thebes and of the Cataracts, of which they were respectively the first persons, were figured on the temples at Memphis; and none were necessarily excluded, provided room could be found for them, except purely local deities.   Those of a neighbouring town were more readily admitted to a place among the contemplar gods; it was at least a neighbourly compliment; and it suited the convenience of the priests, quite as much as the gods themselves.   Many minor divine beings, whose worship was ordained for some particular object, and certain emblems, or sacred animals, were admitted in one and excluded from another place.   Thus the reverence for the crocodile, encouraged in some inland town, in order that the canals might be properly kept up, was found unnecessary in places by the river side, where he was probably held in abhorrence; and the same animal, which was highly regarded in one district, was a symbol of evil in another.

Still all was part of the same system; and however changed and perverted it afterwards became, the original composition of the Pantheon dates from the most remote periods of Egyptian history; and the few innovations introduced in early times occasioned no real alteration in the principle of the religion itself.   Changes certainly took place in the speculations of the Egyptians, as in their mode of representing them; and some foreign deities were occasionally admitted into their Pantheon; yet the original progress of their ideas may readily be traced, from the one God, to the Deity in action under various characters, as well as numerous abstract ideas made into separate gods.   Of these last, two are particularly worthy of notice, from being common to many other religions; which have treated them according to their peculiar views.   They are the Nature gods; sometimes represented as the sun and earth, by people who were inclined to a physical rather than an ideal treatment of the subject; but which the speculative Egyptians considered as the vivifying or generative principle, the abstract idea of "father," and the producing principle of nature, or "mother;" both consequent upon the creative action.   Of these, the latter was originally (as one of the great deities) only the abstract idea of " mother," *Maut,* whose emblem was a vulture ; and if another—Isis (sometimes identified with Athor, the Egyptian Venus), holding the child Horus, her offspring—was a direct representation of the maternal office, she may be considered an offset of the myth.   Two other goddesses also belonged to it, the one of parturition (Lucina), and the other of gestation ; the former connected with the maternal idea by having the vulture as her emblem, the latter related to Isis as the " mother of the child ;" and thus the analogies and relationships of various deities were kept up on one side, while on the other the subdivisions and minute shades of difference increased the number and complication of these ideal beings.   Thus too the relationship of deities in many mythologies may be recognised ; representing as they do the same original idea ; and the Alitta, or Mylitta (*i. e.,* " the child-bearing " goddess) of the Arabs and Assyrians, the Anaitis of Persia, the Syrian Astarte, and Venus-Urania, Cybele, and " the Queen of heaven," the " Mother of the child " found in Western Asia, Egypt, India, ancient Italy, and even in Mexico, the prolific Diana of Ephesus, and others, are various characters of the Nature goddess.

The dress of the priests was simple ; but the robes of ceremony were grand and imposing ; and besides the leopard-skin dress of the prophet were other peculiarities of costume, that marked their respective grades.   Necklaces, bracelets, garlands, and other ornaments were also put on, during the religious ceremonies in the temple.   The material of their robes was linen ; but they sometimes wore cotton garments ; and it was lawful to have an upper one of wool as a cloak ; though they were not permitted to enter a temple with this last, nor to wear woollen garments next the skin. Nor could any body be buried in bandages of that material.

The dresses of the priests consisted of an under garment, like the usual apron worn by the Egyptians, and a loose upper robe with full sleeves, secured by a girdle round the loins ; or of the apron, and a shirt with short, tight sleeves, over which was thrown a loose robe, leaving the right arm exposed.   Sometimes a priest, when officiating in the temple, laid aside the upper vestment, and was satisfied to wear an ample robe bound round the waist, and descending over the apron to his ankles (which answers to

1 2 3 4

5 6 7 8 9

286.   Dresses for Priests.   *Thebes.*
8, 9. Hierogrammat, or sacred scribe.

the dress of the Stolistes mentioned by Clemens, " covering only the lower part of the body ") ; and occasionally he put on a long full garment, reaching from below the arms to the feet, and supported over the neck with straps.* Others again, in the sacred processions, were entirely covered with a dress of this kind, reaching to the throat, and concealing even the hands and arms.†

The costume of the hierogrammat, or sacred scribe,‡ consisted

* *Fig.* 4.   † *Fig.* 5.   ‡ *Fig.* 8.

of a large kelt or apron, either tied in front, or wound round the lower part of the body; and the loose upper robe with full sleeves, which, in all cases, was of the finest linen. He had sometimes one or two feathers on his head, as described by Clemens and Diodorus.* Those who bore the sacred emblems wore a long, full apron reaching to the ankles, tied in front with long bands; and a strap, also of linen, passed over the shoulder to support it.† Sometimes a priest, who offered incense, was clad in this long apron, and the full robe with sleeves, or only in the former; and the dress of the same priest varied on different occasions. Their sandals were made of the papyrus and palm-leaves, and the simplicity of their habits extended to the bed they slept upon, which was sometimes a skin stretched on the ground, or a sort of wicker bedstead of palm branches,‡ covered with a mat or a skin; and their head was supported by a wooden concave pillow.

The same mode of resting the head was common to all the

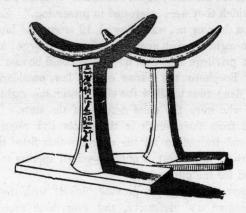

287.   Alabaster pillow for the head.   *Alnwick Museum.*

Egyptians, and a considerable number of these stools § have been found in the tombs of Thebes: generally of sycamore, acacia, or

* Woodcut 286, *fig.* 9.   † *Fig.* 6.   ‡ Woodcut 84, *fig.* 1, p. 71.
                § Woodcuts 287, and 82, 83, p. 71.

tamarisk wood; or of alabaster, not inelegantly formed, and frequently ornamented with coloured hieroglyphics. In Abyssinia, and in parts of Upper Ethiopia, they still adopt the same support for the head; and the materials of which they are made are either wood, stone, or common earthenware. Nor are they peculiar to Abyssinia and the valley of the Nile: the same custom prevails in far distant countries; and we find them used in Japan, China, and Ashantee, and even in the island of Otaheite (Tahiti), where they are also of wood, but longer and less concave than those of Africa.

Next in rank to the priests were the military. To them was assigned one of the three portions into which the land of Egypt was divided by an edict of Sesostris, in order, says Diodorus, " that those who exposed themselves to danger in the field might be more ready to undergo the hazards of war, from the interest they felt in the country as occupiers of the soil; for it would be absurd to commit the safety of the community to those who possessed nothing which they were interested in preserving." Each soldier, whether on duty or no, was allowed 12 arourae of land (a little more than eight English acres) free from all charge; and another important privilege was, that no soldier could be cast into prison for debt; Bocchoris, the framer of this law, considering that it would be dangerous to allow the civil power the right of arresting those who were the chief defence of the state. They were instructed from their youth in the duties and requirements of soldiers, and trained in all the exercises that fitted them for an active career; and a sort of military school appears to have been established for the purpose.

Each man was obliged to provide himself with the necessary arms, offensive and defensive, and everything requisite for a campaign; and he was expected to hold himself in readiness for taking the field when required, or for garrison duty. The principal garrisons were posted in the fortified towns of Pelusium, Marea, Eileithyias, Hieraconpolis, Syene, Elephantine, and other intermediate places; and a large portion of the army was frequently called upon, by their warlike monarchs, to invade a foreign country, or to suppress those rebellions which occasionally broke out in the conquered provinces.

The whole military force, consisting of 410,000, was divided into two corps, the Calasiries and Hermotybies. They furnished a body of men to do the duty of royal guards, 1000 of each being annually selected for that purpose; and each soldier had an additional allowance of " five *minæ* of bread, with two of beef, and four *arusters* of wine," as daily rations, during the period of his service.

The Calasiries (*Klashr*) were the most numerous, and amounted to 250,000 men, at the time that Egypt was most populous. They inhabited the nomes of Thebes, Bubastis, Aphthis, Tanis, Mendes, Sebennytus, Athribis, Pharbæthus, Thmuis, Onuphis, Anysis, and the Isle of Myecphoris, which was opposite Bubastis; and the Hermotybies, who lived in those of Busiris, Saïs, Chemmis, Papremis, the Isle of Prosopitis, and the half of Natho, made up the remaining 160,000. It was here that they abode while retired from military service, and in these nomes their farms or portions of land were situated, which tended to encourage habits of industry, and keep up a taste for active employment.

Besides the native corps they had mercenary troops, who were enrolled either from the nations in alliance with the Egyptians, or from those who had been conquered by them. They were divided into regiments, sometimes disciplined in the same manner as the Egyptians, though allowed to retain their arms and costume; but they were not on the same footing as the native troops; they had no land, and merely received pay, like other hired soldiers. Strabo speaks of them as mercenaries; and the million of men he mentions must have included these foreign auxiliaries. When formally enrolled in the army they were considered a part of it, and accompanied the victorious legions on their return from foreign conquest; and they sometimes assisted in performing garrison duty in Egypt, in the place of those Egyptian troops which were left to guard the conquered provinces.

The strength of the army consisted in archers, whose skill con-

fig. 1.   *fig.* 2.   *fig.* 3.   *fig.* 4.

288.   Allies of the Egyptians.   *Thebes.*

tributed mainly to the successes of the Egyptians; as of our
own ancestors; and their importance is shown by the Egyptian
" soldier " being represented as an archer kneeling, often preceded by the word " *Klashr*," converted by Herodotus into
" *Calasiris*." They fought either on foot or in chariots, and
may therefore be classed under the separate heads of a mounted
and unmounted corps; and they constituted a great part of both
wings. Several bodies of heavy infantry, divided into regiments,
each distinguished by its peculiar arms, formed the centre; and
the cavalry (which, according to the Scriptural accounts, was
numerous) covered and supported the foot.

Though Egyptian horsemen are rarely found on any monuments, they are too frequently and positively noticed in sacred
and profane history to allow us to question their employment;
and an ancient battle-axe represents a mounted soldier on its
blade.*

* Woodcut 355.

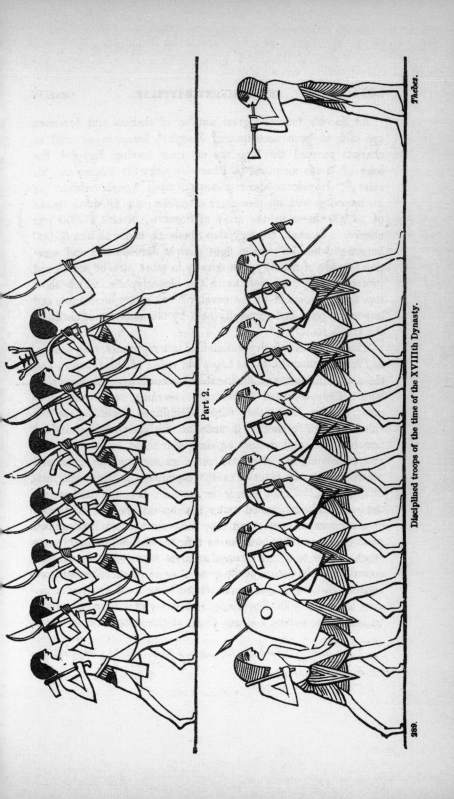

Part 2.

Disciplined troops of the time of the XVIIIth Dynasty.

Thebes.

289.

At Jacob's funeral a great number of chariots and *horsemen* are said to have accompanied Joseph;* *horsemen* as well as chariots pursued the Israelites on their leaving Egypt;† the song of Moses mentions in Pharaoh's army the " horse an his rider ;"‡ Herodotus also represents Amasis " on horseback " in his interview with the messenger of Apries; and Diodorus speaks of 24,000 horse in the army of Sesostris, besides 27,000 war chariots. Shishak, the Egyptian Sheshonk, had with him 60,000 horsemen when he went to fight against Jerusalem;§ and mention is made of the Egyptian cavalry in other parts of sacred and profane history; as well as in the hieroglyphics, which show that the " command of the cavalry " was a very honourable and important post, and generally held by the most distinguished of the king's sons.

The Egyptian infantry was divided into regiments, very similar, as Plutarch observes, to the λοχοι and ταξεις of the Greeks; and these were formed and distinguished according to the arms they bore. They consisted of bowmen, spearmen, swordsmen, clubmen, slingers, and other corps, disciplined according to the rules of regular tactics; || and the regiments being divided into battalions and companies, each officer had his peculiar rank and command, like the chiliarchs, hecatontarchs, decarchs, and others among the Greeks, or the captains over thousands, hundreds, fifties, and tens, among the Jews. ¶ When in battle array, the heavy infantry, armed with spears and shields, and a falchion, or other weapon, was drawn up in the form of an impregnable phalanx ;** and the bowmen as well as the light infantry were taught either to act in line, or to adopt more open movements, according to the nature of the ground, or the state of the enemy's battle. But the phalanx once formed was fixed and unchangeable, and the 10,000 Egyptians in the army of Crœsus could not be induced to oppose a larger front to the enemy, being accus-

---

* Gen. l. 9.   † Exod. xiv. 28: *comp.* 2 Kings, xviii. 24; Isa. xxxvi. 9.
‡ Exod. xv. 21.   § 2 Chron. xii. 3.
|| See woodcuts 289, 290.   ¶ Deut. i. 15.
** See woodcut next page.

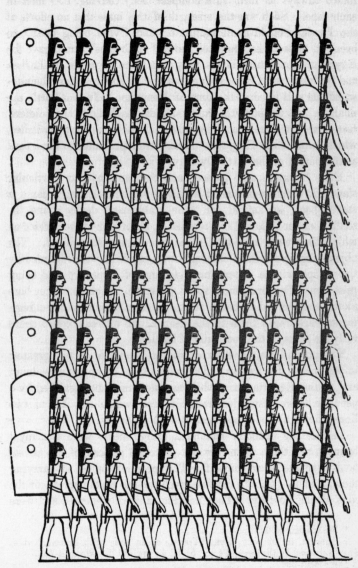

290.   Phalanx of heavy infantry.   *Thebes.*

tomed always to form in a compact body, having 100 men in each face. Such was the strength of this mass that no efforts of the Persians could avail against it; and Cyrus being unable to break it, after he had defeated the rest of Crœsus's army, gave the Egyptians honourable terms, assigning them the cities of Larissa and Cyllene, near Cumæ and the sea, for an abode; where their descendants still lived in the time of Xenophon. In that battle the phalanx had adopted the huge shields, reaching to the soldiers' feet, and completely covering them from the enemy's missiles, which some of the Egyptian infantry are represented to have used at the period of the VIth Dynasty.*

Each battalion, and indeed each company, had its particular standard, which represented a sacred subject,—a king's name, a sacred boat, an animal, or some emblematic device; and the soldiers either followed or preceded it, according to the service on which they were employed, or as circumstances required. The objects chosen for their standards were such as were regarded by the troops with a superstitious feeling of respect;† and being raised, says Diodorus, on a spear (or staff), which an officer bore aloft,‡ they served to point out to the men their respective regiments, encouraged them to the charge, and offered a conspicuous rallying point in the confusion of battle.

The post of standard-bearer was at all times of the greatest importance. He was an officer, and a man of approved valour; and in the Egyptian army he was sometimes distinguished by a peculiar badge suspended from his neck, which consisted of two lions, the emblems of courage, and other devices.

Besides the ordinary standards of regiments were the royal banners, and those borne by the principal persons of the household near the king himself. The peculiar office of carrying these, and the *flabella*, was reserved for the royal princes, or the sons of the nobility. They had the rank of generals, and were

---

* See woodcut 300.
† Solomon, in his Song, says, "Terrible as an army with banners," vi. 4. They were used by the Jews, Ps. xx. 5; lx. 4; Isa. xiii. 2. Woodcut 291.
‡ Woodcut 289.

291.   Egyptian standards.   *Thebes.*

either despatched to take command of a wing, or a division, and remained in attendance upon the monarch; and their post during the royal triumph, the coronation, or other grand ceremonies, was close to his person. Some bore the fans of state behind the throne, or supported the seat on which he was carried to the

292.   Officers of the household.   *Thebes.*

temple; others held the sceptre, and waved flabella before him;
and the privilege of serving on his right, or left, hand depended
on the grade they enjoyed. A wing was called "*horn*," as by
the Greeks and Romans.

The troops were summoned by sound of trumpet *—an instrument, as well as the long drum, used by the Egyptians at the
earliest period ;† and the trumpeters are represented in the battle-
scenes of Thebes either standing still, and summoning the troops
to form, or in the act of leading them to the charge.

The offensive weapons of the Egyptians were the bow, spear,
two species of javelin, sling, a short and straight sword, dagger,
knife, falchion or *ensis falcatus*, axe or hatchet, battle-axe, pole-
axe, mace or club, and the *lissán*,—a curved stick similar to that
still in use among the modern Ethiopians. Their defensive arms
consisted of a helmet of metal, or a quilted headpiece; a cuirass,
or coat of armour, made of metal plates, or quilted with metal

* Woodcut 289.   † See above, woodcuts, pp. 104, 105.

bands, and an ample shield. But they had no greaves; and the only coverings to the arms were a part of the cuirass, forming a short sleeve, and extending about half way to the elbow.

The soldier's chief defence was his shield, which, in length, was equal to about half his height, and generally double its own breadth. It was most commonly covered with bull's hide, having the hair outwards, sometimes strengthened by one or more

293. Shields. *Thebes.*

rims of metal, and studded with nails or metal pins, the inner part being a wooden frame. It was on this account that the shields of the Egyptians, who had fallen in the battle between Artaxerxes and the younger Cyrus, were collected by the Greeks for firewood, together with arrows, baggage-waggons, and other things made of wood.

In shape, the Egyptian shield resembled the ordinary funereal tablets found in the tombs, circular at the summit and squared at the base, frequently with a slight increase or swell towards the top; and near the upper part of the outer surface was a circular

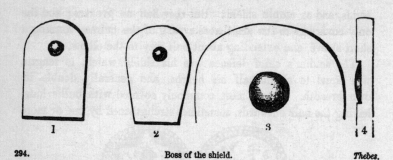

294.   Boss of the shield.   *Thebes.*

cavity in lieu of a boss, the use of which is not easily explained.
To the inside of the shield was attached a thong, by which they

295.   Thong inside the shield.   *Thebes.*

suspended it upon their shoulders, as described by Xenophon;
and an instance occurs of a shield so supported, which is shown

to be concave within; like that used in Assyria.* It appears that
the handle was so made that they might pass their arm through

296. Concave shield. *Thebes.*   297. Mode of carrying the shield. *Thebes.*

it and grasp a spear: but this may only be another mode of representing the shield slung at their back. The handle was sometimes

298.   Handle of shield.   *Thebes*

placed horizontally, across the shield, sometimes vertically; but
the latter was its more usual position.†

* Woodcut 296. Layard, N. and Bab., p. 457.   † Woodcuts 295 and 298.

Some lighter bucklers, furnished with a wooden bar, placed across the upper part, which was held with the hand, are represented at Beni-Hassan; but these appear to have belonged rather to foreigners than to Egyptian soldiers.

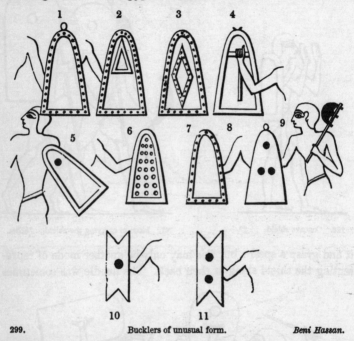

299.   Bucklers of unusual form.   *Beni Hassan.*

Some Egyptian shields were of extraordinary dimensions, and varied in form from those generally used, being pointed at the summit. They were of very early date, having been used before the Shepherd invasion; and were the same that the Egyptian phalanx carried in the army of Crœsus, and again in that of Artaxerxes, mentioned by Xenophon. But they were not generally adopted by the Egyptian troops, who found the common shield sufficiently large, and more convenient.

The Egyptian bow was not unlike that used in later times by European archers. The string was either fixed upon a projecting piece of horn, or inserted into a groove or notch in the wood,

300.   Large shield of early time.   *O'Sioot.*

at either extremity, differing in this respect from that of the
Koofa, and some other Asiatic people, who secured the string by
passing it over a small nut which projected from the circular
ends of the bow.

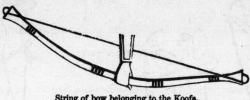

301.   String of bow belonging to the Koofa.   *Thebes.*

The Ethiopians and Libyans, who were famed for their skill
in archery, adopted the same method of fastening the string as
the Egyptians, and their bow was similar in form and size to that
of their neighbours.

The Egyptian bow was a round piece of wood, from five to
five feet and a half in length, either almost straight, and tapering
to a point at both ends; some of which are represented in the
sculptures, and have even been found at Thebes; or curving

fig. 1.

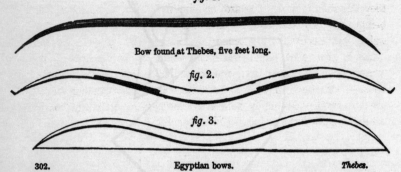

Bow found at Thebes, five feet long.

fig. 2.

fig. 3.

302.   Egyptian bows.   *Thebes.*

inwards in the middle, when unstrung, as in the paintings of the
tombs of the kings; and in some instances a piece of leather
or wood was attached to or let into it, above and below the
centre.

In stringing it, the Egyptians fixed the lower point in the
ground, and, standing or seated, the knee pressed against the

303. Usual mode of stringing the bow. *Thebes and Beni Hassan.*   304. Stringing a bow. *Beni Hassan.*

inner side of the bow, they bent it with one hand, and then
passed the string with the other into the notch at the upper extremity; and one instance occurs of a man resting the bow on

his shoulder, and bracing it in that position.　While shooting, they frequently wore a guard on the left arm, to prevent its being hurt by the string; and this was fastened round the wrist, and secured by a thong tied above the elbow.　Sometimes a groove of metal was fixed upon the fore knuckle, in which the arrow rested and ran when discharged; and the chasseur, whose bow appears to have been less powerful than those used in war, occasionally held spare arrows in his right hand, while he pulled the string.　(*Woodcut* 306.)

305.　　　A guard worn on the wrist.　　　*Thebes.*

Their mode of drawing it was either with the forefinger and thumb, or the two forefingers; and though in the chase they often brought the arrow merely to the breast, (—a sort of snap-shooting adopted in the buffalo hunts of America—), their custom in war, as with the old English archers, was to carry it to the ear, the shaft of the arrow passing very nearly in a line with the eye.

The Egyptian bow-string was generally of catgut; and so great was their confidence in the strength of it and of the bow, that an archer from his car sometimes used them to entangle his opponent, whilst he smote him with a sword.

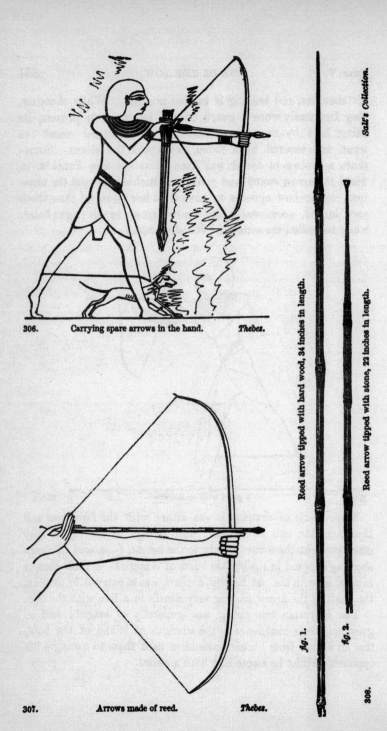

306. Carrying spare arrows in the hand. *Thebes.*

307. Arrows made of reed. *Thebes.*

Reed arrow tipped with hard wood, 34 inches in length.

Reed arrow tipped with stone, 22 inches in length.

Sale's Collection.

fig. 1.

fig. 2.

308.

Their arrows varied from twenty-two to thirty-four inches in length; some were of wood, others of reed;* frequently tipped with a metal head; and winged with three feathers,† glued longitudinally, and at equal distances, upon the other end of the shaft, as on our own arrows. Sometimes, instead of the metal head, a piece of hard wood was inserted into the reed, which terminated in a long tapering point;‡ but these were of too light and powerless a nature to be employed in war, and could only have been intended for the chase; in others, the place of the metal was supplied by a small piece of flint, or other sharp stone, secured by a firm black paste;§ and though used occasionally in battle, they appear from the sculptures to have belonged more particularly to the huntsman; and the arrows of archers are generally represented with bronze heads,‖ some barbed, others

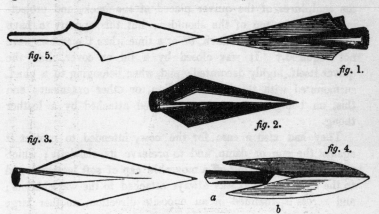

fig. 5.
fig. 1.
fig. 2.
fig. 3.
fig. 4.
a
b

309.   Metal heads of arrows.   *Alnwick Museum and Thebes.*
Fig. 4 had its shank (*a*) let into the hollow end of the shaft, and the projection above *b* acted as
a stop.

triangular, and many with three or four projecting blades, placed at right angles, and meeting in a common point. Stone-tipped arrows were not confined to an ancient era, nor were they peculiar to the Egyptians; the Persians and other eastern people frequently used them, even in war; and recent discoveries have

* Woodcuts 307 and 308.   † Woodcut 306.   ‡ Woodcut 308, *fig.* 1.
   § Woodcut 308, *fig.* 2.   ‖ Woodcuts 309 and 348.

ascertained that they were adopted by the Greeks themselves, several having been found in places unvisited by the troops of Persia, as well as on the plain of Marathon, and other fields of battle where they fought.

Each bowman was furnished with a capacious quiver, about four inches in diameter, and consequently containing a plentiful supply of arrows, which was supported by a belt, passing over the shoulder, and across the breast, to the opposite side. Their mode of carrying it differed from that of the Greeks, who bore it upon their shoulder, and from that of some Asiatic people, who suspended it vertically at their back, almost on a level with the elbow; or at their thigh; the usual custom of the Egyptian soldier being to fix it nearly in a horizontal position, and to draw out the arrows from beneath his arm.* Instances also occur in the sculptures of the quiver placed at the back, and projecting above the top of the shoulder; but this appears to have been only during the march, or at a time when the arrows were not required.† It was closed by a lid or cover, like the quiver itself, highly decorated; and, when belonging to a chief, surmounted with the head of a lion, or other ornament; and this, on being thrown open, remained attached by a leather thong.

They had also a case for the bow, intended to protect it against the sun or damp, and to preserve its elasticity; which was opened by drawing off a moveable cap of soft leather sewed to the upper end. It was always attached to the war-chariots; and across it, inclined in an opposite direction, another large case, containing two spears and an extra supply of arrows;‡ and, besides the quiver he wore, the warrior had frequently three others attached to his car.

Archers of the infantry were furnished with a smaller sheath for the bow,§ of which it covered the centre, leaving the two ends exposed; and, being of a pliable substance, probably leather, it was put round the bow, as they held it in their hand

---

* Woodcut 348.   † Woodcut 325, *fig.* 2.
‡ Woodcuts 326, 327, 331.   § Woodcut 289, part 1.

during a march. Besides the bow, their principal weapon of offence, they, like the mounted archers who fought in cars, were provided with a falchion, dagger, curved stick, mace, or battle-axe, for close combat when their arrows were exhausted ; and their defensive arms were the helmet, or quilted headpiece, and a coat of the same materials; but they had no shield, that being an impediment to the free use of the bow.

The spear, or pike, was of wood,* between five and six feet in length, with a metal head, into which the shaft was inserted and fixed with nails. The head was of bronze or iron, often very large, and with a double edge; but the spear does not appear to have been furnished with a metal point at the other extremity, called σαυρωτηρ by Homer,† which is still adopted in Turkish, modern Egyptian, and other spears, in order to plant them upright in the ground; as the spear of Saul was fixed near his head, while he " lay sleeping within the trench." ‡ Spears of this kind may sometimes come under the denomination of javelins, the metal being intended as well for a counterpoise in their flight as for the purpose above mentioned; but such an addition to those of the heavy-armed infantry was neither requisite nor convenient.

The javelin, lighter and shorter than the spear, was also of wood, and similarly armed with a strong two-edged metal head, of an elongated diamond, or leaf shape, either flat, or increasing in thickness at the centre, and sometimes tapering to a very long point;§ and the upper extremity of its shaft terminated in a bronze knob, surmounted by a ball with two thongs or tassels, intended both as an ornament and a counterpoise to the weight of its point. It was used like a spear, for thrusting, being held with one or with two hands; and occasionally, when the adversary was within reach, it was darted, and still retained in the warrior's grasp; the shaft being allowed to pass through his hand till stopped by the blow, or by the fingers suddenly closing

* Woodcuts 289, 290, 297, 310 a.　　　　† Hom. Il. x, 151.
‡ 1 Sam. xxvi. 7.　Comp. Virg. Æn. xii. 130.
§ Woodcut 355, fig. 9.

on the band of metal at the end; a custom still common among
the modern Nubians and Ababdeh.   They had another javelin,

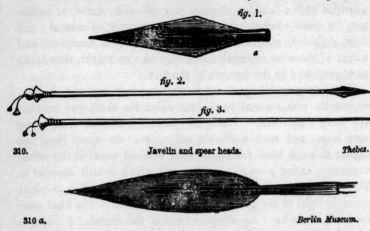

fig. 1.

a

fig. 2.

fig. 3.

310.   Javelin and spear heads.   *Thebes.*

310 *a.*   *Berlin Museum.*

apparently of wood, tapering to a sharp point, without the usual
metal head;* and a still lighter kind, armed with a small bronze

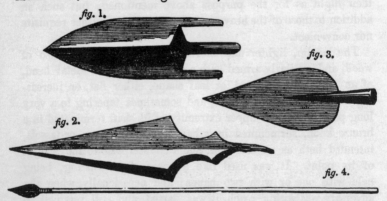

fig. 1.

fig. 3.

fig. 2.

fig. 4.

311.   Heads of small javelins.   *Alnwick Museum and Thebes.*

point,† which was frequently four-sided, three-bladed,‡ or broad
and nearly flat;§ and, from the upper end of the shaft being desti-

* Woodcut 310, *fig.* 3.   † Woodcut 310, *fig.* 1; and woodcut 355, *fig.* 8.
        ‡ Woodcut 311, *fig.* 2.   § *Fig.* 3.

tute of any metal counterpoise,* it resembled a dart now used by
the people of Dar-Foor, and other African tribes, who, without
any scientific knowledge of projectiles, and of the curve of a para-
bola, dexterously strike their enemy with its falling point.

Another inferior kind of javelin was made of reed, with a metal
head; but this can scarcely be considered a military weapon, nor
would it hold a high rank among those employed by the Egyptian
chasseur, most of which were of excellent workmanship.

The sling was a thong of leather, or string plaited;† broad in
the middle, and having a loop at one end, by which it was fixed
upon and firmly held with the hand; the other extremity terminating in a lash, which escaped from the finger as the stone was
thrown: and when used, the slinger whirled it two or three times
over his head, to steady it and increase the impetus.‡

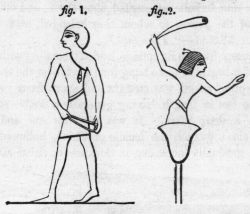

fig. 1.   *fig. 2.*

312.   Slingers.   *Beni Hassan and Thebes.*

It was an arm looked upon by many of the Greeks with great
contempt; but, when exposed to the missiles of the Persians, the
" Ten thousand " found the necessity of adopting it; and the leaden
bullet of the Rhodian slingers proved, by its greater range, its superiority over the large stones thrown by the enemy. Other Greeks

* Woodcut 311, *fig.* 4.
† As that still used in Egypt to drive away birds from the corn-fields.
‡ Woodcuts 49 and 355, *figs.* 4 and 5.

were also skilful with the sling, as the Achæans and Acarnanians; but the people most renowned for it were the natives of the Balearic Islands, who considered the sling of so much importance that the principal care of a parent was to instruct a boy in its use; and he was not permitted to have his breakfast, until he had dislodged it from a beam with the sling. This unpleasant alternative does not appear to have been imposed on the more fortunate sons of an Egyptian family, nor was the same consequence attached to the sling as to the bow and many other weapons.

Most Greeks, who used the sling, threw leaden plummets of an elongated spherical shape, or, rather, like an olive pointed at each end;—proving that the principle of "*the pointed ball*" was not unknown to them; and, indeed, all boys have long since found that an oval-shaped stone goes farther than a round one. Some had a thunderbolt represented upon them; and others bore the name of the person to whom they belonged, or a word, as ΑΓΩΝΙΣ, or ΔΕΞΑΙ—"*Take that.*"

The Achæans, like the Egyptians, loaded their sling with a round pebble; and a bagful of these hung from a belt over the shoulder.*

The Egyptian sword was straight and short, from two and a half to three feet in length, having generally a double edge, and tapering to a sharp point. It was used for cut and thrust. They had also a dagger, the handle of which, hollowed in the centre, and gradually increasing in thickness at either extremity,

fig. 1.

fig. 2.

313.   Daggers in their sheaths, with inlaid handles.   *Thebes.*

was inlaid with costly stones, precious woods, or metals; and the pommel of that worn by the king in his girdle was frequently surmounted by one or two heads of a hawk, the symbol

* Woodcut 312, *fig.* 1.

314.   Stabbing an enemy.   *Thebes.*

of Phrah, or the Sun, the title given to the monarchs of the Nile.
It was much smaller than the sword: its blade was about ten or
seven inches in length, tapering gradually in breadth, from one

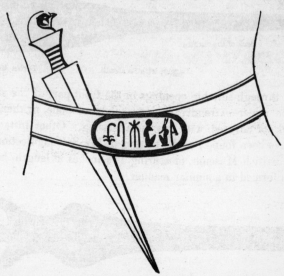

315.   Mode of wearing the dagger.   *Thebes.*

inch and a half to two-thirds of an inch, towards the point; and
the total length, with the handle, only completed a foot or sixteen inches.   The blade was bronze, thicker in the middle than
at the edges, and slightly grooved in that part; and so exquisitely
was the metal worked, that some retain their pliability and spring
after a period of several thousand years, and almost resemble steel
in elasticity.   Such is the dagger of the Berlin collection, which
was discovered in a Theban tomb, together with its leathern
sheath.   The handle is partly covered with metal, and adorned
with numerous small pins and studs of gold, which are purposely

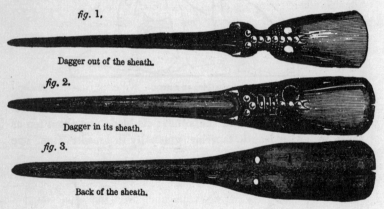

fig. 1.

Dagger out of the sheath.

fig. 2.

Dagger in its sheath.

fig. 3.

Back of the sheath.

316.   Dagger, with its sheath.   *Berlin Museum.*

shown through suitable openings in the front part of the sheath;
but the upper extremity consists solely of bone, neither ornamented nor covered with any metal casing.   Other instances of
this have been found; and a dagger in Mr. Salt's collection, now
in the British Museum, measuring 11½ inches in length, had the
handle formed in a similar manner.

317.   Egyptian dagger, 11¼ inches.   *British Museum.*

I have the blade of a smaller dagger, also of bronze, bearing the Amunoph II., 5¼ inches long, found at Thebes; and a knife, apparently of steel, is represented in the paintings, which had a single edge.

There was also a falchion called Shopsh, or Khopsh; resembling in form and name the κοπις of the Argives, reputed to be an Egyptian colony. It was more generally used than the sword, being borne by light as well as heavy armed troops; and that it was a most efficient weapon is evident, as well from the size and form of the blade as from its weight; the back of this bronze or iron blade being sometimes cased with brass.*

Officers as well as privates carried the falchion; and the king himself is frequently represented in close combat with the enemy, armed with it, or with the hatchet, battle-axe, pole-axe, or mace. A simple stick is more usually seen in the hand of officers commanding corps of infantry; but they had also other weapons; and, in leading their troops to the charge, they were armed in the same manner as the king when he fought on foot.

The axe, or hatchet, was small and simple, seldom exceeding two, or two feet and a half, in length: it had a single blade, and no instance is met with of a double axe resembling the *bipennis* of the Romans. It was of the same form as that used by the Egyptian carpenters; and served for close combat as well as for breaking down the gates of a town, and felling trees to construct engines for an assault. Independent of the bronze pins which secured the blade, the

318.   Axes and hatchets.
Thebes, and Salt's Collection.

* Woodcut 297, *fig.* 1.

handle was bound in that part with thongs of hide, in order
to prevent the wood, grooved to admit the metal, from splitting,
when a blow was struck.

The axe was less ornamented than other weapons: some bore
the figure of an animal, a boat, or fancy device, engraved upon
the blade; and the handle, frequently terminating in the shape
of a gazelle's foot, was marked with circular and diagonal lines,
representing bands, as on the projecting torus of an Egyptian
temple, or like the ligature of the Roman fasces.*   The soldier,
on his march, either held it in his hand, or suspended it at his
back with the blade downwards; but it does not appear from
the sculptures to have been covered by a sheath, nor is any
mode of wearing a sword indicated by them, except as a dagger
in the girdle, the point sloping to the left.†

The blade of the battle-axe was, in form, not unlike the

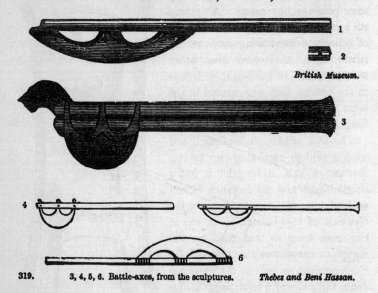

319.   3, 4, 5, 6. Battle-axes, from the sculptures.   *Thebes and Beni Hassan.*

Parthian shield; a segment of a circle, divided at the back into
two smaller segments, whose three points were fastened to the

------

* Woodcuts 318, and 355, *fig.* 3.   † As in woodcut 315.

handle with metal pins. It was of bronze, and sometimes (as the colour of those in the paintings shows) of steel; and the length of the handle was equal to, or more than double that of, the blade. In the British Museum is a portion of one of these weapons.* Its bronze blade is thirteen inches and a half long, and two and a half broad, inserted into a silver tube, secured with nails of the same metal. The wooden handle once fixed into this tube is wanting; but, judging from those represented at Thebes, it was considerably longer than the tube, and even protruded a little beyond the extremity of the blade, where it was sometimes ornamented with the head of a lion or other device, receding slightly,† so as not to interfere with the blow. The total length of these battle-axes may have been from three to four feet, and sometimes much less;‡ and their blades varied slightly in shape.§

The pole-axe was about three feet in length, but apparently more difficult to wield than the preceding, owing to the great weight of a metal ball to which the blade was fixed; and required, like the mace, a powerful as well as a skilful arm. The handle was generally about two feet in length, sometimes much longer; the

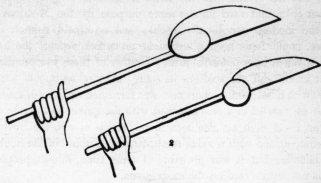

320.   Pole-axe.   *Thebes.*

ball four inches in its greatest diameter, and the blade varied from ten to fourteen inches, by two and three in breadth.

The mace was very similar to the pole-axe, without a blade.

* Woodcut 319, *fig.* 1.   † As *fig.* 3.
‡ As *fig.* 6, which is from the sculptures.   § *Figs.* 3 and 6.

It was of wood, bound with bronze, about two feet and a half in length, and furnished with an angular piece of metal, projecting from the handle, which may have been intended as a guard, though in many instances they represent the hand placed above it, while the blow was given.*

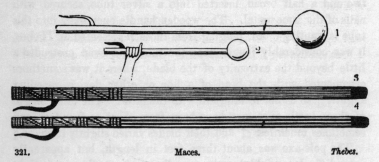

321.   Maces.   *Thebes.*

They had another mace,† similar in many respects to this, without the ball, and, to judge from its frequent occurrence in the sculptures, more generally used, and evidently far more manageable; but the former was the most formidable weapon against armour (like that used for the same purpose by the Memlooks, and the modern people of Cutch); and no shield, helmet, or cuirass, could have been a sufficient protection against the impetus given it by a powerful arm. Neither of these was peculiar to the chiefs: all the soldiers in some infantry regiments were armed with them; and a charioteer was furnished with one or more, which he carried in a case attached with the quiver to the side of his car. ‡ A club has also been found, and is now in the British Museum, armed with wooden teeth, similar to those in the South Sea Islands; but it was probably of some rude, foreign people, and is not represented on the monuments.

In ancient-times, when the fate of a battle was frequently decided by personal valour, the dexterous management of such arms was of great importance; and a band of resolute veterans, headed by a gallant chief, spread dismay among the ranks of an enemy.

* Woodcut 321, *fig.* 2.   † Woodcut 321, *figs.* 3 and 4.
‡ Egyptian chariot, in woodcut 331, p. 376.

They had another kind of mace, sometimes of uniform thickness through its whole length, sometimes broader at the upper end,* without either the ball or guard; and many of their allies carried a rude, heavy club;† but no body of native troops was armed with this last, and it cannot be considered an Egyptian weapon.

The curved stick, or club (now called *lissán* "tongue"), was used by heavy and light-armed troops as well as by archers; and if it does not appear a formidable arm, yet the experience of modern

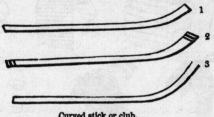

322.   Curved stick or club.   *Thebes.*

times bears ample testimony to its efficacy in close combat. To the Bisharieen it supplies the place of a sword; and the Ababdeh, content with this, their spear, and shield, fear not to encounter other tribes armed with the matchlock and the *yatagán*. In length it is about two feet and a half, and is made of a hard acacia wood.

The helmet was usually quilted; and though bronze helmets are said to have been worn by the Egyptians, they generally adopted the former, which being thick, and well padded, served as an excellent protection to the head, without the inconvenience of metal in so hot a climate. Some of them descended to the shoulder,‡ others only a short distance below the level of the ear;§ and the summit, terminating in an obtuse point, was ornamented with two tassels. ‖ They were of a green, red, or black colour; and a longer one, which fitted less closely to the back of the head, was fringed at the lower edge with a broad border,¶ and in some instances consisted of two parts, or an upper and under fold. ** Another, worn by the spearmen, and many corps of in-

---

* Woodcut 322, *figs.* 1 and 2.   † Woodcut 288, *fig.* 3.
‡ Woodcut 323, *figs.* 1, 2, 3, 4.   § *Figs.* 5, 6, 7.
‖ *Figs.* 3, 4, 5, 6, 7.   ¶ *Fig.* 3.   ** *Fig.* 4.

fantry and charioteers, was also quilted, and descended to the shoulder with a fringe; but it had no tassels, and, fitting close to the top of the head, it widened towards the base, the front, which covered the forehead, being made of a separate piece, attached to the other part. *

There is no representation of an Egyptian helmet with a crest,

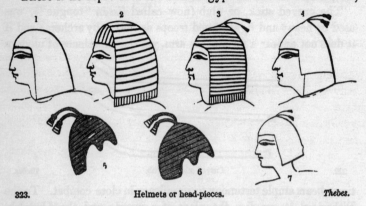

323.   Helmets or head-pieces.   *Thebes.*

but that of the Shairetana, once enemies and afterwards allies of the Pharaohs, shows they were used long before the Trojan war.

The outer surface of the corslet of mail, or coat of scale-armour, consisted of about eleven horizontal rows of metal plates, well secured by bronze pins; and at the hollow of the throat a narrower range of plates was introduced, above which were two more, completing the collar or covering of the neck. The breadth of each plate or scale was little more than an inch, eleven or twelve of them sufficing to cover the front of the body; and the sleeves, which were sometimes so short as to extend less than half way to the elbow, consisted of two rows of similar plates. Many, indeed most, of the corslets were without collars; in some the sleeves were rather longer, reaching nearly to the elbow, and they were worn both by heavy infantry and bowmen. The ordinary corslet may have been little less than two feet and a half in length; it sometimes covered the thighs nearly to the knee; and in order to prevent its pressing heavily upon the shoulder, they bound their girdle

* *Fig.* 2.

over it, and tightened it at the waist. But the thighs, and that part of the body below the girdle, were usually covered by a kelt, or other robe, detached from the corslet; and many of the light and heavy infantry were clad in a quilted vest of the same form as the coat of armour, for which it was a substitute; and

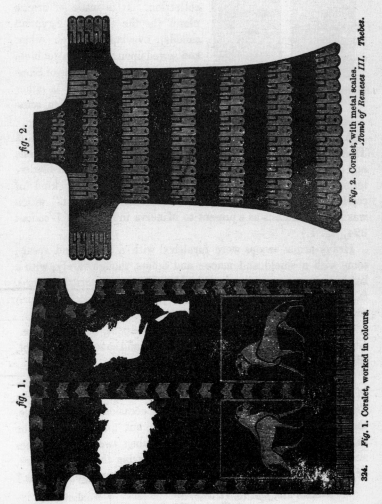

fig. 2.

Fig. 2. Corslet, with metal scales.
Tomb of Remeses III. Thebes.

fig. 1.

Fig. 1. Corslet, worked in colours.

324.

some wore corslets, reaching only from the waist to the upper

324 *a.* Plates of scale-armour.
Fig. 1. With the name of Sheshonk.

part of the breast, and supported by straps over the shoulder, which were faced with bronze plates.* A portion of one is in Dr. Abbott's collection. It is made of bronze plates (in the form of Egyptian shields), overlapping each other, and sewed upon a leathern doublet; two of which have the name of Sheshonk (Shishak), showing it either belonged to that king, or to some great officer of his court.

Among the arms painted in the tomb of Remeses III., at Thebes, is a corslet made of rich stuff, with the figures of lions and other animals worked upon it, and edged with a neat border, terminating below in a fringe; evidently the same kind of corslet, " ornamented with animals embroidered upon it," which was sent by Amasis as a present to Minerva in Lindus. (*Woodcut* 324, *fig.* 1.)

Heavy-armed troops were furnished with a shield and spear; some with a shield and mace; and others, though rarely, with a battle-axe, or a pole-axe, and shield. They also carried a sword, falchion, curved stick or *lissan*, simple mace, or hatchet; which may be looked upon as their side-arms.†

The light troops had nearly the same weapons, but their defensive armour was lighter; and the slingers and some others fought, like the archers, without shields.

The chariot corps constituted a very large and effective portion of the Egyptian army. Each car contained two persons, like the *diphros* (διφρος) of the Greeks. On some occasions it carried three, the charioteer or driver and two chiefs; but this was rarely the case, except in triumphal processions, when two of the princes accompanied the king in their chariot, bearing the regal sceptre, or the *flabella*, and required a third person to manage the reins.‡

---

* Woodcut 325, *figs.* 10, 11, 12.   † Woodcut 325.
‡ Woodcut 326, *fig.* 1.

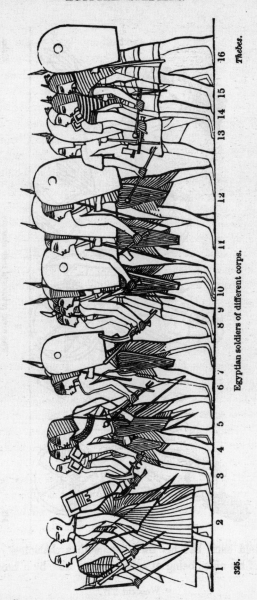

Egyptian soldiers of different corps.

Thebes.

325.

1 2 3 4 5 6 7 8 9 10 11 12 13 14 15 16

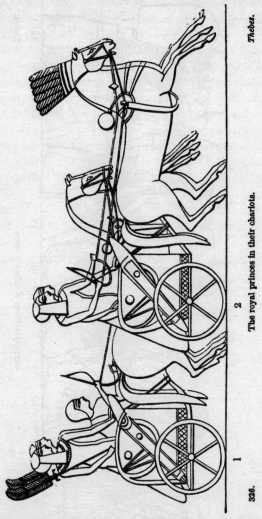

Thebes.

The royal princes in their chariots.

2

1

326.

In the field each had his own car, with a charioteer; and the
insignia of his office being attached behind him by a broad belt,*

* Woodcut 327.

his hands were free for the use of the bow and other arms. The driver generally stood on the off-side, in order to have the whip-hand free; and this interfered less with the use of the bow, than the Greek custom of driving on the near-side; which last was adopted in Greece as being more convenient for throwing the spear. When on an excursion for pleasure, or on a visit to a friend, an Egyptian gentleman mounted alone, and drove himself, footmen and other attendants running before and behind the car;* and sometimes an archer used his bow and acted as his own charioteer.†

In the battle scenes of the Egyptian temples, the king is repre-sented alone in his car, unattended by any charioteer;‡ with the reins fastened round his body, while engaged in bending his bow against the enemy; though it is possible that the driver was omitted, in order not to interfere with the principal figure. The king had always a " second chariot," in order to provide against accidents; as Josiah is stated to have had when defeated by Necho;§ and the same was in attendance on state occasions.‖

327.   The son of King Remeses with his charioteer.   *Thebes.*

The cars of the whole chariot corps contained each two war-

---

* Woodcut 85.   † Woodcut 329.
‡ Like Homer's gods and heroes; Iliad, θ, 116 ; κ, 513; O, 352, &c.
§ 2 Chron. xxxv. 24.   ‖ Gen. xli. 43, " the second chariot."

riors, comrades of equal rank; and the charioteer who accompanied a chief was a person of confidence, as we see from the familiar manner in which one of them is represented conversing with a son of the great Remeses.* (*Woodcut* 327.)

In driving, the Egyptians used a whip, like the heroes and charioteers of Homer; and this, or a short stick, was generally employed even for beasts of burden, and for oxen at the plough, in preference to the goad. The whip consisted of a smooth round wooden handle, and a single or double thong: it sometimes had

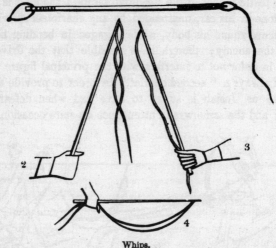

328.   Whips.   *Thebes.*

a lash of leather, or string, about two feet in length, either twisted or plaited; and a loop being attached to the lower end, the archer was enabled to use the bow, while it hung suspended from his wrist.†

When a hero encountered a hostile chief, he sometimes dismounted from his car, and substituting for his bow and quiver the spear, battle-axe, or falchion, he closed with him hand to hand, like the Greeks and Trojans described by Homer: and the lifeless body of the foe being left upon the field, was stripped of its

---

* *Comp.* Hom. Il., θ, 120; and λ, 518.   † Woodcut 329.

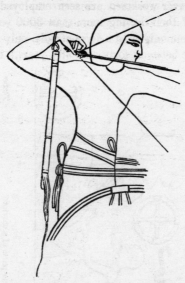

329.   Whip suspended from the wrist of the archer.   *Thebes.*

arms by his companions. Sometimes a wounded adversary, in-
capable of further resistance, having claimed and obtained the
mercy of the victor, was carried from the field in his chariot;
and the ordinary captives, who laid down their arms and yielded
to the Egyptians, were treated as prisoners of war, and were sent
bound to the rear under an escort, to be presented to the monarch,
and to grace his triumph, after the termination of the conflict.
The hands of the slain were then counted before him; and this
return of the enemy's killed was duly registered, to commemorate
his success, and the glories of his reign.

The Egyptian chariots had no seat; but the bottom part consisted of a frame interlaced with thongs or rope, forming a species
of network, in order, by its elasticity, to render the motion of a
carriage without springs more easy: and this was also provided
for by placing the wheels as far back as possible, and resting
much of the weight on the horses, which supported the pole.

That the chariot was of wood is sufficiently proved by the

sculptures, wherever workmen are seen employed in making it; and the fact of their having more than 3000 years ago already invented and commonly used a form of pole, only introduced into our own country between forty and fifty years,* is an instance of

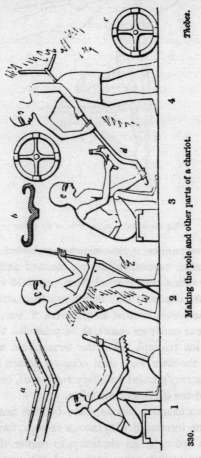

330.   Making the pole and other parts of a chariot.   Thebes.

the truth of Solomon's assertion, "there is no new thing under the sun," and shows the skill of their workmen at that remote time.

* Woodcut 330, *fig.* 3 *d.*

The body of the car was exceedingly light, consisting of a painted wooden framework, strengthened and ornamented with metal and leather binding, like many of those mentioned by Homer: the bottom part rested on the axle-tree and lower extremity of the pole, which was itself inserted into the axle, or a socket attached to it; and some chariots are shown by the monuments to have been "inlaid with silver and gold, others painted;" —the latter, as might be expected, the most numerous, 61 of them being mentioned to 9 of the former. The upper rim of its front was fastened to the pole by a couple of thongs or straps, to steady it, like the straps at the back of our modern chariots and coaches; and when the horses were taken out, the pole was supported on a crutch, or the wooden figure of a man, representing a captive, or enemy, who was considered fitted for this degrading office.

The greater portion of the sides, and the whole of the back, were open; the latter indeed entirely so, without any rim or framework above; and the hinder part of the lateral framework commenced nearly in a line with the centre of the wheel, and rising perpendicularly, or slightly inclined backwards, from the base of the car, extended with a curve, at the height of about two feet and a half, to the front, serving as well for a safeguard to the driver, as a support for his quivers and bow-case. To strengthen it, three thongs of leather were attached at either side, and an upright of wood connected it with the base of the front part immediately above the pole, where the straps before mentioned were fastened.

The bow-case, frequently richly ornamented, with the figure of a lion or other devices, was placed in an inclined position, pointing forwards; its upper edge, immediately below the flexible leather cover, being generally on a level with the summit of the framework of the chariot; so that when the bow was drawn out, the leather cover fell downwards, and left the upper part on an uninterrupted level. In battle this was of course a matter of no importance; but in the city, where the bow-case was considered an elegant part of the ornamental hangings of a car, and conti-

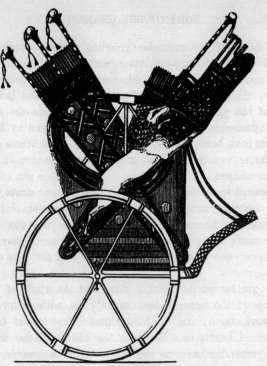

331.   A war chariot, with bow-cases and complete furniture.   *Thebes.*

332.   Chariot of the Rot-u-n.   *Thebes*

nued to be attached to it, they paid some attention to the position and fall of the pendent cover, deprived, as it there was, of its bow; for, as I have observed, the civilised state of Egyptian society required the absence of all arms, except on service. The quivers and spear-cases were suspended in a contrary direction, pointing backwards; sometimes an additional quiver was attached close to the bow-case, with a mace and other arms, and every war chariot containing two men was furnished with the same number of bows.

The processes of making the pole, wheels, and other parts of the chariot are often represented, and even the mode of bending the wood for the purpose.* In the ornamental trappings, hangings, and binding of the framework and cases, leather was principally used, dyed of various hues, and afterwards adorned with metal edges and studs; and the wheels, strengthened at the joints of the felly with bronze or brass bands, were bound with a hoop of metal.† The Egyptians themselves have not failed to point out what parts were the peculiar province of the carpenter, and of the currier. The body and framework of the car, the pole, yoke, and

333.   Cutting leather, and binding a car.   *Thebes.*

* Woodcut 334, next page.   † *Comp.* Hom. Il., ε, 724.

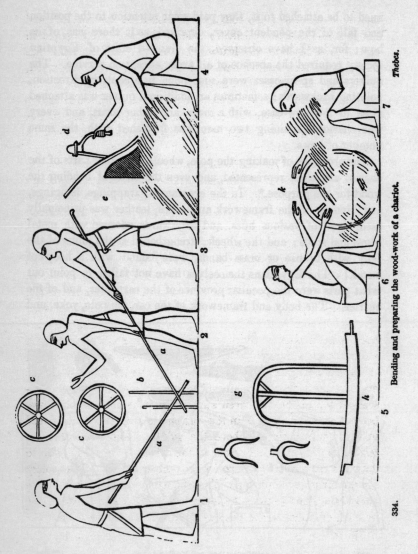

334.   Bending and preparing the wood-work of a chariot.   *Thebes.*

wheels, were the work of the former; the cases for the bows and
other arms, the saddle and harness, the binding of the framework,

and the coverings of the body, were finished by the currier; and lest it should not be sufficiently evident that they are engaged in cutting and bending the leather for this purpose, the artist has distinctly pointed out the nature of the substance they employed, by figuring an entire skin, and the soles of a pair of shoes,* or sandals, suspended in the shop; and we find a semicircular knife† used by the Egyptians to cut leather precisely similar to our own, even in the remote age of king Amunoph II., who lived 14 centuries before our era.

In war chariots, the wheels had six spokes, generally round; in many curricles, or private cars, employed in towns, only four; and the wheel was fixed to the axle by a small linch-pin, sometimes surmounted with a fanciful head, and secured by a thong which passed through the lower end.

The harness of curricles and war chariots was nearly similar; and the pole in either case was supported on a curved yoke fixed to its extremity by a strong pin, and bound with straps or thongs of leather. The yoke, resting upon a small well-padded saddle, was firmly fitted into a groove of metal; and the saddle, placed upon the horses' withers, and furnished with girths and a breastband, was surmounted by an ornamental knob; and in front of it a small hook secured the bearing-rein. The other reins passed through a thong or ring at the side of the saddle, and thence over the projecting extremity of the yoke; and the same thong secured the girths, and even appears in some instances to have been attached to them. In the war chariots, a large ball, placed upon a shaft, projected above the saddle, which was either intended to give a greater power to the driver, by enabling him to draw the reins over a groove in its centre; or was added solely for an ornamental purpose, like the fancy head-dresses of the horses, and fixed to the yoke immediately above the centre of the saddle,‡ or rather to the head of a pin which connected the yoke to the pole.§

* Woodcut 333, *l* and *g*.
† It occurs frequently.　See woodcut 333, *c*.
‡ Woodcut 335, *fig.* 2.　　　　§ Woodcut 335, *fig.* 1.

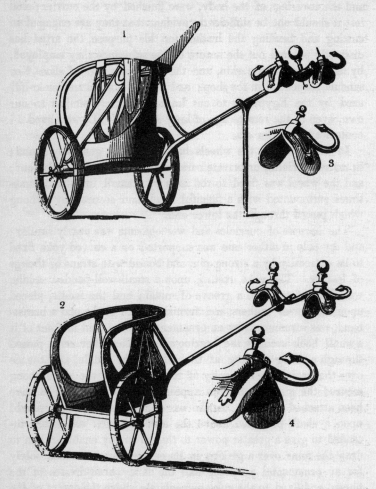

335.   Chariots in perspective, from a comparison of different sculptures.

The traces were single, one only on the inner side of each horse, fastened to the lower part of the pole, and thence extending to the saddle; but no exterior trace was thought necessary:

and no provision was made for attaching it to the car. Indeed
the yoke sufficed for all the purposes of draught as well as for
backing the chariot; and being fixed to the saddle, it kept the
horses at the same distance and in the same relative position, and
prevented their breaking outwards from the line of draught. In
order to render this more intelligible, I shall introduce a pair of
horses yoked to a chariot according to the rules of European
drawing, derived from a comparison of the numerous representations in the sculptures, omitting only their housings and head-
dress, which may be readily understood in an Egyptian picture.
I have also followed the Egyptian fashion of putting a chesnut
and a grey together, which was thought quite as correct in ancient Egypt, as it now is in England.

On grand occasions the Egyptian horses were decked with
fancy ornaments : a rich striped or checkered housing, trimmed
with a broad border and large pendent tassels, covered the
whole body; and two or more feathers inserted in lions' heads,
or some other device of gold, formed a crest upon the summit of
the head-stall. But this display was confined to the chariots of
the monarch, or the military chiefs; and it was thought sufficient, in the harness of other cars, and in the town curricle, to
adorn the bridles with rosettes, which resemble those used in England at the present day.*

They had no blinkers; but the head and upper part of the
neck were frequently enveloped in a rich covering similar to the
housing, trimmed with a leather fringe; and the bridle consisted
of two check pieces, a throat-lash, head-stall, and the forehead
and nose straps.

No instance occurs of Egyptian chariots with more than two
horses; nor is there any representation of a carriage with shafts
drawn by one horse; but a pair of shafts have been found,
with a wheel of curious construction, having a wooden tire to
the felly, and an inner circle, probably of metal, which passed
through, and connected, its six spokes a short distance from the

* Woodcuts 85 and 326.

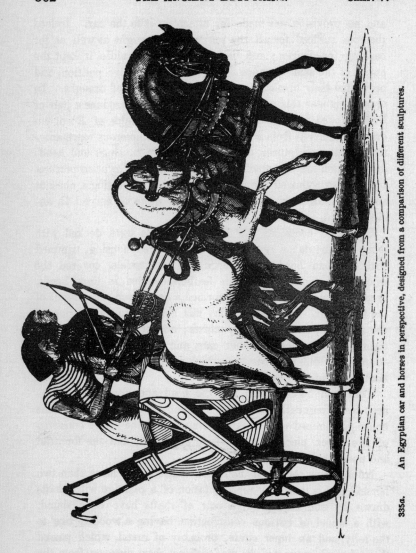

An Egyptian car and horses in perspective, designed from a comparison of different sculptures.

335a.

nave (A A). The diameter of the wheel was about 3 ft. 1 in.
The felly was in six pieces, the end of one overlapping the other;
and the tire was fastened to it by bands of raw hide passing

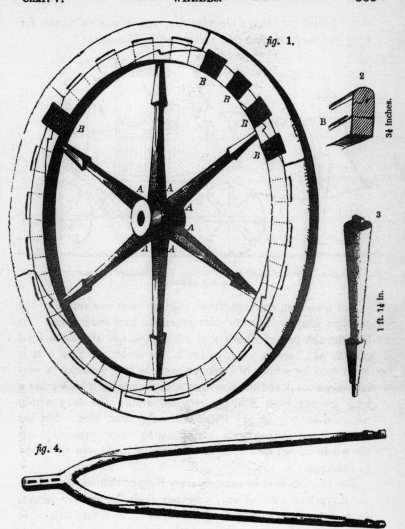

336.　　　**Fig.** 1. Wheel; 3 ft. 1 in. diameter.　　*In the Collection of Dr. Abbott.*
　　　　　Fig. 4. Shafts; 11 feet in total length.

through long narrow holes made to receive them (B B). It is uncertain whether the carriage they belonged to had two or four wheels; for though an instance does occur of an Egyptian

four-wheeled car, it is a singular one, and it was only used for
religious purposes, like that mentioned by Herodotus.*

337.   Singular instance of a four-wheeled carriage, on the bandages of a mummy, belonging
to S. d'Athanasi.

The travelling carriage drawn by two oxen was very like the
common chariot; but the sides appear to have been closed. It
had also one pair of wheels with six spokes, and the same kind
of pole and harness. An umbrella was sometimes fixed over it
when used for women of rank, as over the king's chariot on certain occasions;† and the bow-case with the bow in it shows that a
long journey from Ethiopia required arms; the lady within
being on her way to pay a visit to the Egyptian king. She has
a very large retinue with her, bringing many presents: and
the whole subject calls to mind the visit of the Queen of Sheba
to Solomon.

The chariots used by contemporary Eastern nations, with whom
the Egyptians were at war, were not dissimilar in their general
form, or in the mode of yoking the horses (even if they differed in
the number of persons they contained, having usually three instead of the two in Egyptian and Greek cars); as may be seen
from that which is brought, with its two unyoked horses, as a

* Herod. ii. 63.   † Woodcut 86, in p. 75.

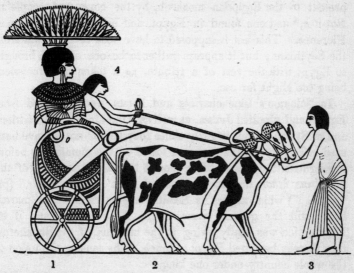

338.   An Ethiopian princess travelling in a *plaustrum*, or car drawn by oxen.   Over her is a
       sort of umbrella. 3. An attendant. 4. The charioteer or driver.   *Thebes.*

339.   Car and bow, in the collection at Florence (from the great work of Professor
                                   Rosellini).

present to the Egyptian monarch, by the conquered people of Rot-ñ-n,* and one found in Egypt, and now in the museum at Florence. This last is supposed to have been taken in war from the Scythians; but it appears rather to be one of those brought to Egypt with the rest of a tribute, as a token of submission, being too slight for use.

In Solomon's time chariots and horses were exported from Egypt, and supplied Judæa, as well as " the kings of the Hittites, and of Syria; " † but in early times they appear not to have been used in Egypt, and they are not found on the monuments before the eighteenth dynasty. For though the Egyptian name of the horse was *hthor*, the *mare* was called, as in Hebrew, " *sûs*," (pl. " *susim ;*") which argues its Semitic origin; *fáras*, " the mare," being still the generic name of the Arab horse; and if its introduction was really owing to the invasion of the Shepherds, they thereby benefited Egypt as much, as by causing the union of the whole country under one king.

The Egyptians sometimes drove a pair of mules, instead of horses, in the chariots used in towns, or in the country; an instance of which occurs in a painting now in the British Museum.

The Egyptian chariot corps, like the infantry, were divided into light and heavy troops, both armed with bows: the former chiefly employed in harassing the enemy with missiles, and in evolutions requiring rapidity of movement; the latter called upon to break through opposing masses of infantry, after having galled them during their advance with a heavy shower of arrows; and, in order to enable them to charge with greater security, they were furnished with a shield, which was not required for the other mounted archers, and a long spear was substituted on these occasions for the missiles they had previously employed. The light-armed chariot corps were also supplied with weapons adapted to close combat, as the sword, club, and javelin; but they had neither spear nor shield. The heavy infantry, and light

Woodcut 339.   † 1 Kings, x. 29.   2 Chron. i. 16, 17.

troops employed in the assault of fortified towns, were all provided with shields, under cover of which they made approaches
to the place; and so closely was the idea of a siege connected
with this arm,* that a figure of the king, who is sometimes introduced in the sculptures, as the representative of the whole army,
advancing with the shield before him, is intended to show that
the place was taken by assault.

In attacking a fortified town, they advanced under cover of
the arrows of the bowmen ; and either instantly applied the
scaling-ladder to the ramparts, or undertook the routine of a
regular siege : in which case, having advanced to the walls, they
posted themselves under cover of *testudos*, and shook and dislodged the stones of the parapet with a species of battering-ram,†
directed and impelled by a body of men expressly chosen for this
service : but when the place held out against these attacks, and
neither a *coup de main*, the ladder, nor the ram, were found to
succeed, they used the testudo for concealing and protecting the
sappers, while they mined the place; and certainly, of all people,
the Egyptians were the most likely to have recourse to this
stratagem of war, from the great practice they had in under-
ground excavations, and in directing shafts through the solid
rock.

The testudo was of frame-work, sometimes supported by poles
having a forked summit, and covered, in all probability, with
hides ; it was sufficiently large to contain several men, and so
placed that the light troops might mount upon the outside, and
thus obtain a footing on more elevated ground, apply the ladders
with greater precision, or obtain some other important advantage; and each party was commanded by an officer of skill, and
frequently by those of the first rank.‡

They also endeavoured to force open the gates of the town, or

---

* Conf. 2 Kings xix. 32. " Nor come before it (the city) with *shield*, nor
cast a bank against it."   Isaiah xxxvii. 33.
† See woodcut 340.
‡ Woodcut 341. Four of the king's sons command the four testudos, *a*,
b, *c*, *d*.

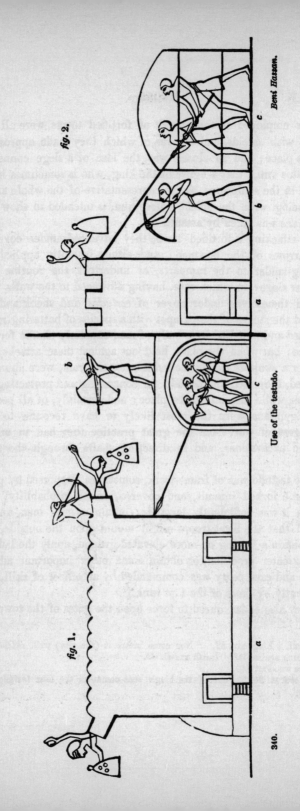

fig. 2.

Beni Hassan.

b   *c*

a

Use of the testudo.

c   *b*

fig. 1.

a

340.

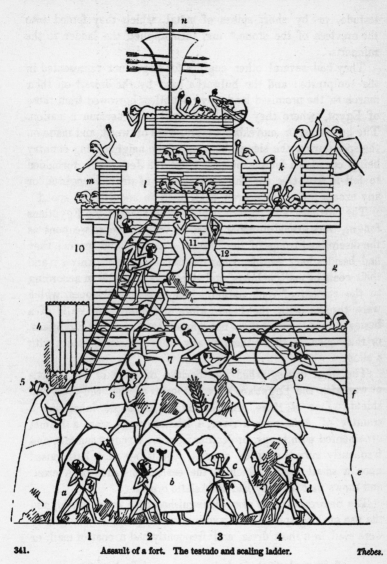

341.   Assault of a fort. The testudo and scaling ladder.   *Thebes.*

hew them down with axes; and when the fort was built upon
a rock, they escaladed the precipitous part by means of the

testudo, or by short spikes of metal, which they forced into the crevices of the stone,* and then applied the ladder to the ramparts.

They had several other engines for sieges not represented in the sculptures; and the bulwarks used by the Jews,† on their march to the promised land, were doubtless borrowed from those of Egypt, where they had lived until they became a nation. The bulwarks, or moveable towers, were of wood, and made on the spot during the siege, the trees of the neighbouring country being cut down for the purpose: but the Jews were forbidden to fell a fruit-tree for the construction of warlike engines, or any except those which grew wild, or in an uncultivated spot.‡

The northern and eastern tribes, against whom the Egyptians fought, were armed in many instances with the same weapons as the disciplined troops of the Pharaohs, as bows and spears; they had besides long swords, rude massive clubs, and knives; and their coats of mail, helmets, and shields varied in form according to the custom of each nation. They also used stones, which were thrown with the hand, while defending the walls of a besieged town; but it does not appear that either the Egyptians, or their enemies, threw them on any other occasions, except with a sling.

The most distinguished peculiarities of some of the nations at war with the Egyptians were the forms of the head-dress and shield. One of these, the Shairetana, a people inhabiting a country of Asia, near a river, a lake, or a sea, wore a helmet ornamented with horns, projecting from its circular summit, and frequently surmounted by a crest, consisting of a ball raised upon a small shaft; which is the earliest instance of a crest, and shows that it really had an Asiatic origin.

The Shairetana were also distinguished by a round shield, and the use of long spears and javelins, with a pointed sword; they were clad in a short dress, and frequently had a coat of mail, or

---

* See woodcut 341, *fig.* 5.   † Deut. xx. 20.
‡ " For the tree of the field is man's life." Deut. xx. 19.

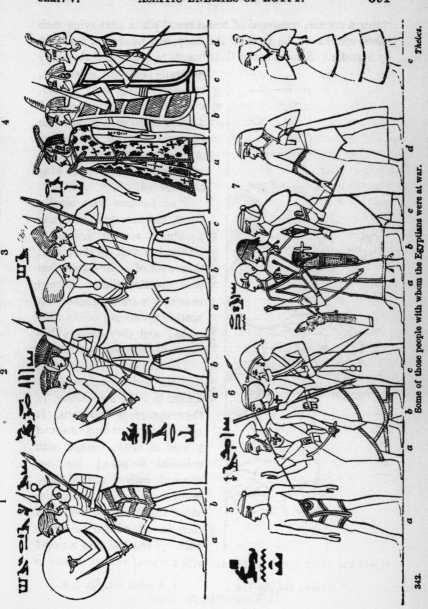

Some of those people with whom the Egyptians were at war.

Thebes.

342.

rather a cuirass, composed of broad metal plates overlaying each other, adapted to the form of the body, and secured at the waist by a girdle. Some allowed their beards to grow; and they very generally adopted a custom, common to most early nations, of wearing large ear-rings.* Layard supposes them to be the Sharutinians (near the modern Antioch) mentioned among the conquests of the Assyrian king at Nimroud.

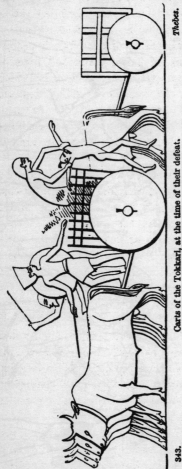

Their features were usually large, the nose prominent and aquiline; and in their complexion, as well as their hair, they were of a far lighter hue than the Egyptians. At one time they were the enemies, at another the allies,† of the Pharaohs: and they assisted Remeses II. against the Khita.

The Tokkari wore a helmet, in form and appearance very similar to those represented in the sculptures of Persepolis. It appears to have been made of a kind of cloth, marked with coloured stripes; ‡ the rim adorned with a row of large beads or other ornamental devices, and it was secured by a thong or riband tied below the chin. They had also a round shield and short dress, frequently with a coat of armour similar to

* Woodcut 342, *fig.* 1, *a, b.*   † Woodcut 341, *figs* 5, 6.
‡ Woodcut 342, *fig.* 2, *a, b.*

that of the Shairetana; and their offensive weapons consisted principally of a spear, and a large pointed knife, or straight sword. They sometimes, though rarely, had a beard, which was still more unusual with the chiefs: their features were regular, the nose slightly aquiline: and whenever the Egyptian artists have represented them on a large scale, their face presents a more pleasing outline than the generality of these Asiatic people. They fought, like the Egyptians, in chariots; and had carts or waggons, with two solid wheels, drawn by a pair of oxen; which appear to have been placed in the rear, as in the Scythian and Tartar armies, and were used for carrying off the old men, women, and children, in defeat. They were also at one time allies of the Pharaohs, and assisted them in their long wars against the Rebo.

Another people, whose name is lost,* were distinguished by a costume of a very Oriental character, consisting of a high fur-cap, not unlike one worn by the ancient Persians and that of the modern Tartars; a tight dress, with the usual girdle; and a short kelt, common to many Asiatic nations, which, apparently divided and folding over in front, was tied at the bottom with strings. Round their neck, and falling upon the breast, was a large round amulet,† very similar to those of agate worn by the dervishes of the East, in which they resembled the Assyrian captives of Tirhakah, represented on the walls of Medeenet Haboo.‡ Their features were remarkable; and though in the sculptures they occasionally vary in appearance, from the presence or the absence of a beard, the strongly defined contour of the face and the high bridge of their prominent nose sufficiently distinguish them from other people, and show that the artist has intended to convey a notion of these peculiar characteristics.

Their arms consisted of two javelins, a club, and falchion, and a shield like that of the Egyptians, with a round summit. They were on terms of friendship with the third Remeses, and assisted

---

* It begins with the letters Sha . . . . Woodcuts 288, *fig.* 2, and 342, *fig.* 3.
† Woodcut 342, *fig.* 3 *a.*   ‡ Woodcut 344, *fig.* 1.

him in his wars against the Rebo ; and though they occur among the foreigners who had been conquered by the arms of Egypt, the same feeling of inveterate enmity, arising from a repeated succession of conflicts, did not exist towards them as towards many other Asiatic tribes. The same remark applies to another people, represented at Medeenet Haboo,* as allies of the Egyptians, whose name has been unfortunately lost : they were clad in a short tight dress, and carried a shield, like the former, with a bow and a heavy club ; but of their features we have little or no knowledge, owing to the imperfect state of the sculptures.

Among the most formidable Asiatic enemies encountered by the Egyptians were the Rebo,† with whom they had frequent and severe contests.

One of the principal military events in the glorious reign of the great Remeses was his success against them ; and three victories gained over the Rebo by Remeses III., about a century later, were great triumphs for the Egyptians.

From the style of their costume, and the lightness of their complexion, it is evident they inhabited a northern as well as an Asiatic country, very distant from Egypt, and of a far more temperate climate. Their dress consisted of an under garment, with the usual short kelt, and a long outer robe, highly coloured, and frequently ornamented with fancy devices, or a broad rich border, which descended to the ankles, and was fastened at the neck with a large bow, or by a strap over the shoulder, the lower part being open in front. Beneath this they wore a highly ornamented girdle, the end of which, falling down in front, terminated in a large tassel ; and so fond were they of decorating their persons, that besides earrings, necklaces, and trinkets, common to Asiatic and other tribes, the chiefs decked their heads with feathers, and some painted or tattooed their arms and legs.

They were evidently a people of consequence, being selected as the type of Asia, or of the nations of the East, in the tombs of the kings at Thebes.

---

* See the allies, in woodcut 288, *fig.* 3.   † Woodcut 342, *fig.* 4.

Their hair was not less singular than their dress: it was divided into separate parts, one of which fell in ringlets over the forehead, and the other over the back of the head; and a plaited lock of great length, passing nearly over the ear, descended to the breast, and terminated in a curled point. In features they were as remarkable as in costume; and the Egyptians have not failed to indicate their most striking peculiarities, as blue eyes, aquiline nose, and small red beards. Their arms consisted principally of the bow, and a long straight sword, with an exceedingly sharp point; and it is probable that, to their skill in the use of the former, we may attribute their effectual resistance to the repeated invasions of the Egyptians.

Another Eastern nation, with whom the Egyptians were already at war in the remote age of Amun-m-he II., nearly 2000 years before our era, was the Pount;* who were tributary to Egypt in the reign of the third Thothmes.

Their features were less marked than those of many Oriental people represented in the sculptures: they shaved their beards, and wore their hair enveloped in a large cap, bound with a fillet, like many of the tribes of the interior, and the Syrians who bordered upon Egypt. Their dress consisted chiefly of a short kelt, secured with the usual girdle: and they appear to have inhabited a region lying more to the south than the Rot-n-n, or the Koofa, who were also tributary at the same period to Thothmes III. They probably lived on the borders of Arabia; and some suppose there was one tribe of this name in Africa, and another in Asia. Among the presents brought by them to the Egyptian monarch were some gold, with a little silver, the ibex, leopard, baboon, ape, ostrich eggs and feathers, dried fruits and skins, baskets full of a brown substance called *ana* (?), with two obelisks made of it, and a red mineral (?), called " *min* " (apparently *minium*, " red lead," or vermilion); and exotic shrubs, with ebony and ivory, seem to prove that they lived in a cultivated country as well as a warm climate.

The Shari were another Asiatic people, against whom the

* Or Pouônt. Woodcut 342, *fig.* 5.

Egyptians waged a successful war, principally in the reigns of Osirei (or Sethos) and his son, the great Remeses. I am inclined to think them a tribe of Northern Arabia, or *Shur;* and their name seems to agree with that of the Arabian Gulf, called by the Egyptians "the Sea of Shari." Their features were marked by a prominent aquiline nose and high cheek bones : they had a large beard ; and their head-dress consisted either of a cap bound, like that of the Pount, with a fillet, or a skull-cap fitting loosely to the head, secured by a band, and terminating at the end, which fell down behind, in a ball or tassel.* Their dress consisted of a long loose robe reaching to the ankles, and fastened at the waist by a girdle, the upper part furnished with ample sleeves. The girdle was sometimes highly ornamented : men as well as women wore earrings ; and they frequently had a small cross suspended to a necklace, or to the collar of their dress. The adoption of this last was not peculiar to them ; it was also appended to, or figured upon, the robes of the Rot-n̄-n ; and traces of it may be

344.   Prisoners of Tirhaka.   *Thebes.*

* Woodcut 342, *fig.* 6 c.

seen in the fancy ornaments of the Rebo, showing that this very simple device was already in use as early as the 15th century before the Christian era.

Some wore a sort of double belt, crossing the body, and passing over each shoulder, which, together with the pointed cap, resembles the dress of Tirhaka's captives.* Their principal arms were the bow, spear, two javelins, and a sword or club; and their country was defended by several strongly fortified towns.

The Rot-n-no,† or Rot-ñ-n, were a nation with whom the Egyptians waged a long war, commencing at least as early as, and perhaps prior to, the reign of the third Thothmes. Their white complexion, tight dresses, and long gloves,‡ decide them to have been natives of a much colder climate than Egypt or Southern Syria; and the productions of their country, which they bring as a tribute to the victorious Pharaoh, pronounce them to have lived in the East. These consist of horses, and even chariots, with four spoked wheels,§ (very similar to the Egyptian curricle,) rare woods, ivory, elephants and bears, a profusion of elegant gold and silver vases, with rings of the same precious metals, porcelain, and jars filled with choice gums and resins used for making incense, as well as bitumen, called "zift," the common name for "pitch" in Arabic and Hebrew. And it is a curious fact that one of the same kind of jars is now in the British Museum, having on it the word "tribute." Their country was in the vicinity, or part, of Mesopotamia, and consisted of an "Upper and Lower" province; and in the record of the tributes paid to Thothmes III. at Karnak, the Rot-ñ-n are mentioned with Nahrayn (Mesopotamia), Neniee (Nineveh), Shinar (Singar), Babel, and other places.

Their features were regular, without the very prominent nose that characterises some Eastern people represented in the sculptures; and they were of a very light colour, with brown or red hair, and blue eyes. Their long dress, usually furnished with

---

* Woodcut 344.   † Woodcut 342, fig. 7.

‡ There are other instances of gloves in Egyptian sculptures; but they are very rare. The expression shoe, in Ruth iv. 7, is in the Targum "right-hand glove."   § Woodcut 332.

tight sleeves, and fastened by strings round the neck, was either
closed or folded over in front, and was sometimes secured by a
girdle.   Beneath the outer robe they wore a kelt; and an ample
cloak, probably woollen, like the modern *herám*, or blanket, of
the coast of Barbary, was thrown over the whole dress;* the
head being generally covered with a close cap, or a fuller one,
bound by a fillet.

   The women wore a long garment secured by a girdle, and
trimmed in the lower part with three rows of flounces; the
sleeves sometimes large and open, sometimes fastened tight round
the wrist; and the hair was either covered with a cap, to which
a long tassel was appended, or descending in ringlets was encir-
cled by a simple band.†

   The Toersha,‡ a people who lived near a river or the sea,
are also mentioned among the enemies of Egypt, and their close
cap, from whose pointed summit a crest of hair falls to the
back of the neck, readily distinguishes them from other Eastern
tribes. Their features offer no peculiarity; and we know them
only by being introduced among the tribes conquered by the
third Remeses. The same applies to the Mashoash,§ another
Asiatic nation; who resemble the former in their general features,
and the shape of their beards; but their head-dress is low, and

1   2

345.   Other enemies of the Egyptians.   *Thebes.*

rather more like that of some of Tirhaka's prisoners,‖ descending
in two points at the side and back of the head, and bound with
a fillet.

   * Woodcuts 353, and 342, *fig.* 7, *d.*   † Woodcuts 353, and 342, *fig.* 7, *e.*
   ‡ Woodcut 345, *fig.* 1.   § Woodcut 345, *fig.* 2.   ‖ Woodcut 344.

The people of Kufa (Koofa) were also an Asiatic race; and their long hair, rich dresses, and sandals of the most varied form and colour, render them remarkable among the nations represented in Egyptian sculpture. In complexion they were much darker than the Rot-ñ-n, but far more fair than the Egyptians; and to judge from the tribute they brought to the Pharaohs, they were a rich people, and, like the Rot-ñ-n, far advanced in the arts and customs of civilised life. This tribute, which is shown to have been paid to the Egyptians as early as the reign of Thothmes III., consisted almost entirely of gold and silver, in rings and bars, and vases of the same metals. Many of the latter were silver, inlaid with gold, tastefully ornamented, of elegant form, and similar to those already in use among the Egyptians; and from the almost exclusive introduction of the precious metals, and the absence of animals, woods, and such productions as were brought to Egypt by other people, we may suppose the artist intended to convey a notion of the great mineral riches of their country; where silver seems to have been even more abundant than gold. They are occasionally represented carrying knives or daggers, beads, a small quantity of ivory, leathern bottles, and a few bronze and porcelain cups. Their dress was a simple kelt, richly worked and of varied colour, folding over in front, and fastened with a girdle; and their sandals, which, being closed like boots, differed entirely from those of the Egyptians, appear to have been of cloth or leather, highly ornamented, and reaching considerably above the ankle. Their long hair hung loosely in tresses, reaching more than half way down the back; and from the top of the head projected three or four curls, either of real or artificial hair. (*Woodcut* 347, *fig.* 1.)

The Khita, or Sheta, were a warlike people of Asia, who had made considerable progress in military tactics, both with regard to manœuvres in the field, and the art of fortifying towns; some of which they surrounded with a double fosse, crossed by *bridges*. But whether these were supported on arches, or simply of wooden rafters resting on piers of the same materials, we are unable to decide, since the view is given as seen from above, and

is therefore confined to the level upper surface.* Their troops
were disciplined; and the close array of their phalanxes of

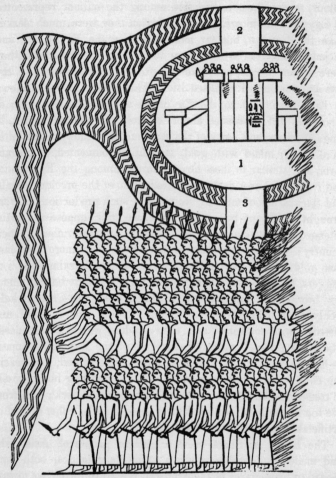

346. Phalanx of the Sheta, drawn up as a corps de réserve, with the fortified town, sur-
      rounded by double ditches, over which are *bridges* (figs. 2 and 3).   *Thebes.*

infantry, the style of their chariots, and the arms they used, indicate a great superiority in military tactics, compared with other

* Woodcut 346, *figs.* 2 and 3.

Eastern nations of that early period. The wars waged against the Khita by the Egyptians, and the victories obtained over them by the great Remeses, are pictured on the walls of his palace at Thebes,* and are again alluded to in the sculptures of Remeses III., at Medeenet Haboo, where this people occurs in the list of nations conquered by the Pharaohs. Their arms were the bow, sword, and spear; and their principal defence was a wicker shield, either rectangular, or concave at the sides and convex at each end, approaching in form the Theban buckler.

Their dress consisted of a long robe, reaching to the ankles, with short sleeves, open or folding over in front, and secured by a girdle round the waist; but though frequently made of a very thick stuff, and perhaps even quilted, it was by no means an effectual substitute for armour, nor could it resist the spear or the metal-pointed arrow. They either wore a close or a full cap; and their arms were occasionally decked with bracelets, as their dresses with brilliant colours. Their cars were drawn by two horses, like those of Egypt, but they each contained three men, and some had wheels with four instead of six spokes; in both which respects they differed from those of their opponents. They had some cavalry: but large masses of infantry, with a formidable body of chariots, constituted the principal force of their numerous and well-appointed army; and if, from the manner in which they posted their *corps de réserve*, we may infer them to have been a people skilled in war, some idea may also be formed of the strength of their army from the numbers composing that division, which amounted to 24,000 men,† drawn up in three close phalanxes, consisting each of 8000.

The nation of Khita seems to have been composed of two distinct tribes,‡ both comprehended under the same name. They differed in their costume and general appearance; one having a large cap, and the long loose robe, with open sleeves or capes covering the shoulders, worn by many Asiatic people already mentioned, a square or oblong shield, and sometimes a large

* Usually called the Memnonium.   † At the Memnonium.
          ‡ Woodcut 347, *figs.* 2, 3, 4, and 5.

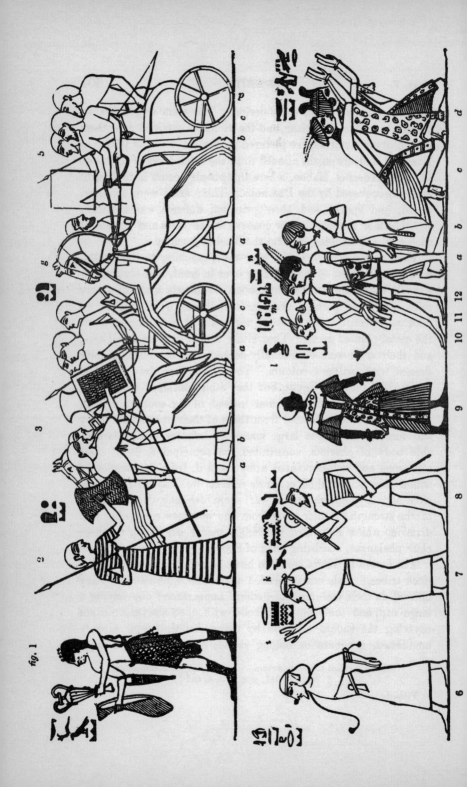

fig. 1

beard; the other the dress and shield before described, and no beard. They both fought in cars, and used the same weapons; and we find they lived together, or garrisoned the same towns.

They were evidently in the vicinity of Mesopotamia, or " Nahrayn;" and the strong fort of Atesh, or Kadesh,* belonged to them. It is supposed that they were the Hittites.

Several other nations and tribes, who inhabited parts of Asia, are shown by the monuments to have been invaded and reduced to subjection by the arms of the Pharaohs; and in the names of some we recognise towns or districts of Syria, as in Asmaori (Samaria?), Lemanon, Kanana, or Kanaan, and Ascalon. The inhabitants of the two first are figured with a round full head-dress, bound with a fillet: and those of Kanaan are distinguished by a coat of mail and helmet, and the use of spears, javelins, and a battle-axe similar to that of Egypt.† (*Woodcut* 347, figs. 6, 7, 8.)

The country of Lemanon is shown by the artist to have been mountainous, inaccessible to chariots, and abounding in lofty trees, which the affrighted mountaineers are engaged in felling, in order to impede the advance of the invading army. Having taken by assault the fortified towns on the frontier, the Egyptian monarch advances with his light infantry in pursuit of the fugitives, who had escaped, and taken refuge in the woods; and sending a herald to offer terms on condition of their surrender, the chiefs are induced to trust to his clemency, and return to their allegiance; as are those of Kanaan, whose strongholds yield in like manner to the arms of the conqueror.

These two names seem to point out the inhabitants of Mount Lebanon and Canaan, since the campaign is said to have taken place in the first year, or soon after the accession, of Osirei, or Sethi, the father of the great Remeses; and the events which previously occurred in Egypt, during the rule of the Stranger kings, may have given an opportunity to these people, though so near Egypt, to rebel, and assert their independence.

Many black nations were also conquered by the early mon-

* Woodcut 346, *fig.* 1.	† Woodcut 347, *fig.* 8.

archs of the 18th and 19th dynasties, as the Toreses, the Tareáo, the Cush,* or Ethiopians, and others.

The Blacks, like the Ethiopians, wore short aprons of bulls' hides, or the skins of wild beasts, frequently drawn by the Egyptian artists with the tail projecting from the girdle, for the purpose of adding to their grotesque appearance: the chiefs, decked with ostrich and other feathers, had large circular gold earrings, collars, and bracelets; and many of the Ethiopian grandees were clad in garments of fine linen, with leathern girdles highly ornamented, a leopard skin being occasionally thrown over their shoulder.† The chief arms of the Ethiopians and Blacks were the bow, the spear, and club: they fought mostly on foot, and the tactics of a disciplined army appear to have been unknown to them.

The Ethiopian tribute consisted of gold, mostly in dust, a little silver, *shishm* perhaps "antimony," ostrich feathers, skins, ebony, ivory, apes, oxen of the long-horned breed still found in Abyssinia, lions, oryxes, leopards, giraffes, and hounds; and they were obliged to supply the victors with slaves, which the Egyptians sometimes exacted even from the conquered countries of Asia.

When an expedition was resolved upon against a foreign nation, each province furnished its quotum of men. The troops were generally commanded by the king in person; but in some instances a general was appointed to that post, and intrusted with the sole conduct of the war. A place of rendezvous was fixed, in early times generally at Thebes, Memphis, or Pelusium; and the troops having assembled in the vicinity, remained encamped there, awaiting the leader of the expedition. As soon as he arrived, the necessary preparations were made; a sacrifice was performed to the gods whose assistance was invoked in the approaching conflict; and orders having been issued for their march, a signal was given by sound of trumpet; the troops fell in, and with a profound bow each soldier in the ranks saluted the

---

* It is the Scriptural as well as the hieroglyphical name. Woodcut 347, *fig.* 13, *a, b, c,* and *d.*

† Woodcut 347, *fig.* 13, *c, d.*

royal general, and prepared to follow him to the field. The march then commenced, as Clemens and the sculptures inform us, to the sound of the drum; the chariots led the van; and the king, mounted in his car of war, and attended by his chief officers carrying flabella, took his post in the centre, preceded and followed by bodies of infantry armed with bows, spears, or other weapons, according to their respective corps.

On commencing the attack in the open field, a signal was again made by sound of trumpet. The archers drawn up in line first discharged a shower of arrows on the enemy's front, and a considerable mass of chariots advanced to the charge; the heavy infantry, armed with spears or clubs, and covered with their shields, moved forwards at the same time in close array, flanked by chariots and cavalry, and pressed upon the centre and wings of the enemy, the archers still galling the hostile columns with their arrows, and endeavouring to create disorder in their ranks.

348.   A body of archers.   *Thebes.*

Their mode of warfare was not like that of nations in their infancy, or in a state of barbarism; and it is evident, from the number of prisoners they took, that they spared the prostrate who asked for quarter: and the representations of persons slaughtered by the Egyptians, who have overtaken them, are intended to allude to what happened in the heat of action, and not to any wanton cruelty on the part of the victors.   Indeed in the naval fight of Remeses III., the Egyptians, both in the ships and on the shore, are seen rescuing the enemy, whose galley has been sunk, from a watery grave; and the humanity of that people is strongly argued, whose artists deem it a virtue, worthy of being recorded among the glorious actions of their countrymen.

Those who sued for mercy and laid down their arms, were spared and sent bound from the field; and the hands of the slain being cut off, and placed in heaps before the king, immediately after the action, were counted by the military secretaries in his presence, who thus ascertained and reported to him the amount of the enemy's slain.   Sometimes their tongues, and occasionally other members, were laid before him in the same manner; in all instances being intended as authentic returns of the loss of the foe: for which the soldiers received a proportionate reward, divided among the whole army: the capture of prisoners probably claiming a higher premium, exclusively enjoyed by the captor.

The arms, horses, chariots, and booty, taken in the field or in the camp, were also collected, and the same officers wrote an account of them, and presented it to the monarch.   The booty was sometimes collected in an open space, surrounded by a temporary wall, indicated in the sculptures by the representation of shields placed erect, with a wicker gate, on the inner and outer face of which a strong guard was posted, the sentries walking to and fro with drawn swords.   It was forbidden to the Spartan soldier, when on guard, to have his shield, in order that, being deprived of this defence, he might be more cautious not to fall asleep; and the same appears to have been a custom of the Egyptians, as the watch here on duty at the camp-gates are only armed with swords and maces, though belonging to the heavy-armed corps, who, on other occasions, were in the habit of carrying a shield.

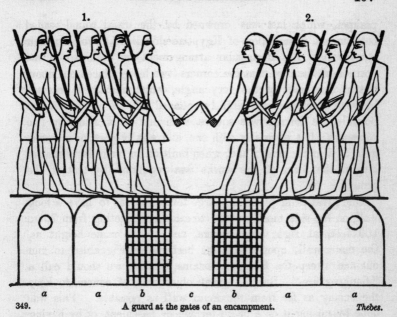

349.   A guard at the gates of an encampment.   *Thebes.*

The sculptures at the Memnonium in Thebes show their mode
of encamping on the field, when they had been victorious and no
longer feared an attack; but the permanent station, or regular
encampment, was constructed with greater attention to the principles of defence, and furnished with ditches and a strong efficient
rampart.

A system of regular fortification was adopted in the earliest
times. The form of the fortresses was quadrangular; the walls
of crude brick 15 feet thick, and often 50 feet high, with square
towers at intervals along each face. These were generally the
same height as the walls, and when they only reached part of the
way up they were rather buttresses; and sometimes the whole wall
was doubled by an outer casing, leaving a space between the two,
filled in here and there by a solid buttress, which strengthened
and united them, and prevented any one passing freely round the
inner wall when the outer one was broken through. The
towers, like the rest of the walls, consisted of a rampart and

parapet, which last was crowned by the usual round-headed battlements, in imitation of Egyptian shields, like those on their stone walls. But a singular arrangement was followed in the position of the towers at the corners, two being placed not upon, but at each side of the very angle, which remained recessed between them, and was slightly rounded off. Whenever it was possible, the fortress was square, with one or occasionally two entrances; but generally with one, and a sally-port, or a water-gate, if near the river: and, when built on an irregularly-shaped height, the form of the works was regulated by that of the ground.

One great principle in the large fortresses was to have a long wall, on the side most exposed to attack, projecting from 70 to 100 feet, at right angles from, and at the same height as, the main wall, upon which the besieged were enabled to run out and sweep the faces, or curtains, by what we should call a "flanking fire." But the great object was, of course, to keep the enemy as far from the main wall as possible. This was done by raising it on a broad terrace or basement, or by having an outer circuit, or low wall of circumvallation, parallel to the main wall, and distant from it, on every side, from 13 to 20 feet; and a tower stood at each side of the entrance, which was towards one corner of the least exposed face. This low wall answered the purpose of a second rampart and ditch; it served to keep the besiegers' moveable towers and battering rams at a distance from the main wall, who had to carry the outer circuit before they could attempt a breach in, or an assault on, the body of the fortress; while, from the lowness of the outer circuit, they were exposed to the missiles of the besieged.

Another more effectual defence, adopted in larger fortifications, was a ditch with a counterscarp, and in the centre of the ditch a continuous stone wall, parallel to the face of the curtain and the counterscarp (—a sort of ravelin, or a tenaille), and then came the scarp of the platform on which the fortress stood. Over the ditch was a wooden bridge, which was removed during a siege.

Occasionally, as at Semneh, there was a glacis of stone, sloping

down from the counterscarp of the ditch towards the level
country ; so that they had in those early days some of the peculiarities of our modern works, the glacis, scarps, and counter-
scarps, and a sort of ravelin (or a tenaille) in the ditch.   But
though some were kept up after the accession of the 18th
dynasty, the practice of fortifying towns seems to have been
discontinued, and fortresses or walled towns were not then used,
except on the edge of the desert, and on the frontiers where
large garrisons were required.   To supply their place, the
temples were provided with lofty pyramidal stone towers, which,
projecting beyond the walls, enabled the besieged to command
and rake them, while the parapet-wall over the gateway shielded
the soldiers who defended the entrance; and the whole plan of
an outer wall of circumvallation was carried out by the large
crude brick enclosure of the *temenos*, within which the temple
stood.   Each temple was thus a detached fort, and was thought
as sufficient a protection for itself and for the town as a continuous wall, which required a large garrison to defend it; and
neither Thebes nor Memphis, the two capitals, were walled cities.

The field encampment was either a square, or a parallelogram,
with a principal entrance in one of the faces; and near the centre
were the general's tent, and those of the principal officers.   The
general's tent was sometimes surrounded by a double rampart or
fosse, enclosing two distinct areas, the outer one containing three
tents, probably of the next in command, or of the officers on the
staff; and the guards slept or watched in the open air.   Other
tents were pitched outside these enclosures; and near the external circuit, a space was set apart for feeding horses and beasts
of burthen, and another for ranging the chariots and baggage.
It was near the general's tent, and within the same area, that
the altars of the gods, or whatever related to religious matters,
the standards, and the military chest, were kept; and the sacred
emblems were deposited beneath a canopy, within an enclosure
similar to that of the general's tent.

To judge from the mode of binding their prisoners, we might
suppose they treated them with unnecessary harshness and even

cruelty, at the moment of their capture, and during their march
with the army. They tied their hands behind their backs, or

over their heads, in the most strained
positions, and a rope passing round
their neck fastened them to each
other ; and some had their hands enclosed in an elongated fetter of wood,
made of two opposite segments, nailed
together at each end; such as are
used for securing prisoners in Egypt,
at the present day. In the capture
of a town some were beaten with
sticks, in order to force from them
the secret of the booty that had been
concealed ; many were compelled to
labour for the benefit of the vic-

A captive secured by a handcuff.
350.   *Thebes.*

tors ; and others were insulted by the wanton soldiery, who
pulled their beards and derided their appearance. But when we
remember how frequently instances of harsh treatment have
occurred, even among civilized Europeans, at an epoch which
deemed itself much more enlightened than the fourteenth century
before our era, we are disposed to excuse the occasional inso-
lence of an Egyptian soldier ; and the unfavourable impressions
conveyed by such scenes are more than counterbalanced by the
proofs of Egyptian humanity, as in the sea-fight above mentioned. Allowance is also to be made for a licence of the
sculptors, who, as Gibbon observes, " in every age have felt the
truth of a system, which derives the sublime from the principle
of terror."

Indeed, when compared with the Assyrians, and other Asiatic
conquerors, the Egyptians hold a high position among the nations
of antiquity from their conduct to their prisoners ; and the cruel
custom of flaying them alive, and the tortures represented in the
sculptures of Nineveh, show the Assyrians were guilty of bar-
barities, at a period long after the Egyptians had been accustomed to the refinements of civilized communities.

The captives, too, represented on the façades of their temples, bound at the feet of the king, who holds them by the hair of the head, and with an uplifted arm appears about to immolate them in the presence of the deity, are merely an emblematical record of his successes over the enemies of Egypt;* as is shown by the same subject being represented on monuments erected by the Ptolemies and Cæsars.†

The sailors of the " king's ships," or royal navy, were part of the military class, a certain number of whom were specially trained for the sea; though all the soldiers were capable of handling galleys, from their constant practice at the oar on the Nile. The Egyptian troops were therefore employed on board ship by Xerxes, in his war against Greece, "being," as Herodotus says, "all sailors." And as ships of war then depended on the skill of their crews in the use of the oar, the employment of the Egyptian soldiers in a sea fight is not so extraordinary. Many, too, of the Nile boats were built purposely for war, and were used in the expeditions of the Pharaohs into Ethiopia; officers who commanded them are often mentioned on the monuments; and chief, or captain, of the king's ships is not an uncommon title.

Herodotus and Diodorus both mention the fleet of long vessels, or ships of war, fitted out by Sesostris on the Arabian Gulf. They were four hundred in number; and there is every reason to believe that the trade, and the means of protecting it by ships of war, existed there at least as early as the 12th dynasty, about two thousand years before our era.

The galleys, or ships of war, used in their wars out of Egypt differed from those of the Nile. They were less raised at the head and stern; and on each side, throughout the whole length of the vessel, a wooden bulwark, rising considerably above the gunwale, sheltered the rowers, who sat behind it, from the missiles of the enemy; the handles of the oars passing through an aperture at the lower part.

* Herodotus justly blames the Greeks for their ignorance of the Egyptian character, in taking literally their allegorical tales of human sacrifices, ii. 45.
† At E'Dayr, near E'sné, at Dendera, and other places.

The ships in the sea fight represented at Thebes fully confirm the statement of Herodotus that the Egyptian soldiers were employed on board them; as their arms and dress are exactly the same as those of the heavy infantry and archers of the army; and the quilted helmet of the rowers shows they also were part of the same corps. Besides the archers in the raised poop and forecastle, a body of slingers was stationed in the tops, where they could with more facility manage that weapon, and employ it with effect on the enemy.

351.   War galley; the sail being pulled up during the action.   *Thebes.*
a. Raised forecastle, in which the archers were posted.   c. Another post for the archers,
  and the pilot d.   e. A bulwark, to protect the rowers.   f. Slingers, in the top.

On advancing to engage a hostile fleet, the sail was used till they came within a certain distance, when the signal or order having been given to clear for action, it was reefed by means of ropes running in pulleys, or loops, upon the yard. The ends of these ropes, which were usually four in number, dividing the sail as it rose into five folds, descended and were attached to the lower part of the mast, so as to be readily worked, when the sail required to be pulled up at a moment's notice, either in a squall of wind or on any other occasion; and in this respect, and in the absence of a lower yard, the sail of the war galley greatly differed from that of the boats on the Nile. Having prepared for the attack, the rowers, whose strength had been hitherto reserved, plied their oars; the head was directed towards an enemy's vessel, and showers of missiles were thrown from the forecastle and tops as they advanced. It was of great importance to strike their opponent on the side; and when the steersman, by a skilful manœuvre, could succeed in this, the shock was so great that they sank it, or obtained a considerable advantage by crippling the oars.

The small Egyptian galleys do not appear to have been furnished with a beak, like those of the Romans, which being of bronze sharply pointed, and sometimes below the water's surface, often sank a vessel at once; but a lion's head fixed to the prow supplied its place, and being probably covered with metal, was capable of doing great execution, when the galley was impelled by the force of sixteen or twenty oars. This head occasionally varied in form, and perhaps served to indicate the rank of the commander, the name of the vessel, or the deity under whose protection they sailed; unless indeed the lion was always chosen for their war galleys, and the ram, oryx, and others, confined to the boats connected with the service of religion.

Some of the war galleys on the Nile were furnished with forty-four oars, twenty-two being represented on one side; which, allowing for the steerage and prow, would require their total length to be about 120 feet. They were furnished, like all the others, with one large square sail; but the mast, instead of being single, was made of two limbs of equal length, sufficiently open at the top to admit the yard between them, and secured by several strong stays, one of which extended to the prow, and others to the steerage of the boat. Over the top of the mast a light rope was passed, probably intended for furling the sail, which last, from the horizontal lines represented upon it, appears to have been like those of the Chinese, and is a curious instance of a sail, apparently made of the papyrus.

This double mast was common of old, during the 4th and other early dynasties; but it afterwards gave place entirely to the single one, with bars, or rollers, at the upper part, serving

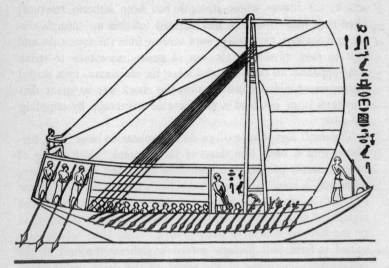

352. Large boat with sail, apparently made of the papyrus, a double mast, and many
       rowers.   *In a tomb at Kom Ahmar, above Minieh.*

for pulleys, over which the ropes passed; and sometimes rings
were fixed to it, in which the halliards worked.

In this, as in other Egyptian boats, the braces were fixed to the
end of the yard; which being held by a man seated in the steerage,
or upon the cabin, served to turn the sail to the right and left;
they were common to all boats; and at the lower end of the sail
(which in these boats had no yard) were the sheets, which were
secured within the gunwale. The mode of steering is different
from that usually described in the Egyptian paintings; and
instead of a rudder in the centre of the stern, or at either side,
it is furnished with three on the same side: a peculiarity which,
like the double mast and the folding sail, was afterwards abandoned as cumbrous and imperfect. This boat shows satisfactorily
their mode of arranging the oars, while not required during a
favourable wind: they were drawn up, through the ring or band
in which they turned, and they were probably held in that position
by a thong or loop passing over the handle. The ordinary boats

of the Nile were of a different construction; which will be mentioned in describing the boat-builders, one of the members of the fourth class of the Egyptian community.

On returning from war, the troops marched according to the post assigned to each regiment, observing the same order and regularity as during their advance through the enemy's country: and the allies who came with them occupied a position towards the rear of the army, and were followed by a strong corps of Egyptians. Rewards were afterwards distributed to the soldiers, and the triumphant procession of the conqueror was graced by the presence of the captives, who were conducted in bonds beside his chariot.

On traversing countries tributary to, or in alliance with, Egypt, the monarch received the homage of the friendly inhabitants, who, greeting his arrival with joyful acclamations and rich presents, complimented him on the victory he had obtained; and the army, as it passed through Egypt, was met at each of the principal cities by a concourse of people, who, headed by the priests, and chief men of the place, bearing bouquets of flowers, green boughs, and palm branches, received them with loud acclamations, and welcomed their return. Then addressing themselves to the king, the priests celebrated his praises; and, enumerating the many benefits he had conferred on Egypt by the conquest of foreign nations, the enemies of his country, they affirmed that his power was exalted in the world " like the sun " in the heavens, and his beneficence only equalled by that of the deities themselves.

Having reached the capital, preparations commenced for a general thanksgiving in the principal temple : and suitable offerings were made to the presiding deity, the guardian of the city, by whose special favour and intercession the victory was supposed to have been obtained. The prisoners were presented to him, as well as the spoils taken from the enemy, and the monarch acknowledged the manifest power of his all-protecting hand, and his own gratitude for so distinguished a proof of heavenly favour to him and to the nation. And these subjects, represented on

the walls of the temples, not only served as a record of the
victory, but tended to impress the people with a religious veneration for the deity, towards whom their sovereign set them so
marked an example of respect.   The troops were also required
to attend during the performance of the prescribed ceremonies,
and to return thanks for the victories they had obtained, as well
as for their personal preservation; and a priest offered incense,
meat offerings, and libations, in their presence.*

The captives, being brought to Egypt, were employed in the
service of the monarch, in building temples, cutting canals,
raising dykes and embankments, and other public works: and
some, who were purchased by the grandees, were employed in
the same capacity as the Memlooks of the present day.   Women
slaves were also engaged in the service of families, like the
Greeks and Circassians in modern Egypt, and other parts of the
Turkish empire; and from finding them represented in the
sculptures of Thebes, accompanying men of their own nation,

353.   Women of the Rot-n-n sent to Egypt.   *Thebes.*

* *See* above, p. 278.

354.   Black slaves, with their women and children.   *Thebes.*

who bear tribute to the Egyptian monarch, we may conclude
that a certain number were annually sent to Egypt from the
conquered provinces of the North and East, as well as from
Ethiopia. It is evident that both white and black slaves were
employed as servants: they attended on the guests when invited
to the house of their master; and from their being in the families
of priests, as well as of the military chiefs, we may infer that
they were purchased with money, and that the right of possessing
slaves was not confined to those who had taken them in war.
The traffic in slaves was tolerated by the Egyptians; and doubtless many persons were engaged, as at present, in bringing them
to Egypt for public sale, independent of those who were sent as
part of the tribute; and the Ishmaelites,* who bought Joseph from
his brethren, sold him to Potiphar on arriving in Egypt. It was
the common custom in those days: the Jews had their bondsmen
bought with money;† the Phœnicians, who traded in slaves,
sold "the children of Judah and Jerusalem" to the Greeks;‡
and the people of the Caucasus sent their boys and girls to

---

* Gen. xxxvii. 28. *See* also Gen. xliv. 9.   † Levit. xxv. 44, &c.
‡ Amos iii. 6.

Persia*, as the modern Circassians do to that country and to Turkey.

Diodorus, in mentioning the military punishments of the Egyptians, says that they were not actuated by any spirit of vengeance; but solely by the hope of reclaiming an offender, and of preventing for the future the commission of a similar crime. They were, therefore, averse to making desertion and insubordination capital offences : the soldier was degraded, and condemned publicly to wear some conspicuous mark of ignominy, which rendered him an object of reproach to his comrades; and, without fixing any time for his release, he was doomed to bear it, till his subsequent good conduct had retrieved his character, and obtained for him the forgiveness of his superiors. " For," says the historian, " by rendering the stigma a more odious disgrace than death itself, the legislator hoped to make it the most severe of punishments, at the same time that it had a great advantage in not depriving the state of the services of the offender; and deeming it natural to every one, who had been degraded from his post, to desire to regain the station and character he had lost, they cherished the hope that he might eventually reform, and become a worthy member of the society to which he belonged." For minor offences they inflicted the bastinado, which was commonly employed for punishing peasants and other people; but the soldier who treacherously held communication with the enemy was sentenced to the excision of his tongue; in accordance with the ancient practice of punishing the offending member.

This brief outline of the military customs of Egypt suffices to show that the monuments contain abundant records of those early days; and though many others have long since perished, some belonging to the most glorious periods have fortunately been preserved; and the sculptures of Thothmes III., of the Amunophs, of Sethos, of the Second and Third Remeses, and other kings, confirm the testimony of historians respecting the power of ancient Egypt.

* Herod. iii. 97.

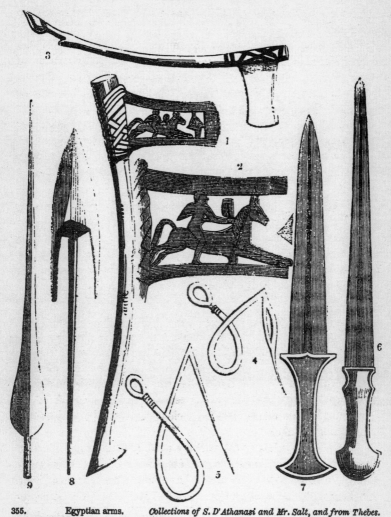

355.   Egyptian arms.   *Collections of S. D'Athanasi and Mr. Salt, and from Thebes.*

Fig. 1. Hatchet, 1 foot 5 inches in length.
    4 and 5. Slings, from the sculptures.
    6. Dagger, 15¾ inches in length.

Fig. 7. Dagger, 10½ inches long.
    8. Head of dart, 3 inches.
    9. Javelin head, 14 inches long.

INDEX

Please note that page references prefigured by *ii* refer to the companion *The Ancient Egyptians – Their Life and Customs Vol. Two.* Page references prefigured by *i* relate to this first volume.

Aaron, embroidered fine linen coat of, ii. 81.

Abbott, collection of Dr., i. 194, 195, 368, 383.

Abrek, Berek, " bow the knee," ii. 203.

Abstract ideas, i. 327, 328, 330.

Abydus, Temple of. Osiris at, i. 301, 307.

—— false arch at, ii. 301.

——, some preferred to be buried at, ii. 377.

Abyssinia. *See* Monkies.

Abyssinian branch of the Nile, ii. 19.

—— called " *blue*" properly " *black* river," ii. 20.

Abyssinians do not eat geese and ducks, i. 166.

Acacia, or Mimosa, several kinds of, i. 57 ; ii. 28, 37, 38. See *Sont.*

——, a sensitive —, in Ethiopia, ii. 28.

—— *séál,* of the Eastern desert, ii. 38, 106.

Acanthus, or *Sont,* groves of, ii. 28, 37, 110.

Adaptability. *See* Taste, i. 21 ; ii. 288.

Admired the knick-knacks and furniture of the rooms, i. 146.

Ægyptus the old name of the Nile, i. 303.

—— not the land of Egypt, in Homer, i. 303.

African enemies of Egypt, i. 403, 404.

Agathodæmon, the Asp, i. 46.

Age, respect for old, ii. 226.

Agesilaus took back chaplets of papyrus to Sparta, i. 57, 81.

—— entertained by Tachos, i. 81.

Agility. *See* Feats of —.

Agriculture, ii. 3-54.

Agriculture. *See* Land, Plants, Plough.

—— led to scientific discoveries, ii. 247-250.

—— led to the adjustment of the year, ii. 251, 252.

—— and manufactures of Egypt, ii. 255.

Agweh, preserve of dates, i. 55.

Alabaster used for vases and bottles, i. 156, 157 ; ii. 70, 342.

——, walls lined with, ii. 288, 292.

Alabastron, vase called, ii. 342.

Alcaline plant called *Boréeth,* ii. 106.

Alexander's conquest of Egypt, i. 309.

Alexandria, population of, i. 305.

——, number of persons who sold vegetables in, i. 168.

—— much wine to be obtained at, i. 54.

Alitta or Mylitta, i. 333.

Alloys in bronze, i. 148.

Almond tree in Egypt, i. 57 ; ii. 27.

—— oil, ii. 24, 27.

Alluvial deposit in the Valley of the Nile, i. 306 ; ii. 8, 9.

—— rise of, and proportion of the, ii. 8, 9. *See* Nile.

—— quality, and analysis of the, ii. 19.

Alphabet, twenty-five letters said to compose the Egyptian, i. 291.

Altars, ii. 361.

Amasis, wisdom of, ii. 228.

—— population of Egypt under, i. 304.

—— foreigners saw little of Egypt till after reign of, ii. 231.

Amenti, or Hades, i. 285 ; ii. 357, 358.

——, Four genii of, ii. 381, 382, 390, 391, 396, 399.

America and England, ii. 240.

Americans, North, like Europeans, i. 303.

Ames, or Amosis, i. 111, 307.

" Ames," a harper called, i. (woodcut, 122) 112.

Amphoræ, or wine-jars, i. 47, 48.

——, how fixed upright, i. 48, 49.

——, stopped and sealed, i. 48.

—— pitch, or resinous sediment in, i. 48.

Amun (God of Thebes), i. 327, 328, 331, 332.

Amun expelled from the Pantheon, i. 308.
——, women of, i. 133.
Amunophs, i. 306, 308.
Amunoph III. *See* Lions.
Amusements of Egyptians lively, i. 210.
Analysis of alluvial deposit, ii. 19.
Animal magnetism, use of, ii. 353.
Animals of Egypt, list of the, i. 245–255.
—— chiefly hunted, i. 224.
—— of Egypt, most noted, i. 227.
——, fabulous, or fanciful, i. 226; ii. 263.
—— not represented, i. 244.
—— sometimes placed entire on the altars, i. 173, 263.
—— skill in rearing, ii. 169.
Anointing the King, i. 275.
—— the statues of gods, i. 275.
——; a customary ceremony, i. 77, 275.
—— guests at a party, i. 77, 78.
Antelopes, various, i. 227, 247.
Anthylla, wine of, i. 50.
Anubis, ii. 358, 378, 381, 382, 396.
——, rites of, i. 129.
Aphôphis, Apôp, the "giant," the "great serpent," the emblem of sin, i. 330.
Apis, the soul of Osiris, i. 288.
——, fête of, i. 288, 291.
——, fête of, lasted seven days, i. 291.
—— called Epaphus, i. 288, 290.
—— and Mnevis, i. 288, 289.
——, colour and marks of, i. 289.
——, clean oxen belonged to, i. 290.
—— called Hapi, i. 290. *See* ii. 390, *note.*
—— kept at Memphis, i. 290.
——, stables of, i. 290, 295.
—— shown to strangers, i. 290.
—— said to have been drowned after living twenty-five years, i. 291.
—— embalmed and buried with great pomp, i. 291.
—— died and another chosen, i. 291.
——, children prophetic who smelt the breath of, and attended the processions in honour of, i. 291, 295.
——, expense of the funeral of, i. 292.
——, discovery of burial-place of, i. 292.
—— generally lived 17 to 20 years, i. 292.
——, rejoicings on finding the new, i. 293, 294.

Apis consulted as an oracle, and omens drawn from him, i. 294.
—— the living image of Osiris, i. 288, 294, 300.
——, mode of consulting, i. 295.
——'s influence on crocodiles, i. 295.
——, care respecting food and water given to, i. 293, 295, 322.
Apollinopolis. *See* Crocodile.
Apries took Gaza and Sidon, i. 309.
Arab invaders of Egypt, i. 2.
Arabs had very fine parchment, ii. 100.
—— used at first the shoulder-blades of sheep to write upon, ii. 100.
Arch, bricks led to the invention of the, i. 18; ii. 304.
——, bricks and stones at first placed lengthways in forming the, ii. 304.
—— in Egypt very ancient, i. 18, 31; ii. 300.
—— in Greece, ii. 302.
——, true and false, ii. 302, 303.
—— of brick, ii. 300–303.
—— of stone, ii. 300, 301, 303.
——, principle of the, not depending on the material, nor on the key-stone, ii. 300.
——, the pent roof the predecessor of the, ii. 303.
——, pointed, very early, ii. 304.
——, pointed, very early, at Tusculum, in Italy (woodcut), ii. 261.
——, substitutes for, and origin of the, ii. 302–304.
Archers of Egypt, i. 337.
—— of the infantry, i. 354.
——, attack of, i. 405.
Architecture of Egypt, derived much from natural productions, ii. 280, 288.
——, some parts from wood, ii. 280.
——, at first simple, ii. 297.
—— a creation of the mind, ii. 271.
——, constructed — borrowed pillar from the quarry, but rock-temples and tombs took other members from constructed—ii. 281.
——, Byzantine, and Romanesque, Lombard, Saxon, Norman, Saracenic, pointed, ii. 305.
——, progress and modification of styles of, ii. 305. *See* Saracenic.
Ark, or boat, of Sokari, i. 284, 285.
Arks. *See* Shrines.
Armed troops, light and heavy, i. 338, 340, 368.
Arms of Egyptian soldiers, i. 344–369.

Arms of their allies, i. 338.
—— of heavy and light armed troops, i. 368.
Army, amount of the, i. 337.
——, discipline of the, i. 337, 338, 340.
——, regiments of the, i. 338, 340. *See* Soldiers.
——, standards of the, i. 342, 343.
——, return of the. *See* War.
Aroura, or *Arura*, land measure, ii. 256.
Arouras, twelve given to each soldier, i. 336 ; ii. 228.
Arrivals of guests at a party, i. 73–76, 141.
Arrows, length of, i. 353.
—— of reed, i. 352, 353 ; ii. 30.
—— tipped with metal, or with flint, i. 222, 353.
—— with flint heads used by the Greeks also, and others, i. 353, 354.
——, spare, i. 351, 352.
Arsinoë, on the Red Sea, ii. 235, 236.
——, or Crocodilopolis, i. 307.
Arsinoïte nome, i. 242 ; ii. 28.
Artificial flowers, i. 57.
Arts, ii. 277–280. *See* Taste.
—— of production and arts of design, ii. 295.
—— and inventions older than we suppose, ii. 57.
Aryandes coined money in Egypt, ii. 150.
Ascalon and Asmaor (Samaria?), i. 403.
Ashúr of ten strings, a Jewish instrument, i. 126, 130.
Asiatic enemies of Egypt. *See* Enemies.
A'Souán, or Syene, Cuphic inscriptions at, ii. 142.
——, quarries at, ii. 309, 311.
Asp, or Agathodæmon, guarding a store-room, i. 46.
—— sacred to Neph (Nû, or Núm), i. 253.
Assemblies, the great, i. 280.
Asses numerous in Egypt, i. 231.
——, wild, not represented, i. 244.
Assessors, ii. 369, 376, 381.
——, forty-two, ii. 376, 382.
Assyria, i. 308.
Assyrian art borrowed, and archaïc style of, not yet found, ii. 263. *See* Nimroud Sculptures and Cylinders.
Assyrians, cruelty of the, i. 3, 410.
Astarte, i. 333.
Atesh, or Kadesh, fort of, i. 403.

Athenian coins of commerce had the old type, ii. 151.
Athor, cow or heifer the emblem of, i. 260, 261, 299.
——, Venus of Egypt, i. 333.
——, the Persea the sacred tree of, ii. 383.
Athribis (or Crocodilopolis), i. 307.
Attendants collecting the game, i. 236.
Axe, or hatchet, used in war, i. 361, 362, 419.
——, with a metal blade, used by peasants also, ii. 18.
A'zrek means " black" as well as " blue," ii. 20.

Baalbek, large stones of, ii. 299.
——, mode of removing large stones from the quarry at, ii. 316.
Babel (Babylon), tribute from, i. 397.
Babylon, arched tunnel under the Euphrates at, ii. 302.
——, mode of carrying Gods of, i. 269.
——, golden statues at, ii. 243.
Babylonian embroidered cloths, and cloths of different colours, ii. 81.
Babylonians, pole, sun-dial, and division of day, from the, ii. 319.
Bacchus, fête of, i. 287.
——, resemblance of, to Osiris, i. 285.
Bags containing gold dust, i. 148.
Bagpipes of the Abruzzi, i. 129.
Bais, palm branches, i. 71.
Baker and cook formerly the same office, i. 177.
Balance, ii. 148, 152. *See* Scales.
Balanites. *See* Egleeg.
Ball, or bullet, the pointed, i. 358.
——, games of, i. 198–200.
——, they mounted on each other's backs while playing at, i. 198, 200.
Balsam, ii. 27.
Bargains, length of time in concluding, ii. 104.
Barley, ii. 21. *See* Wheat, and Beer.
Barrels not wanted in Egypt, ii. 166.
Basin of Amasis, golden, i. 186.
Baskets for fruit when gathered, i. 43.
Bastinado, punishment of the, i. 418 ; ii. 4, 210, 211, 215.
—— of women, ii. 211.
—— of workmen, ii. 212.
—— of *shereefs* and great men, ii. 212.
—— of a Copt at Cairo, ii. 213.
Baths, ii. 349.

Bats represented, i. 234.

Battle axe, i. 362, 363.

—— with bronze blade and silver casing to the handle, i. 363.

Battles formerly decided by hand-to-hand fighting, i. 364.

Beads, ii. 64, 65, 339, 340.

Beans and other vegetables eaten, but not by the priests, i. 323.

Bear, i. 228, 245.

Beards, false, ii. 329.

—— of gods, kings, and private individuals, ii. 329.

Bedroom furniture, i. 70, 71.

Bedsteads, i 72.

Beef and goose favourite meats of the Egyptians, i. 66.

—— not wholesome, i. 66.

Beer, men drunk with, i. 54.

—— offered, i. 266.

—— called barley-wine, and zythos (zythus), i. 53–55.

Bees and hives, i. 36.

—— taken on the Nile in boats, i. 36.

Bellows worked by the feet, i. 174.

Benha-el-Assal, or "Benha of honey," town of, i. 37.

Beni-Hassan, strange shields at, i. 348.

——, wrestlers at, i. 204, 205.

——, dwarfs and deformed persons at, i. 204.

Benno sacred bird of Osiris (apparently the Phœnix), i. 251, 252.

Berek. See Abrek.

Berenice, on the Red Sea, ii. 235–237.

Berkel, pyramids of Gebel, ii. 301, 304.

Bersheh. See Colossus.

Bident spear, i. 237–239.

Biot, reign of Thothmes fixed by, ii. 255.

Birds of Egypt, i. 232–234, 249–252.

——, fanciful and allegorical, i. 252; ii. 396.

——, salted and dried, i. 173; ii. 184, 185.

—— sometimes placed whole on the altar, i. 173, 263.

—— served up with the feet and pinion-joints taken off, i. 173.

—— caught in nets and traps, ii. 180–185.

Birthday of the King celebrated, and of Typho, i. 281.

Bitumen called sift, or zift "pitch," i. 397; ii. 259. See Rot-n-n.

Black slave holding a plate, i. 141.

Black and white slaves. See Slaves.

—— puddings made in Egypt, i. 170.

Blades of tools, and weapons, mode of fastening, ii. 113, 164.

Blocks. See Stones.

Blood used for cooking, i. 170.

Boar, wild, in Egypt, i. 244.

——, wild, eaten by some people about Damietta, i. 244.

Boards, mode of joining two, ii. 111, 112.

Boat towed on a lake in the grounds of a villa, i. 25.

—— with sail made of papyrus, i. 413, 414.

—— of the dead, or Baris, ii. 355.

Boat-builders of two kinds, ii. 119.

Boatmen of the fleet, or navy. See Sailors.

—— of the Nile, of the 3rd class, ii. 55.

—— of guard ships, ii. 55.

——, steersman a high office among, ii. 55.

Boats of Egypt, i. 414; ii. 119–131. See Ships.

—— with double mast in early times, i. 413, 414.

——, punts, or canoes of papyrus, osiers, &c., pitched, ii. 119, 120, 123.

——, various kinds of, in Egypt, ii. 123, 130.

—— going up and down the Nile, ii. 122–124.

——, sails of, like those of China, but generally of sailcloth, ii. 123.

—— of burthen, ii. 121, 122.

—— of large size only used during high Nile, ii. 125.

—— made of the papyrus, ii. 119–123.

——, mentioned by Pliny and Strabo, at the Cataracts, ii. 119, 121.

—— of the papyrus safe against crocodiles, ii. 120.

—— of papyrus not sent to India, as Pliny pretends, ii. 122.

—— of the Armenians covered with hide, ii. 121.

—— of Egypt had no beaks, ii. 128.

——, construction of, ii. 130.

——, lotus painted on, ii. 127.

——, eye on prow of, confined to the funeral boats, ii. 127, 367.

——, eye on Maltese and Indian, ii. 127.

——, ornaments on head and stern of, ii. 128.

Boats, streamers of, ii. 127.
——, raised places at the head and stern of, i. 413; ii. 128.
——, painted, ii. 127.
——, clean and well washed, ii. 129.
—— made of *sont*, or Acacia wood, ii. 129.
——, pullies, doubtful if used in, ii. 130, 131.
——, rigging of, ii. 130.
—— built with ribs, and little or no keel, ii. 126.
—— with and without a cabin, ii. 123–125, 127, 129.
——, of burthen, cabins of, ii. 129.
——, square sails of, ii. 126, 128.
—— with coloured and embroidered sails, ii. 131, *cut* 167.
——, sails of, how reefed and furled, i. 412; ii. 126, 130.
—— sails of, had yard at the top and bottom, ii. 126, 128.
—— sails of, had one yard in old times, ii. 126.
Bocchoris the Wise, a great legislator, ii. 217.
Body, reason for preserving the, ii. 380.
Boiled meats seldom eaten by Homer's heroes, i. 173.
Bottle held on the thumb, i. 165.
Bottles, i. 155, 157, 158, 164, 165.
—— and vases stopped with leaves, i. 165.
Bouquet of the Mareotic wine, i. 49.
Bouquets at parties, i. 57.
—— among the offerings to the Gods, i. 257, 258.
Bow of the Koofa, i 349.
—— of Egypt, i. 349, 350.
——, mode of stringing the, i. 350.
——, mode of drawing the, i. 222, 351.
——, guard on the wrist, in using the, i. 351.
—— and arrows for the chase, i. 221.
—— cover used by infantry, i. 354.
—— case, i. 354.
—— suspended at the side of a chariot, i. 375.
—— string of catgut, i. 351.
—— string used for entangling an enemy, i. 351.
Bow the knee, *abrek, bérek*, ii. 203.
Box, curious mode of fastening the lid of a, i. 163, 164.
Boxes of wood of various forms for ornament, and for the toilet table, i. 159–164.

Boxes and furniture, ii. 110, 111, 115–117.
—— veneered with rare woods, i. 163; ii. 115.
—— of ivory, i. 158.
—— in the form of geese, i. 161.
—— with handle in form of a fox, or a fox-dog, i. 161.
——, lids of, ii. 115–117.
—— of ebony and ivory, ii. 117.
—— with pointed top, i. 164; ii. 115, 116.
——, mode of opening, ii. 116, 117.
Boy. *See* Child.
Boys watched the grapes, i. 43.
Brass cups, i. 82, 180.
—— money, ii. 150.
Bread with seeds, i. 177, 179.
——, cakes of, in form of leaves, crocodile's head, &c., i. 177, 266.
——, shape of rolls of, i. 176, 177, 179, 266.
—— made of wheat, or barley, or *doora*, i. 179. See *Doora*.
——, error of Herodotus respecting wheaten, i. 180.
Brickmakers. *See* Bricks.
—— with taskmasters, as described in the Bible, ii. 195.
Bricks led to the invention of the arch, i. 18; ii. 304.
——, houses of crude, i. 6, 18; ii. 8.
——, houses of crude, stuccoed, i. 6.
—— derived from mass of mud first used for building, ii. 281.
——, captives and Egyptians made, ii. 195.
—— made with, and without, straw, ii. 194.
—— preserved to this day, ii. 194.
——, horizontal courses of, in curved lines, ii. 194.
——, burnt, of Roman time, ii. 194.
—— a government monopoly, ii. 194, 195.
——, stamped, ii. 195.
——, great use of, ii. 194, 195.
——, Jews made, but not represented on the monuments, ii. 195, 197.
—— called *Tobi*, as in Arabic, ii. 197.
British bronze weapons, perhaps Phœnician, ii. 136.
Bronze, or brass, cups, i. 82, 180.
——, alloys in, i. 148.
—— blades elastic, i. 148; ii. 159.
—— of excellent quality, i. 148.
——, the earliest cast, ii. 160, 161.
——, use of, ii. 152–155.

Bronze, gilt, ii. 146, 147, 159.
—— tools for cutting stone, ii. 156, 158.
—— used at least 2000 years B.C., ii. 134.
—— weapons in Britain. *See* British.
—— tools, how tempered, ii. 156.
—— chisel found at Thebes, ii. 158.
——, patina upon, ii. 159. *See* Metals, and Metallurgy.
Bruce's harpers, i. 108–110.
Bubastis, Tel Basta. *See* Fête.
—— raised more than any town, as a protection against the inundation, ii. 9, 209.
Buffoonery, the Egyptians fond of, i. 73, 100, 210.
Buffoons, i. 100–103.
Buildings. *See* Architecture.
——, oldest, were of limestone, ii. 305.
Bull-fights, i. 209, 300, 301.
Bulls, sacred, i. 248, 288, 289. *See* Apis.
Bureaucratie in Egypt, ii. 176.
Burial refused, i. 325; ii. 376.
—— refused even to a king if bad, i. 314, 379.
Bushes dragged over the mud, ii. 11.
Butchers sharpening knives on a steel, i. 169, 170.
Buto, fête of Latona at, i. 296, 298.
Byblus. *See* Papyrus.
Byrsa, the citadel of Carthage, ii. 93.
——, a name found in the East, ii. 93.
Byssus is linen, not cotton, ii. 73.
Byzantine and other styles of architecture, ii. 305.

Cabbages eaten to excite them to drink, i. 53.
Cabinet-makers. *See* Carpenters.
Cabins. *See* Boats.
Calasiries (*Klashr*) soldiers, i. 337, 338.
Calasiris, fringed dress called, ii. 91, 321.
Cambyses invaded Egypt, i. 309.
Caffass of palm branches, i. 71.
Cairo, *Mulkufs* on the houses of, vignette A, i. 1.
Cakes of various shapes in offerings, i. 266.
—— with seeds, i. 177, 266; ii. 31.
Calf, golden, i. 140.
Camel not represented, i. 234.
Camp, i. 406, 407.
Camp-stools, i. 63.

Canals carrying the water through the lands, ii. 5, 7, 10.
——, mouths of the, dammed up to keep in the water, ii. 11.
Canopus vase, ii. 391.
Captives. *See* Prisoners. *See* Enemies.
—— represented supporting tables and chairs, and on sandals, i. 68, 69; ii. 287, 333.
—— represented slain by the king on the façades of the temples, allegorical, and found on the monuments of the Ptolemies and Cæsars, i. 411.
Car. *See* Chariot.
Carchemish, defeat of Necho at, i. 309.
——, fortified town of, i. 308, 309.
Caricatures of women, i. 52; ii. 276.
Carpenters and Cabinetmakers, ii. 109, 111–119.
——, tools of the, ii. 111–114.
——, work of the, ii. 111–119.
Carpets, i. 68; ii. 92, 93.
Carriage with four wheels, i. 384.
—— for travelling (or *plaustrum*), i. 384, 385.
Carthamus, ii. 22, 34.
Cartonage of mummies, ii. 396, 397.
Carts of the Tokkari, i. 392.
Cassiterides, ii. 134–136.
Castes. *See* Classes.
Castor Oil, and castorberry tree, ii. 23, 24, 29.
——, mode of extracting, ii. 23, 24.
Cat used as a retriever, i. 236, 238.
——, sacred, i. 246.
——, wild, or *chaus*, i. 230, 246.
Catgut strings of lyre and other instruments, i. 118, 122, 123, 125.
Cattle of different kinds, i. 231.
——, stall fed, i. 27; ii. 49.
——, marked with a hot iron, i. 217, 218.
——, account of, given to a steward, ii. 178. *See* Shepherds. *See* Superintendents.
Cavalry of Egypt, i. 338, 340.
Cedar and fir wood, from Syria, ii. 38.
Celtes not found in Egypt, ii. 164.
Cerberus, ii. 377, 378.
Ceremonies of Egypt, i. 267–288, 296–301.
——, other, i. 280, 285, 287.
——, the Egyptians delighted in, i. 267.

INDEX.

Ceres and Isis, i. 297.
——, wolves led a priest to the temple of, i. 299.
Chair, a monkey tied to the leg of a, i. 145.
Chairs, i. 58–65.
——, double and single, i. 62.
——, the Egyptians sat on, i. 58.
——, kangaroo, i. 64, 65.
Changes made in the Egyptian religion, i. 328–330.
Chaplets, numerous, i. 57.
—— of nightshade in Egypt, ii. 33.
Character of the Egyptians, i. 2, 3, 210; ii. 210, 227. *See* Conquest.
——, modes of telling the, i. 210, 211.
Chariot with complete furniture, i. 376.
—— held two persons, i. 368, 370.
—— sometimes held three, i. 368, 370.
——, the king alone in his, i. 371.
——, the king had a " second," i. 371.
—— had no seat, i. 373.
—— was of wood, i. 373.
——, bent pole of the, i. 374.
——, driver was on the off side of the, i. 371.
——, parts of the, i. 375.
——, process of making a, i. 377, 378.
——, partly made by carpenters, partly by curriers, i. 377.
—— makers, ii. 117.
——, bow and arrow, and spear cases suspended on the, i. 377.
——, wheels of the, i. 379.
——, drawing of, in perspective, i. 380, 382.
——, mode of fastening, and parts of the harness of a war, i. 379, 381.
—— had only two horses, i. 381.
—— for travelling (or *plaustrum*), i. 384, 385.
—— or car in the Florence Museum, i. 385, 386.
—— with mules, i. 384, 385.
—— of the Rot-ñ-n, i. 376.
Chariot-corps, i. 368, 371, 386.
Charioteer, i. 368, 370, 371.
—— often a person of consequence, i. 372.
Chariots of silver and gold, others painted, i. 375.
——, guests arrived in, i. 73, 74, 76.
—— of gentlemen in towns, i. 371.
—— of princes, i. 370.
Charms, ii. 352.
——, or bullas, worn by children, ii. 330.

Charon, origin of, ii. 375, 377.
Chase, i. 212, 214, 218, 221, 224.
—— a favourite pastime, i. 212.
—— in the grounds of grandees, and nets enclosing a space for the, i. 213.
Chemistry and metallic oxides, knowledge of, ii. 67.
—— and dyeing cloths, ii. 67.
Cherubim like the winged figures of Truth in the arks, i. 271.
Chevron ornament in Egypt, ii. 290.
Chickens, or fowls, treatment of, ii. 184.
Child, lock of hair indicative of a, i. 311, 372.
—— accompanied its parents when fishing and fowling, i. 235, 237.
Children of priests, education of, i. 321.
——'s hair, ii. 328.
——, education of, ii. 226.
—— of common people, i. 322.
—— of slaves, ii. 225.
——, severity of duties of, ii. 225.
——, respect of, to parents, ii. 225.
——, not swaddled, and mode of carrying, ii. 330.
Chinese bottles, ii. 68, 69, 70.
——, probable date of, ii. 70.
Chisels, ii. 113, 114. *See* Bronze.
Choristers, i. 92.
—— often blind, i. 94, 95.
Chorus of many persons, i. 92.
Christian story offers fine subjects for art, ii. 294.
Clappers, or *Crotala*, i. 99, 100, 129, 130, 135, 296.
—— used in dances, i. 135.
Clapping the hands, i. 92. *See* Hands.
Class the 1st and the 2nd, priests and soldiers, i. 316; ii. 2.
Class 3rd, huntsmen, gardeners, boatmen, peasants, &c., ii. 2, 54, 55.
Class 4th, members of the, ii. 2, 56.
Class 5th, members of the, ii. 2.
Classes, five, of the Egyptians, not castes, i. 316; ii. 2.
—— according to Herodotus, Diodorus, Strabo, and Plato, ii. 1, 2.
Clay used for pottery, ii. 107.
—— kneaded by the foot, ii. 107.
Cloth, manufacture of, ii. 85, 86, 89.
——, calendering, ii. 91, 92.
Clover, dried, called in Arabic *Drees*, ii. 21, 48, 49.
Club of rude shape, i. 364.
—— (*lissán*) or curved stick, i. 365.
—— used by foreigners (woodcut), i. 338, 365.

Cock's head. See *Rhyton*.
Cocks and hens, not represented, i. 234.
—— originally from Asia, i. 234.
Coffin makers, ii. 117–119.
Coffins, ii. 119, 368, 375, 397.
—— of foreign woods, i. 19.
Coin of Athens, of old type, being known in commerce, ii. 151.
Coinage, oldest, ii. 147, 150.
Coins of Electrum, Lydian, ii. 150.
—— of real gold were of Darius, ii. 150.
—— oldest silver, ii. 147, 150. *See* Gold.
Colossi. *See* Statues.
Colossus on a sledge, at El Bersheh, ii. 307, 308. *See* Frontispiece to vol. ii.
Colour of temples, ii. 281, 290, 291.
—— of statues, ii. 279.
Colours, nature of their, ii. 292.
—— taste in the arrangement of, ii. 293.
—— applied to wood on a coating of stucco, ii. 111.
Coloured, and glazed tiles, ii. 288, 292.
Column thrown down by one of the guests at a party, i. 146.
—— supporting a statue, not good taste, i. 21.
Columns, eight orders of Egyptian, ii. 285, 286.
——, palm tree and other, ii. 283.
——, Caryatide from the Osiride, ii. 286.
——, slender, reaching to the top of the house, i. 20, 21; ii. 286.
—— of our modern houses, i. 20.
——, variety of, in the same hall, ii. 296, 297.
——, square, or pillars, the oldest, ii. 281.
——, polygonal, ii. 282–284.
——, half drums of, ii. 284.
Combs, ii. 342, 343.
Committees never responsible, ii. 295.
Commutation. *See* Punishments.
Confectioners, i. 174, 177.
Confession of the dead, ii. 201.
Conquest of a country does not entirely change the character of a people, i. 2; ii. 227.
Conquests of the Egyptians, i. 308, 390–416.
Convent, or college, of women, i. 319.
Conversation considered the charm of society, i. 146.

Cook. *See* Baker.
Cooking meat, i. 174, 175, 178.
Cooks, i. 170, 174–178.
Coopers, ii. 117.
——, occupation of, ii. 166.
Copper, use of, or bronze, when alloyed with tin, ii. 152, 158.
—— mines in Egypt, ii. 155. *See* Bronze.
Copt, refusing to pay taxes, story of, ii. 213.
Coptos, pottery of, ii. 107.
Corbag whips, i. 240.
Corn, six ears of, offered by the king. i. 273.
—— and other produce sown, ii. 39. *See* Wheat.
Corn country, i. 173.
Coronation. *See* King.
Corslet, or coat of scale armour, i. 366, 367.
—— worked in colours, i. 367, 368.
—— bronze, scales of, with the name of Sheshonk (Shishak), i. 368.
—— of Amasis, with gold thread, ii. 81, 82.
Cotton cloth, ii. 74.
—— used by the priests, ii. 74.
—— not Byssus, ii. 73.
Couches, i. 68, 69.
Cow. *See* Athor.
Cow's head on a pilaster, ii. 286.
Credulity, reaction of, i. 211.
——, injury arising from, i. 325, 328.
Criminals. *See* Punishments. *See* Bastinado.
—— when not transported, ii. 215.
Crocodile, mode of catching the, i. 241, 242, 244.
—— venerated in some, hated in other places, i. 242, 332.
—— attacked by the Tentyrites, i. 242.
—— a timid animal, i. 242.
——, mode of attack of the, i. 243.
——, size of the, i. 243.
—— eaten at Apollinopolis, i. 241.
—— held in abhorrence at Apollinopolis, Tentyris, and Heracleopolis, i. 242.
—— and the trochilus, i. 243.
—— moves the lower jaw, i. 197.
——, toy of the, i. 197.
——, eggs of the, i. 243.
Crocodile's eggs destroyed by the ichneumon, i. 229.
Crocodilopolis. *See* Arsinoë. *See* Athribis.

Crops, several, ii. 20, 21, 25, 39, 49, 50. *See* Plants.

Cross, sign of life put for the, i. 277.

Cross-legged, poor people sat, i. 58.

——, they did not generally sit, i. 58.

Crotala, or clappers. *See* Clappers.

Crown of Upper and Lower Egypt (called *Pshent*), i. 257, 269 ; ii. 323, 325.

—— put on by the king, i. 273.

—— put on the king's head by the gods, i. 276.

Cruelty of Asiatics, i. 3.

—— not commonly practised by the Egyptians, i. 3, 406, 410.

——, occasional acts of, i. 410.

Cubit, ii. 256–259.

—— of same length at different times, ii. 257.

—— of the Nilometer, ii. 257–259.

Cullenders. *See* Strainers.

Cups, i. 180. *See* Vases.

Cups of brass, or bronze, i. 82.

Curriers and shoemakers, ii. 10–105.

Cush, or Ethiopia, i. 402, 404.

Cutch, club of the people of, i. 364.

Cylinders very ancient in Egypt, long before, and not borrowed from, the Assyrians, ii. 341.

Cymbals, i. 99, 100.

Cyperus, various kinds of, ii. 96.

Daggers, i. 358.

——, mode of wearing and using, i. 359.

—— with sheaths, and ornamented handles, i. 360.

—— of bronze, i. 360, 361.

Damaskening, art of, ii. 159, 161, 162.

Damietta, wild boar eaten by some people about, i. 244.

Dance, i. 133-140.

——, steps in the, i. 139.

——, figure, i. 137, 140.

——, gestures in the, i. 133–135, 138.

—— of the lower orders, i. 139.

Dancers, i. 96.

Dancing not taught to the upper classes, i. 135.

—— of the Greeks and Romans, i. 135, 138.

—— of Hippoclides, i. 135.

——, posture in, i. 138.

——, pirouette in, i. 138.

—— women, dresses of the, i. 138.

——, sacred, i. 140.

—— taught to slaves, i. 138.

Dancing, clapped their hands while, i. 135.

—— in the temple, i. 140.

Darabooka drum, i. 93, 98.

Darics gold coins, ii. 150, 151.

Darius introduced good laws into Egypt, ii. 229.

Date-wine, i. 56.

Dates, i. 55.

——, preserve of, i. 181.

—— of *Korayn*, called *Amaree*, ii. 37.

David danced, i. 140.

——, gold and silver collected by, ii. 243.

Days of the Epact, the 5 days added to the 360, i. 281 ; ii. 252, 254.

—— and night divided into 12 hours, ii. 319.

Dead, did not cut themselves for the, ii. 374.

——, no degradation offered to the, ii. 379.

——, numerous ceremonies of the, ii. 119, 357–363, 365–375, 383–390.

—— body, if found, was embalmed at the expense of the district, ii. 388.

——, trial of the, ii. 375, 377, 378.

——, intestines of the, ii. 388, 390, 391.

——, lake of the, ii. 377.

——, objects buried with the, ii. 319.

Death of individuals, songs on the, i. 97.

Death, soul after, ii. 329, 357.

Debt, laws respecting, ii. 217, 218.

——, no arrest for, ii. 217.

——, gave tomb of a parent as a pledge for, ii. 218, 376.

—— increased by luxury, and fondness for imitation, ii. 218, 219.

Decimal and duodecimal calculation, ii. 178.

Decorative design, the province of, ii. 288.

——works by celebrated artists, ii. 280.

Decoy bird, i. 236.

Dedication of a temple, i. 271, 272.

Deeds, mode of executing, ii. 219.

——, number of witnesses for, ii. 219, 222.

——, form of, for sale of small property, ii. 220–222.

Deity, division of the, into his attributes, i. 327, 329

——, unity of the, i. 327.

Delta, villages of the, like islands during the inundation, ii. 7.

——, the water and the land rise less in the, ii. 7, 9.

Dentists, ii. 350.

Desert, edge of the, cultivated, ii. 20.

Diana. *See* Pasht.

Dice, i. 195, 196.

Dido and the bull's hide, ii. 93. *See* Byrsa.

Dining, mode of, i. 167.

Dinner, they sat round a small table at, i. 167, 181, 182.

——, number of dishes at, i. 167, 180.

——, preparation of, i. 165.

—— at noon, i. 73, 174, 179.

——, occupation of guests before, i. 76.

Discoveries and inventions often effects of chance, ii. 84.

Dishes of various kinds, i. 167, 180.

Divans, i. 58.

Doctors, ii. 350–352.

——, feeling the pulse, ii. 352.

Dog, mummies of the fox-, i. 231.

Dogs in fashion at different times, i. 231.

—— often appear to be chosen for their ugliness, i. 231.

——, breeds of, i. 230, 231.

——, hunting with, i. 218.

—— coupled, i. 218, 219.

Dôm tree, or Theban palm, i. 56, 57.

——, nut of the fruit of the, i. 56 ; ii. 28, 113.

——, fruit of the, like our gingerbread, i. 56.

Doora, or *holcus* sorghum, bread of the, i. 179 ; ii. 3, 22, 25.

——, plucked up by the roots, and the head stripped off by a spiked instrument, ii. 50, 51.

Doors, i. 13, 15–17, 28.

——, hinges, and keys, i. 15, 16.

——, single and double valves, opened inwards, i. 17.

——, sentences written over, i. 6.

—— of store-rooms for grain, i. 14, 32.

Doorways, i. 9, 15–17, 26.

Doqáq, of ground lupins, for washing, instead of soap, i. 186.

Double pipe, i. 128, 129.

—— used in sacred music, i. 129.

Dovetailing, ii. 111.

Doura. See *Doora.*

Dramatic entertainments, Greek, i. 100.

Draughts, game of, i. 189, 190, 191, 192, 193.

Drawing much studied in France, ii. 275.

—— and sculpture preceded writing, ii. 270.

Dress, leopard skin, of the priests, i. 319. *See* Leopard-skin Dress.

—— of a king and a queen, i. 317.

Dresses of dancing women, i. 138.

—— of huntsmen, i. 215.

—— of priests, i. 319, 320, 333–335.

—— of soldiers, i. 365, 366.

—— of mercenary troops, i. 337.

—— and arms of foreign people the enemies of Egypt, i. 390–404.

—— of the kings. i. 317 ; ii. 322–325.

—— of the queens, i. 317.

—— of men, ii. 320–322.

—— of women, i. 318–335.

—— of children, ii. 329, 330.

—— at a party, i. 81.

—— simple, like that of a river god, ii. 320.

—— embroidered and coloured, ii. 81, 83.

—— with fringes, i. 333 ; ii. 91, 320, 321.

——, head, of men, ii. 325.

——, head, of women, ii. 335.

—— of poor people, ii. 320.

—— not fully described on the monuments, ii. 320.

Drill (or centrebit), i. 56 ; ii. 94, 111–113.

Drinking to each other, i. 82.

—— excesses in, i. 52, 53.

Drum, i. 98, 104, 105, 106, 107.

Drum. See *Darabooka* Drum.

Drumstick, i. 107.

Drums of columns, ii. 284.

Dwarfs and deformed persons in the service of grandees, i. 203, 204.

Dykes, ii. 5, 7, 10.

—— watched by guards and kept up at a great expense, ii. 7.

——, punishment for injuring the, ii. 7.

Dynasty, Thinite, Memphite, Theban, i. 307. *See* Saïte.

——, 18th, i. 308.

Earrings, women talking about, i. 145.

——, patterns of, ii. 335, 338, 345.

Education of the priests and other classes, i. 321, 322.

—— of youth, strict, ii. 226.

Egleeg, or Balanites, tree, ii. 28, 37, 38, 110.

Eglon, King of Moab, parlour of, i. 11.

Egypt, influence of, on Greece, i. 1.

—— influence of, on early civilization, i. 3.

Egypt, antiquity of, i. 3, 4.

——, treatment of women in, i. 4; ii. 223.

——, plants and trees of, i. 57.

—— famous for medicinal plants and drugs, i. 50; ii. 351.

——, history of, i. 307–309.

——, Menes, the first king of, i. 307.

——, dynasties of the kings of, i. 307.

—— once divided into several independent kingdoms, i. 307.

—— Ames (or Amosis) became sole king of, i. 111, 307.

——, Shepherds invaded, and were driven out of, i. 307, 308.

——, lost all its conquests in Asia, i. 309.

—— conquered by Cambyses, i. 309.

—— recovered by native kings, i. 309.

——, Alexander conquers, i. 309.

——, rule of the Ptolemies in, i. 309.

——, rule of the Romans in, i. 310.

—— of limited extent, i. 304.

——, number of square miles in, i. 304.

——, towns and villages of ancient, i. 304.

——, population of, i. 305.

—— had Ethiopians, Libyans, and others under its sway, i. 305.

——, produce of, greater in old times, but capable of producing more now, i. 305.

——, no great encroachments of sand in, i. 306.

——, some towns of, placed on the edge of the desert, i. 306, 307.

—— glass. See Glass. See Etruscans

—— has more cultivable land now than formerly, i. 306.

—— emblems, and crowns, of Upper and Lower, i. 257, 269 ; ii. 323, 325.

——, productiveness of, ii. 2, 3.

—— called " the world," ii. 227.

—— nomes or provinces, and limits of, ii. 229.

——, divisions of, at different times, ii. 229, 230, 231.

——, foreigners confined to certain parts of, ii. 231.

—— became commercial after the fall of Tyre and building of Alexandria, ii. 133.

——, long the dominant nation, and set the fashion in art, &c., ii. 263.

——, foreign woods imported into, ii. 111.

—— produced little wood for ornamental purposes, ii. 109.

Egypt, boats of. See Boats.

—— wealth of, ii. 238, 239, 242. See Tribute.

——, wines of, ii. 238, 239, 240.

——, known to foreigners for its manufactures, ii. 247. See Agriculture.

——, exports of, ii. 233, 234, 256.

——, offices in, at different times, ii. 231.

——, Greek information respecting, imperfect, ii. 231, 389.

—— under the Romans, ii. 233.

" Egyptian," artificial flowers called, i. 57.

Egyptian. See Embroidery. See Chemistry.

—— yarn, ii. 84.

—— architecture, ii. 280–304.

—— architecture, all painted, ii. 290. See Architecture.

— painters and scribes, ii. 275, 276, 277.

—— inkstands and sketches, ii. 276.

—— art, ii. 262.

—— paintings on panel, ii. 277.

—— laws, sanctity of old, ii. 227.

—— lawgivers, ii. 226.

—— temples, subjects of the sculpture in, ii. 295, 296.

—— colours, ii. 292, 293.

—— scribes with a pen behind the ear, ii. 275.

—— figures drawn in squares, ii. 266, 267.

—— figures often spirited, but wanting in life and reality, ii. 268.

—— statues, ii. 272.

—— sculptures in low relief and intaglio, ii. 272.

—— sculptures of a new style of Remeses III., ii. 273.

—— sculpture, revival of, ii. 274.

Egyptians, origin of the, i. 302, 303.

——, a Caucasian race, i. 302.

—— went to Egypt as conquerors, i. 303.

—— placed some towns on the edge of the desert, i. 306, 307.

——, early government of the, hierarchical, i. 307.

—— restless under all foreign rulers, i. 310.

—— social habits of the, i. 3, 4, 5, 144.

—— not guilty of great cruelty. See Cruelty. See Humanity.

—— thought to be a gloomy people, i. 2.

——, character of the, i. 2, 3, 210.

Egyptians, character of the modern,
i. 2 ; ii. 210, 227.
—— very fond of their country, ii.
227.
—— fond of flowers, i. 19, 57.
—— fond of wine, i. 53.
—— fond of variety, i. 58 ; ii. 297.
—— fond of ceremonies and religious
pomp, i 267.
—— sat on chairs, i. 58.
—— did not recline at meals, i. 58.
—— victories and power of. See
Conquests.
—— had only one wife, i. 5 ; ii. 224.
—— kept to their old customs, 226.
—— "wisdom of the," i. 325 ; ii. 202.
—— gratitude of the, ii. 227.
—— had some elegant vases, but generally deficient in taste, and very
inferior to the Greeks, ii. 109.
—— had the *guilloche*, *chevron*, and
other patterns at a very early time,
ii. 290.
—— coated walls with stucco, ii. 291.
—— used gilding, ii. 293.
—— avoided uniformity and studied
variety in their architecture, ii. 296,
297, 298.
—— had columns of different styles
in the same hall, ii. 296, 297.
—— skill of the, in drawing lines, ii.
274.
—— pencils and brushes of the, ii. 275.
—— did not bear innovation in sacred
subjects, ii. 264.
—— did not alter their style of drawing, and were bound by fixed rules,
ii. 264, 266.
—— deficient in taste, ii. 265–269,
272.
—— drew animals better than men,
ii. 269.
——, "all equally noble," ii. 357.
—— first who taught that soul of man
was immortal, ii. 379.
Elasticity of bronze, i. 154, 360 ; ii.
159.
Electric fish, called in Arabic Raad
" thunder," ii. 192.
Electrum, coins of, ii. 150.
Elizabethan rooms, i. 58.
Embalmers, ii. 119, 374, 387.
Embalming process, 383–387.
——, supposed reason for, ii. 380.
——, when given up, ii. 398, 399.
Emblems offered, i. 260.
——, sacred and other, i. 257.
Embroidery of the Egyptians, Hebrews, Babylonians, and Romans,
ii. 81.
Embroidery, with gold, ii. 81.
Emeralds, false, in glass. ii. 63, 64.
——, large statues of, ii. 63.
Enamelling on gold, ii. 70.
*Encaustu*n, the colours burnt in, ii. 70.
Enemies of Egypt, Asiatic, i. 390, 391–
403.
——, African, i. 402, 403, 404.
——, wounded, i. 373.
——, heads of, represented on win-
dow-sills, i. 68 ; ii. 287.
Epact, the five days of the. See Days.
——, third day of the, Typho's birth-
day, i. 281.
Epaphus, clean oxen belonged to, i.
250. See Apis.
Ethiopia, Jupiter going into, i. 269.
——, gods taking refuge in, i. 269.
——, a princess of, coming to an
Egyptian king, i. 384, 385.
Ethiopian kings of Egypt, i. 308.
Ethiopians, tribute of the, i. 404.
Etruscans, Greeks, and Assyrians
had some bottles and vases from
Egypt, ii. 70, 71.
Evil, ii. 372.
Europe had an indigenous population,
i. 303.
Europeans differ from Asiatics, i. 303.
Excesses of men and women in drink-
ing, i. 52, 53.
—— in eating and drinking, i. 173.
Expenses of the Egyptians trifling, the
necessary, ii 219. See Food.
Extremities of the world possess the
greatest treasures, ii. 240.
Ex-votos, ii. 354.
Eye of Osiris, i. 257.
—— signifying " Egypt," i. 244, 257.
—— on boats, ii. 127. See Boats.
Eyes painted, or blackened with *Kohl*,
ii. 343.

Falchion, *Shopsh*, or *Khopsh*, i. 361.
Fanbearer of the king a high office,
i. 283, 284.
——, investiture to the office of, i. 283.
Father, abstract idea of, i. 327, 332.
——, murder of a, ii. 209.
——'s trade followed by a son. See
Son.
Fauteuil of the master of the house, i.
145.
—— some pet animal tied to the leg of
a, i. 145.
Fauteuils, i. 60, 61, 62.

INDEX.

Fauteuils, highly ornamented, i. 60, 61.

Feas', ruler of the, i. 82.

Feats of strength and dexterity, i. 201, 205, 207.

—— of agility, i. 188, 189.

Feet, clay kneaded with the, ii. 107.

——, paste kneaded with the, i. 177.

Fescennine verses of Italy, i. 101.

Festivals, i. 280–287. *See* Fêtes. *See* Sacred.

—— connected with agriculture, ii. 52, 53, 54.

—— of harvest-home, i. 282.

Fête of Diana at Bubastis, i. 296, 297.

—— of Isis at Busiris, i. 296, 297.

—— of Minerva, or Neith, at Saïs, i. 296, 298.

—— of burning lamps, ii. 71.

—— of the Sun at Heliopolis, i. 296, 298, 301.

—— of Latona at Buto, and of Mars at Papremis, i. 296, 298.

—— of Thoth, i. 299.

—— in honour of the daughter of Mycerinus, i. 299.

Fêtes, many, in the year, i. 296.

—— at the new and full moon, i. 299.

—— other, i. 301. *See* Sacred.

—— of the peasants during the high Nile, ii. 52. *See* Festivals.

Fig trees and vines, i. 41, 57.

——, wild, ii. 30.

Figs, i. 54.

——, sycamore, 44, 57, 181, 259. *See* Sycamore.

—— and grapes, fond of, i. 181.

—— and grapes on altars, i. 262.

—— in a basket, the hieroglyphic signifying "wife," i. 323.

Figl (or *Raphanus*), i. 167, 259, 323.

Figure, proportions and Egyptian mode of drawing the human, ii. 266, 267.

Figure. *See* Foot, the standard for the.

Firmán, or royal order; custom of kissing, ii. 203.

First fruits, offerings of the, i. 274, 299.

Fish not eaten by the priests, i. 322.

——, sacred, i. 254; ii. 191, 192.

—— and meat at dinner, i. 167.

——, how brought to table, i. 173.

—— of Egypt most prized, ii. 191.

—— of the Nile of muddy flavour, ii. 193.

——, great consumption of, ii. 189, 193.

Fish, dried, ii. 181, 189, 190.

—— of Egypt regretted by the Israelites, ii. 191.

——, electric. *See* Electric.

—— of the sea not appreciated, ii. 193.

Fishponds, i. 37, 215.

Fisheries, revenue from the, ii. 193.

—— of the Lake Mœris, ii. 193.

Fishermen, ii. 181, 186.

Fishing, ii. 181, 186–193.

Fishing, an amusement of gentlemen, i. 238.

——, they sat on a mat, or in a chair, while, i. 238.

—— with a fly unknown, i. 239.

——nets and leads of, ii. 187–189.

Fishing-rod and hook, i. 239; ii. 186.

Flax, process of cultivating, or steeping, and preparing for cloth, ii. 88, 89.

——, comb for preparing, ii. 90, 91.

—— used for ropes, ii. 93.

——, nets of string, made of, ii. 95.

——, much in Egypt, ii. 50.

Flaxman, the, great taste of, ii. 289.

Flower offered from each other's bouquet, i. 146.

—— garden, i. 37, 57.

—— of the lotus, i. 39. *See* Lotus.

Flowers, as emblems, i. 257.

—— presented as offerings, i. 257–259.

—— produced in Egypt, i. 57.

—— much used, i. 19, 57.

——, artificial, called "Egyptian," i. 57.

—— presented to guests, i. 78–81, 141.

——, wreaths of, i. 57, 79.

——, stands for, i. 79.

——, fondness of the Egyptians for, i. 19, 57.

——, bowl crowned with, i. 80.

—— brought as part of a foreign tribute, i. 57, 395.

—— of the lotus much used for chaplets and wreaths, i. 57.

——, tables decked with, i. 57.

—— and plants of Egypt, from Pliny, ii. 27–32. *See* Plants.

—— in the paintings, ii. 36.

——, "*immortelles*," placed in the tomb, ii. 374.

Flute, length of the Egyptian, i. 127.

——, antiquity of the, i. 126, 127.

—— of reed, bone, wood, or ivory, i. 127.

—— not allowed in the rites of Osiris and Anubis, i. 129.

Flute, Minerva's aversion for the, i. 127.
Fly-fishing. *See* Fishing.
Food, i. 166–168.
—— of the peasants, i. 167; ii. 3.
—— of the poor people and shepherds, ii. 175.
—— of poor people simple and cheap, i. 179; ii. 219, 330.
"Fool or a physician at forty," origin of, ii. 352.
Foot, watering with the, i. 34.
——, standard, or unit for the human figure, ii. 266.
Foot-machine, i. 34.
Footmen, running, i. 76.
Footstools, i. 68.
Foreleg and shoulder, called "the chosen part," i. 264.
Forks not used at dinner, i. 181.
—— known to the Jews and Etruscans, but not used at table, i. 182.
—— used in an Egyptian kitchen, i. 174, 175.
—— of wood used by the peasants, ii. 42, 45.
Fortification, regular system of, i. 407.
Fowling, a great amusement, i. 234.
Fox, i. 227, 245.
—— dog, i. 231.
Fringes on dresses (sometimes sewed on). ii. 91, 322. *See* Dresses with fringes.
Fruit in wicker baskets, i. 43.
—— gathering, i. 40, 41, 43, 44.
Fruit trees, i. 36, 55, 57.
Fruits on the altar, i. 259.
Fullers, ii. 106.
Funerals, mourners at, ii. 366.
Funerals of kings, ii. 366.
——, some grand, ii. 366–373.
Furniture of Egyptian rooms, i. 58–72.
Fyoom, or Arsinoïte nome, i. 49, 229, 244, 304.
——, extremity of the, artificially irrigated, i. 307.
——, remains of vineyards on the western borders of, i. 49; ii. 20.
——, wild boars found in the, i. 244.

Game, preserves for, i. 37.
——, parks and covers for, i. 215.
Game-cart, substitute for the, i. 218.
Games in honour of the gods, i. 282.
—— most usual, i. 188, 189.
—— of ball, i. 198–200.
Games, various, i. 192–207.
—— of single-stick, i. 206, 207.
——, board of, found by Dr. Abbott, i. 194, 195. See *Mora* and Draughts.
Gardens, i. 25, 32, 35–37.
Garlands or chaplets, i. 57, 79–81.
Garments worn at feasts, i. 81.
Gazelle, i. 214–216, 219, 220, 223–225, 227, 247.
Geese, boxes in the form of, i. 161.
—— fed, i. 215. *See* Goose.
—— potted, ii. 185.
Geography, in the books of Hermes, i. 274.
Geometry, i. 321.
——, arithmetic, and astronomy, ii. 319.
—— invented in Egypt, ii. 248, 251.
Gilding, ii. 145–147.
Giraffe, i. 231, 247.
Gladiators not employed in Egypt, i. 210.
Glass, early use of—blowers, bottles and blowpipe, and glazed pottery, ii. 58.
—— bottles, ii. 58, 67.
—— bottles of various colours, ii. 60.
—— beads with name of Amun-m-het, ii. 59.
—— beads, ii. 64, 65. *See* Beads.
—— beads rarely found with a name, ii. 60.
——, discovery or invention of, ii. 60.
——, Egyptians famed for particular kinds of, ii. 60.
——, counterfeits of precious stones, ii. 60, 63. *See* Precious Stones.
—— shows advance of luxury, ii. 65.
—— of many colours attempted at Venice, ii. 61.
—— mosaics of pictures in Venice, ii. 61, 63.
——, false emeralds of, ii. 63, 64.
——, coloured, 60, 63–65, 67, 71.
——, coloured imitations of murrhine vases, ii. 71.
—— applied to various uses, ii. 65.
—— coloured porcelain, ii. 66, 71. *See* Vitrified.
——, cut, ground, and cast, ii. 67.
—— cut by the diamond, emery powder and wheel, ii. 67.
—— bottles inclosed in wicker casing, ii. 67, 68.
—— lamps, ii. 71, 72.
Glazed tiles in Egypt, ii. 287, 292.
Gloves, i. 283; ii. 336.
—— brought by the Rot-ñ-n, i. 397.

Glue, ii. 114, 115.
Goats browsing on vines after the vintage, i. 45.
God, division of, into various attributes, i. 327.
——, spirit of, was Nef, Nû, Núm, or Nûb, i. 327.
——, or Goddess, with several names, i. 329.
Gods of Egypt, i. 327, 328, 330, 331.
——, figures of the, i. 328.
——, nature, i. 332, 333.
—— worshipped throughout Egypt, i. 331.
—— of different cities, i. 331, 332.
Goddesses with various names, in different countries, really the same, i. 333.
Goeffreying machine, ii. 92.
Gold-dust in bags, i. 148, 260, 261; ii. 149.
Gold in Egypt and in Britain, and quartz veins broken up, ii. 141.
—— thread, ii. 81.
—— wire, ii. 82.
—— workers, ii. 137, 138.
——, great use of, for ornaments, ii. 138, 140, 141.
——, hieroglyphic signifying, ii. 149. (Woodcut, figs. a, b.)
——, fusing, ii. 139.
——, washing ore of, ii. 139.
——, vases of, ii. 140, 141.
—— mines of Egypt and Ethiopia in the Bisharee desert, and Mr. Bonomi's account of them, ii. 141.
—— of Australia and California, ii. 143.
—— mines described by Diodorus, ii. 143, 144.
——, cruelty to people condemned to the mines, ii. 144, 145.
—— at first used very pure, ii. 145.
—— leaf, at first thick, ii. 145.
—— on vases, mummies, &c., ii. 146.
—— beating, improvements in, ii. 146.
—— used before silver, shown by the latter being called "Whitegold," ii. 147, 241. (Woodcut 408, fig. c.)
—— used for overlaying humbler materials, ii. 147.
—— greater use of, for ornamental purposes, ii. 147.
——, rings of, as money, ii. 149.
——, a quantity in bags already counted, ii. 149.
—— darics of Persia, ii. 150.
—— staters, the oldest coins, originally mere dumps, ii. 150.

Gold, fetters of, in Ethiopia, ii. 155.
—— of Colchis, ii. 240.
—— of Spain, ii. 240, 242.
—— and silver, ii. 238-247.
—— and silver, relative value of, at different times, ii. 242.
——. See Precious Metals, Wealth, and Jewelry, ii. 243, 244.
——, quantity of in ancient countries, ii. 243.
——, teeth stopped with, ii. 350.
——, statues of, ii. 243.
—— of David and Solomon, ii. 243.
—— loss by wear and other causes, ii. 245.
—— in Rome, ii. 244, 245.
—— before and after the discovery of America, ii. 246.
Golden-calf ground and reduced to powder, ii. 136.
——, mode of worshipping with dances, i. 140.
—— mosaics. See Mosaics.
—— ewer and basin, i. 76, 77.
Good, Goodness, i. 327; ii. 358. See Osiris.
Goose and beef much eaten, i. 66.
——. See Abyssinians.
——, emblem of the God Seb, i. 251.
—— and globe, "son of the Sun," of Egypt, found on Greek vases. See Vases.
Grace before meals, i. 186.
Grain, pigs and other animals trod in the, ii. 11, 12, 13.
Grain, abundance of, ii. 3.
—— of "seven plenteous years" laid up, shows the abundance of, ii. 3.
—— exported and belonging to Government stores, ii. 3.
Granaries, i. 13, 31, 32; ii. 43, 46.
—— with vaulted roofs, i. 31, 32.
Granite, difficulty of cutting, ii. 157.
—— not cut and worked when less hard, ii. 157.
——, stunning the crystals of, ii. 157.
——, early use of squared, ii. 287.
——, painted, ii. 291.
——, imitation of, ii. 292.
——, walls cased with, ii. 292.
Grapes, gathering of, i. 40-43.
—— watched by boys, i. 43.
Gratitude of the Egyptians, ii. 227.
Grease used in moving large stones, ii. 309.
Greece, pictures of, ii., 278, 279.
—— in its infancy, when Egypt had long been the leading nation, ii. 263.

Greece borrowed from Egypt, ii. 264, 283.
——, influence of Egypt on, i. 1, 4; ii. 263.
Greek temples traced from wooden buildings, i. 5.
—— lyres. *See* Lyres.
—— instruments, name of, i. 126.
—— flute, name of, i. 126.
—— mercenaries in Egypt, i. 309.
—— statues coloured, ii. 279, 280.
—— artists painted on panel, not on walls, the best, ii. 278, 280.
—— pictures in temples and galleries, ii. 279.
—— pictures carried off to Rome, ii. 279.
——, oldest paintings monochrome, ii. 279.
—— statues and bas-reliefs coloured, ii. 279, 291.
—— colours, ii. 291.
—— taste, colour, form, and proportion, ii, 293.
—— architecture at first simple, ii. 297.
—— towns wanted lofty buildings, i. 21.
——, Ionic, and Corinthian capitals, ii. 297.
—— and Egyptian temples of a different character, ii. 298.
—— architecture and bas-reliefs coloured, ii. 291.
Greeks claimed discoveries of others, ii. 109.
——, vases of the, far superior to those of Egyptians in taste, ii. 109.
—— did not copy natural objects for ornament, ii. 288.
—— copied from the "Barbarian" what was beautiful, and made it their own, ii. 289.
—— knew but did not use the arch in buildings, ii. 302.
—— considered music a necessary accomplishment, i. 94.
—— indebted to Asia for stringed instruments, i. 111.
——, long-haired, ii. 327.
Grove or *Temenos*. *See* explanation of Frontispiece, List of woodcuts, vol. i.
—— or *Temenos*, i. 409.
Guard at the gate of a camp, i. 407.
—— had no shield, i. 406.
Guards, royal, i. 337.
Guests, reception of, and arrival of, i. 73.

Guests had flowers and wine brought them on arriving, i. 81, 141.
—— anointed on arriving, i. 78.
—— received bouquets of flowers and necklaces, i. 78, 79.
—— crowned with flowers, i. 78, 80.
—— admired the furniture and knick-knacks, i. 76, 146.
—— at dinner sat on the ground, or on chairs, i. 181, 182.
—— amused with music and dancing, i. 141.
Guilloche ornament, i. 19; ii. 290.
Guitar of 3 strings, i. 84, 86, 123, 124.
—— knowledge required for the invention of the, i. 84.
—— *Kithára, Chitarra*, i. 124, 129.
—— an instrument found at Thebes not unlike the, i. 125.
Gûsla of Montenegro, with one string, i. 125.

Hair of women, ii. 335.
—— of children, i. 312; ii. 328. *See* Child.
—— of men shaved, i. 312; ii. 327.
—— of servants, ii. 334.
Halfeh or *Poa* grass, i. 57.
Hand-writing to tell a character, i. 211.
Hands cut off, as a return of the enemy's killed, i. 373.
—— clapping the, i. 89, 90, 92, 95, 101, 128, 135, 139, 296.
Handles of vases, i. 153, 154.
Hare, i. 227, 228, 246.
Harness. *See* Chariot.
Harp of the Paris Collection, i. 113, 114.
—— unknown to the Greeks, i. 111.
—— head of a, from Thebes, i. 110.
Harps, the oldest, i. 85, 111.
—— of various sizes, i. 110, 111.
——, catgut strings of. *See* Catgut.
—— with a support, i. 87, 111, 112.
—— of wood covered with bull's hide, i. 87, 113.
—— of tortoiseshell, i. 87, 113.
—— of coloured leather, i. 88, 89, 90, 113.
——, shortening the strings of the, i. 113.
—— had no pedals and no pole, i.113.
—— used for religious services, i. 113, 129, 130.
—— in the hands of Deities, i. 113.
Harpers, i. 108–112.
—— of the tomb of Remeses III., called Bruce's, i. 108–110.

Harpers standing to play, i. 86, 87, 88, 89, 90, 108, 10), 111, 112.
Harpocrates, with his finger to his mouth, not silence, ii. 182.
—— ii. 53. *See* Horus.
——, or reproduction on dissolution, ii. 382.
Harvest home, i. 282.
Hatchet, or axe, i. 361, 362, 419; ii. 114.
Hatching eggs artificially, ii. 170.
——, the modern oven for, ii. 170–172.
Hawking, no instance of, i. 221.
Head of an animal given to a poor man, i. 171.
—— cut off first, i. 170, 263.
—— placed on altars and taken to the kitchen, i. 172.
—— said by Herodotus not to have been eaten, i. 172.
——, imprecations on the, as on the scapegoat, probably not extended to every one, i. 172. *See* Enemies.
Heads, men and women carried loads on their, i. 177.
Heads of Egyptians, hard, ii. 328.
Head-stools, or wooden pillows, i. 63, 71, 335, 336.
Hearse of the dead, ii. 368, 373, 375.
Heavy-armed troops, arms of, i. 368.
Hedgehog, i. 227, 229, 245.
Heliopolis, wine not taken into the temple at, i. 51.
—— Re, the Sun, was the God of, i. 296, 298, 300, 331; ii. 312.
——, Mnevis, the sacred bull of, i. 288.
—— said to have been founded by Arabs (or a Semitic race), i. 302.
Helmet, quilted, i. 365, 366.
—— with crest, from Asia, i. 366.
Henneh, ii. 345.
Heracleopolis, i. 243.
Hermæ of Greece not the origin of statues, ii. 271.
Hermes, books of, i. 274; ii. 251. *See* Medicine.
——, or Mercury, ii. 228. *See* Thoth.
Hermotybies, soldiers, i. 337.
Heroes, no divine honours paid to, i. 328.
Hieraphori, bearers of standards, images, &c., i. 273, 284, 285.
Hierogrammat (sacred scribe), *Hieroscopus*, and *Stolistes*, i. 276.
Hieroglyphics cut to great depth in granite, ii. 156.

Hippopotamus hide, use of the, i. 240. *See* Corbag and Shields.
——, blade for spearing the, i. 241.
—— chase of the, i. 239–241.
—— emblem of Typho, i. 288.
—— cakes with, stamped on them, i. 288.
—— sacred to Mars, i. 246.
History of Egypt, i 307–309.
Hoe, ii. 11, 14, 16, 17, 18.
—— used with and without the plough, ii. 12, 18.
—— called *Tóré*, and put for the letter M, ii. 17.
—— had not a metal blade in early times, ii. 17.
Holydays, i. 281.
—— of peasants, ii. 52.
Hoop, game with a, i. 194, 195.
Horizontal courses of masonry, great antiquity of, ii. 287.
Horizontal line in architecture, i. 20.
Horns for instruments, i. 105.
Hors d'œuvres to excite the appetite, i. 174.
Horses exported from Egypt, i. 386.
—— originally from Asia, i. 234, 386.
—— called *Sûs* as in Hebrew, i. 386.
—— abundant, i. 231.
—— of Egypt esteemed, i. 234.
——, trappings of, i. 381.
Horus, or Orus, i. 242, 275, 288, 300, 312, 330.
——, the child, or Harpocrates, i. 256, 312, 333; ii. 182, 382.
House in the British Museum, model of a, i. 13, 14.
Houses, plans of, i. 11, 12.
——, they slept in summer on the roofs of, i. 7.
——, small, i. 13.
——, large, 20, 24, 27, 29.
—— at Karnak, i. 14.
——, remains of, i. 11.
—— of crude brick, i. 6.
—— of priests, luxurious, i. 7, 322.
——, plans and number of stories of, i. 8.
—— irregular in plan, i. 11, 28.
——, they sought coolness in their, i. 5, 6.
——, tombs, and temples painted, ii. 290–292.
—— painted, in Greece, ii. 278.
Human sacrifices in Egypt, no, ii. 411.
Human figure. *See* Figure.

Humanity of the Egyptians recorded by their sculptors, i. 406. *See* Cruelty.
Hunting, mode of, i. 218, 221, 224.
Huntsmen, i. 213, 215, 218.
—— of the 3rd class. *See* Class 3rd.
Hyæna, i. 213, 224, 227, 246.
—— caught, i. 213, 224.
—— apparently not eaten, i. 224.
——, spotted, i. 227, 246.
Hyrax, or *Wabber*, i. 228, 247.

Jackal, i. 227, 246.
Javelin lighter than the spear, i. 355.
—— of reed, an inferior kind of, i. 357.
Ibex, i. 227, 247.
Ibis, two kinds of, sacred, i. 251.
——, shoulder of an, broken and set, ii. 172
Ichneumon, i. 227, 229, 246.
—— destroys serpents and the eggs of crocodiles, i. 229, 243.
Jerboa, i. 227, 230, 246.
Jerusalem, temple of, pillaged, i. 308, 340.
Jewels of silver and gold, &c., i. 146; ii. 147, 336–341.
Jewish music, i. 94, 95.
—— musicians, numerous, i. 96.
—— instruments and music, i. 94, 96, 98, 105, 120, 129, 130, 140.
—— trumpets, i. 96, 104, 105.
Jews, features of the, ii. 197.
—— included among Syrians by the Egyptians, ii. 197.
—— anointed the king, i. 275.
—— brought in the ark, i. 268.
—— mourning and songs at funerals, i. 98.
—— embalmed the dead, ii. 387.
—— had forks; not at table, i. 182.
——, investiture to office among the, i. 275.
—— sold as slaves by the Phœnicians, i. 417.
——, brickmakers at Thebes not, ii. 195, 197.
——, features of Eastern not like those of Western, ii. 197–199.
—— features of Western, not given to the Saviour, ii. 198.
Jingling instrument, i. 89, 92, 93.
Immigration does not always destroy the aborigines, and conquest never, i. 2; ii. 227.
Inapplicableness and adaptability, i. 21; ii. 288.

Incense, i. 265.
—— offered, i. 324.
—— offered to the dead, ii. 358.
—— brought from Asia, ii. 397.
India, resemblance of the religions of Egypt and, i. 329.
——, arrival of the Hindoos in, i. 329.
——, aborigines of Scythian origin in, i. 329.
—— trade with, ii. 134, 234, 235, 237.
——, Solomon's trade with, ii. 235.
——, trade of Tyrians with, ii. 235.
Indian productions went to Egypt, ii. 134, 235, 237.
Indigo used by the Egyptians, ii. 78, 79.
Infantry, heavy and light, i. 386, 387.
Inn, this life only an, i. 187; ii. 356.
Insects of Egypt, i. 255.
—— fabulous, i. 255.
Instruments. *See* Musical.
—— with a neck for shortening the strings, i. 84.
—— with three strings, i. 84.
——, unknown, i. 133.
—— to which they danced, i. 133.
—— resembling lyres, i. 118–122.
—— of sacred music, i. 129.
——, triangular, i. 118, 119, 126.
—— names of Greek, i. 126.
—— of jingling sound, i. 89, 92, 93, 119.
—— held on the shoulder, i. 121.
—— found at Thebes not unlike a guitar, i. 125.
—— of one string, i. 125.
Interest not allowed to increase beyond double the original sum lent, ii. 217.
Intestines of the dead, how buried, ii. 388, 390, 391.
Inventions, few represented, ii. 320.
—— of the Egyptians, ii. 315–319.
Inventions, many older than we suppose, ii. 57.
Investiture to office, i. 275, 282, 283.
Inundation, water of the, retained by dykes, ii. 11.
—— kept out from certain crops, ii. 11.
——, subsiding of the, ii. 11.
——, the land dries quickly after the, ii. 11.
—— beginning of the, ii. 5.
—— caused by rains of Abyssinia, ii. 5.
—— Nile red and green, and red again in the, ii. 5.

Inundation as described by Virgil (Georg. IV. 28.), ii. 5.
—— makes the villages of the Delta like Islands, as of old, ii. 7.
——, height of the, ii. 8, 9.
—— same height as of old, ii. 8, 9.
—— artificially improved when low, ii. 7.
——, plough and hoe used after the, ii. 11.
—— now rises high above the base of old monuments, ii. 9. *See* Bubastis.
——, cattle rescued from the, ii. 6, 7. *See* Vignette at head of Chap. VIII.
——, fêtes of peasants during the, ii. 52.
——, observations on the, ii. 248–250, 255.
—— led to the invention of sluices, Nilometers, levelling, geometry, &c., ii. 249.
Joints of meat, i. 170, 171.
—— of peculiar form, i. 171.
—— on the altar, i. 264.
—— boiled and roasted, i. 173.
Ionic movements, i. 138.
Joseph sold, i. 417.
Joseph's brethren sat according to age, i. 58, 179.
—— silver cup, i. 82.
Iron, use of, very ancient, ii. 153–155.
—— use of, in Egypt, ii. 155.
—— bedsteads. *See* Og.
—— mentioned in Homer as tempered by plunging, ii. 153.
—— blades sharpened on a steel, ii. 155.
—— easily decomposed and not likely to be found, ii. 155.
—— known to the Egyptians, ii. 154.
——" *Ferrum* " Latin for sword, ii. 155.
Irrigation, i. 32–34; ii. 4, 5, 11.
—— prolonged, ii. 7, 11.
Isaac, savoury meats brought to, i. 173.
Isis "with ten thousand names," i. 329.
—— the mother of the child, i. 333.
—— and Athor (Venus), i. 300.
—— and Ceres of the Greeks, i. 297.
——, festival of, i. 296, 297.
Isis and Nepthys, the beginning and the end, ii. 381.
Isle. *See* Wight, Isle of.
Israelites regretted the fish of Egypt; the onions, and other vegetables, i. 167, 169.
Israelites. *See* Jews, *see* Jewish.

Italian Pantomime and Fescennine Verses, i. 101.
Judgment, the future, i. 331. *See* Osiris.
——, mode of passing, ii. 207.
—— scenes, ii. 380, 381.
Judge, the king was, ii. 202.
—— of the dead. *See* Osiris.
Judges received salary from Government, ii. 204.
——, ii. 229, 232.
——, figures of, without hands, ii. 206.
——, bench of, ii. 30, 203.
——, the Arch Judge chief of, ii. 203, 206.
Judging a case, mode of, ii. 206, 207.
Justice given gratuitously, ii. 204.
Justice, goddess of, without a head, ii. 382.
——, figure of, i. 272. *See* Truth.
Jupiter going into Ethiopia, i. 269.
Jupiters, several, i. 329.
Juvenile offenders, ii. 215.
Jvy, i. 256, 285; ii. 33.

Kanaan (Canaan), i. 403.
Karnak, temple of, i. 397.
—— and our churches, ii. 302.
Kasr-Kharóon (in the Fyoom), i. 307.
Kebsh, wild sheep, i. 227, 247.
Khem, the God, the abstract idea of father, i. 273, 327, 332.
——, or Amun-Khem, or Amun-Re *generator*, i. 273.
——, or Pan, i. 286.
Khita, or Sheta, i. 399, 401.
——, supposed to be the Hittites, i. 403.
——, fort of the, called Atesh or Kadesh, i. 400.
——, bridges over a river and ditch of the, i. 399, 400.
Khonfud, or clod-crushing machine, ii. 1, 14.
Killed, hands of the, i. 373.
King called Phrah, " the Sun " (Pharaoh), i. 280, 310. (First observed by the D. of Northumberland and Colonel Felix.)
——, feelings towards the, i. 310.
——, hereditary title of, i. 310.
——, either of the priestly or of the military class, i. 311.
——, duties of the, i. 312.
——, companions of the, i. 312.
——, rules for the conduct of the, i. 312–314.

King could do no wrong, and never died, i. 313.

——, prayer for the, and praise of the, by the priest, i. 313.

——, mourning for the death of the, and funeral of the, i. 315; ii. 366, 378.

——, people could prevent the, being buried in his tomb, i. 326 ; ii. 378.

——, Coronation of the, i. 272, 273.

——, anointed, i. 275.

——, Gods laid their hands on the, i. 276.

—— passing through towns on his return from victory, i. 278.

—— sacrificed daily in the temple, i. 281, 313.

——, confidential advisers, or ministers of the, i. 316 ; ii. 202.

——, respect for, ii. 226.

——, was judge, ii. 202.

—— could commute punishments, ii. 209.

—— wore his helmet or a wig in battle, ii. 324.

King's birth-day celebrated, i. 281.

Kisirka, or Nubian lyre, i. 117.

Kissing a royal order, ii. 203.

Kitchen (woodcuts), i. 175, 176.

——, cooks and others in the, i. 177, 178.

Knee, bow the. *See* Bow, *see Abrek*.

Kneph, with a ram's head. *See* Nû.

Knife, semicircular, for cutting leather, ii. 103.

Knives, stone. *See* Stone and Metal.

Koofa (Kufa), i. 395, 399.

Korayn, A'maree, dates of, ii. 37.

Labour, division of, ii. 185.

Ladles of bronze gilt, i. 185.

Lake of the dead at every large city, ii. 377.

Lamps, festival of burning, i. 298; ii. 71.

Land rented from the kings and others, ii. 4.

—— cultivated with little labour, ii. 14. *See* Sowing and Grain.

——, overseer of the. *See* Steward.

——, alluvial deposit on the, ii. 11.

——, dries soon after the inundation subsides, ii. 11.

Land, levels of the, different, ii. 10, 11.

——, rise of the, ii. 8, 9.

Land, varies in different parts, ii. 8, 9.

——, lower near the edge of the desert than on the banks of the Nile, ii. 7, 10.

Large blocks of stone. *See* Stone.

Lasso, use of the, i. 213, 220.

Laws of Egyp , ii. 202-218.

——, respect for the, ii. 207.

——, primitive character of some, ii. 214.

——, sanctity of old, ii. 227.

Lawgivers, ii. 207, 218, 228.

Lazarus, swathed in bandages, ii. 387.

Leather, twisting, ii. 93.

—— cutters of Thebes, ii. 93.

——, circular cu⁺ of, ii. 93, 94.

—— used for writing paper, ii. 99.

——, tanning of, ii. 102.

—— cutters, ii. 102.

—— stamped of time of Shishak, ii. 102.

——, objects made of, ii. 102.

——, curing skins for, ii. 102.

——, stretching and binding, ii. 103.

——, semicircular knife for cutting, ii. 103.

—— cutter, holding strap with his toes, ii. 104.

——, great use of, ii. 105.

Lemanon, i. 403.

Lentils, much eaten, i. 167, 177, 181.

—— supposed by Strabo to be imbedded in the rock at the Pyramids, i. 167.

—— of Pelusium, famous, i. 167.

——, porridge or soup of, i. 177.

Leopard skin dress, i. 291, 319. *See* Prophet, *see Nebris.*

Leopard's spotted skin suspended on a staff near Osiris, i. 285.

Lepidotus, fish, ii. 192.

Levels of the land. *See* Land.

Libation, they first began with a, i. 264.

—— of wine, i. 265.

—— vases used in, i. 266.

Life given to the king, i. 277.

—— sign of, taken by the Christians as a cross, i. 277.

——, or *Crux ansata*, i. 257.

——, mode of, account given before magistrates of, ii. 199-201.

Light armed troops, arms of, i. 368 386.

Limestone used in the oldest Egyptian buildings, ii. 305.

Linen corslet of Amasis, ii. 80.

Linen, fine, of Egypt, exported, ii. 72, 73, 80.
—— bandages of mummies, ii. 73, 74, 77.
—— experiments respecting, ii. 73.
——, peculiarity in the manufacture of, in the number of threads of the warp and woof, ii. 76, 77, 80.
—— threads double, ii. 76.
—— threads coloured before worked in, ii. 79.
—— cloths fringed, ii. 77, 91, 320, 321. See Calasiris.
——, beauty of texture of, ii. 75, 76.
——, singularly fine piece of, ii. 75, 80.
——, selvages of, dyed with Indigo, as of modern Nubians, ii. 77–79.
——, dresses worn by votaries of Isis in Italy, ii. 74.
——, the word ειλικρινης, "sincere," taken from fine, ii. 80.
—— different qualities of, ii. 80. See Byssus.
Linus, song of, i. 97.
Lion, i. 224, 229, 246.
—— formerly in Syria and Greece, i. 229.
—— hunting, i. 224 ; ii. 341.
Lions trained for the chase, i. 221.
—— killed by Amunoph III., i. 224.
Liturgies. See Services.
Lively character of the Egyptians, i. 2, 210.
Locust in the sculptures, i. 234.
Looms, horizontal and upright, ii. 85, 86, 87.
——, rude, but the work fine, ii. 75.
Lots, casting of, i. 196.
Lotus, i. 34, 36, 57 ; ii. 29. See Nufar.
—— eaten, i. 168 ; ii. 3.
—— a symbol, i. 257.
—— presented to guests, i. 79.
—— a favourite flower, i. 57.
——, or nelumbium, not represented except by the Romans, i. 57.
——, or Lotos, of Cyrene (a thorny tree, an acacia), ii. 121.
Lowbgeh, or palm wine, i. 55.
Lupins, ii. 21. See Doqáq.
Luxury increasing, led to debt, ii. 219.
Lyre, fabulous invention of the, i. 114, 115.
—— ornamented with heads of animals, i. 114.
——, number of strings of the, i. 115.
—— used in sacred music, i. 129.
—— of the Greeks, i. 115–117.

Lyre of Greece, with three strings, i. 124.
——, construction of the, i. 115–117.
—— of the Berlin and Leyden Museums, i. 116, 117.
——, or Kissírka, of Nubia, i. 117.
——, mode of tuning the, i. 117.
——, other instruments resembling the, i. 118, 119.
——, standing, i. 119, 120.
—— of three strings really a guitar, i. 86, 123.
—— of 18 strings, i. 115.
—— with many strings might be invented at an early time, i. 84.

Maabdeh, crocodile mummies at, i. 242.
Maces, weapons with metal head, i. 364.
Machine for crushing clods. See Khonfud.
Magic, by a boy, &c., ii. 352, 353.
Magnetism, animal, effect on nerves, ii. 353.
Mándara, or reception-room, i. 10.
Maneros, song of, i. 97.
Manufactures of Egypt, ii. 247, 255.
Marathon and other places, flint arrow-heads found at, i. 354.
March of the army, i. 342, 404.
—— of the army home after war, i. 415.
Mareotic wine, i. 49.
Mareotis belonged to Egypt, ii. 229.
Marriage ceremony and contracts not found, ii. 223.
—— with sisters, ii. 224.
Marriages of the Egyptian royal family with foreigners, i. 308.
Mars. See Papremis.
Masara, quarries of El, ii. 306.
Mashoash, an Asiatic people, i. 398.
Mast of the old ships of Egypt was double, i. 413.
Master and mistress of the house sat on one chair, i. 145.
Mat-making, ii. 86.
Mats, i. 68.
Maut, the abstract idea of mother, i. 333. See Mother.
—— " proceeded from herself," or her own mother, i. 327.
Measure of land, of length (stadium), ii. 256. See Cubit, Weights.
Measures of capacity, ii. 260.
—— of liquids, ii. 261.
—— for grain, made of wood, ii. 167.

Meat eaten without being kept, i. 165, 174.

——, great quantity of, served up, i. 166.

Mecca. *See* Mekkeh.

Medeenet Haboo, i. 73, 272, 284, 285, 394, 401.

Medicinal plants in Egypt, i. 50; ii. 351.

Medicine, six books of, ii. 355.

Medicines, ii. 351, 352.

Medusa's head like that of the Typhonian monster in Egypt, i. 153; ii. 263.

Mekaukes, Coptic governor of Egypt, i. 37.

Mekkeh pilgrims, the number of, made up by angels, i. 297.

Memlooks, club (or *dabós*) of the, i. 364.

Memnonium, palace-temple of Remeses II., usually called the, i. 401, 407.

Memphis, i. 209, 290, 295, 307, 331.
—— Pthah. the god of, i. 331.

——, capital of Lower Egypt, ii. 229, 230.

—— "Menofr," ii. 96.

Memphite dynasties and kings, i. 307.

Men and women sat together at a party, i. 144.

Menes first king of Egypt, i. 307.
—— introduced luxury, i. 173.
—— changed the course of the Nile, ii. 249, 251, 287.

——, science before the time of, ii. 251, 287

——, Amun of Ptolemaic time would have been recognized by, ii. 264.

Menophres, the Egyptian name of, uncertain, ii. 255.

Mercenaries. *See* Soldiers.

Mercury, the inventor of the lyre and of music, i. 84, 118, 123.

Mesopotamia, i. 308, 397, 403.
——, Egyptian conquests in, i. 308.
——, tribute from, i. 397.

Mesoré, offering in the month of, i. 299.

Metal implements of Egypt and Europe of a different character, ii. 164.

——, stones used for arms and tools before, ii. 163.

Metals, skill in the compounding of, i. 148; ii. 159.

——, inlaying of. *See* Damaskening.

Metals, oldest casting of, ii. 160. *See* Bronze and Metallurgy.

——, Samians famous for casting, ii. 160.

——, soldering, ii. 162.

Metallurgy, skill in, ii. 133, 136, 156, 158, 159.

—— carried to perfection in Egypt and at Sidon, ii. 133.

Military class, i. 336.
—— punishments, i. 418.
—— music, i. 104–106.
—— bands of music, i. 104.

Milk offered to the gods, i. 266.

Mimosa. *See* Acacia.

Mina, *men*, or *mna*, weight, ii. 259, 260.

Miuerva, fête of, at Saïs, i. 296, 298.

—— reputed inventress of the trumpet, i. 104.

——. *See* Neith.

Minervas, several, i. 329.

Ministers and confidential advisers of the king, i. 316; ii. 202.

Minos, Æacus, and Rhadamanthos, Egyptian names, ii. 381.

Mirrors of metal, ii. 346, 347.

Mnevis, the black bull, i. 289.

——, the sacred bull of Heliopolis, i. 288.

Mœris, king, i. 307.

——, revenues from the fish of the lake, ii. 193.

Money, sheep and oxen valued as, ii. 117.

—— formerly taken by weight, ii. 148

—— in rings, ii. 149.

——, Persian, the first coined, in Egypt, ii. 150.

——, oldest coined, ii. 150. *See* Gold. *See* Silver.

Monkey, or other pet, tied to the leg of a chair, i. 145.

Monkies assisting to gather fruit, i. 44.

—— in Abyssinia held torches, i. 44.

Monochordium of one string, i. 125.

Monolith of Saïs, and of Buto, ii. 310. *See* Saïs.

Months originally lunar, i. 299; ii. 252.

—— and seasons of the year, ii. 252, 253.

Moon, fêtes at the new and full, i. 287, 299.

——, erroneously supposed to be related to Osiris, i. 289.

—— was the god Thoth, i. 328. *See* Thoth.

Mora, game of, i. 188, 189, 190.
Mordants, the use of, ii. 83, 84.
Mosaics, golden, ii. 305.
—— in vaults and ceilings, ii. 305.
Moses broke down the superstitions of Egypt, i. 325.
—— did not mention the future judgment, reason why, i. 331.
Mother, goddess, i. 332, 333.
——. *See* Maut.
—— of the child found in Asia, Egypt, India, Italy, Mexico, the nature goddess, i. 333.
Mourners, hired, ii. 366.
——, chief, or type of mourning, ii. 371, 373.
Mud, after the inundation, bushes dragged over the, ii. 11.
—— of the Nile. *See* Nile and Alluvial deposit.
Mulkuf on houses, i. 6.
Mummies, making coffins and bandaging, ii. 117–119.
——, embalming of, ii. 383, 387.
——, classification of, ii. 391, 394.
——, offering and services to, ii. 358–360, 362.
—— of poor people, ii. 365.
—— strewed over the ground by Christian excavators, ii. 364.
——, different qualities of, ii. 391-396.
Mummy cases, old, resold, ii. 363.
—— cloths, of linen, some coarse, ii. 75-78. *See* Linen.
Mummy pit. *See* Vignette, ii. 400.
—— pits, ii. 363, 364.
Mummy's head seen in the coffin at an open panel, ii. 368.
Murder of a child by a parent, ii. 209.
—— of a parent by a son, ii. 209.
—— of a slave, punished by death, ii. 208, 209.
Murrhine vases, doubtful of what stone, ii. 71.
——, false, probably a glass-porcelain, ii. 71.
Music, i. 82–133.
—— before dinner, i. 82.
—— after dinner, i. 188.
——, style of, i. 83.
—— studied by the priests, i. 83.
——, Egyptians fond of, i. 83, 84.
—— at Greek entertainments, i. 83.
—— part of education, i. 83, 94.
——, skill of the Egyptians in, i. 83, 84, 86.
——, at first metrical, i. 83.

Music, a Greek accomplishment, i. 94.
—— of the Jews, i. 94, 95, 96.
——, military, i. 104, 105.
—— allowed in religious ceremonies, i. 301.
—— not in the temple of Osiris, i. 301.
—— of mournful kind, i. 301.
Musical notation, i. 96.
—— instruments, the oldest were those of percussion, i. 83.
—— instruments at first rude, i. 84.
—— instruments, combination of many, i. 86, 89, 91, 92.
—— instruments of jingling kind, i. 89, 92, 93, 119.
—— instruments had strings of catgut, i. 118, 122, 123, 125.
Musicians, six hundred, together, i. 91.
——, hired, i. 96.
——, great number of Jewish, i. 96.
Mutton not eaten at Thebes, i. 166.
—— not eaten by the priests, i. 324.
Mycerinus, fête in honour of the daughter of king, i. 299.
Mylitta, or Alitta, i. 333.
Myos Hormos, port on the Red Sea, ii. 235-237.
Mysteries, greater and less, i. 321.
—— of Osiris, i. 298, 331.

Nabl, or viol, of the Jews, i. 121, 126.
Nahrayn, i. 397. *See* Mesopotamia.
Napkin brought for wiping the mouth after drinking, i. 144.
Nations gifted with certain qualities, i. 3.
Natron lakes, nome of Nitriotis, i. 166; ii. 229.
Natural productions for decorative purposes, a mistake to copy, ii. 288.
—— objects, the Greeks preferred taking the sentiment of, ii. 288.
—— objects not always imitated by the Egyptians, ii. 290.
Nature gods, i. 332, 333.
—— Goddess, i. 333.
——, the vivifying and producing principles of, i. 332, 333.
Navigation, origin of, ii. 132.
—— indebted to the Phœnicians, ii. 132.
Navy included in the army, i. 311.
Neboot, or long pole, game with the, i. 207-209.
Nebris, or fawn of Bacchus, taken

from the spotted leopard-skin suspended near Osiris, i. 235.

Nebris and the leopard-skin dress of priests in Egypt, i. 291.

Nebuchadnezzar deprived Egypt of its influence in Syria, i. 309.

Nechesia and the Leucos Portus, ii. 235, 237.

Necho lost all the conquests of Egypt in Asia, i. 309.

Necklaces, ii. 339–340, 341.

—— and jewellery offered in the temple, i. 260.

Nectanebo, i. 309.

Needles, ii. 344, 345.

Nef, or Nûm. See Nû.

Neith, i. 296, 298, 328. See Minerva.

Nelumbium not represented growing in Egypt, i. 57.

—— only represented by the Romans, i. 57.

Nepenthes probably the Hashéesh (or opium?), ii. 35.

Netpe, i. 181, 256; ii. 396, 397. See Sycamore.

Netting needles, ii. 91, 95.

Nets of different kinds, i. 214.

—— enclosing part of the desert, i.214.

—— of flax string, ii. 95.

—— of very fine quality, ii. 80.

—— for birds, ii. 180–185.

—— for fishing. See Fishing-nets.

"Newest" things recommended instead of the "best," ii. 289.

Nightshade used in Egypt for chaplets, ii. 33.

Nile, valley of the, has more arable land than formerly, i. 306.

—— deposit the same throughout its course from Abyssinia, ii. 19. See Alluvial.

—— water, fattening properties of the, i. 293, 295, 322.

—— water red and green at the beginning of the inundation, ii. 5.

—— water laid up in jars before it is green, and error of Aristides, ii. 5.

——, Osiris the beneficent property of the, i. 298.

——, white and Blue, properly "Black," ii. 19, 20.

——, fertilizing properties of the, ii. 20.

Niloa, festival of the Nile, i. 282.

Nilometer of Elephantine, ii. 257.

Nilometers made, ii. 249.

——, daily rise according to the, ii. 52, 249.

Nilus, the god, of a blue and red colour, ii. 5.

—— called "Hapi." See List of Woodcuts, 278.

Nimroud or Nineveh sculptures, i. 152; ii. 263. See Nineveh.

——, weights brought by Mr. Layard from, ii. 260.

Nineveh (Niniee), tribute from, i. 397.

—— sculptures, cruelty of the Assyrians shown by the, i. 3, 410.

—— marbles not so old as some have supposed, ii. 263.

—— ornaments, i. 152, 153.

—— ornaments late compared to those of Egypt, ii. 290.

Nisroch, the head of a bird on a vase like that of the god, i. 152.

Nitriotis See Natron Lakes.

Nitrous top-dressing, on the land, ii. 19.

Nofre (or Nofr), Atmoo, i. 256, 284, 285. See Nuiar.

Nomarchs, ii. 230, 231.

Nomes of Egypt, furnishing soldiers, i. 337.

——, thirty-six, afterwards fifty-three, ii. 229.

Nóreg, probably used of old, answering to the Hebrew moreg, ii. 47.

——, like the Roman tribulum, ii. 48.

Notaries, public, ii. 165.

—— or public scribes punished for fraud, ii. 214, 217.

Nû, Nûm, Noub, Nef, Neph, or Kneph (Chnuphis), the god, i. 271, 327, 332.

——, the spirit, i. 327. See Asp or Agathodæmon.

Nufar, name of the lotus, perhaps related to Nofr, "Good," i. 256.

Numbers placed over cattle, sheep, &c., ii. 178, 179.

Nummulite rock at the Pyramids, i. 167.

Oar, of boats, ii. 126.

Oasis, i. 55, 277; ii. 191, 229.

Obelisk, object of, to contrast with the horizontal line, ii. 311.

——, barbarous additions to the point of, ii. 311.

—— in a quarry, ii. 311.

Obelisks, transported from quarries of Syene, ii. 309.

——, the largest, ii. 309, 312.

——, effect of, i. 21.

Obelisks, removed to Europe, ii. 311.

Offerings of various kinds, i. 323.

—— to different Gods at various periods of the year, i. 263.

—— most common, i. 263.

—— of flowers, fruits, ointment, i. 259-261.

—— of emblems, jewels, i. 260.

—— for the dead, ii. 362.

Og, King of Bashan, iron bedstead of, i. 72.

Oils, ii. 23, 24, 27, 29, 30, 32.

Ointment. See Anointing.

——, offering of, i. 259, 260.

—— on heads of guests, i. 77, 78.

—— to anoint the statue of a God, i. 259.

—— of various kinds, i. 259; ii. 23, 24, 27, 32.

—— found in jars in the tombs, i. 78.

——, pots of different materials for holding, i. 155, 157.

——, sagdas, or psugdæ, i. 259; ii. 342.

Olive, i. 57; ii. 24, 28.

——, soldiers carried a twig of, at the sacrifice of thanks for victory, i. 279.

Ombos (Ombite nome), i. 242.

Onions, i. 168, 169.

—— offered and eaten, i. 323, 324.

——, a particular mode of presenting, i. 324; ii. 357.

——, error respecting, i. 168.

—— of Egypt of excellent flavour, i. 169.

——, stories respecting, i. 169.

Orchard, i. 37-39.

Ornaments worn by women, ii. 336-346.

Ornan, threshing instruments of, ii. 46, 47.

O'Sioót, or O'sioút, (formerly Lycopolis,) wolf mummies at, i. 228.

Osirei, King. See Sethi.

Osiris, loss of, Osiris found, i. 287, 300.

——, fêtes in honour of, i. 286-288, 300.

——, offerings to, ii. 358.

——. See Benno, sacred bird of.

—— worshipped under the form of Apis, i. 288-291.

——, Judge of the dead, i. 331; ii. 377.

——, allegorical history of, i. 298.

——, character and mysteries of, i. 298, 331.

Osiris, history of, the great mystery, i. 298.

——, the abstract idea of good, or goodness, i. 330; ii. 356.

——, before 18th dynasty only kings called after death, ii. 329.

— —, after that time all good men called, ii. 357, 367, 380.

——, souls of good men returned to, ii. 329, 357.

——, remarkable and peculiar character of, i. 331.

——, eye of, i. 244, 257; ii. 127, 367, 386, 391.

——, sceptres of, i. 257, 266; ii. 381.

——, chamber of, at Philæ, i. 257.

——, they beat themselves in honour of, i. 264.

——, or Bacchus, i. 286. See Bacchus.

—— and Anubis, rites of, i. 129. See Flute.

——, rites of, i. 129, 299, 301.

—— and the Nile, i. 298. See Nile.

—— invented the pipe, i. 127.

—— the Great, Deity of the future state, i. 331.

—— mummies in form of, ii. 383, 385.

——, small figures of the dead, in the form of, ii. 367, 400.

——, wooden figure of, brought to table, i. 186, 187.

——, allegories connected with the land of Egypt, and, i. 300; ii. 53.

Osirtasen I., i. 204, 307.

—— the original Sesostris, i. 307.

Osirtasens, fashionable dogs in the reigns of the, i. 231.

Ostrich feathers and eggs, i. 224.

—— caught for its eggs and plumes, ii. 54.

Ottomans, i. 58, 67.

Oxen for sacrifice not necessarily free from black spots, i. 290.

——, clean, belonged to Epaphus, or Apis, i. 290.

Oxyrhinchus, city of, i. 307.

—— fish, i. 254; ii. 191.

Paamylia, i. 286.

Painted walls and panels, i. 19-21.

—— houses and temples, ii. 290, 291, 292.

Painters, and carvers in stone, distinct from sculptors, ii. 56.

Painting before sculpture, ii. 281.

—— and sculpture, origin of, ii. 270, 271.

——. See Greek.

Painting, oldest in Egypt and Greece, ii. 277, 279.
—— on panel in Egypt, ii. 277.
—— in fresco, not in Egypt, ii. 278.
Palace. *See* Pavilion.
Palimpsests, ii. 99.
Palanquins, i. 73, 75; ii. 119.
Pallaces, Pallacides, Pellices Jovis, i. 96, 133, 317.
Palm, or date tree, split, and used for roofing, i. 18.
Palm-tree, i. 39, 55–57.
——, used for various purposes, parts of the, i. 56.
—— miscalled "of the desert," i. 55, 168.
—— requires water to enable it to grow, i. 168.
—— a great gift to the people, i. 168.
—— branch type of a year, i. 256.
——, the *Dôm*, or Theban, i. 56, 57. See *Dôm* tree.
—— formerly said to be sterile in Lower Egypt, ii. 36.
Palm-wine, i. 55.
—— of the Oasis called *Lowbgeh*, i. 55.
—— used in the embalming process, ii. 383, 385.
Panegyries, or assemblies, i. 280.
Panels, houses with painted, i. 19–21.
——, walls with, i. 28, 29.
Pantheism, i. 323.
Pantomime, Italian, i. 101.
Paper, earliest substitutes for, ii. 100.
—— when first made from linen rags, ii. 101.
—— of cotton and silk, ii. 101.
—— in Arabic called "leaf," ii. 100.
——, leaves used for, ii. 100.
—— very old in China, ii. 101.
—— when first used in England, ii. 101.
Papremis, or Mars, fête of, i. 209, 298.
Papyrus or byblus plant, ii. 26, 29, 95, 96.
—— used for making punts, baskets, &c , a more common kind, ii. 95, 96.
—— of different kinds, ii. 96.
——, early use of the, ii. 98.
—— or book, i. 274.
—— eaten, i. 168 ; ii. 3.
—— garlands, i. 57, 81.
—— punts, i. 236 ; ii. 5.
—— punt a security against crocodiles, i. 236.
—— and another water plant, emblems of Upper and Lower Egypt, i. 257.

Papyrus not now in Egypt, ii. 97, 100.
—— grows only in Sicily and Syria, ii. 97, 100.
—— prophecy fulfilled respecting the, ii. 100.
——, its name perpetuated in " paper," ii. 100.
——, modern paper made from the, ii. 97.
——, or paper, when found very brittle, ii. 96.
——, mode of making, ii. 96–98.
——, different qualities of, ii. 98.
—— of fine quality, ii. 96.
——, Pliny wrong in supposing, not used before the time of Alexander, ii. 98.
——, breadth of sheets of, ii. 98.
—— continued in use till time of Charlemagne, ii. 98.
——, monopoly of, resold, the original writing erased, ii. 99.
——, substitutes for, of pottery, board, &c., ii. 98–100.
Parchment, invention of, ii. 98, 99.
——, excellent Arab, ii. 100.
Parks and covers, i. 37, 215.
Parlour, i. 11.
Party. *See* Guests.
Pasht, Bubastis, Diana, i. 296.
Passport system in Egypt, ii. 200, 201.
Paste kneaded by the hands, and the feet, i. 174, 177.
Pastry, i. 174, 177.
Pavilion and palace of the King, i. 22.
Pavilions, i. 22.
Payment, evasion of, ii. 200, 211, 213.
Peasants, frugal mode of living of the, i. 168 ; ii. 3.
—— allowed to grow the crops they chose, ii. 3.
—— rented the land from the King and others, ii. 4.
——, agricultural skill of the, ii. 3.
——, fêtes of the, during the high Nile, ii. 52. *See* Festivals.
Pelusiam beer famous, i. 54.
—— lentils, i. 167.
Pelusium, i 404.
People, task to be performed by different, i. 3.
Periploca secamone, or *ghulga* plant, i. 256 ; ii. 36, 38.
—— used for curing skins, ii. 103.
Perpendicular style abandoned the variety of the original pointed architecture, ii. 297.

Persea tree, ii. 28. *See* Egleeg.
—— sacred to Athor, i. 256.
Phalanx of infantry, Egyptian, i. 340-342.
——, Egyptian, in the army of Crœsus, i. 342.
Pharaoh. *See* Phrah.
Pharos never was a day's sail from the shore, i. 303.
Philæ, view of (vignette F), i. 212.
Philoteras Portus, on the Red Sea, ii. 235, 236.
Phœnicians traded in slaves, i. 417.
—— the great navigators of old, ii. 132.
—— doubled the Cape of Good Hope, ii. 133.
—— traded in tin, ii. 133. *See* Tin.
—— exchanged manufactures for tin, ii. 136.
—— went to Britain for tin, ii. 134, 135.
——, commercial jealousy of the, ii. 134.
——, trade of the, ii. 133-136. *See* Spain, and Gold.
Phœnix, bird, apparently the *Benno*, i. 252.
Phrah, "the sun," changed into Pharaoh, i. 310. *See* King.
Physician, origin of saying "a fool or a, after forty," ii. 352.
Pig sacrificed to the moon, i. 286.
—— to Typho, i. 323.
—— paste figure of a, offered by poor people, i. 337.
——'s flesh abhorred by the priests, i. 322, 324.
——, treatment of, not kept in a sty, i. 231.
—— eaten sometimes by the Egyptians, i. 323.
—— turned into the fields, ii. 18, 19.
—— rarely found in the sculptures, and never before the 18th dynasty (woodcut), ii. 18.
Pillows, or head stools, of wood and other materials, i. 63, 71, 335, 336.
Pins, ii. 344, 345.
Pipe, the Egyptian, very old, i. 127.
—— of reed and of straw, i. 127-129.
—— invented by Osiris, i. 127.
——, double, i. 128, 129.
——, double, was among the sacred instruments, i. 129.
——, double, of modern Egypt, or *Zummara*, i. 128.
Pipes and flutes at first rude, i. 84.

Pirouette danced 4000 years ago, i. 138.
Pitch called "*zift*" or "*sift*," i. 397; ii. 120, 259.
Plants of Egypt, i. 57, 167-169; ii. 20-22, 25, 26.
—— from Pliny, ii. 23, 24, 27-35.
—— sacred, i. 256.
—— brought as part of a foreign tribute, i. 57, 395.
—— number of, in Egypt about 1300, ii. 26.
—— producing oil. *See* Oils.
—— raised in ancient Egypt, ii. 26.
—— now grown before and after the inundation, ii. 21, 22, 25.
——, wild and indigenous, of the desert; few introduced into Egypt, ii. 26.
Plate, or silver, few pieces of Greek or Roman, ii. 147.
Plaustrum, or travelling carriage, drawn by two oxen, i. 384, 385.
Plough, ii. 13-16.
——, light furrows made by the, ii. 14.
——, oxen and cows yoked to the, ii. 15.
—— perhaps shod with metal, ii. 15, 17.
Ploughing the land, ii. 13, 14.
—— with an ox and an ass, not in Egypt, ii. 16.
Pointed ball, the principle of the, known to the Greeks, i. 358.
Pole and bucket, or *Shadóof*, i. 33, 35, 72. *See* Shadóof.
Pole-axe, i. 363.
Pomegranate, i. 36, 54, 57, 256.
—— tree represented, i. 36.
——, the *Rhodon* (rose) that gave its name to Rhodes, ii. 29.
Pompeii, red panels, and "reeds for columns" painted at, i. 19-21.
Population of Egypt in old times, i. 304, 305.
—— of the world the same now as of old, i. 305.
—— of Alexandria, i. 305.
Porcelain, or glass-porcelain, ii. 66, 70, 71.
—— of many colours, yellow put on afterwards, and parts added to, ii. 66.
Porches, i. 9.
Porcupine, i. 216, 225, 228, 246.
Porte, the Sublime, or "High Gate," ii. 202.
Potters, ii. 107, 108.

Potter's wheel, ii. 107.

Pottery, &c., used for writing upon, ii. 99.

——, Coptic names for different kinds of, ii. 107.

—— of modern Egypt has succeeded to that of old time, ii. 107.

—— Egyptian, far inferior in taste to that of Greece, ii. 109.

Poulterers, ii. 184, 185.

Poultry. See Cocks and hens.

Pounders, ii. 165, 166.

—— used stone mortars, ii. 165, 166.

Pount, Asiatic people of, i. 396.

Power of Egypt, i. 308, 418; ii. 263.

Precious stones imitated in glass, ii. 60, 63.

—— cut with the diamond, ii. 67.

—— metals formerly used, ii. 245.

——, amount of, in old times, ii. 247. See Gold, Wealth.

Preserves, or covers, i. 37, 215.

Prevention of crime in youth a modern suggestion, ii. 215.

Priest, each, had one wife, i. 5; ii. 224.

Priestesses, i. 316, 317. See Women, holy.

Priesthood kept up their influence partly by pomp and ceremonies, i. 267.

Priests, worldly possessions of the, i. 7.

——, the law was in the hands of the, i. 311.

—— and military class had the highest rank, i. 316.

—— of various grades, i. 316, 319.

—— of the King, i. 316.

——, dress of the, i. 333, 334.

—— dressed in fawn (or leopard) skins, i. 291.

—— who wore the leopard-skin dress. See Prophet.

——, chief, and the prophets called "Sem," i. 270, 319. S·e Prophet.

—— enjoyed great privileges, i. 319, 321, 325.

—— paid no taxes, but had public allowance of food, &c., i. 319.

—— initiated into the mysteries, i. 321.

——, education of the children of the, i. 321.

—— had great ascendency over the people, i. 321, 325, 326.

——, abstinence of the, i. 322, 324, 325.

Priests abstained from pork, fish, beans, &c., i. 322, 324, 325.

—— abstained from salt on certain occasions, i. 324.

——, ablutions of the, i. 324.

—— fond of cleanliness, ii. 327.

—— left the people in ignorance, i. 325.

—— raised their own class, and degraded the people, i. 325.

—— were moral, and set a good example, i. 322, 325.

—— did not disregard social ties, performed the duties of fathers and husbands, i. 326.

—— governed the country well, i. 326.

—— did not assume power over the King as the Ethiopian pontiffs did, i. 326.

——, system of the, not suited to all times, and too unbending, i. 326.

—— slept on a wooden pillow, i. 335, 336.

—— brought in the shrine, i. 269.

—— carrying the table, or stand,. i. 268.

—— wore the leopard-skin dress when with the shrines, one of the, i. 269.

Primitive habits traced long after a people have been settled, i. 5.

—— mountains in the desert, i. 228.

Princes, dress of the, i. 311.

——, lock of hair, the badge of, i. 312; ii. 322.

—— in chariots, i. 370.

——, office of, i. 311, 342, 344.

—— carried flabella, i. 342, 344.

—— commanded parts of the army, i. 342.

Principles of nature, the vivifying and producing, i. 332, 333.

Prisoners of war, i. 373, 416.

——, treatment of, i. 406, 410.

——, employment of, i. 416.

Private life gives an insight into character, i. 5, 210.

Prizes for gymnastic exercises, cattle, dresses, and skins, i. 210; ii. 52.

Procession of the ark of Sokari, i. 284, 285.

—— at the King's coronation, i. 272, 273.

Processions, order of, from Clemens, i. 274.

Professions, only two, i. 311; ii. 1.

Prophet clad in the leopard-skin

dress, he was called "*Sɛm*," i. 270, 275, 284, 319, 320, 324.

Prophet, duty of the, i. 319.

Proportion understood by the Egyptians, but particularly by the Greeks, and now by the Italians, ii. 293.

Prostration before great people, i. 58; ii. 203.

Psaydæ, ointment, i. 259; ii. 342.

Psalms of David, some written after the captivity, ii. 251.

Psammitichus, Psammaticus, or Psamatik, court for Apis of, i. 290.

"*Pshent*," double crown called, i. 269; ii. 323. *See* Crown.

Pthah, the creative power, i. 327.

——, Memphis the city of, i. 331.

—— accompanied by the figure of Truth, i. 327.

Pthah-Sokari-Osiris, i. 204.

——, boat of, i. 284, 285.

Ptolemies, titles of some of the, in a deed, ii. 220.

——, tyranny of the, ii. 229.

——, corruptions under the later, ii. 232.

Pullies known in Egypt, but may not have been used in boats, ii. 130, 131.

Pump, ii. 318.

Punishment of the offending member, ii. 214, 217.

——. *See* Prevention of crime.

—— for adultery, ii. 210. *See* Murder.

Punishments. *See* Bastinado.

——, military, i. 418; ii. 210.

—— with the corbag whip and the bastinado, i. 240, 418.

——, commutation of, ii. 209.

—— of great men now in Egypt, ii. 212.

—— of public weighers, notaries, shopkeepers, forgers, and others, for fraud, ii. 214, 217.

Pyramid, granite casing of the Third, ii. 292.

——, pent roof construction over entrance-passage of the Great, ii. 303.

Pyramidal, or sloping, line, and in rock temples, ii. 298.

Pyramids, i. 307.

—— during the inundation (vignette G), i. 302.

——, tombs near the. *See* Tombs.

——, dimensions of the, ii. 256.

——, claim of superiority of brick over stone, ii. 304.

Pyramids, arches of crude brick, ii. 301-303.

—— of Gebel Berkel in Ethiopia, ii. 301, 304.

—— the oldest monuments, ii. 287.

Quails, numerous, i. 234.

Quarry, mode of beginning a, ii. 303, 306.

Quarries of Syene, ii. 309, 311.

Quartz veins broken up for gold, ii. 141.

Queens, sceptre of, i. 276.

—— held priestly offices, i. 317.

Quiver, mode of carrying the, i. 314.

Rahab, an instrument of one string, i. 125.

Rain, very little, in Egypt, i. 7; ii. 250.

—— falls occasionally, and signs of heavy rain at the tombs of the Kings, at Thebes, ii. 250.

Raphanus, or *figl*, i. 167; ii. 23, 30.

—— among the offerings, i. 259.

—— gives an oil, ii. 23, 30.

Rebo, an Asiatic people, i. 393-395.

—— chosen as the type of Asia, i. 394.

Reclining, not an Egyptian custom, i. 58.

Red paint on walls, censured by Vitruvius, i. 19.

—— Sea, ports on the, ii. 235-237.

Religion of Egypt, system of the, i. 326, 327.

——, changes in the, i. 329, 330, 332.

——, doctrines of the, i. 327.

——, abuses crept into the, i. 326.

—— a Pantheism rather than a Polytheism, i. 328.

—— had no mixture of Sabæism, i. 328.

——, subjects connected with, i. 257-301, 313-334. *See* Sacred.

Remeses II., or the Great, i. 308, 392, 396, 401, 403, 418.

——, name of Sesostris transferred from an older king to, i. 307.

Remeses III., pavilion of, i. 73 (Vignette C, 401).

——, treasury of, i. 155.

——, probably the same as the Rhampsinitus of Herodotus, i. 155.

——, change in the sculptures, in the reign of, ii. 273.

—— conquests of, i. 308, 394, 398, 401, 418.

Remeses III., naval fight in reign of, i. 406, 410.
—— playing at draughts, i. 191–193.
Reptiles of Egypt, i. 252, 253.
——, fabulous, i. 253.
Rhampsinitus probably the same as Remeses III., i. 155.
——, story of the daughter of, i. 299.
——, treasury of, i. 15, 155.
——, strength of the trap set in the, ii. 182.
Rhyton, or drinking-cup, i. 153, 154.
—— in form of a cock's head, i. 153.
Ring-finger, third of the left hand, ii. 337.
Rings, ii. 336, 339, 341.
Robbers, chief of the, a man of integrity, like their modern Shekh, ii. 216.
Romans, state of Egypt under the, ii. 233.
Roof of houses of palm branches and mud, i. 7; ii. 280, 281.
——, they slept in summer on the, i. 7.
—— and floors of palm-tree beams, i. 18.
Roofs vaulted, i. 18; ii. 301, 302, 303.
Ropes of flax and date fibres, and of twisted leather, ii. 93.
Rose, or *rhodon*. *See* Pomegranate.
Rot-n̄-n, a people of Asia, i. 153, 395–397.
——, women of the, i. 397, 398, 416.
——, tribute of the, i. 397.
—— mentioned with Nahrayn, or Mesopotamia, i. 397. *See* Gloves.
——, vases of the, i. 153.
—— brought bitumen to Egypt, called *zift*, i. 397.
Rudders of boats, ii. 125, 129.

Sabaco, i. 308.
—— raised the towns, especially Bubastis, to protect them from the inundation, ii. 9.
Sabæism not part of the Egyptian religion, i. 328.
Sacred music, instruments of, i. 129–133, 108, 109.
—— rites. *See* Religion.
—— scribe, dress of the, i. 334.
—— trees and vegetables, i. 256.
—— animals, i. 245–256.
—— emblems, i. 257.
—— fêtes, or festivals, i. 272, 286, 288, 296–301.
—— dancing, i. 140.

Sacred, subjects in painting had prescribed rules, ii. 264, 266.
Sacrifice, i. 264. *See* Offerings.
—— daily in the temple, attended by the king, i. 281.
—— after victory, i. 279, 416.
Sacrifices, human, not in Egypt, i. 411.
Sagdas. See *Psagdæ.*
Sails of some boats, of the papyrus, resembling those of the Chinese, i. 413, 414.
—— furled in ships of war, i. 412.
Sailors of Egypt, i. 411.
——. *See* Boatmen.
—— of the fleet, or "king's ships," ranked with the soldiers, i. 411; ii. 55.
Sails of modern lighters and Ethiopian boats, ii. 126. *See* Boats.
Sais, city of, i. 296, 298, 299.
——, lake of, i. 298.
——, nome of, i. 337.
—— monolith, ii. 55, 309, 310.
Saïte Dynasty, Kings, i. 309.
Salt sometimes excluded from the tables of the priests, i. 324.
Sandals of the priests, i. 335.
—— of women and others, ii. 331–333.
Sands, error respecting the great encroachment of the, i. 306.
Sandstone generally used after the 12th dynasty, ii. 306.
Sapt, "the chosen part," i. 264.
Saracenic architecture, progress of, ii. 305.
—— gave us the pointed arch, ii. 305.
Sarapeum of Memphis discovered, i. 292.
Sarapis, temple of, i. 292.
Sarcophagi, ii. 397, 398.
Sarcophagus, ii. 368, 374.
Satan, the Manichæan, i. 330.
Saviour, portrait of the, ii. 198.
Saw, ii. 113, 114, 118.
Sawing, mode of, ii. 114, 118.
Saxon, Norman, and Lombard styles, ii. 305.
Scales for weighing, ii. 136.
—— gold, ii. 151, 152.
Scarabæi, ii. 341, 335, 397.
Scarabæus, or beetle, i. 255.
Sceptre hereditary, i. 310.
—— of Queens, i. 276.
Sceptres of Osiris, i. 257, 266; ii. 381.
Science in Egypt advanced by the effects of the Nile, ii. 248–250.
—— already advanced in time of Menes, ii. 251, 287.

Scorpion, i. 254.

Scourers or fullers, ii. 106.

Scouring plants, used by fullers, ii. 106.

Sea-fight, i. 406, 410, 411.

Seáleh, or acacia Seál, i. 228; ii. 38, 106.

Seals on doors, i. 15, 16.

—— of tombs, ii. 364, 365.

Seats of chairs and stools, i. 64.

Seb, goose, emblem of, i. 251.

Seb and Nepte, the children of, i. 330.

Semneh, fortresses of, i. 408.

Sennacherib, i. 309.

Serapis. See Sarapis.

Services or liturgies performed for the dead, ii. 357-362, 373.

Sesostris, ships of, i. 311, 411. See Ships.

——, a name transferred to Remeses II., i. 307.

—— gave lands to the soldiers, i. 336.

——, division of the country by, ii. 230.

Seth, i. 275, 330, 331.

——, the brother of Osiris, banished from the Pantheon, i. 330.

——, the abstract idea of Evil, i. 330, 331.

—— and Horus pouring emblems over the king, i. 275, 330.

——, with Hor-Hat, i. 275.

—— the same as Typho, or Typhon, i. 330.

Sethi, or Sethos, or Osirei I., i. 308, 396, 403, 418.

Seventy days, time of embalming, ii. 374, 383, 384, 387.

Shadóof, or pole and bucket, i. 33-35; ii. 4, 5, 22, 26.

——. Vignette, i. 72.

Shafts of a cart or carriage, found, i. 383.

Sharetana, an Asiatic people, i. 390-392.

—— had a helmet with horns, i. 390.

Shart, a people of northern Arabia, i. 396.

——, name of the Red Sea, i. 396.

Shaved their beards, priests, ii. 327.

—— their whole body, ii. 327.

—— heads of children, ii. 328.

Sheaves bound up, ii. 47.

Shekel, meaning weight, ii. 148.

Sheep, fear of diminishing the stock of, i. 166.

——, large flocks of, i. 166; ii. 172.

—— valuable for their wool, i. 166.

Shepherds, invasion of the, i. 111, 307.

—— invasion and their expulsion, i. 307, 308.

——, music dated before the, i. 111.

Shepherds hated in Egypt, ii. 168, 169.

—— caricatured in the paintings, ii. 169, 175.

——, care of breeds of sheep by the, ii. 172.

——, various grades of, ii. 175.

—— chosen by the steward, ii. 176, 177.

—— gave account of the stock to the scribes, ii. 176.

Sheshonk (Shishak) took Jerusalem, i. 308, 340.

——, i. 308, 330, 340.

Shield of the Egyptians, i. 345.

——, battlements in the form of the, i. 23, 408.

—— used as an umbrella, i. 73, 75.

——, boss of the, i. 349.

——, form and handle of the, i. 345, 347.

—— slung at the back, i. 346, 347.

——, concave form of the, i. 347.

—— covered with hide, i. 345.

——, a light kind of, perhaps foreign, i. 348.

—— a large kind of, i. 349.

Shields of the Egyptians used by the Greeks for firewood, i. 345.

—— made of hide of hippopotamus and crocodile, i. 240.

Shinar (Shingar, Sinjar), tribute from, i. 397.

Ships of war, i. 411-413; ii. 130.

——, rigging of, i. 412, 414; ii. 130.

—— of Sesostris in the Arabian Gulf, i. 411; ii. 133.

—— of great size, ii. 131, 132.

—— originally mere rafts, ii. 132.

Shishak pillaged temple of Jerusalem, i. 308, 340. See Sheshonk.

Shoemakers and curriers, ii. 103.

Shops, ii. 103, 184.

——, name and occupation of the owner put up over, ii. 105.

"Shrine of King Ptolemy," i. 268.

Shrines, or arks, or sacred boats, i. 267-272, 284, 285.

—— procession of, i. 267-270.

——, golden, i. 268.

Sieges of fortified towns, i. 387-390.

Sieves of string, the oldest of rushes, ii. 95.

Sift. See Zift.

Silence, Egyptian mode of indicating, ii. 182.

——, God of. See Harpocrates.

Silsilis, large quarries at, ii. 306.

Silver, use of, for money in Abraham's time, ii. 148, 240.

—— called "white gold," ii. 147, 241. See Gold.

Silver, hieroglyphic signifying, ii. 149. (Woodcut, fig. c.)

—— much used for money, ii. 147.

—— soon followed gold, ii. 148.

—— thread and wire, ii. 82.

Simple dress of the Egyptians, like a River God's, ii. 320.

Simpula, or ladles, i. 184, 185.

—— with a hinge, i. 184, 185.

Simsim, or sesame, gives an oil, ii. 23, 26, 31.

"Sincere," ειλικρινης, ii. 80.

Singing and music after dinner, i. 188. See Music and Songs.

—— at work, ii. 308.

——, a solo, i. 92.

Single-stick, i. 206, 207.

Siphons, i. 174, 175; ii. 317, 318.

Sistrum, i. 131–133.

—— held by women, i. 133.

—— has been found, i. 132, 133.

Sitting on their heels, i. 58.

Sketches made on pieces of stone, board, &c., ii. 99, 276.

Skins imported into Egypt and part of tribute, ii. 105, 106.

——, tanning and curing, ii. 102, 106.

Skins. See Leopard skins; see Water skins; see Prizes.

Slave, a black woman, holding a plate in the way the African women now do, i. 141.

——, murder of a, capital offence, ii. 208.

Slaves, black and white, i. 416, 417; ii. 225.

——, traffic in, customary in those days, i. 417.

——, the Jews also had, i. 417.

——, Caucasian, like the modern Circassian, i. 418.

——, treatment of, i. 417.

——, children by, ii. 225.

Slaughtering for the table, i. 169.

Sling, i. 357, 419.

—— looked upon with contempt by some of the Greeks, i. 357.

—— used by some of the Greeks. i. 358.

——, the people of the Balearic Islands famed for their skill with the, i. 358.

Sling, the Greeks used a leaden-pointed ball for their, i. 358.

—— — bullets of Egypt were round pebbles, i. 358.

Snakes of Egypt, i. 253.

——, sacred, i. 46, 253. See Asp.

——, horned, i. 253.

Soap, i. 186.

—— plant, ii. 106.

——, earths, steatite, ground lupins, &c., used for, i. 186.

Sokari. See Pthah-Sokari-Osiris.

——, necklace of, i. 260, 261.

——, ark of, i. 284, 285.

Soldering metals. See Metals.

Soldiers. See Army; see Class 2nd.

——, pay and rations of the, i. 336, 337.

—— from certain nomes or provinces of Egypt, i. 337.

——, mercenary, auxiliaries and allies, i. 337, 338.

—— of different corps, i. 369. See Olive; see Frontispiece of vol. ii.

Solomon's trade, ii. 235.

—— wealth, ii. 243.

Soltána Valideh, influence of the, i. 4.

Sons followed the profession of their fathers, but not always, i. 316; ii. 57.

Song, a solo, i. 92.

—— of Maneros or Linus, i. 97.

—— of the thrashers, ii. 43.

Songs, or dirges, on the death of individuals, i. 97; ii. 370, 372.

Sont, Mimosa, or Acacia, Nilotica, ii. 28, 37, 38, 106, 110, 129.

——, pods of the, used for tanning, ii. 106.

——, groves of, ii. 28, 37, 110.

Sooez (Suez), ii. 236, 237.

Sothic period, ii. 255.

—— and solar year, ii. 253–255.

Sothis, rising of, in reign of Thothmes III., ii. 254, 255.

Soul, transmigration of the, ii. 379.

—— immortal, first taught by the Egyptians, ii. 379.

Sowing the land, ii. 11, 12.

—— broadcast, ii. 39.

Spear, or pike, with metal head, i. 355.

—— had nothing at the lower end to fix it in the ground, i. 355.

—— and javelin heads, i. 355, 356.

Sphinx, i. 226, 248.

Sphinxes, ii. 290, 315, 324.

Spiked stand for offering birds, i. 263.

—— instrument. *See Doora.*

Spindles, ii. 84–88.

Spinning, employment of women, ii. 84, 85.

Spoil of the enemy, i. 406.

Spoonbill, i. 251.

Spoons, i. 183, 184.

Stables, i. 30.

Stag, i. 227, 247.

Stamps. *See* Seals.

Standards of the Egyptians, i. 342, 343.

Stands for flowers, i. 79.

Staters, the oldest coins, ii. 150.

Statue on a column, not good taste, an instance of inadaptability, i. 21.

—— on a sledge at El Bersheh, ii. 307, 308.

Statues of the Greeks, some as large as those of Egypt, ii. 300.

—— painted, ii. 279, 280.

——, large, ii. 309, 310, 314, 315.

—— at Thebes, ii. 309, 310.

—— of great size, not good taste, i. 21.

——, early, ii. 270, 271.

——. *See* Greek Statues; *see* Hermæ.

——, polishing and painting granite, ii. 314, 315. *See* Granite.

Steel. *See* Iron.

Steelyard of Roman time, ii. 152.

Steersman a high office, ii. 55.

Steward, or overseer of lands, i. 32; ii. 4.

Stick. '*See* Throw-stick; *see* Walking-stick.

Sticks, fights with, i. 206–209, 298.

Stimulants for drinking, i. 53.

Stone, large blocks of, used in other countries as well as in Egypt, ii. 299.

—— knives of early time, and long retained, ii. 163, 164.

—— on a sledge, taken from a quarry, ii. 306.

——, mode of squaring, ii. 313, 315.

Stones of very great size taken by land, ii. 307, 309.

Stones on sledges, ii. 306.

——, transport of large, ii. 307–312.

——, mode of squaring, ii. 313, 315.

—— dragged for Temple of Isis, ii. 307.

——, men condemned to hew, ii. 307.

Stools, i. 58, 61–65, 67.

VOL. II.

Stools for the head. *See* Pillows.

Story of the man and his wife and the jars of gold, i. 23, 24.

Strainers or cullenders of bronze, i. 185.

Stranger Kings, i. 308, 330, 403.

Straw for provender, ii. 48.

—— in making bricks, ii. 194.

String, instruments of one, i. 125.

Strings of catgut, i. 111, 118, 122, 125.

—— not of wire, i. 125.

——, mode of shortening, by a neck, i. 84.

—— limited to three, shows an improvement in music, i. 84.

Styx, the dead who remained on the wrong side of the, ii. 377.

Suez. *See* Sooez.

Sun, worship of the, i. 328, 329, 339.

——, distinct from Sabæism, i. 328.

——, festivals in honour of the, i. 296, 298, 300, 301.

—— worship introduced by the Stranger kings, i. 308.

—— worshipped at Heliopolis, i. 331. *See* Heliopolis. *See* Phrah.

——, the bull Mnevis said to be sacred to the, i. 289.

Superintendents of cattle, a high post, ii. 176, 178.

Surveying, land, or mensuration, ii. 248.

Swineherds in Egypt and India despised, ii. 2.

—— most ignoble, ii. 169.

Swine. *See* Pig.

Swords and daggers, i. 358, 419.

Sycamore, i. 44, 57, 259; ii. 27, 37, 110.

—— figs heavenly fruit, i. 181.

—— figs if eaten supposed to ensure a return to Egypt, ii. 110.

—— tree sacred to Netpe, i. 256; ii. 383.

Symmetry avoided, ii. 296. *See* Variety.

Symphony, the triple, i. 86.

Syringe, ii. 318.

Table for dinner, i. 167, 179, 128.

—— not covered with linen, i. 179.

——, mode of sitting at, i. 179.

Tables, i. 69, 70, 167, 179, 182, 190.

—— brought in and removed with the dishes, i. 180, 181.

Tables, offerings in the tombs on small, ii. 362.

Tabret, or timbrel (the *Taph* of the Jews), i. 129, 130, 140.

Talent, ii. 259, 260.

Tamarisk, ii. 37.

—— wood, use of, ii. 110.

—— tree, sacred to Osiris, i. 256.

Tambourine, i. 98, 129.

—— of various kinds, i. 129.

—— used in sacred music, i. 129.

—— played by goddesses, i. 129.

Tanning skins; pods of the acacia (*sont*), bark of *séáleh* and rhus, for, ii. 106.

Tapestry (*tapeta*) carpets, ii. 92.

Taste, ii. 288, 289. *See* Inapplicableness.

——, encouragement of, ii. 293–295.

Taxes, very great in Egypt, ii. 234.

Temenos. *See* Grove.

Temperance, exhortations to, i. 53, 187.

Temple, dedication of a, i. 271, 272.

——, a complete. *See* Frontispiece, vol. i.

Temples, subjects represented in the, i. 264.

——, coloured, ii. 290.

——, sculptures of, ii. 295.

—— not derived from excavated monuments, ii. 298.

——, or sanctuaries, at first small, ii. 299.

Tentyris (now Dendera), i. 242, 307.

Tentyrites overcame the crocodile, i. 242.

Testudo and battering ram, i. 387–389.

Thales, improbable story of, teaching his instructors, ii. 109, 319.

Thanksgivings, i. 260. *See* Grace.

—— after victory, i. 278, 416.

Theban dynasty, i. 307.

Thebes, pavilion of Remeses III.; two colossi of the plain before the temple of Amunoph III.; vignettes C, E, i. 73, 141, 306.

——, i. 306, 331, 407.

——, capital of Upper Egypt, ii. 229, 230.

—— and Memphis had no walls round them, i. 409.

——, tombs of the kings at, i. 394.

——, plain of, formerly of less breadth, i. 306.

Theft, ii. 216.

——, mode of discovering, by divination, ii. 353.

Thieves had a chief, to whom they reported what they stole, and to whom the person robbed applied, ii. 216.

Thimble-rig, i. 203.

This, the Thinite dynasty, i. 307.

Thomson, Mr., on linen and mummy cloths, ii. 73–77, 79, 80.

Thoth, the Mercury or Hermes of Egypt, i. 274, 275.

——, books of Hermes, or, i. 274.

——, fête of, i. 299.

——, the intellect, i. 123.

——month of, i. 299.

——, the Moon and God of letters, with an Ibis head, i. 328.

——, answered to Time, ii. 381.

Thothmes, the kings, i. 308.

—— III., i. 153, 308, 395, 397, 399, 418.

——, rising of Sothis in reign of, and date of, ii. 255.

Threshers, song of the, ii. 43.

Threshing. *See* Wheat; *see* Ornan.

Throwstick, i. 235, 237.

—— not on the principle of the *boomerang* of Australia, i. 235.

Thummim. *See* Truth.

Thyrsus carried by the priests, i. 291.

—— suggested by the staff or ivy-bound flower, i. 285.

Tiles, glazed, ii. 288, 292.

Tin, early use of, ii. 133, 134.

—— taken to the Isle of Wight as a depôt, ii. 135.

—— called *Kassiteros* in Greek, and *Kastira* in Sanscrit, ii. 133.

—— sought in Britain by the Phœnicians, ii. 134, 135.

——, some found in Spain even now, ii. 134.

Tirhaka, i. 308.

——, captives of, i. 393, 395–398.

Tnephachthus' curse of Menes, i. 173.

Toersha, a people of Asia, i. 398.

Toes, a strap held between the, ii. 104.

Tokkari, an Asiatic people, i. 392.

——, carts of the, i. 392.

Tomb of Remeses III., i. 77, 108.

——, some not allowed to be buried in their own, i. 314, 325; ii. 376, 379.

Tombs and funeral rites, ii. 356–400.

——, visit of women to the (as at present), i. 93; ii. 364.

—— of the kings, i. 394.

—— of poor people, ii. 365.

—— all finished except the name of the owner, and ready for sale, ii. 363.

——, seals of the, ii. 364.

Tombs, of great size, ii. 365.
——, gardens at the, ii. 365.
—— at base of mountains of Thebes, ii. 372.
—— never circular in Egypt, ii. 365.
—— at the Pyramids, i. 111 ; ii. 287, 365.
Tomtom drum, i. 103–106.
Towers, moveable, used in sieges, i. 390.
Towns raised above the inundation, ii. 9.
Toys for children, i. 196, 197.
Trade of Egypt, ii. 134, 234, 235, 237.
—— of a father generally followed by his son, ii. 57.
Tradesmen not allowed to meddle with politics, nor to follow more than one pursuit, ii. 57.
Transmigration of the soul, ii. 379.
—— in India, ii. 380.
Traps for birds, ii. 180, 182.
——, spring, very strong, ii. 182.
Treasure, story of, found, i. 23, 24.
Treasury. *See* Remeses III.
Trees of Egypt, i. 35–37, 57.
——, sacred, i. 256.
—— represented on monuments, ii. 36–38.
Triad of gods, i. 329–332.
Trial of the dead, i. 325 ; ii. 376, 379.
Tribute paid to Egypt, i. 396, 397, 399, 404, 417 ; ii. 233, 241.
—— of Ethiopia, i. 404.
——, jar of, i. 397.
—— from Asia and Africa, ii. 233.
——, vases brought as part of a, i. 152, 153, 397, 399.
Triclinium not used by the Egyptians, i. 58.
Trimalchio's exhortation at his feast, i. 187.
Triumph of the king after victory, i. 277. *See* Thanksgiving.
Trochilus, story of the, i. 243.
Trumpet, i. 104, 105.
——, troops summoned by the, i. 344.
—— of the Israelites, Greeks, and Romans, i. 105. *See* Jewish instruments.
Truth, the figure of, i. 260, 271, 272, 327.
Truth, i. 271, called *Thmei* (θεμις). *See* Pthah.
—— and Justice, i. 272 ; ii. 205.
——, the two figures of Thmei or, answer to *Thummim*, ii. 205, 382.

Truth, or Justice, the great cardinal virtue, ii. 207.
——, goddess of, with her eyes closed, ii. 205.
Turkish tent traced in the house, i. 5.
Typho or Typhon, or Seth, i. 105, 241, 242, 244, 249, 288, 323, 330.
——, the 3rd day of the Epact the birthday of, i. 281.
——, sow sacrificed to, i. 323.
——, chase of a boar by, i. 244.
——, hippopotamus and crocodile, emblems of, i. 241, 288.
Typhonian monster, i. 152, 153.
——, head of, resembled that of Medusa, i. 153 ; ii. 263.

Variety, the Egyptians fond of, i. 58 ; ii. 296.
Vase like a caldron, i. 154.
—— of bronze, with an elastic cover, i. 154, 158.
Vases, i. 147–158.
—— of glass and porcelain, i. 78, 82.
—— with the head of a bird and of a Typhonian monster, i. 152, 153.
—— with a human head for a cover, i. 155.
—— of porcelain, or of enamel on gold, i. 152.
—— from Asia, i. 152, 153.
—— often of as bad shape as our flower-pots, i. 153.
—— and bottles in a case, i. 80.
—— and bottles, closed with leaves, i. 142, 165, 262.
—— of gold and silver, and other materials, i. 82, 148.
—— of gold, with so-called Greek patterns, i. 147.
—— of same form as some Greek, but most ancient, i. 147.
—— used in the temple and the kitchen, i. 154, 156.
—— of bronze, glass, and other materials, i. 148.
—— studded with precious stones, i. 148.
—— variously ornamented with animals, &c., i. 152, 153.
—— of the Greeks, with the "Goose and Sun" of Egypt (first noticed by Mr. Stuart Poole), ii. 263.
—— of elegant form in Egypt, sometimes imbricated, with plates of metal, ii. 162.

Vases from Egypt. *See* Etruscans.
Vaults, vaulting. *See* Arches.
Vectis. *See* Wight, Isle of.
Vegetables, great quantity of, at dinner, i. 166.
Vegetables forbidden to the priests, some. *See* Beans.
Vegetables, food of the lower orders, i. 167. *See* Food.
——, great number of people in Egypt who sold, i. 168.
——, sacred, i. 256.
Veneering with rare woods, i. 19; ii. 114, 115.
Vertical line in architecture, i. 21; ii. 302.
Veterinary art in Egypt, ii. 173, 174.
Victim, mode of slaying and cutting-up a, i. 263, 264.
Victory, return of a king after, i. 277–279, 415.
——, thanksgiving after, i. 279, 416.
Villa, arrangement of a large, i. 27, 28.
—— boat towed on a lake in the grounds of a, i. 28.
Villas, i. 24–28.
—— of irregular plan, i. 28.
——, entrances to, i. 25.
Vine, i. 39–45; ii. 29, 36.
Vines trained, i. 38, 41.
—— browsed on by kids after the vintage, i. 45.
—— grown on the edge of the desert, i. 49; ii. 20.
Vineyard, i. 38, 41–43.
Vitrified coating over figures and sarcophagi of stone, ii. 64, 65, 70.
Vitruvius censures quantities of red paint on walls, and "reeds for columns," i. 19, 21.
Umbrella over a chariot, i. 73, 75, 76, 384, 385.
——, shield used for an, i. 73, 75.
Undertakers, ii. 119, 387.
Volutes from Egypt, ii. 297.
Vows, public and private, i. 261.
Usury condemned, ii. 217.

Wabber, or *hyrax* (a sort of marmotte), i. 228, 247.
Walking-sticks, ii. 347, 348.
War, preparation for, i. 404.
——, mode of attack in, i. 405.
——, return of the army from, i. 278, 415, 416.
Wars of the Egyptians, i. 390–416.

Washerwomen, ii. 92.
Washing before dinner, i. 76, 77.
—— after dinner, i. 185.
Water of the Nile. *See* Nile.
—— pitcher or *hydria*, i. 287.
—— skins, i. 35, 213.
—— wheel, hydraulic screw, and foot machine, i. 34.
Wealth of ancient people, ii. 243, 244, 245.
—— of individuals at Rome, ii. 244, 245.
Weighers, public, ii. 165.
——, public, confidence in, and punishment of, ii. 214, 217.
Weighing rings of gold and silver, ii. 148.
Weight, *shekel*, meaning, ii. 148.
——, money taken by, ii. 148.
——, things sold by, ii. 165. *See* Scales.
Weights, game of raising, i. 207.
—— and measures, ii. 259–261.
——, talent, mina, and other, ii. 259, 260.
Wheat, ii. 21.
—— and barley, when cut, the best, ii. 39.
——, all bearded, the seven-eared, quality of, ii. 39.
—— found in tombs, said to have been grown in England, ii. 39.
—— cropped a little below the ear, ii. 39, 48.
—— cropped now close to the ground, ii. 47.
—— carried to the threshing floor, ii. 39.
——, sowing, reaping, carrying, threshing, winnowing, and housing, ii. 40, 41, 44–46.
——, treading out, or *tritura*, with oxen, ii. 41–46.
——, oxen unmuzzled when treading out the, ii. 46.
Wheaten bread, i. 180. *See* Bread.
Wheel and shafts of a cart found by Dr. Abbott, i. 383.
Wheels of chariots, i. 374, 376–380, 384.
——, had four or six spokes, 374, 379, 384.
Wheelwrights, ii. 117.
Wheeled carriage, four, i. 384.
Whip, i. 372.
—— suspended from the wrist, i. 373.
Wife, hieroglyphic signifying, i. 323.

Wife, the priests and other Egyptians had only one, i. 5; ii. 224.

"Wife" and weaving, ii. 84.

—— said to rule at home, ii. 223.

—— of Potiphar, ii. 224.

Wight, Isle of, made the depôt for tin, and the port of traders from the continent, ii. 135.

Wigs, ii. 325, 326, 329.

Wild animals kept for the table, i. 215.

—— animals, i. 226–231, 239–248.

—— ass and wild boar not represented, i. 244.

Wild boar, i. 244, 247. See Damietta.

—— ox or cow, a species of antelope (the Antilope Defassa), i. 227, 247.

Windows of houses, i. 14, 20, 22.

—— not covered with hangings, i. 22.

—— hanging up between columns, i. 20.

Wine of various kinds, i. 49–51, 266.

—— in the cellar, i. 49.

—— presented to guests, i. 81, 141.

—— presented before dinner, i. 82.

—— brought by an upper servant, i. 141.

——, it was not rude to refuse, i. 144.

—— not forbidden to women, i. 51, 52.

—— presented with a complimentary speech, i. 144.

—— offered in two cups to the gods, i. 266.

—— offered to the gods, i. 51. See Heliopolis.

—— called Erp, i. 48, 266.

—— of the Upper and Lower country, i. 266.

—— of the palm. See Palm-wine.

—— also imported from Phœnicia and Greece, i. 53.

—— used medicinally, i. 50.

Wines of a choice kind confined to the rich, i. 54.

——, fictitious or medicated, i. 50.

Wine-cellars, i. 47, 48.

Wine-jars, or amphoræ, i. 48.

——, resinous substance put into the, i. 48.

—— press, i. 45–47.

Wire, when first drawn, ii. 82.

"Wisdom of the Egyptians," i. 325; ii. 202.

Witnessing a murder or any violence, without giving information, was participation in guilt, ii. 208.

Witnesses, number of, required for deeds, ii. 176.

Wolf, i. 227, 228, 245.

Wolf mummies at O'Sioót. See O'Sioót.

Women, treatment and influence of, in Egypt, ascended the throne, i. 4; ii. 223.

—— sat with the men, i. 144.

—— in Greece secluded, i. 144; ii. 224.

—— not secluded in Rome, i. 144.

—— attended festivals, ii. 224.

—— sacred, or holy, i. 316–319.

—— held offices connected with religion, i. 317, 318.

—— of Amun, i. 133. See Pallaces.

——, a sort of college or convent of, i. 319.

——, rights and duties of, i. 4.

—— talked about their earrings, i. 145.

—— carried loads on their heads, sometimes on their shoulders, i. 177.

—— occupied in weaving, and other occupations in doors, ii. 223.

—— of the hareem, ii. 225.

—— guilty of capital crimes, punishment of, ii. 209–211.

——, dresses of, ii. 334.

Wood brought from Syria and other countries, i. 18; ii. 38, 111.

——, little, in Egypt, ii. 109.

—— painted on a coating of stucco, ii. 111.

Woods, veneering. See Veneering.

—— most used in Egypt, ii. 38.

Wooden figure of Osiris at table, i. 186, 187.

Woof pushed upwards and downwards, ii. 85.

Wool. See Sheep.

Woollen cloths, none buried in, i. 353; ii. 72.

—— cloths worn by common people, i. 333.

—— upper garment worn by priests, ii. 72.

World not more peopled now than formerly, i. 305.

Wounded enemies, i. 373.

Wreaths of flowers, i. 57, 79, 80.

Wrestling, i. 204–206.

Writing, everything done in, ii. 176.

Writing-paper, leather used instead of, ii. 99. See Paper; see Papyrus.

Year, division of the, ii. 251–254.

—— of 365 and 365¼ days, ii. 252–254.

—— intercalated, ii. 254, 255.

Yoke for carrying waterpots and other things, i. 33.
—— of a plough, ii. 15.
—— of a chariot, i. 379, 381.
Yoking oxen and cows to the plough, ii. 15.
Young animals for stocking preserves, i. 215, 216.

Zift, or bitumen, brought in tribute from Asia, i. 397; ii. 120. *See* Rot-n̄-n.
Zummára, a double pipe of modern Egypt, i. 128.
Zythus, or *Zythos*, beer, i. 53–55.